INSIDERS' GUIDE® TO

WILLIAMSBURG

and Virginia's Historic Triangle

SIXTEENTH EDITION

SUE CORBETT

INSIDERS' GUIDE

GUILFORD, CONNECTICUT
AN IMPRINT OF GLOBE PEQUOT PRESS

All the information in this guidebook is subject to change. We recommend that you call ahead to obtain current information before traveling.

To buy books in quantity for corporate use or incentives, call **(800) 962–0973** or e-mail **premiums@GlobePequot.com**.

INSIDERS' GUIDE ®

Editor: Kevin Sirois
Project Editor: Heather Santiago
Text Design: Sheryl Kober
Maps: XNR Productions, Inc. © Morris Book Publishing, LLC.

ISSN 1541-454X
ISBN 978-0-7627-5704-6

Printed in the United States of America
10 9 8 7 6 5 4 3 2 1

CONTENTS

How to Use This Book 1

History 2

Getting Here, Getting Around 7

Accommodations 15

Bed-and-Breakfasts and Guest Homes 29

Regional Cuisine and Restaurants 41

Nightlife 67

Shopping 72

Attractions 84

Jamestown and Yorktown 112

Kidstuff 130

Virginia's Indian Culture 133

Our Military Heritage 137

The Arts 143

Annual Events 149

Newport News and Hampton 158

Parks and Recreation 174

Golf 185

Day Trips 189

Appendix: Living Here **207**

Relocation 208

Retirement 219

Education 225

Health Care 231

Media 233

Index **237**

Directory of Maps

Williamsburg and the Virginia Peninsula vi

Virginia's Historic Triangle. vii

Colonial Williamsburg viii

Jamestown. ix

Yorktown. x

ABOUT THE AUTHOR

Sue Corbett is a contributor to *People* magazine, *Publishers Weekly,* and has been a journalist for more than 20 years. She is also the author of several books for children including *The 12 Days of Christmas in Virginia,* an illustrated travelogue. She lives in Newport News with her husband and three children.

ACKNOWLEDGEMENTS

The author would like to thank Tom Davidson, who helped immeasurably in the writing and research of this book, in large part by joining me to eat our way around Williamsburg. She also apologizes to her kids, who were mostly patient when mom was working on "the Williamsburg book." But most of all she bows at the feet of Beth Minick, a true Billsburg insider, who pointed her to all the right places.

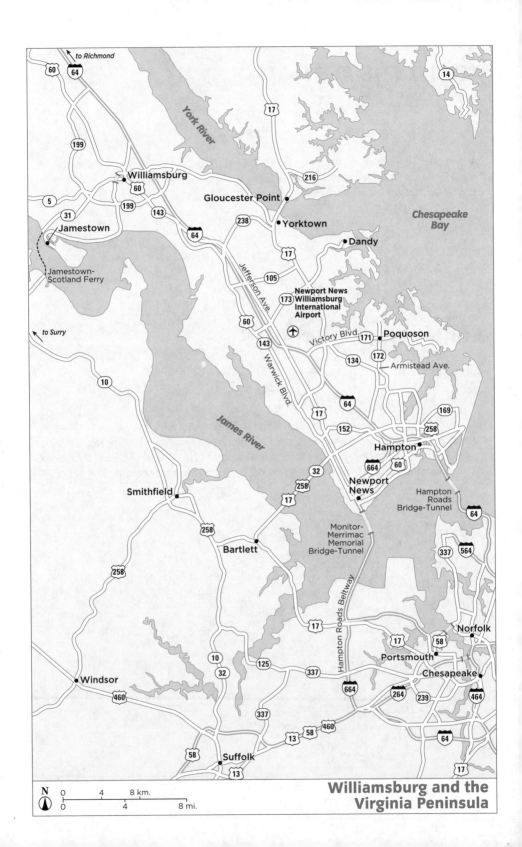

Williamsburg and the Virginia Peninsula

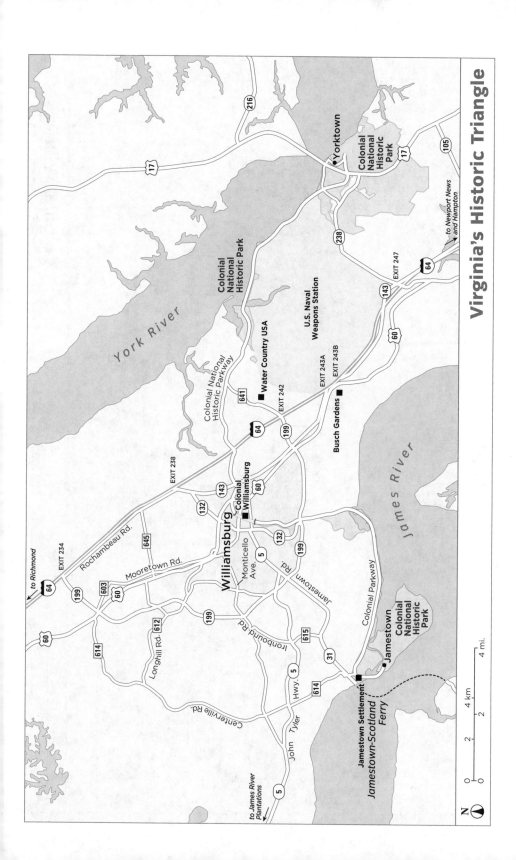

Virginia's Historic Triangle

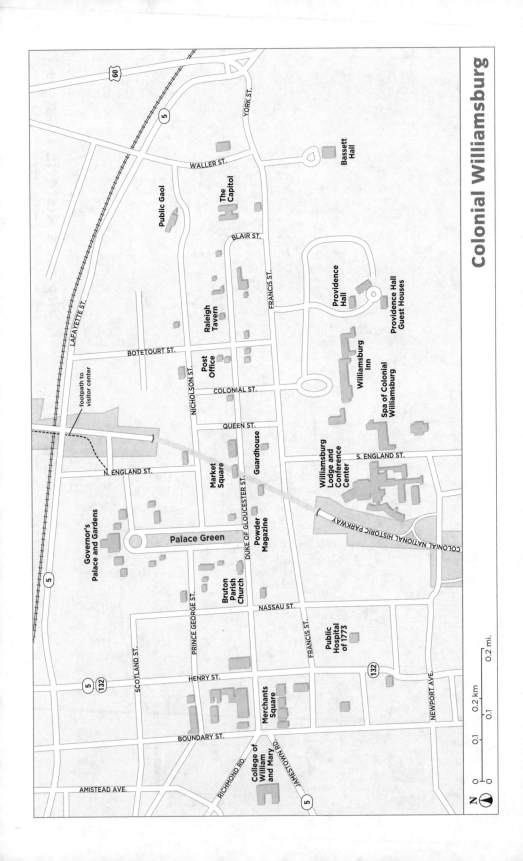

Colonial Williamsburg

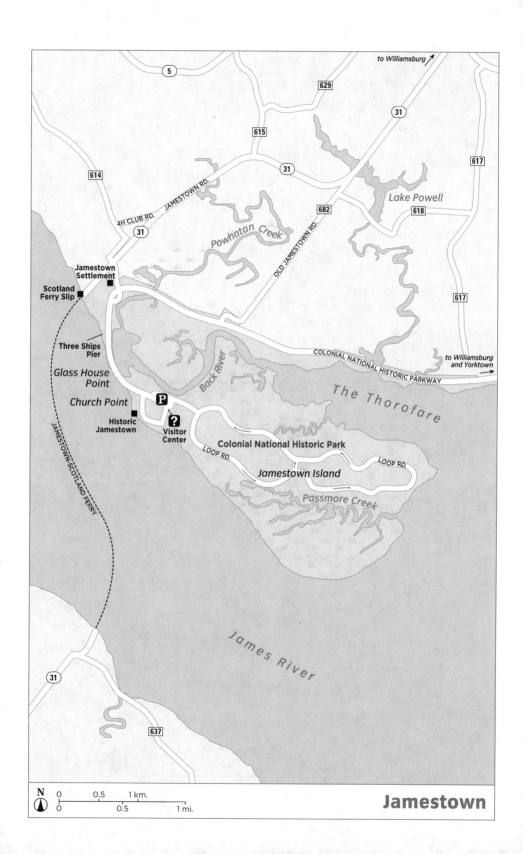

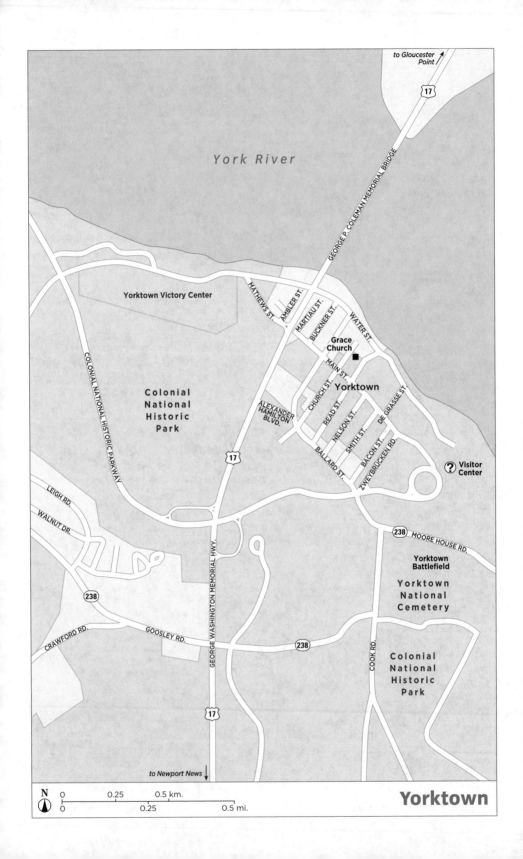

to Gloucester
Point

17

York River

to Newport News

Yorktown Victory Center

MATHEWS ST.

AMBLER ST.

MARTIAU ST.

BUCKNER ST.

WATER ST.

GEORGE P. COLEMAN MEMORIAL BRIDGE

Grace
Church

MAIN ST.

CHURCH ST.

READ ST.

NELSON ST.

SMITH ST.

BACON ST.

DE GRASSE ST.

Yorktown

ALEXANDER
HAMILTON
BLVD.

BALLARD ST.

ZWEYBRUCKEN RD.

COLONIAL NATIONAL HISTORIC PARKWAY

**Colonial
National
Historic
Park**

17

? **Visitor
Center**

LEIGH RD.

WALNUT DR.

238

GEORGE WASHINGTON MEMORIAL HWY.

238 MOORE HOUSE RD.

**Yorktown
Battlefield**

**Yorktown
National
Cemetery**

COOK RD.

CRAWFORD RD.

GOOSLEY RD.

238

**Colonial
National
Historic
Park**

17

N

0   0.25   0.5 km.

0   0.25   0.5 mi.

Yorktown

HOW TO USE THIS BOOK

This book lays out the best sites to see, things to do, places to eat and stay. Recognizing that families are always on the lookout for adventures that will broaden their children's horizons, we've added more activities that can be enjoyed in the great outdoors to our Kidstuff and Parks and Recreation chapters. Likewise, Colonial Williamsburg offers a long list of programs designed to entertain and enlighten the entire family. It's a selection you can review with your children as you sit down and plan your vacation. For readers well beyond childhood who remain "young at heart," we have a list of services and activities outlined in our Retirement chapter.

To help you decide where to rest your weary head, our Accommodations and Bed-and-Breakfasts chapters give you a choice of more than 100 places. All entries are in alphabetical order within these categories and include a pricing key. In our Restaurants chapter, eateries are listed in alphabetical order. So you don't strain your budget, we have included an easy-to-use pricing guide.

A detailed guide to shopping is divided geographically, working from the center of the colonial city outward,

Our chapters highlighting attractions begin with Colonial Williamsburg. General Attractions follow, providing information on Busch Gardens theme park, Water Country USA and other destinations, from Jamestown and Yorktown to beautiful plantation houses and churches that are centuries old.

If there's a duffer in your party, peruse our chapter on golf for the lowdown on all of our local courses and a sampling of fees you can expect to pay. Other outdoor pursuits are explored in Parks and Recreation, which directs you to places where you can hike, bike, swim, or drop that hook, line, and sinker in and around the Williamsburg area. Our Day Trips chapter can tell you how to get to points of interest outside the Historic Triangle and what to do once you reach them.

As in previous editions, we have dedicated considerable attention and space to Newport News and Hampton, adjacent cities on the Virginia Peninsula that are just a short jaunt east of Williamsburg on I-64. This in-depth chapter includes information on attractions, restaurants, accommodations, and shopping. In essence, it's a microcosm of the information we give you on Williamsburg and certainly shares enough data for planning a separate vacation to this area, dubbed the Lower Peninsula.

We have also provided special chapters on other topics of interest, including Virginia's Indian Culture, Media, and Our Military Heritage.

Moving to Virginia or already live here? Be sure to check out the blue-tabbed pages at the back of the book, where you will find the **Living Here** appendix that offers sections on relocation, retirement, education, health care and media.

HISTORY

Williamsburg claims a long and fascinating history. In its three centuries, Virginia's former capital enjoyed both periods of great fortune and dramatic decline before reinventing itself through an unprecedented restoration process that began in the mid-1920s.

This successful effort at re-creating Williamsburg's past in a way it can be enjoyed in the present is what draws vast numbers of visitors to the 18th-century buildings and brick-paved streets of the city. Most find themselves moved and inspired by seeing this re-creation of early American life spread out in front of them. In town in the late '90s to discuss his well-known documentary on Thomas Jefferson, filmmaker and historian Ken Burns called his visit to Williamsburg "the highlight of my professional life."

Speaking at a convention at the College of William and Mary several years ago, Pulitzer Prize–winning historian David McCullough said exploring the past is "an antidote to self-pity" because no matter how bad off we might think ourselves now, "others have had it worse."

Of course, we don't think for one minute that you're here in Williamsburg to gloat over your forefathers' misfortunes. We do believe, however, that if you have come to town to seek a little respite from the cares and speed-of-light pace of 21st-century life, you're in the right place.

WHY WILLIAMSBURG?

Did you ever wonder why the early colonists chose Williamsburg as the seat of government for Virginia? Believe it or not, you can thank the lowly mosquito for getting Williamsburg off the ground. When English settlers set foot on New World soil in 1607, they made their homes in Jamestown, which became the center of the Virginia Colony's government. But Jamestown lay on a low, marshy island that was also home to a well-established (and quite nasty) population of stinging and biting insects. Some settlers, fearing island conditions could lead to epidemics and finding the current site not grand enough for the capital city of America's largest colony, lobbied for relocation to a place called Middle Plantation, five miles inland. This settlement, which had grown up around a 17th-century palisade built as a defense against Indian attack, by 1690 was a small village composed of stores, mills, a tavern, a church, and an assortment of homes. In reality, there was nothing grand about it, but it sat on

relatively high ground and had access to both the James and York Rivers via navigable creeks.

For those who advocated moving inland, serendipity struck in the form of fire, when the Jamestown Statehouse burned for the fourth time in 1698. Thus, the basically unformed village of Middle Plantation became the locus for colonists who envisioned a capital city equal to their aspirations. The name Middle Plantation, more rural than regal, was changed to Williamsburg in honor of William III, king of England, and building began.

The new capital was laid out in a distinctly geometrical fashion, dictated by the colonists' current ideas about proper urban planning. The Market Square, or town commons, and a main street stretching from the Capitol building to the newly established College of William and Mary were the key structural elements of the plan. The Capitol and the college, along with Bruton Parish Church, represented stability and continuity to early settlers.

By the mid-18th century, Williamsburg was a thriving center of commerce and government. Close to 2,000 people, half of them slaves, called the city home on the eve of the American Revolution. Tailors, carpenters, bakers, gunsmiths, wheelwrights, merchants, clerks, and slaves all worked to form the support system for the capital city's growing number of—what else—politicians and lawyers. While the latter two professions wielded power and enjoyed considerable prestige, there are those who would argue that the most important persons in town were the tavern keepers. Taverns were not just for drinking, after all; they were the political, social, and cultural heart of colonial life. If the walls of the Raleigh Tavern could speak, surely they would tell of the clandestine sessions held there by Virginia's burgesses. They could also tell tales of a more scandalous and less heroic sort. Thomas Jefferson didn't brand the town "Devilsburg" for nothing.

i *In Virginia, if you are looking for the experience of living history, you'll find nearly every era represented at numerous special events and destinations year-round. For free brochures on African-American, Native American, and Hispanic heritage, or for information on Civil War battlefields and sites, call the Virginia tourism hotline at (800) 321-3244.*

The prominent role Williamsburg played in events leading to the Revolutionary War is well known. In 1765 Patrick Henry delivered his rousing (some said treasonous) Stamp Act speech at the House of Burgesses here. The First Continental Congress was called from here in 1774. And, for all intents and purposes, the Revolution ended a dozen miles away, with the surrender of Cornwallis to Washington on the fields of Yorktown in 1781.

FROM RICHES TO RAGS

But as the Revolutionary War wound down, Williamsburg's days as a center of government were over. In 1780, shortly after Jefferson was elected to succeed Patrick Henry as Virginia's governor, the capital was moved to Richmond.

Jefferson, who came from the western part of what is now the state of Virginia, had long advocated moving the capital west to lessen traveling distances for officials coming from the far reaches of the colony (then stretching as far as Illinois). Richmond also was judged a safer site, in terms of both climate and military defense.

As Richmond moved into the spotlight, Williamsburg suffered through a decline and loss of prestige and vitality. Taverns closed; public buildings fell into ruin. The number of residents dwindled to about 1,400. Shortly after the Revolution, the empty Governor's Palace and Capitol burned. Only two institutions of note remained: the college, with enrollment greatly diminished, and the Public Hospital for the Insane. (Town wags liked to say that the only difference between the two was that the latter required some proof of improvement before letting you leave.)

The Civil War did little to enhance Williamsburg's fortunes. Though most of the 18th-century buildings survived, Federal troops occupied the town for three years, and the college was forced to close after its Wren Building burned. In 1862, McClellan's Union forces battled through in their attempt to reach Richmond, the Confederate capital.

The arrival of the railroad in 1880 revived the town a little. The C&O's Fast Flying Virginian, also called the Cannonball Express, ran daily from its southern terminus in Newport News, through Williamsburg and on to Toledo, Ohio. (Dinner in the dining car cost less than a dollar, and that included whiskey.) New houses sprang up near the C&O depot, roads were paved, William and Mary added dorms, a library, and a gymnasium. But Williamsburg remained a quiet college burg, rather insulated, until the mid-1920s, when a Rockefeller came to town.

BACK TO RICHES AGAIN

Luckily for Williamsburg, Dr. W. A. R. Goodwin, rector of Bruton Parish Church, was a man of vast imagination. He saw past the shabby exteriors of the many old buildings and dreamed of restoring the town's faded heritage. Goodwin was also a persuasive fellow and was able to interest philanthropist John D. Rockefeller Jr. in his vision of a vibrant Williamsburg. The two men teamed up and, in 1926, work on the restoration of the colonial capital began. Rockefeller not only provided funds but also personally devoted himself to the ambitious project by directing the measurements of buildings and spearheading research efforts.

i A number of U.S. presidents have visited the historic Colonial Williamsburg area, including Franklin Roosevelt, Harry Truman, Dwight Eisenhower, Lyndon Johnson, Richard Nixon, Gerald Ford, Jimmy Carter, Ronald Reagan, and Bill Clinton.

Fittingly, the Raleigh Tavern was the first restored building opened to the public, in 1932. Soon the Governor's Palace and reconstructed Capitol were ready for viewing as well. Colonial Williamsburg, repository of the American past, was well on its way to becoming the fascinating domain that it is today. Tourists arrived in small numbers at first, but after Queen Elizabeth's visit to the Historic Area in 1957, the public began coming in droves. Hotels, motels, restaurants, and shopping centers sprang up to serve them.

Benefiting from the ready audience Colonial Williamsburg provided, a number of nearby Historic Triangle attractions decided to put on the ritz. National Park Service properties at Jamestown and Yorktown were improved. Jamestown Settlement, adjacent to Jamestown Island, opened in 1957. Yorktown Victory Center opened in 1976. In 2009, paid attendance at the two attractions surpassed 600,000.

Anheuser-Busch arrived in the area, first with a brewery, then with the enormously popular Busch Gardens theme park, which will celebrate its 35th anniversary in 2010. The Williamsburg Pottery Factory grew from a roadside stand into a vast and somewhat indescribable retail complex that has drawn millions of shoppers annually.

By the time Water Country USA opened its doors in 1984, Williamsburg had reinvented itself again—this time as a vacation destination with something for everyone to enjoy, not just the history buffs.

ABOUT THE ECONOMY

Attracting tourists isn't the only business of the Historic Triangle. Industry, commerce, and professional services have grown dramatically in the region. Regionally, the economy has long been driven by the military and related contractors—shipbuilding historically, but increasingly such high-technology fields as remote sensing and computer-driven simulations.

In and around Williamsburg proper, Anheuser-Busch has been a key driver over the past 35 years—so the sale of the brewery to Belgian-based beer conglomerate InBev in late 2008 is still rippling through the economy.

The brewery itself has gone through rounds of cost-cutting, but still employs around 800. It's also responsible for spin-off jobs at suppliers such as Owens-Illinois bottle-making plant and Ball Metal Container's can-manufacturing plant.

The former Busch theme parks—including Busch Gardens and Water Country USA—were sold to the private-equity group Blackstone Inc. in late 2009. As of early 2010, Busch's Kingsmill Resort was also for sale, and InBev in late 2009 announced it was discontinuing its sponsorship of the LPGA Michelob Ultra Open, held annually at Kingsmill.

Other major local employers in and around Williamsburg include timeshare resorts such as Williamsburg Plantation; Eastern State Hospital, a state-funded mental-health facility; the College of William and Mary; and Sentara Williamsburg Regional Medical Center.

The region's population growth has also been a critical economic factor, especially in the areas immediately surrounding the city of Williamsburg. James City County, for example, almost doubled in population between 1990 and 2010, to nearly 70,000, and is projected to grow by another 25 percent by 2020. That has meant

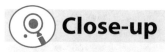

Close-up

A Williamsburg Chronology

1683: Bruton Parish completes its first church building.

1693: King William III and Queen Mary II grant a charter for the College of William and Mary in Virginia; bricks are laid in 1695.

1699: The colonial capital moves from Jamestown to Williamsburg, previously called "Middle Plantation." On June 7, 1699, the city officially is renamed Williamsburg when the General Assembly passes the act to build the statehouse.

1715: The second Bruton Parish Church structure replaces the first.

1765: Patrick Henry gives his Stamp Act Speech in the House of Burgesses.

1774: The First Continental Congress meets in Williamsburg.

1780: Thomas Jefferson becomes the elected Revolutionary Governor; the capital moves to Richmond for better security.

1781: The "Frenchman's Map" of the city, later used in restoration of Colonial Williamsburg, shows the city streets and structures after Lafayette's troops help Revolutionary forces win the Battle of Yorktown.

1862: Williamsburg falls to Federal forces that garrison at the College of William and Mary.

1880: The C&O Railroad (now CSX) arrives in town, bringing with it some recovery from the economic damages of war and decline.

1924–1927: The Reverend W. A. R. Goodwin obtains John D. Rockefeller Jr.'s support in restoring Williamsburg's 18th-century heritage.

1932: The Raleigh Tavern, Colonial Williamsburg's first completed restoration, opens to the public. The Governor's Palace follows in 1934.

1957: Queen Elizabeth II tours the Historic Area; Colonial Williamsburg's Information Center and the Jamestown Festival Park (now Jamestown Settlement) open.

1975: Anheuser-Busch develops its Busch Gardens theme park.

1976: Network television carries the debate between President Gerald Ford and Democratic nominee Jimmy Carter, held at William and Mary's Phi Beta Kappa Hall.

1983: The Summit of Industrialized Nations meets here, bringing together heads of state from the United States, Japan, France, West Germany, Italy, Great Britain, Canada, and the European Economic Community. President Ronald Reagan serves as host.

1988: Democratic presidential candidates debate in Phi Beta Kappa Hall.

1993: The College of William and Mary celebrates the 300th anniversary of the year it was chartered in England.

August 1995: The College of William and Mary throws a 300th birthday party for the Christopher Wren Building, the nation's oldest academic building in continuous use, built two years after the college was chartered.

October 1995: Defense ministers from each of the 16 North Atlantic Treaty Organization (NATO) nations meet in Williamsburg. It is their first meeting in the United States in four decades.

Dec. 31, 1998: Williamsburg begins its 300th anniversary celebration at annual First Night festivities.

1999: Williamsburg commemorates its 300th anniversary with special events throughout the year.

2001: Colonial Williamsburg celebrates its 75th anniversary with extended hours, reduced rates, and grand reopenings of several renovated properties.

2007: Jamestown celebrates its 400th anniversary.

significant spending and jobs in construction, both of homes and commercial facilities. Jobs in those industries took a hit with the 2008–9 recession: employment in construction fell more than 10 percent, for example, particularly as the pace of home construction slowed.

Still, the region's unemployment rate has remained roughly two percentage points below the national average, largely because of the cushioning effect of military spending and other government programs. Those programs stretch far beyond building ships and maintaining military bases. For instance, the region has one of the highest concentrations of scientists and engineers in the country—and they don't just work at shipyards. They're also at places like NASA's Lang-

ley Research Center in Hampton, which specializes in aeronautics, and the U.S. Department of Energy's Jefferson Lab in Newport News, where particle accelerators and high-energy lasers gives scientists peeks at the basic nature of atoms.

If you need to know more about the area's economy, there are a number of useful resources. Both *The Virginia Gazette* and the *Daily Press* cover regional economic news. More broadly, the Virginia Employment Commission (www.vec.virginia.gov) has excellent economic data available (look for "Labor Marketing Information"), and the University of Virginia's Wheldon Cooper Center is a one-stop directory for all types of in-depth private and government statistics and trends.

GETTING HERE, GETTING AROUND

ne thing to always remember around Williamsburg and most of Virginia: No road runs compass-straight. Ever. The hilly, river-crossed terrain doesn't lend itself to it. Locals joke that some roads run the way they do because some native or settler wandered crookedly centuries ago.

So remember that Williamsburg, Jamestown, and Yorktown are small, and roads in the heart of the localities are paved versions of the early paths of the colonists: quaint, sometimes narrow, and often congested. Give yourself plenty of time to make it to your destination at the desired hour.

Before you can hope to find your way around, it's essential you get a brief geography lesson.

Williamsburg is the northwestern-most city in a region called the Virginia Peninsula. The peninsula also includes the cities of Hampton, Newport News, and Poquoson, and the counties of James City and York.

Across the York River to the north is Gloucester County. Across the James River to the south is South Hampton Roads or Southside—the cities of Norfolk, Portsmouth, Chesapeake, Suffolk, and Virginia Beach. Taken together, the Virginia Peninsula and South Hampton Roads make up a geographic area dubbed Hampton Roads, which is also the name of the harbor at the mouth of the James River around which most of these cities are located.

With a population of almost 1.7 million, Hampton Roads is the nation's 35th-largest MSA, about the same size at Charlotte, North Carolina, or Austin, Texas.

GETTING HERE

By Automobile

The Virginia Peninsula is sometimes called the World's Largest Cul-de-Sac. People driving to the area have a limited number of routes to choose from.

From the north or south, most visitors arrive via I-95, cutting onto I-64 near Richmond. I-64 runs like a spine down the peninsula, then crosses over to the Norfolk area via tunnel at the wide harbor where the James River meets the Chesapeake Bay.

If you're of a mind to ditch the interstates, two scenic alternatives come to mind: From the Washington area, take US 301 to US 17 across Virginia's Northern Neck and Middle Peninsula. You'll cross the York River at Gloucester Point (there's a $2 toll,

collected only from northbound vehicles). You'll pass right by the historic Yorktown Battlefield and can connect to Williamsburg on the gorgeous Colonial National Historic Parkway.

Another alternative from farther north: Ditch I-95 at Philadelphia and use the Delaware Turnpike and US 13 to the Chesapeake Bridge-Tunnel (touted as an engineering wonder, a series of causeways, bridges, and two tunnels that span more than 17 miles at the mouth of the bay). There's a $12 toll each way—expensive, but often less than the aggravation of gridlock on the Washington Beltway or I-95.

From the Richmond area, the scenic alternatives to I-64 are US Route 60, which intersects with I-295 east of Richmond. It's two lanes each direction, divided in most places, but with frequent turnoffs and occasional traffic lights. The other choice is Route 5, the old plantation route between Williamsburg and Richmond. Protected as a Scenic Byway, Route 5 is a two-lane road through pretty countryside. It is especially picturesque during autumn and provides a cooler, tree-shaded—if slower—option during the heat of summer.

Traveling at legal speed on any of these three highways, you are within an hour of Williamsburg from downtown Richmond. One note about speeding: Besides authorities' usual vigilance, radar detectors are illegal in Virginia. Get caught with one and you'll get *another* ticket in addition to the one for speeding.

From the south—including the Norfolk area and Outer Banks—the main route to the peninsula is the Hampton Roads Bridge Tunnel, one of the most maddeningly unpredictable water crossings you'll find anywhere. It's free—although the toll it extracts in time can be incalculable. Rush hours (both directions, morning and afternoon, from commuters, especially to and from the nearby Norfolk Navy Base) are guaranteed to clog. Friday and Sunday afternoons in summer, too, as weekend travelers to the Outer Banks of North Carolina add to the flow. But the tunnel can jam up for almost no apparent reason at just about any time of day or night—all it takes is for one of the two lanes either direction to shut down because of a vehicle breakdown, accident, or road maintenance.

The alternatives: The Monitor-Merrimac Bridge-Tunnel (yes, it runs roughly at the place where the famous ironclad battle occurred) is an extension of I-264, the western leg of the Hampton Roads Beltway. Once on the peninsula, stay on I-264 until it connects with I-64, then continue northwest to Williamsburg.

The second alternate is the James River Bridge: Hop over to US 17 (either from the I-264 beltway, or from US 58 at Suffolk. Once across the bridge, continue up Mercury Boulevard to I-64.

Perhaps the most leisurely—and memorable—route is the (free) Jamestown-Scotland ferry from Surry County. Approach Surry on State Route 31 until it ends at the James River. Ferries run roughly every half-hour during the day and evening, hourly overnight. The trip takes about 15 minutes, and deposits you at the foot of Jamestown Road. (The ferry and its fleet of four vessels is an attraction in itself. For more, see our entry in the Day Trips chapter.)

i **Route 199 helps motorists circumvent downtown traffic and makes the trip from Busch Gardens, Williamsburg, or Water Country USA to the Williamsburg Pottery Factory area in record time. The northwestern two-thirds is a limited-access highway, so drivers can exit at any number of points en route.**

By Plane

Three commercial airports provide service to the area. All offer a choice of major airlines.

NEWPORT NEWS/WILLIAMSBURG INTERNATIONAL AIRPORT
900 Bland Blvd., I-64, exit 255B
(757) 877-0221
www.nnwairport.com
The Newport News/Williamsburg International Airport (formerly "Patrick Henry International") is only 17 miles from the heart of Williamsburg.

Depending on your departure point, this can be a quick, cheap entry point to the area. Service is provided by **AirTran** (800) 248-8726; **U.S. Airways** (800) 428-4322; and **Delta** (800-221-1212). **Frontier Airlines** (800) 432-1359, is scheduled to start nonstop service to and from Denver, four days a week, beginning in May 2010.

The downside of Newport News: Other than AirTran, most of the flights into the airport are commuter planes. There are around 50 flights daily, including frequent direct service to Atlanta, Charlotte, and Philadelphia, and once- or twice-daily direct service to Boston, New York-LaGuardia and Orlando. (All other service is via connections.) A $23 million terminal expansion is scheduled to be completed in 2010.

Once you're on the ground, you can catch a taxi (the fare will run about $40). Several companies offer shared shuttle services for around $35 per person one way. Both options are located outside the

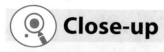 **Close-up**

The Williamsburg Trolley

Parking in the Historic Area is tight. And traffic during high season around Busch Gardens, Water Country USA, and Richmond Road can be very congested. For years, one of the best amenities of staying in Colonial Williamsburg lodging was being able to leave your car behind for the day and hop on a CW bus, which circulates through and around the Historic Area, stopping at major points of interest. (Ticket holders may board at any stop.)

In 2009, the city added trolley service to expand the public transportation options outside the historic area. The red-and-green trolleys look traditional but have modern features like bicycle racks, air-conditioning, and full wheelchair accessibility.

The trolleys will run from Merchants Square, along Richmond Road to the Williamsburg Shopping Center and High Street (home to a movie theater and several restaurants) and then west on Monticello Avenue to the New Town area (see our Close-up in the Shopping chapter). Service will be available from 3 to 10 p.m. Mon to Thurs, 3 to 11 p.m. Fri and Sat and from noon to 8 p.m. Sun.

A complete loop takes 30 minutes and costs 50 cents, 25 cents for seniors (exact fare only). Area middle and high school students and students of the College of William and Mary ride for free with an official school ID card. Children under 6 ride free. The trolley does not operate on Thanksgiving, Christmas, or New Year's Day.

Look for the round "Williamsburg Trolley" signs at several locations in New Town and High Street. The trolley stops on Richmond Road near the Williamsburg Shopping Center and the Williamsburg Hospitality House and near the Peanut Shop on Prince George Street and near Talbots in Merchants Square.

More information about the trolley is available online at www.williamsburgtransport.com, or by calling (757) 220-5493 ext. 200, from 8 a.m. to 5 p.m. Mon through Fri.

terminal (advance reservations are recommended for the shuttles; more information is under "ground transportation" on the airport's Web site). It's about a 25-minute ride to Williamsburg.

Car rental companies at the airport are **Avis** (800) 331-1212; **Budget** (800) 527-0700; **Enterprise** (800) 261-7331; **Hertz** (800) 654-3131; and **National** (800) 227-7368.

NORFOLK INTERNATIONAL AIRPORT
2200 Norview Ave., I-64, exit 279
(757) 857-3351
www.norfolkairport.com

Norfolk's airport lies 40 miles southeast of Williamsburg. It has roughly 180 flights a day, including direct flights to 20 cities, and frequent service to the Northeast. Southwest Airlines' arrival in 2001 has moderated fares to many cities.

Against those pros, add one big con: the Hampton Roads Bridge-Tunnel, which takes I-64 across the Hampton Roads harbor. Sometimes, it's a free-flowing breeze. Other times—especially rush hours and weekends—it can back up for miles. Allow extra time.

Airlines serving Norfolk International include **American** (800) 433-7300; **Continental** (800) 525-0280; **Delta** (800) 221-1212; **Northwest** (800) 225-2525 (as of press time; Northwest and Delta are in the process of merging, with all flights expected to be combined at Delta in mid-2010); **Southwest** (800) 435-9792; **United** (800) 241-6522; and **U.S. Airways** (800) 428-4322.

Rental car companies have desks on the lower level of the arrivals terminal near baggage claim. On-terminal rental companies are **Alamo** (800) 462-5266; **Avis** (800) 831-2847; **Budget** (800) 527-

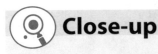 # Close-up

Colonial National Historic Parkway

A visit to the Historic Triangle wouldn't be complete without a leisurely drive along Colonial National ParkwayParkway, a 23-mile corridor specifically built to link the beginning and the end of the British colonial experience in America, with beautiful views of the James and York Rivers, and the rolling, wooded land between them.

The Colonial Parkway has limited exits and no amenities, commercial advertising, or trucks. But there is **wildlife**—deer, squirrels, muskrats, and possums may wander across the road. The waterways you encounter are home to fish, crabs, egrets, and waterfowl. Think of it as a "linear park," shielded from development. The drive is especially enchanting in spring, when the dogwood and redbud are blooming, and in the fall, when the hardwoods turn.

A warning to the lead-footed: This is a federal road and the speed limits, which range from 25 mph to 45 mph, are strictly enforced. Getting a ticket means appearing in federal court, where few beat the offense. Moreover, the road is made of river gravel set in concrete. Driving much faster than 45 gets noisy.

Points of interest are marked by numerous turnouts with informative signs. These often give historical information not covered by visits to individual sites, so the drive will complement tours of Jamestown, Williamsburg, or Yorktown. Above all, it demonstrates how history and the prosperity of the Historic Triangle are intertwined with the waterways, from colonial times to today.

Leaving Jamestown, you'll pass through woodlands of silver maples, river birches, pine, and spruce. The James River runs along your right. You'll note dozens of duck blinds in the marshes and creeks. The river is a flyway for many ducks as well as Canada geese.

Each turnout contains a historical marker. One on the Jamestown end notes the site of an early community called **Archer's Hope.** All five inhabitants were among the one-quarter of Virginia's colonists killed during the Great Indian Massacre on March 22, 1622. A little farther down the road toward Williamsburg, a marker notes the site of an early attempted settlement that actually predated Jamestown. In September 1570 a group of Spanish Jesuits landed along College Creek. They crossed the peninsula to the York River, where they established a mission. But six months later all of them, except one young boy, were wiped out during a massacre. The young boy survived in the woods until he was rescued by a relief expedition in 1572.

After reading that marker, turn around and look across the James River. On a clear day, you may spy the **"Ghost Fleet,"** a collection of mothballed U.S. Navy ships (technically part of the National Defense Reserve Fleet).

The road then turns inland (and the speed limit drops to 35) as you pass Williamsburg. Just beyond a short tunnel (you'll pass under Duke of Gloucester Street in the heart of the his-

---

0700; **Dollar** (800) 800-3665; **Enterprise** (800) 736-8227; **Hertz** (800) 654-3131; **National** (800) 227-7368; and **Thrifty** (800) 367-2277.

Ground transportation to Williamsburg from Norfolk includes several taxi services and a ground shuttle service by **Airport Express** (757) 963-0433 or (866) 823-4626.

The shuttle to Williamsburg leaves every 30 minutes on the half-hour and the hour and costs $50, and $10 for additional riders. When you're heading back to the airport, call the day before to schedule a pickup at the door of your hotel. Cab fare will run almost $100. (Check around baggage claims—you can often find someone else heading for Williamsburg to split the ride.)

toric area), you'll see **Robertson's Windmill,** dating from the 18th century, on your left. The windmill suffered a blow to its status as a landmark in 2009 when one its blades fell off and Colonial Williamsburg removed the other three, citing safety concerns. There's a turnoff to the Colonial Williamsburg visitor center; to stay on the Colonial Parkway, bear to your right and keep going straight.

Yorktown is 13 miles away, but there's plenty to see before you get there. Among the historical markers: the site of a Union Army advance on Williamsburg during the Civil War; Jones Mill Pond, a favorite local fishing hole; and the sites of Ringfield and Bellfield Plantations. Once you pass over King's Creek, the banks of the majestic York River open up before you. On the left side of the river is Gloucester County, a place full of a history all its own.

On this side of the river, a long dock stretching into the river is the loading pier of **Cheatham Annex,** an ammunition supply depot for the Norfolk Naval Base. Nearby a marker that points out Werewocomoco, Powhatan's "chiefest habitation" and the place where Captain John Smith was held captive in 1607.

The York River, known as the Pamunkey by Virginia Indians, flows over the deepest natural channel of any in the Chesapeake Bay tributary. That's why a little farther downriver you'll come across another pier. This one is located adjacent to the Yorktown Naval Weapons Station, established in 1918 to support the Atlantic Fleet, home ported in nearby Norfolk. If you pull over into the Bracken's Pond turnout, you may see large naval ships taking on supplies. If you see armed guards along the parkway, red lights on the pier, or a ship flying a red flag, you'll know that's the business at hand.

Within minutes you'll come upon a left-hand exit for **Yorktown,** site of the British surrender to the American Continental Army in 1781, when the American Revolution came to a close. If you choose instead to do a driving tour of the Yorktown battlefield, stay on the Colonial Parkway until it ends, which puts you right on the battlefield road.

The best way to enjoy the parkway is to set aside a few hours to explore. Ingredients for a picnic can be gathered at **The Fresh Market** or the **Cheese Shop** in Williamsburg, or the **Jamestown Pie Co.** closer to the road's southern end. You'll find plenty of places to pull over and enjoy a waterside vista.

NOTE: The western end of the parkway was closed in 2009 following an accident in which a barge hit a piling, seriously damaging the bridge crossing Powhatan Creek. Scheduled to reopen by summer 2010, work is running behind mostly due to uncooperative weather. From Williamsburg, the parkway remains open to traffic headed east to Yorktown and as far west as the intersection with Route 199. A marked detour utilizing Route 199 and Jamestown Road (Route 31) will guide you to Jamestown if the parkway has not yet reopened in its entirety.

RICHMOND INTERNATIONAL AIRPORT
1 Richard East Byrd Terminal Dr.
(804) 226-3000
www.flyrichmond.com
Richmond International Airport, exit 197A off I-64, is about 45 miles west of Williamsburg and offers nonstop flights to 22 destinations and connecting flights to worldwide destinations.

The airport terminal and parking garages went through a $120 million project to replace the terminal, completed in 2007. The expansion solved a critical problem at the airport—all the gates were full, preventing low-cost carriers from entering the market and keeping airfares among the highest in the nation.

Since the expansion, low-fare specialists like AirTran and JetBlue have started serving Rich-

A Word about Routes

In Virginia, state and national high-ways are referred to as "routes." So if you ask for directions to Route 5, you'll get an answer immediately. Ask for *Highway* 5, and you might get a blank stare.

mond, and fares have moderated. The airport handles about 170 flights daily.

Airlines serving Richmond International include **American** (800) 433-7300; **Continental** (800) 525-0280; **Delta** (800) 221-1212; **JetBlue** (800) 538-2583; **Northwest** (800) 225-2525 (note: Delta and Northwest should complete their merger in mid-2010, combining under the Delta name); **United** (800) 241-6522; **U.S. Airways** (800) 428-4322; and **AirCanada** (888) 247-2262.

You'll find the rental car companies adjacent to the baggage claim area. Companies that serve this airport include **Alamo** (877) 222-9075; **Avis** (800) 831-2847; **Budget** (800) 527-0700; **Dollar** (800) 800-3665; **Enterprise** (800) 261-7331; **Hertz** (800) 654-3131; **National** (800) 227-7368; and **Thrifty** (800) 367-2277.

Ground transportation to Williamsburg from the Richmond airport includes several taxi services (fares to Williamsburg will run close to $100) and a ground shuttle by **Groome Transportation** at (800) 552-7911. The shuttle to Williamsburg leaves every hour on the hour and costs $44, or $27.50 per person for two or more. While reservations aren't necessary if you're traveling from the airport to Williamsburg, it is best to call

ℹ️ Call it a quirk: Most of the airlines at Norfolk are crammed into Terminal B. Only U.S. Airways and Southwest go out of Terminal A—so security lines there tend to be short. The other airlines? Allow extra time for long security lines, especially early in the morning.

a day or two in advance to make a reservation for a return trip from Williamsburg to the Richmond airport. (Round-trip service is $78 for one person if you buy it before leaving Richmond.)

By Rail

AMTRAK
The Williamsburg Transportation Center
468 North Boundary St.
(757) 229-8750, (800) 872-7245
www.amtrak.com
Amtrak's Northeast Regional service generally halts in Richmond, but two trains a day (three on Fridays) stretch on to Williamsburg. The Amtrak terminal, housed in what is now called the Williamsburg Transportation Center, is just three blocks from the historic district. Taxi service, provided by several companies, is available.

Amtrak provides good connections through Washington, D.C., to all points north and west. Connections to the north and south are frequent from Richmond as well.

Two daily westward departures serve Richmond and Washington, D.C., generally mid-morning and early afternoon (precise times change every few months).

Advice for train travelers: The major car rental companies' offices are some distance from the station. However, B&W Rental & Colonial Rent-A-Car Inc., a locally owned company, has an office in the Transportation Center. If you make a reservation with them, a company representative will meet your train with keys and a contract for a rental car in hand. Their services may save visitors taxi fare to hotels and an overnight wait for a car. Call (757) 220-3399 or (888) 220-9941 for specifics.

By Bus

GREYHOUND BUS SYSTEM
The Williamsburg Transportation Center
468 North Boundary St.
(757) 229-1460
Greyhound offers nationwide service to and from the Williamsburg area. Arrivals and departures

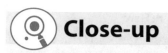 **Close-up**

Pronunciation Guide

The last thing newcomers need to add to their lists of things to do is to learn a foreign language. English is spoken here, and some locals may remind you it's been spoken here longer than anywhere else in North America. (Of course, those very people are likely to have the old Virginia accent that makes "about" sound like a piece of footwear).

Here are some names and pronunciations that date to the first meetings of Native Americans and the colonials.

Botetourt: BOT-a-tot. Lord Botetourt was the Virginia Colony's governor from 1768 to 1770. You'll see his name on area streets and the occasional room or hall of a public building.

Chickahominy River: chick-a-HOM-i-nee. This Indian word means "land of much grain." The river is in New Kent County, and meets the James just west of Williamsburg.

DOG Street: Students and locals use this acronym for Duke of Gloucester Street, Colonial Williamsburg's central pedestrian thoroughfare.

Fort Eustis: fort YOU-stess. An army base in northern Newport News. See our Newport News and Hampton and Our Military Heritage chapters for more information on this fort and its transportation museum.

Gaol: jail. At the Publick Gaol behind the Capitol on Nicholson Street in Colonial Williamsburg, visitors can see the small, dank cells where 18th-century criminals and debtors were incarcerated. The English are to blame for the funny spelling.

Gloucester: GLOSS-ter. This county north of the York River is named after an English city.

Isle of Wight: Ile-of-white. Named after an English island, this county lies south of the James River.

Mattaponi River: mat-ta-pa-NI. The name of this York River tributary is derived from an Indian language.

Monticello: Thomas Jefferson's estate outside Charlottesville may be mont-a-CHEL-lo, but Monticello Road in Williamsburg should be pronounced mont-a-SELL-o.

Norfolk: NAW-fok. Even natives sometimes disagree about the right way to say this city's name, which is another borrowing from the British, who have a Norfolk County. No matter how you say it, be careful! The best advice probably is to say it quickly.

Pamunkey: puh-MUN-key. An Indian tribe whose reservation is in King William County.

Poquoson: puh-KO-sen. Derived from the Indian for "low ground" or "swamp," this peninsula city (next to York County) is a popular suburb with the scientists and air crew from nearby Langley Air Force base and NASA Langley Research Center.

Powhatan: POW-a-tan. This famous Indian chief, father of Pocahontas, might be surprised to see his moniker used not only on streets but also as a name for a time-share development.

Rochambeau: row-sham-BOW. This French general was Washington's ally at Yorktown during the Revolutionary War.

Taliaferro: TOL-liv-er. This old Virginia family, originally Italian, saw their name anglicized. General William Booth Taliaferro was a wealthy planter and greatly aided the devastated College of William and Mary after the Civil War.

Toano: toe-AN-oh. This town in western James City County takes its name from an Indian believed to have been a member of Powhatan's tribe.

Wythe: with. George Wythe signed the Declaration of Independence, was William and Mary's first professor of law, and eventually became chancellor of Virginia. The Wythe House in Colonial Williamsburg was once his property.

are from the Williamsburg Transportation Center. Buses heading to major destinations such as Washington, D.C. ($40 one-way), Philadelphia ($80 one-way), and New York City ($75 one-way) leave throughout the day with as many as six departures in a 24-hour period. No reservations are required, but making an advance purchase could save you a substantial amount of money. (Advance purchase can reduce the fare to New York, for instance, to as little as $39 one way.) Passengers are asked to arrive at the station at least half an hour ahead of departure time to allow ample time to buy tickets, stow baggage, and get ready for boarding.

i When asking for directions, don't even try to figure out the compass directions (most locals don't bother). Because so few roads run by the compass (and not many more actually stay *straight* for very long), it's easier to have a destination in mind when you ask a local for directions: "Is that Route 60 toward the outlet center, or Route 60 toward Busch Gardens?" or "Are you looking for I-64 toward Richmond or toward Norfolk?"

Once You're Here

Here's an easy trick: Think of the region as a cross, with the Colonial Williamsburg Visitor Center at the center. The Colonial Parkway, the upright portion of the cross, has Yorktown at the top and Jamestown at the bottom. US 60, the crossing arm, has Toano, Lightfoot, and the outlets to the left and Busch Gardens to the right.

For getting around Williamsburg on your own, it might help to orient yourself by thinking of US 60 as the spine of the city. Toward the north and west from downtown Williamsburg, US 60 is named Richmond Road, the major commercial artery. From the William and Mary campus eastward, it travels Francis Street to York Street, where it turns east and is the route to Busch Gardens. A parallel Bypass Route 60 north of the center of town features motels and restaurants and is a good route for avoiding traffic when traveling from Busch Gardens to Richmond Road locations.

The fastest way to go *around* town is Route 199, which will get you from I-64 near Busch Gardens to I-64 near Lightfoot, bypassing the historic area altogether. Most of the route is limited access, restricting the number of stoplights.

ACCOMMODATIONS

The pineapple was the colonial symbol of hospitality, and it still signifies gracious accommodation. Today you'll have a much easier time finding welcome here than did the British, French, and Continental armies, and later the Civil War's Yankee soldiers. They boarded at the colonial inns and taverns in the Historic Area, the true antecedents of today's hotels, motels, and inns. Your stay should be much more comfortable.

The Williamsburg area offers more than 10,000 hotel and motel rooms in a wide range of prices, so you should have no difficulty finding something that suits you. If you're coming at Christmas, however, we recommend that you make your reservations well in advance.

A toll-free reservation service, (800) 999-4485, is operated by the Williamsburg Hotel/Motel Association and can advise you on a choice of accommodations as well as make your reservation with member properties. Most accommodations, in turn, will make dinner reservations for you, and tickets to Colonial Williamsburg and Busch Gardens can be purchased at many of the check-in desks. Or visit www.gowilliamsburg.com to explore all the options and make reservations.

While we give you up-to-date details on amenities at the time of publication, some things can change abruptly. To ensure your satisfaction, we strongly recommend you ask about details on specifics such as ground-floor rooms, elevators, separate heating and cooling controls, mattress sizes, showers or tubs, age of the establishment, whether your four-footed family members are welcome, and availability of cable TV or Internet access when you make your reservation.

You might also inquire about proximity to highways, or CSX railroad noise. Other considerations are distance to your local touring destination and directions from I-64 or whichever route you plan to travel.

When making a reservation, inquire about special discounted rates for AAA members, children, senior citizens, members of the military, and government travelers. You may also want to ask about changes in pricing between in-season and out-of-season times. These periods are defined by the individual lodging, but generally in-season or peak season is from late March to November and again during the winter holiday season. Off-season months are generally January, February, and much, if not all, of March, though this can change, depending on when Easter Sunday falls. Reservations made well in advance are almost a necessity in peak season.

The accommodations listed below accept major credit cards unless otherwise noted. And, unless we tell you differently, assume that the lodgings allow smoking and children, and that the facility is wheelchair accessible. Although it's certainly possible to find a pet-friendly hotel or motel in the Historic Triangle, it's not the norm. If pets are not mentioned in a hotel's description, assume that you and your family are welcome there, but pets are not.

Hotels and Motels Price Code

Based on information available at the time of publication, we offer the following price code as a general guide, with the warning that fluctuations in price and availability, and even chain allegiance, of lodgings often occur. The figures indicate an average charge for double occupancy during peak season.

$ . . . . Less than $100
$$ . . . . $101 to $175
$$$ . . . . $176 to $250
$$$$ . . . . More than $250

BASSETT MOTEL $
800 York St.
(757) 229-5175
http://bassettmotel.com
This motel is conveniently located within a short walk or drive from most of Williamsburg's attractions—the Historic Area, Busch Gardens, Water County USA, etc. Eighteen ground-floor rooms offer individual heat and air-conditioning controls, and full baths. Open year-round.

BEST WESTERN HISTORIC AREA INN $
201 Bypass Rd.
(757) 220-0880, (800) 446-1062
www.bestwestern.com
This hotel is conveniently located between the historic area and the outlet shopping district and popular with both tourists and business travelers. Continental breakfast and wireless Internet access are included in the room rate. An indoor heated pool and Jacuzzi will please the kids or offer relief at the end of a day traveling or touring. Uno's Chicago Grill, serving pizza, seafood, and grilled meats, is adjacent, and Cracker Barrel, Dairy Queen, and Golden Corral are across the (busy) street. There are smoking rooms available, but pets are prohibited. Discounts are offered to senior citizens, military, government employees, and AAA members.

BUDGET INN $
800 Capitol Landing Rd.
(757) 229-2374
There are 23 rooms at this older but clean motel. Guests will enjoy the tree-shaded grounds and the outdoor swimming pool. Each room has cable TV. Internet access is available without an additional charge.

CLARION HOTEL—HISTORIC DISTRICT $$
351 York St.
(757) 229-4100
www.clarionwilliamsburg.com
This hotel has 143 deluxe guest rooms, all a very short walk from the eastern end of the Historic Area. Busch Gardens and Water Country USA are within a five-minute drive.

The well-appointed guest rooms have coffeemakers, work desks, hair dryers, irons, ironing boards, Nintendo game systems, pillow-top mattresses, voice mail, and cable television. Select rooms have down pillows, kitchen facilities with microwaves and refrigerators, safes, and sofa sleepers. Wheelchair-accessible rooms can be requested.

Coffee, a daily newspaper, local phone calls, and wireless Internet access are included in the room rate. There is an on-site business center with a public computer and copy and fax services. After hours, guests can relax in the indoor heated pool or Jacuzzi. A billiard room, game room, fitness center, and full-service restaurant, the Bourbon Street Grille, are located on the property. Banquet and meeting rooms can accommodate up to 330 people for most business or social functions. Senior citizen and other discounts are offered. The hotel is 100 percent smoke-free.

COLONEL WALLER MOTEL $
917 Capitol Landing Rd.
(757) 253-0999, (800) 368-5006
Families like the inexpensive, all-suite configuration of this 28-room motel's large, comfortable

offerings, conveniently located near the eastern edge of the Historic Area. After supper, if you have a ticket, you can wander over to the Colonial Williamsburg Visitor Center and catch the bus into Merchants Square for an ice-cream cone or fresh-roasted Virginia peanuts. The outdoor pool will take your mind off your sore feet while you review your day's touring. Senior citizen, AAA, and other discounts are offered, except on holidays. There are refrigerators in all the rooms.

COMFORT INN—CENTRAL $
2007 Richmond Rd.
(757) 220-3888, (800) 221-2222
www.choicehotels.com
Located along Richmond Road's commercial district, this budget hotel has an indoor heated swimming pool with exterior sundeck, and 127 rooms, all with complimentary wireless Internet access, cable TV, coffeemakers, hair dryers, irons, and ironing boards. Continental breakfast, weekday newspaper, and local phone calls are included in the room rate. Designated smoking rooms are available, but pets are prohibited. Pretty much whatever you feel like eating is available within walking distance—Red Lobster, Carrabas, the Fireside Chop House, and Old Mill Waffle and Pancake House are among the choices nearby. Business travelers may appreciate the availability of fax and copy services. Wheelchair-accessible rooms and whirlpool suites are also available. Military and government employees, senior citizens, and AAA members are eligible for discounts.

COMFORT INN—HISTORIC AREA $
706 Bypass Rd.
(757) 229-9230, (800) 358-8003
www.choicehotels.com
This budget hotel lets you swim year-round with two pools, a heated indoor pool with hot tub and sauna, and an outdoor pool open during the warm summer months. There are 157 rooms, some with king-size beds and Jacuzzis. All rooms are equipped with hair dryers and cable television. Continental breakfast and wireless Internet

access are included in the room rate. The building is wheelchair accessible, and there are laundry facilities for guest use. Smoking is allowed in certain rooms, but no pets. There is no restaurant on the property, but Cracker Barrel and Golden Corral are within walking distance without crossing a busy street. The location puts you 10 minutes from the Historic Area, Busch Gardens, and Prime Outlets. For business travelers, there is a copy and fax service and a meeting room which can accommodate up to 100 people. Discounts for senior citizen, AAA, and military personnel are offered

COMFORT SUITES $
220-A Bypass Rd.
(757) 645-4646
www.choicehotels.com
This brand-spanking new all-suite hotel opened in March 2010 in a location convenient to all of Williamsburg's attractions. Every room has either two queen-size beds or a king, with a pullout sleeper sofa in the sitting room. The kitchen area offers a refrigerator and microwave. The entire building has wireless Internet, and the whole place is smoke-free. There is an indoor pool with spa and a fitness center. Daily newspapers and continental breakfast are included in your room charge. The Cracker Barrel and Golden Corral restaurants are just across the parking lot.

COUNTRY HEARTH INN & SUITES $
924 Capitol Landing Rd.
(757) 229-5215, (800) 368-8383
www.countryhearth.com
This motel offers 58 guest rooms all with cable TV, free phone calls and wireless Internet access, wheelchair-accessible rooms, nine suites with full kitchens, a game room, an outdoor pool, guest laundry facilities, and a picnic area with grill. Continental breakfast is included in the room rate. Located in a part of the city that is not as busy as the Richmond Road corridor, the quiet here may be more attractive to some visitors. Children younger than 17 stay free with their parents. Cribs are available for infants.

Close-up

Colonial Williamsburg Lodgings

Lodging in one of Colonial Williamsburg's properties offers advantages. These hotels and motels are closest to the Historic Area, so you can park upon arrival and either walk or ride the CW bus for free to get around. But the three best perks are priority for tee times, priority for dining reservations, and the convenience that anything you purchase from Colonial Williamsburg stores during your stay will be delivered free to your room.

Guests of the Williamsburg Inn, Providence Hall, Colonial Houses, and Williamsburg Lodge can use the Spa of Colonial Williamsburg's fitness center and pool free of charge. Check out details about the following six properties on the Internet at www.colonialwilliamsburg.com.

Colonial Houses (136 East Francis St., at the Williamsburg Inn; 800-HISTORY; $$$–$$$$). If you've ever dreamt of waking up in the 18th century, staying in one of these houses is probably the closest you'll come to wish fulfillment. The Colonial Houses offer 75 guest accommodations in 26 separate buildings, some as small as one room, and others as large as 16 rooms. Multiple rooms can be combined within a house to accommodate parties of up to 32. Scattered throughout the Historic Area, many houses overlook brick courtyards, gardens, or Duke of Gloucester Street. Furnished with authentic period reproductions and antiques, many of the houses have canopy beds, sitting rooms, or fireplaces. Guests of the Colonial Houses have recreation privileges at the Williamsburg Inn. *NOTE*: Inquire as early as possible about availability and about the accommodations unique to each. Many book as much as a year in advance for Christmas and Thanksgiving.

Providence Hall Guesthouses (305 South England St.; 800-HISTORY; $$$–$$$$). Located a short walk from the main Williamsburg Inn building, these rooms offer a tranquil view of a wooded area with a pond from private patios and balconies. The interior decor is contemporary with Asian accents, for those who like a change from colonial architecture for at least part of the day. King- and queen-size beds are available.

The Williamsburg Inn (136 East Francis St.; 800-HISTORY; $$$$). This is arguably the premier accommodation in Hampton Roads, justly proud of its pedigree as a luxury hotel. It is situated in a dignified, beautifully landscaped setting with the Historic Area and The Golden Horseshoe Golf Course on its periphery. Opened in 1937 and built to the exacting standards of John D. Rockefeller and his wife, Abby Aldrich, the Inn underwent extensive renovations in 2001. A businessman like Rockefeller would no doubt approve of the changes that brought the Inn into the 21st century—the addition of desks in each room, Internet access, larger televisions, minibars, and in-room safes. The main dining room, The Regency Room, is a four-star restaurant in its own right. Afternoon tea is served in the Terrace Room. Cocktails can be had in the Restoration Bar.

COUNTRY INN & SUITES BY
CARLSON WILLIAMSBURG EAST $$
7135 Pocahontas Trail (US Route 60)
(757) 229-6900
www.countryinns.com
Formerly the Park Inn, this 88-room property was renovated in 2006. Located between Busch Gardens and the Historic Area, the entire hotel is nonsmoking. Continental breakfast, wireless Internet access, and cable TV are included in the room rate. Kids can splash in an outdoor pool during warm weather. The inn is wheelchair accessible.

COUNTRY INN & SUITES BY CARLSON
WILLIAMSBURG HISTORIC AREA $$
400 Bypass Rd.
(757) 259-7990, (800) 456-4000
www.countryinns.com
This modern, 66-room hotel is a favorite for

Don't leave without having your picture taken on the sweeping, spiral Queen's Staircase, so named because Queen Elizabeth II was photographed while descending it on her way to dinner during her 1957 visit.

The Williamsburg Lodge (310 South England St.; 800-HISTORY; $$–$$$$). The Williamsburg Lodge specializes in accommodating big groups, with 45,000 square feet of conference meeting space, two ballrooms, and 323 rooms in eight separate buildings, connected by covered, brick walkways. In addition to refurbished guest rooms in the main building, built in 1939, the Tazewell Hall offers rooms with rocking chairs on the patio or balcony and three suites with fireplaces. Four brand-new guesthouses—the Ashby and Custis houses with 30 new rooms each, and the Nicholas and Tyler houses with 38 new rooms each—have also been added to the complex. Rooms in the guesthouses feature modern amenities such as Wi-Fi, and are decorated in "historic colors," with furnishings inspired by folk art from the Abby Aldrich Rockefeller Museum, located across the street. Guests of the Lodge have access to the fitness center at the Spa of Colonial Williamsburg, two outdoor pools, and one indoor lap pool. A business center provides a fax, computer, and printer for office needs. The Lodge restaurant, on the premises, serves cuisine with contemporary southern and Chesapeake influences.

Woodlands Hotel and Suites (102 Visitor Center Dr.; 800-HISTORY; $–$$). This contemporary three-story facility, with brick and glass exterior, is set amid a pine forest, adjacent to the Colonial Williamsburg Visitor Center. The spacious lobby, bathed in natural light from cathedral ceiling skylights, includes a separate space for a continental breakfast buffet. For full-service dining, a family-friendly, 125-seat restaurant is located across from the lobby along the pedestrian promenade to the Visitor Center. All 204 guest rooms are accessed from interior hallways. Each has two full-size beds, a sitting area with a desk, two chairs, and a comfortable lounge chair (that converts to a single bed). The 96 suites have king-size beds, a sitting area with a queen-size sofa bed and upholstered chairs, a desk, TV, and a kitchen area with a small refrigerator, microwave, and sink.

In the summer months, guests may enjoy an outdoor swimming pool and recreational amenities, including miniature golf, horseshoes, volleyball, badminton, table tennis, and shuffleboard. From June through August, the "Colonial Kids Club," offers supervised activities for children ages 5 to 12, including arts and crafts, 18th-century children's games, and visits to sites in the Historic Area. Lunch is provided. Activities vary daily.

The Woodlands fitness center, which is located on the promenade leading to Colonial Williamsburg's Visitor Center, provides guests the opportunity to stay in shape with free weights, treadmill, elliptical machines, a Smith machine, and a stationary bike. Towels and bathroom services are offered on-site.

families who need a little extra space. In addition to standard guest rooms—all with country-style decor—the hotel offers a variety of suites. Kids will love the indoor pool and Jacuzzi, and their parents can check out the fitness room. The hotel also provides a free continental breakfast, free newspaper, and free wireless Internet. Each room has a television with a DVD player. For lunch or dinner, there are several restaurants within walking distance.

CROWNE PLAZA WILLIAMSBURG HOTEL AND CONFERENCE CENTER $$
6945 Pocahontas Trail (US Route 60)
(757) 220-2250, (800) 227-6963
www.cpwilliamsburghotel.com

Convenient to both I-64 and the Historic Area, the most interesting facet of this upscale hotel's location is how close it was to the action 150 years ago: it sits on the site of the Civil War's 1862 Battle of Williamsburg. With 303 guest rooms, this is one of the larger hotels in the area and a popular conference location. Visitors can gaze at an actual redoubt from the earthworks of Fort Magruder on the hotel's grounds and examine Civil War artifacts on display in the hotel lobby. The 26,000 square feet of conference space honors the location's role in the War Between the States with meeting rooms named Lee's Redoubt, Grant's Redoubt, and one that always stops first-time visitors in their tracks: Hooker's Redoubt—named for the Union general. All guest rooms have cable TV and complimentary high-speed Internet access. You'll also find a seasonal outdoor pool, indoor pool, fitness center, gift shop, lighted tennis courts, and two restaurants—Veranda's, offering breakfast, lunch, and dinner, and JB's Tavern. Room service is also available 24 hours. Smoking is permitted in some rooms but not in the public areas. The hotel has twelve ADA-accessible rooms, including four with roll-in showers. Pets under 40 pounds are welcome, with a one-time cleaning charge of $45 per stay.

DAYS INN—CENTRAL $
1900 Richmond Rd.
(757) 229-6600, (800) 329-7466
The Days Inn in Williamsburg was completely renovated in 2006, and is a short driving distance from all the major attractions. The 85 guest rooms have small refrigerators, irons and ironing boards, AM-FM clock radios, and cable TV with HBO. Wireless Internet access, local calls, and breakfast are included in the room rate. There is a business center on the property and an outdoor pool, open seasonally. Wheelchair-accessible rooms are available, as are nonsmoking rooms. There are many restaurants within walking distance, as well as Yankee Candle store and the Ripley's Believe It or Not attraction, which is across the street.

DAYS INN—COLONIAL DOWNTOWN $
902 Richmond Rd.
(757) 229-5060, (800) 743-4883
www.showhotel.com/daysinn/2318501
This two-story, 100-room Days Inn is very popular due to its location within walking distance of both the Historic Area and the College of William

and Mary. Renovated in 2005, it has the amenities expected from this national chain—clean rooms, friendly service, cable TV, an outdoor pool, meeting rooms, and a complimentary continental breakfast. Wireless Internet access is included in the room rate. A good choice if your destination is any of the in-town attractions, it's also only a short drive to shopping, Busch Gardens, or Water Country USA. Nonsmoking rooms and wheelchair-accessible rooms are available.

DAYS INN—COLONIAL RESORT $
720 Lightfoot Rd.
(757) 220-0062, (888) 345-3470
www.williamsburgvacations.com
Hanging plants and wicker rockers on the front porch gives this Days Inn, closest to the outlet shopping area, an inviting country-home feel. Inside, the cozy lobby is equally inviting with a fireplace, comfy sofas, and a pot of freshly brewed coffee. This 120-room hotel features an indoor pool that opens to an outdoor sundeck. If you didn't get enough walking during the day, there is a treadmill in the fitness center. Younger visitors may prefer the game room. This five-story inn opened in August 2000 with a meeting room, hospitality suite, and deluxe rooms with either two doubles or one king-size bed. Guests also have access to a coin-operated washer and dryer. You can sit back and watch cable TV with HBO in the evening and start your day off with a continental breakfast. High-speed Internet access throughout the building is included in the room rate.

DAYS INN—HISTORIC AREA $–$$
331 Bypass Rd.
(757) 253-1166, (800) 759-1166
www.williamsburgvacations.com
Free coffee, tea, and cookies all day are a nice touch at this 120-room motel, just a short drive from the Historic Area, Richmond Road shopping, Busch Gardens, and Water Country USA. AARP members receive a 10 percent discount. Other amenities include small group meeting rooms, a heated outdoor pool and Jacuzzi, a game room, volleyball court, and even a cozy lobby with a fireplace. At this hotel, guests also find cable TV, wheelchair-

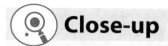

Close-up

Babysitting Services for Visitors

Though Williamsburg is an exceedingly family friendly destination, there are things to do—tour the Williamsburg Winery, sample the fare at Aleworks Microbrewery, dine at the fabulous French restaurant Le Yaca—that would be more fun without your little darlings. For you *and* them.

Due to liability concerns, few hotels offer to arrange babysitting services anymore, though both the **Kingsmill Resort** and the lodgings at **Colonial Williamsburg** are exceptions. (Both also offer summer day camps for kids.)

Another option is the referral list maintained by the **Child and Family Connection**, a non-profit organization. Child care providers on this agency's babysitting list have completed criminal background checks and are certified in CPR and first aid. "Most of the people on the list are people who work in child care during the day and have to have those qualifications anyway," said Mary Minor, the agency's director.

Though Minor's agency will provide referrals, the fee is negotiated between the provider and the family seeking babysitting services.

People relocating to Williamsburg may also find this agency helpful in finding ongoing child care. The connection has a directory of licensed, home-based care providers, day-care centers, and nanny services. The staff also maintains a resource library of books and videos pertaining to many aspects of parenting, including immunizations and health care. It offers support services to parents interested in shared care (matching up mothers of toddlers interested in trading days off), and to people interested in starting a home-based child care business. For any of the services mentioned above, call the Connection at (757) 229-7940.

---

accessible rooms, and nonsmoking rooms. Wireless Internet access is included in the room rate, and there is a business center on the property. The entire fourth floor is a penthouse with a king-size brass bed in the master bedroom. A complimentary continental breakfast is included with your stay, and several restaurants are within walking distance of the hotel, including the Gazebo, located next-door, open for breakfast and lunch.

ECONO LODGE PARKWAY/
HISTORIC AREA $
442 Parkway Dr.
(757) 229-7564
www.econolodgewilliamsburgva.com
This hotel, located within walking distance of many restaurants and close to the Historic Area, received a complete makeover in 2009, with remodeled bathrooms, new bedspreads and window treatments in guest rooms, and new

carpet throughout. There is an outdoor pool, free continental breakfast and a guest laundry. Wireless Internet access is included in the room rate. Each room has cable TV, a microwave, and a refrigerator. A second Econo Lodge, located at 216 Parkway Dr., has different ownership and is open seasonally. For information on that location, call (757) 253-6450, in season.

EMBASSY SUITES—WILLIAMSBURG $$
3006 Mooretown Rd.
(757) 229-6800, (800) 333-0924
www.embassysuites.com
This suites-only hotel is tucked behind the Kingsgate Greene (Kmart) Shopping Center, offering more quiet than other locations but quick access to all attractions and shopping. The 168 suites here feature a king-size bed or two doubles in the bedroom and a sleeper sofa, wet bar, refrigerator, and microwave in the living room.

A cooked-to-order breakfast and a daily evening manager's reception are included in the rate. You also can enjoy the whirlpool adjacent to the indoor heated pool. Wheelchair-accessible suites, a lounge, a full workout room, and a restaurant are also on the premises. A laundry facility and a meeting room for parties of up to 65 people are available. The hotel is five minutes from the Historic Area and ten minutes from all other attractions around the city. Group, corporate, military, AARP, and government rates are available. Children younger than 17 stay for free.

FAIRFIELD INN AND SUITES $$
1402 Richmond Rd.
(757) 645-3600, (800) 228-2800
www.fairfieldinn.com
This hotel is centrally located in Williamsburg. As part of the Marriott chain, it shows off a new decor with luxury features such as down pillows in each room. Rooms also have such staples as coffeemakers, irons and ironing boards, cable TV, and complimentary Internet access through Ethernet cables. (Wireless Internet is available in the lobby and other public areas.) The hotel has 148 rooms and suites on four floors with elevators. Wheelchair-accessible rooms are available. There is an indoor swimming pool, whirlpool, and fitness center. Continental breakfast is included in the room rate. No pets are allowed. The hotel is 100 percent smoke-free.

GREAT WOLF LODGE $$$$$
549 East Rochambeau Dr.
(757) 229-9700, (800) 551-WOLF
www.williamsburg.greatwolflodge.com
The big attraction at this hotel is its indoor water park—a massive attraction that is noisy and irresistibly fun to anybody who likes to splash. However, get ready to pay for the fun. This is one of the priciest places to lay your head in the Williamsburg area.

The lodge is a four-story faux-log structure, with a stone fireplace in the lobby, wood beam ceilings, and wild animal decoys. There are a variety of rooms and suites, all with modern amenities and all clad in a burgundy and forest green decor with rustic pine furniture. Many have fireplaces, whirlpools, and vaulted ceilings. Some have log forts or tent areas—complete with televisions—within the rooms for children.

With all that this theme complex offers, you may never make it outside. The 55,000-square-foot indoor water park includes eight water-slides, an interactive tree house, a wave pool, two 7,000-gallon hot tubs, a water basketball court, and a rock-climbing wall. An outdoor pool, open only in summer months, has water "geysers" that kids love to splash through. There are more than 60 lifeguards on duty throughout the complex. There are also several restaurants on the premises, ranging from fast food and snack bar.

Reservations must include a deposit of the first night's charge, plus tax, and reservations cancelled up to 72 hours before the stay incur a $25 charge. Reservations cancelled within 72 hours will incur a charge of the first night's rate.

HAMPTON INN & SUITES—CENTRAL $-$$
718 Bypass Rd.
(757) 229-7330
www.hamptoninn.hilton.com
This hotel opened in 2009 in a location about equidistant from all of Williamsburg's major attractions. Its 105 rooms offer a mix of king- and queen-size beds; suites that sleep four are available.

Each room is equipped with a desk, coffeemaker, hair dryer, iron, and ironing board. Continental breakfast and wireless Internet access are included in the room rate.

Though there is cable TV in every room with free HBO, that is no excuse to laze about, the hotel offers both indoor and outdoor pools, a Jacuzzi, and a fitness center equipped with treadmills, elliptical machines, weight stations, and medicine balls. A full service business center, open 24 hours, and meeting rooms are also available.

HAMPTON INN & SUITES— HISTORIC DISTRICT $-$$
911 Capitol Landing Rd.
(757) 941-1777
www.williamsburghistoricdistrictsuites
.hamptoninn.com

This hotel one mile north of the historic district is popular with families visiting Busch Gardens and Water Country USA. The hotel has 109 well-equipped rooms, including five designed for wheelchair accessibility. There are four guests rooms reserved for smoking. Included in the room rate is continental breakfast, an indoor pool and Jacuzzi, and cable TV with HBO. There is complimentary Internet access through the building—wireless in the lobby and public areas and via Ethernet cables in the guest rooms. All rooms have microwaves, refrigerators, and hair dryers; some have separate living rooms. There is a business center and a guest laundry.

HAMPTON INN & SUITES— WILLIAMSBURG $-$$
1880 Richmond Rd.
(757) 229-4900, (800) 346-3055
www.hamptoninn.com

One of the more convenient motels in town is this imposing property on Richmond Road at the edge of the city. Aside from a choice of 100 rooms and suites, this property is convenient to local dining, shopping, eating, and sightseeing. Standard rooms offer queen- and king-size beds, as do all the suites. There are an indoor pool and exercise room available for use by guests year-round. The motel offers a deluxe continental breakfast each morning from 6 until 10 a.m., and wheelchair-accessible rooms and nonsmoking rooms are available. Wireless Internet access is included in the room rate; there is also a business center with copy and fax services.

HILTON GARDEN INN $$
1624 Richmond Rd.
(757) 253-9400, (877) 609-9400
www.hilton.com

This four-story inn in the heart of town offers just about everything to make a family or busi-ness traveler right at home. There are 119 rooms, including 17 suites, all offering cable TV with HBO, refrigerator, coffeemaker, microwave, hair dryer, iron and ironing board, complimentary wireless Internet, and two phones. Guests can use the hotel's 24-hour business center, which provides a fax, copier, printer, computer with modem, and phone lines. Also on the property are wheelchair-accessible rooms, a gift shop, and an indoor heated pool, whirlpool, and fitness center, all of which are available 24 hours. A good choice for family reunions, the inn offers a meeting room able to accommodate up to 100 people, or to be split in half, as needed. The restaurant on premises serves breakfast only. A local favorite, The Seafare of Wil-liamsburg, provides evening room service, and a Red Hot & Blue barbecue restaurant is located in front of the hotel. There are a limited number of guest rooms in which smoking is permitted.

HOLIDAY INN—GATEWAY $$
515 Bypass Rd.
(757) 229-9990, (800) HOLIDAY
www.holidayinn.com

This five-story inn opened in 2006 in a location convenient to all of Williamsburg's attractions. The rooms are well-equipped with all the stan-dard amenities, plus microwave and refrigerator. Kids eat free at the on-site restaurant, Bistro 515, and they'll enjoy the heated indoor pool and whirlpool. There's also a fitness center, business center, and meeting rooms which can accom-modate up to 235. Wireless Internet access is included in the room rate.

HOLIDAY INN—PATRIOT $$
3032 Richmond Rd.
(757) 565-2600, (800) 446-6001
www.hipatriot.com

Located on the western border of Williamsburg, this hotel and conference center is a good choice for those whose primary aim is to shop. There are 160 rooms, all of which include wireless Internet, microwave, refrigerator, coffeemaker, iron and ironing board, and hair dryers. A kidney-shaped outdoor pool, an indoor pool, and a hot tub will offer balm to tired feet after a grueling day at the outlets. There's a restaurant and lounge on-site. Smoking and wheelchair-accessible rooms are available, as are discounts for senior citizens.

HOMEWOOD SUITES BY HILTON $$-$$$
601 Bypass Rd.
(757) 259-1199, (888) CALLHOME (225-5400)
www.homewoodsuites.com
This property prides itself on being "a hotel that's like home," offering 61 guest accommodations, including one- and two-bedroom suites with queen- and king-size beds, separate dressing areas, and residential-style bathrooms. In addition, each suite features a fully equipped kitchen with microwave, refrigerator, and dishwasher as well as TVs in the living area and bedroom. Wireless Internet access in every room is included in the room rate. Honeymoon suites offer Jacuzzis. A well-equipped fitness center features an indoor swimming pool. Also on the premises is a shop where guests can buy things they might need while in residence, including groceries. Guests are invited to a daily pantry breakfast, and the "Manager's Reception," with a light meal, Mon through Thurs, from 5 to 7 p.m. Wheelchair-accessible rooms are available, as are nonsmoking suites. A full laundry facility is provided. This property is conveniently located on the US Route 60 bypass, about a mile from the city's Historic Area, Merchants Square shopping, and the College of William and Mary. AAA and AARP discounts are available.

HOWARD JOHNSON $
505 York St.
(757) 220-3100
www.howardjohnson.com
The 85 rooms here include access to a large, indoor swimming pool with spa and sauna. Each room has a cable TV, refrigerator, and microwave. Continental breakfast, wireless Internet access, and local phone calls are included in the room charge. There is a public computer in the lobby for those without a laptop. Wheelchair-accessible and smoking rooms are also available. The motel is less than a five-minute walk from the eastern part of the Historic Area and is 2.5 miles from Busch Gardens.

KINGSMILL RESORT $$$
1010 Kingsmill Rd.
(757) 253-1703, (800) 832-5665
www.kingsmill.com
Designated a "four-diamond" property by AAA, Kingsmill offers a multitude of things to do in a gorgeous setting: tennis, golf, swimming, and a variety of relaxing and restorative treatments at the organic, nature-based spa.

The property overlooks the wide James River on one side, and three world-class golf courses surround the property. (The River Course has played host to PGA and LPGA tournaments for three decades.) As a guest, you can play any of the three 18-hole golf courses, as well as the 9-hole par 3 course, which is great for families and players of all skill levels.

All area attractions are a short drive away, but you can almost get to Busch Gardens without hitting a traffic light. The resort also offers a free shuttle service to Busch Gardens, Water Country USA, and Colonial Williamsburg. On summer Saturdays, a full or half-day "Kids Kamp" is available for an additional fee. Children ages 5 to 12 play sports, swim, play at the beach, do arts and crafts, and visit the game room. A healthy lunch and snack are provided.

There are 425 villa-style rooms, including one-, two-, and three-bedroom suites, some providing working fireplaces with complimentary wood during the winter.

Kitchenettes, swimming (indoor and outdoor pools), tennis, racquetball, fitness equipment, billiards, meeting rooms, and five restaurants are available to guests. A marina with boat slips allows guests to cruise to Williamsburg via the James River and dock at Kingsmill. Various packages are also available, so inquire about them during your initial contact. This is one of the most pleasant accommodations in the Williamsburg area.

MARRIOTT'S MANOR CLUB AT FORD'S COLONY $$-$$$
101 St. Andrews Dr.
(757) 258-1120
www.marriott.com

Nestled in the woodlands of Virginia's rolling countryside, but still within a short drive of historic Williamsburg, is the exclusive Marriott's Manor Club at Ford's Colony, a graceful resort set within a planned community. Choose from one- and two-bedroom private villas with full kitchens, separate living and dining areas, washer/dryers, enclosed balconies or patios, fireplaces, and wireless Internet access.

The resort's on-site spa, fitness centers, indoor and outdoor pools, sport court, and Activities Centers provide a broad array of entertainment. There is also championship golf at the adjacent Ford's Colony Country Club, which also offers four-star dining. (See the Restaurants chapter for the Dining Room at Ford's Colony.) Jogging and hiking trails throughout the development offer more options for enjoying the outdoors.

PATRIOT INN & SUITES $$
1420 Richmond Rd.
(757) 229-2981
www.patriotinnandsuites.com

This hotel in the heart of the retail-and-restaurant corridor offers 110 rooms ranging from double rooms to two-room/two-bath suites. Each room is equipped with iron and ironing board, coffeemaker, hair dryer, cable TV, and in-room safes. All suites have a microwave and a refrigerator. Continental breakfast with hot food is included in the room rate. There is an outdoor pool and self-service laundry facilities.

There is a business center and free wireless Internet access in the lobby (but not in the rooms). Smoking rooms are available and the hotel is accessible to wheelchairs. The IHOP next door is open late, and the High Street development on the other side of the inn has a Movie Tavern and the very popular Five Guys hamburger restaurant.

QUALITY INN—COLONY $
309 Page St.
(757) 229-1855, (800) 228-5151
www.choicehotels.com

This small motel manages to convey colonial-era charm while still offering up-to-date amenities. The 59 rooms have shower baths, TVs with DVDs, and free high-speed Internet access via Ethernet cables. (Wireless connections are available in the lobby and breakfast room.) An outdoor pool provides a spot for relaxation in warm weather. All rooms are modestly furnished but clean and well kept. A complimentary continental breakfast begins the day. A great Mexican restaurant, La Tolteca, is just around the corner, as is another popular restaurant, Second Street. Wheelchair-accessible rooms are available, as are refrigerators and whirlpools in some rooms. Senior citizen and other discounts are offered.

QUALITY INN—HISTORIC AREA $
600 Bypass Rd.
(757) 220-2800, (800) 4-CHOICE
www.choicehotels.com

This 143-room hotel is one mile from the Colonial Williamsburg Visitor Center and within easy driving distance of Busch Gardens and Water Country USA. Except for the wheelchair-accessible rooms, all rooms open on an interior corridor of the hotel. A deluxe continental breakfast, which includes waffles, biscuits and gravy, and fresh fruit, is offered from 6 to 9 a.m. daily. Wireless Internet access is included in the room rate as is a daily newspaper, use of the fitness center, the game room, and the outdoor pool, which is open seasonally. There are a small number of rooms set aside for smokers.

QUALITY INN—KINGSMILL $$
480 McLaws Circle
(757) 220-1100, (800) 296-4667
www.choicehotels.com

This hotel is close to I-64 along a stretch of US Route 60 that offers a pleasing array of amenities and convenient access to Busch Gardens and Water Country USA. There are 111 rooms, including some adapted for wheelchair accessibility. Continental breakfast, indoor and outdoor pools, free wireless Internet access, a game room, some king-size beds, refrigerators, microwaves, and an adjacent seafood restaurant, The Whaling Company, are among the amenities; being an affordable choice that is also very close to the Kingsmill resort, with its championship golf and tennis facilities, is another. With the money you save, you can treat yourself to a lovely French dinner at this exquisite Le Yaca, located in the Kingsmill Shops across US Route 60, or a delicious Italian meal at Maurizio's in the Festival Marketplace just east of the hotel. This hotel is 100 percent smoke-free.

QUARTERPATH INN $
620 York St.
(757) 220-0960, (800) 446-9222
www.quarterpathinn.com

The friendly management at this inn offers 130 rooms a short walk from Colonial Williamsburg's eastern boundary and five minutes by car from Busch Gardens and Water Country USA. Complimentary coffee and free lodging for children younger than 18 are indicators of the hospitality you will find here. Wheelchair-accessible rooms, an adjacent steak and seafood restaurant, outdoor swimming pool, king suites, and whirlpool tubs make the Quarterpath Inn a comfortable place to stay. Senior citizen and other discounts are offered. Small pets are welcome at no charge, but please notify the innkeeper of their presence so the housekeepers can be made aware. There are a limited number of rooms for smokers. Those who would like wireless Internet access should request it. The inn is in the process of upgrading its system, and some rooms have better connectivity than others. Wi-Fi is always available in the lobby for no charge.

RESIDENCE INN BY MARRIOTT $$
1648 Richmond Rd.
(757) 941-2000, (800) 331-3131
www.residenceinn.com

This elegant, conveniently located hotel offers 108 rooms—all of them suites with fully equipped kitchens. Guests can select from studio suites with king-size beds or one- or two-bedroom suites. Other guest amenities include a daily breakfast buffet, evening "hospitality socials" on select nights with beverages and appetizers, high-speed Internet access, an outdoor pool, and a fitness room. While there is no restaurant on the premises, this property is within easy walking distance of several national chain restaurants and the local favorite, Food for Thought. Pets are allowed with a $75 nonrefundable fee. Discounts are offered to military and AAA and AARP members depending on room availability. This facility is 100 percent smoke-free.

RODEWAY INN & SUITES $–$$
7224 Merrimac Trail
(800) 228-2000
www.rodewayinn.com

This 32-room motel gets praise from families on a budget for its large, no-frills suites and its location near Busch Gardens and Water Country USA. Rooms are equipped with a refrigerator, microwave, and wireless Internet access. Continental breakfast is included in the room charge, and there is a large outdoor pool to splash around in during the warm months. This is a nonsmoking facility. Wheelchair access is very limited.

SLEEP INN HISTORIC $
220 Bypass Rd.
(757) 259-1700, (888) 228-9698
www.sleepinn.com

This attractive motel has an inviting roadside appearance with its handsome stucco exterior and neatly landscaped gardens. It also offers fine accommodations in a range of prices. In addition to 65 rooms, this property offers two Jacuzzi rooms, each with two king-size beds and, yes, a Jacuzzi for two. All rooms here provide guests with cable TV, high-speed wireless Internet, phones, alarm clocks, walk-in showers, and tasteful, traditional decor. Everyone who stays here is treated to a full continental breakfast. The indoor swimming pool and exercise room are open year-round. Wheelchair-accessible rooms are available, and they feature queen-size beds. Most rooms are for nonsmokers, though a few rooms have been set aside for those who do smoke. While there is no restaurant on the premises, Cracker Barrel and Golden Corral are steps away, and Uno's Chicago Grill is just across the street. No pets are allowed. AAA and AARP discounts are available.

SPRING HILL SUITES BY MARRIOTT $$
1644 Richmond Rd.
(757) 941-3000, (888) 287-9400
www.springhillsuites.com

This pristine yet moderately priced all-suites property is located conveniently in the heart of Richmond Road's commercial corridor. It offers guests a choice of 120 rooms, all suites, with sleeper sofas and a choice of two queen-size beds or one king. The rooms have separate eating areas and a pantry with a refrigerator. Other amenities include a deluxe continental breakfast, an indoor pool, whirlpool, and exercise room. The entire hotel offers wireless Internet access, and the property is 100 percent smoke-free. Several national chain restaurants—Chili's, Applebee's, Friendly's, and more—are located within easy walking distance of the hotel. Ripley's Believe It or Not attraction is directly across the street.

Wheelchair-accessible rooms are available upon request. AAA and AARP discounts are available, so inquire when you make your reservation.

SUPER 8 MOTEL—WILLIAMSBURG/
HISTORIC AREA $$–$$$
304 Second St.
(757) 229-0500
www.super8.com

This renovated property is a half-mile from Colonial Williamsburg and only a short drive to all the Williamsburg attractions. Its 104 guest rooms have wireless Internet access, microwaves, refrigerators, irons and ironing boards, hair dryers, coffeemakers, and cable TV. It has an outdoor pool and grills for guests' use, and it also offers a continental breakfast. The South of the Border and Second Street Tavern restaurants, as well as several fast-food restaurants, are within walking distance. Pets can be accommodated for a $10 per night fee, and smoking is permitted in certain rooms. A second Super

8 location, 1233 Richmond Rd., (757) 253-1087, has similar amenities for the same price but is closer to the College of William and Mary.

i Many hotels require a two-night minimum stay during the peak season, which in Williamsburg is June through Labor Day and also the holiday season in November and December.

TRAVELODGE—HISTORIC AREA $
120 Bypass Rd.
(757) 229-2000 (800) 544-7774
www.travelodge.com

A short drive from all of Williamsburg's attractions, this budget-priced inn has 122 rooms and suites and one of the area's largest outdoor pools. It's also conveniently located just across the street from the only minigolf in Williamsburg, the nautical-themed Pirate's Cove. There are volleyball and picnic areas on the inn's property, as well as laundry facilities and a small game room. Wireless Internet access is included in the room charge. Nonsmoking and wheelchair-accessible rooms are available. A continental breakfast is complimentary. For other meals, there are dining options including Uno's Chicago Grill and the Cracker Barrel, within an easy walk.

WILLIAMSBURG COURTYARD
BY MARRIOTT $$
470 McLaws Circle,
Busch Corporate Center
(757) 221-0700, (800) 393-2506

The 151 rooms here are popular with travelers who have business at the Busch Corporate Park which surrounds the hotel, and with families who like its location halfway between Busch Gardens and Water Country USA. It's also convenient to the Kingsmill championship golf course and just a short drive from the Historic Area. The property is entirely smoke-free and all rooms have luxury bed linens, a mini-refrigerator, and a cable TV with premium channels. Free Internet access is offered in the lobby (wireless) and in guest rooms (Ethernet). Guests can relax in an indoor and outdoor heated pool, or work out in the fitness center. Laundry facilities are available on the premises. An on-site restaurant is open for breakfast only, but there are excellent dining options nearby—around the corner in the Festival Marketplace—Maurizio's, Emerald Thai—and across the street in the Village shops—Doraldo's, good Italian food suitable for families, and Le Yaca, upscale French. Wheelchair-accessible rooms and meeting rooms are available. Senior citizen and other discounts are offered.

WILLIAMSBURG HOSPITALITY HOUSE $$
415 Richmond Rd.
(757) 229-4020, (800) 932-9192
www.williamsburghosphouse.com
This stately hotel with 295 rooms is directly opposite the College of William and Mary's football stadium and Alumni House, which makes it popular with visiting parents, alumni, and sports fans. Inside, all is quiet elegance and deeply polished woodwork. You'll enjoy efficient attention to your needs. Merchants Square is a two-block walk. Busch Gardens, Water Country USA, and the shopping outlets are short drives. Wheelchair-accessible rooms, a gift shop, and an outdoor swimming pool are offered. Wireless Internet access is available for an additional charge. Meetings of up to 750 people can be accommodated,

and free parking is provided in the attached garage. The restaurant's atmosphere is refined, traditional, and comfortable, and the lounge is a popular gathering spot for Tribe fans. Senior citizen and other discounts are offered, based on availability.

WILLIAMSBURG MARRIOTT $$
50 Kingsmill Rd.
(757) 220-2500, (800) 228-9290
www.marriott.com
If Busch Gardens is your destination, you couldn't get closer. There are many amenities at your disposal. Racquetball, indoor and outdoor swimming, a health club, saunas, and a Jacuzzi all cater to your workout needs, and a fine restaurant and lounge are featured here. Guest rooms have large desks and high-speed Internet access. Tennis courts, meeting rooms, and wheelchair-accessible rooms are also offered. The hotel has 295 rooms, some of which are suites. The excellent on-site restaurant, The Harvest Grille, lives up to Marriott's reputation for fine food, and Pitchers is a friendly, entertaining lounge. The Williamsburg Cafe offers sandwiches and lighter fare. If you are meeting friends for a foursome for golf at Kingsmill, this is a very convenient lodging. Senior citizen and other discounts are offered.

BED-AND-BREAKFASTS AND GUEST HOMES

Newcomers to Virginia soon learn that there is a history to everything here and if you choose to lodge with Williamsburg residents, you will learn you are continuing a tradition dating back more than 200 years, when, during "publick times" twice each year, the legal and governmental business of the colony took place, and the city was as crowded with visitors as it can get during high season today.

In the early days of the Historic Area restoration, there were no hotels in town. The response was to do what folks in the 'Burg have always done: open doors to visitors and offer them hospitality. And while a contemporary hotel/motel room may meet your lodging needs, staying in a tastefully appointed bed-and-breakfast sets a certain tone for your visit. The people who run Williamsburg's small inns and B&Bs are also some of the most knowledgeable residents when it comes to directing you for making best use of your time.

Today, Williamsburg has a well-established roster of exquisite bed-and-breakfasts, some of them world-class, national-award winners. Each has a unique decor and personality all its own. Each offers different amenities. Some are close to the Historic Area, while others are as far afield as Charles City County—you could even stay in a true southern plantation house dating from colonial times, if you're willing to drive a bit.

Keep in mind, too, that the bed-and-breakfast establishments offer some of the finest food served in the area. Breakfasts take on grand proportions in some of the lodgings, and no, you don't have to sit at a large table with a bunch of strangers in all cases. "That's one thing we learned over the years," said Sandy Hirz, who along with her husband, Brad, runs the lovely Liberty Rose Bed and Breakfast. "We discovered that some people simply prefer to enjoy a quiet, private breakfast at a table for two."

Price Code

The dollar signs in each entry indicate a range of rates for double occupancy (two persons) per night. During peak season (generally anytime other than Jan, Feb, and Mar), rates are higher Also, some establishments offer lower rates for single occupancy, and some may require a minimum two-night reservation on select weekends. Please confirm your rate with your hosts at the time you book your visit.

$ . . . . **Less than $100**
$$ . . . . **$101 to $175**
$$$ . . . . **$176 to $250**
$$$$ . . . . **More than $250**

Today's hosts will not require you to sleep three or more to a bed and to bring your linen—and your meals—as was customary in colonial times. Rather, they offer privacy in gracious settings where you can make yourself at home. Most houses date from the Colonial Revival of the 1920s onward. The City of Williamsburg's Architectural Review Board in 1993 designated several of the houses as "historically significant" in helping define the city's character and representing architectural styles and cultural periods from the city's past: Applewood, Colonial Capital, Liberty Rose, and Williamsburg Manor. The West Williamsburg Heights Architecture Preservation

District includes some of the listings, and you may wish to discuss the architectural importance of the area with your hosts.

Most of the homes take their own reservations. But many of the bed-and-breakfast owners have also joined the **Williamsburg Hotel-Motel Association** (800-211-7165; www.visitwilliamsburg.com) for bed-and-breakfast reservations.

Most establishments accept Visa and MasterCard. If you plan to use another credit card, a personal check, or traveler's checks, confirm this with the inn when you make your reservation. Wheelchair accessibility can be tricky at bed-and-breakfasts. Discuss any special needs with your host ahead of time.

Many bed-and-breakfasts also offer special seasonal packages, particularly romance packages, where guests can stay two or more nights and receive extras such as gift certificates to dinner or flowers and champagne in their room for a special price. Often, this information is listed on their Web site but be sure to mention any special occasion you're celebrating when you make your reservation. Some of the larger residences also host weddings and other events as well.

Some of the bed-and-breakfasts sell tickets to local attractions. Be sure to ask your hosts when you make your reservation if they provide this added-value service.

NOTE: There are three charming bed-and-breakfasts—the Marl Inn, Moss Cottage, and the York River Inn—located in Yorktown, 15 miles northeast of Williamsburg, and close to the Yorktown historical attractions and the Riverwalk shopping and dining district. See our complete description in the Jamestown and Yorktown chapter later in this book.

Bed-and-Breakfasts

ALICE PERSON HOUSE $$–$$$
616 Richmond Rd.
(757) 220-9263, (800) 370-9428,
Access Code 41
www.alicepersonhouse.com
Innkeepers Jean and Harry Matthews operate this Colonial Revival home, located within walking distance of the College of William and Mary and the city's Historic Area. Built in 1929, the house is reminiscent of early-20th-century Williamsburg accommodations, replete with high ceilings and spacious rooms, furnished with antiques and Oriental rugs. It is located on one of the city's main streets, once lined with stately old homes and venerable old trees. The house features a formal parlor with a fireplace on the first floor, available for guest use, and three guest rooms, each with private bath, cable TV, and VCR. The house is equipped with secure wireless Internet access for guest use.

The Queen Room features a queen-size, four-poster bed, while the King Room offers an extra-large, king-size, four-poster bed, as well as an antique chest-on-chest. If you would prefer more room, the Capitol Suite is available. The bathrooms feature plush towels; European linens are used on the beds. There is a two-night minimum stay during high season, and a three-night minimum stay on holiday weekends.

Breakfasts are served family style and often include biscuits, quiche, crepes, and waffles served with Virginia sausage or bacon, seasonal fresh fruits, yogurts, fresh-ground coffees, and teas.

Off-street parking is available, but no pets and no smoking. Children ages 10 and older are welcome.

APPLEWOOD COLONIAL BED
AND BREAKFAST $$
605 Richmond Rd.
(757) 903-4306
www.williamsburgbandb.com
This elegantly appointed home is located four short blocks from the city's Historic Area, near the College of William and Mary. A brick walkway leads up to the Georgian doorway and into the home's front parlor. Built by a Colonial Williamsburg craftsman, the house dates from 1928 and features Flemish bond brickwork, colonial decor, fireplaces, and antiques throughout. Each room is appointed with a queen-size bed, cable TV, free Wi-Fi, a small refrigerator with refreshments to

get you started, a coffeemaker, iron and ironing board, and a private bath.

Mrs. Holland's Blue Room is a cozy, romantic second-floor accommodation with a canopy bed, tub, and shower. The Twin Elms is a spacious room on the second floor with a fireplace. The Tree Top suite, on the third floor, has a bedroom with fireplace, two TVs, and a separate sitting area with a daybed and trundle.

Guests enjoy a full breakfast in the dining room, offering treats such as peach French toast, hash brown quiche, baked oatmeal, eggs, meats, rolls, and muffins, all served on an period-style antique table.

Innkeepers Marty and Denise Fleck are happy to work with guests who have dietary restrictions. Please let them know at the time the room is booked. The Flecks are also happy to help make special occasions more memorable by having any particular items in the room before arrival.

Children, ages 10 and older, can be accommodated. This is a nonsmoking, air-conditioned house. A private patio in back is available for relaxing as are bicycles for two-wheel touring of the surrounding area.

BENTLY MANOR INN $$–$$$
720 College Terrace
(757) 253-0202, (877) 334-0641
www.bentleymanorinn.com
Jane and Fred Garland were owners of a B&B near Kennebunkport, Maine, when they came to Williamsburg as tourists and fell in love. They searched for years before finding a home to buy and relocating their business, in 2007, to a warmer climate.

The inn they bought and renamed is on a shady side street, a few blocks off the main drag—a good choice for those whose sleep might be disturbed by the noise of traffic on busy Richmond Road. The Garlands can provide permits for on-street parking on College Terrace which allows guests to forgo having to worry about where to park downtown and instead take a 10-minute stroll through William and Mary's beautiful campus to Merchants Square, six-tenths

of a mile away. The Williamsburg Trolley stops nearby, and Fred regularly picks up guests at Williamsburg's quaint Amtrak Station, if they want to forget their cars altogether.

Bentley Manor has four lovely bedrooms, each with a queen-size bed, remodeled private bath, cable television, and small refrigerator. Wireless Internet is available throughout the house for no charge.

The Garlands serve a full breakfast from 8:30 to 9:30 a.m. consisting of hot entrees (omelettes, sour cream blueberry pancakes), fresh fruit, and baked goods. Afternoon snacks and beverages are made available, weather permitting on the screened-in sunporch. Older children (15 and up) are welcome, but there's no smoking and no pets allowed.

A BOXWOOD INN OF WILLIAMSBURG $$–$$$
708 Richmond Rd.
(757) 221-6607, (888) 798-4333
www.boxwoodinn.com
This extensively renovated 1928 home has won accolades from guests for its peaceful garden setting. It features luxurious king- or queen-size beds, private baths, whirlpool tubs, TVs, antiques, a cozy fireplace, a spacious sunroom, and Williamsburg's "nicest back porch." It is located in the Architectural Preservation District within walking distance of historical Colonial Williamsburg, and it is 2 blocks from the College of William and Mary. Garden lovers will be impressed with the inn's grounds, which have won beautification and garden club awards.

The inn features three rooms, which are decorated with traditional cherry furnishings, and one private suite, the Washington Carriage House, which features an in-room fireplace and Jacuzzi for two and is ideal for honeymoons and anniversaries.

Innkeepers Sandi and Steve Zareski serve a full breakfast each day on a 9-foot-long cherry Shaker farm table made expressly for the inn.

The inn does not permit children or pets.

THE CEDARS OF WILLIAMSBURG $$–$$$
616 Jamestown Rd.
(757) 229-3591, (800) 296-3591
www.cedarsofwilliamsburg.com

A front garden welcomes guests to The Cedars, located across from the William and Mary campus and a short walk from Merchants Square. This establishment, run by owner Bob Tubbs, offers a variety of accommodations. For complete privacy, choose the freestanding Cottage Suite, which has two rooms, one with a king-size bed, one with a queen, and a fireplace. A two-room suite, the William and Mary, is in the main house. The George Washington Suite provides a queen-size bed in the bedroom and a daybed in a sitting room, as well as a private bath. The William and Mary Suite has two rooms joined by a bath and is furnished with a four-poster bed in one and twin beds in the other. The other six sleeping rooms all have private baths. Antiques and 18th-century reproductions throughout the house convey an elegant, historic ambience, fitting to the place known as "Williamsburg's oldest and largest guesthouse."

Brace yourself for a day of touring with a full gourmet breakfast featuring fresh-baked muffins, a hot entree that might include baked oatmeal with brandied raisins or crème brûlée French toast, coffee, tea, juice, and fruit. The Cedars is a nonsmoking house. You'll find off-street parking in the rear.

i When you inquire about a bed-and-breakfast or guest home, ask lots of questions. If you have particular desires regarding decor, air-conditioning, type of breakfast, shower or bathtub availability and location, dietary needs, check-in or cancellation policies, provisions for children or pets, or even the kind of bedding you will have, just ask. When phoning, you are likely to be speaking to one of the owners, and the rapport you establish at this time may be an indicator of your satisfaction later.

COLONIAL CAPITAL BED AND BREAKFAST $$–$$$
501 Richmond Rd.
(757) 229-0233, (800) 776-0570
www.ccbb.com

Three blocks from the Historic Area and opposite William and Mary's football stadium, George and Sharon Hollingsworth host guests in their three-story Colonial Revival home, built about 1926. Antique furnishing and Oriental rugs throughout the house suggest luxury; a plantation parlor on the main floor is kept cozy by a wood-burning fireplace in winter. In the warmer months, you can enjoy the outdoors on the deck, patio, or screened side porch.

Five large guest rooms, each with private bath, offer a variety of accommodations. The Chesapeake features a handcrafted pencil-post, queen-size bed and an unusual corner sink. The James has four-poster pencil-post twin beds handcrafted from a single tree by master craftsman Fred Craver. The third-floor Pamlico has windows on three sides and can be combined with the sitting room across the hall with its half-bath and sleeping accommodations for two, making the entire floor a private suite. Terry robes are provided for the private hall bath.

The Potomac Room has an en suite bath and a private porch with rocking chairs and features a king-size bed with canopied half-tester. The York is a favored room for honeymoons (package plans available) and anniversaries, with its queen-size, turned-post canopied high rope bed and en suite bath with original claw-foot tub.

All rooms have remote-controlled ceiling fans, TVs, and VCRs. Beds are turned down nightly—look for a pillow mint. There is zoned central air-conditioning, free wireless Internet access, and in-room phones.

Breakfast is a decadent affair with French toast, western omelets, soufflés, and a variety of casseroles.

Pickup from Newport News/Williamsburg International Airport or Amtrak is available upon request. Children older than eight years old with well-behaved parents are welcome.

Single occupancy rates are available year-round. This is a nonsmoking inn.

COLONIAL GARDENS BED & BREAKFAST $$$
1109 Jamestown Rd.
(757) 220-8087, (800) 886-9715
www.colonial-gardens.com

This split-level brick home, located a mile beyond the William and Mary campus, sits on a land-scaped acre that lends a country air to its central location. Romantic getaways are the specialty—the entire inn can be rented out for weddings, and owner Karen Watkins has six marriage commissioners in her Rolodex for those who want to say "I do" on the lush grounds.

The house has four guest rooms, each with private bath, telephone, and flat panel TV with DVD and VHS capability and cable. All beds have luxury mattresses and fine linens. Plush bath-robes are provided to all guests.

The Rhododendron Suite features a king-size bed and a sitting area in a sunny alcove overlook-ing the garden for which it is named. The Azalea Suite provides a plantation rice-carved, canopied queen-size bed and a private sitting room which can double as a second bedroom with a twin-size daybed. The Primrose Room has a queen-size bed, and as with the all the upstairs bedrooms, a working fireplace and a music system for CDs or an MP-3 player.

The Library Room is a handy first-floor guest room that features the home's original built-in bookshelves.

Breakfasts are "elaborate": eggs, meat, carbs, fresh fruit. We might have Bananas Foster crepe with baked eggs or poached pears with honey. "I'm a good cook," Watkins says. Complimentary afternoon refreshments are served in the sun-room, overlooking the gardens when they are in bloom. In the winter months, the formal dining room is open to guests returning from a day of sightseeing. A designated refrigerator holds wine, sodas, and water for whenever guests need to slake their thirst. Hot tea, coffee, chips, biscotti, and fresh fruit are offered to nosh on throughout the day.

Colonial Gardens hosts an average of 40 weddings a year, and prospective brides and grooms can view photographs of previous cer-emonies on the home's excellent Web site listed above.

Children older than 12 are welcome, but no pets. This is a nonsmoking inn.

EDGEWOOD PLANTATION $$–$$$
4800 John Tyler Memorial Hwy. (Route 5)
Charles City County
(804) 829-2962
www.edgewoodplantation.com

This historic plantation is located 30 miles west of Williamsburg, but provides a unique lodging experience. The mansion, with its double spiral staircase and 10 fireplaces, is a National Historic Landmark. A gristmill on the property dates from 1725.

There is a ghost. On one bedroom window upstairs, Elizabeth "Lizzie" Rowland wrote her name with a diamond. Legend has it that she died of a broken heart waiting in vain for her lover to return from the Civil War. Don't let her intimi-date you. There's a good night's sleep in any one of the seven bedrooms or Prissy's Quarters, a cabin behind the main house. Gone with the Wind fans will enjoy the third floor, with its sitting and common area rooms, called Scarlett's Room and Melanie's Room. All rooms have king- or queen-size canopy beds.

On the grounds you will find formal gardens and a swimming pool. Breakfast is candlelit, and it may include fresh fruit, orange juice, crepes, quiche, croissants filled with fruit and cheese—or sometimes a country breakfast of Smithfield ham biscuits and fried apples. Special features avail-able upon request include Victorian teas and tours, including a haunted tour. If Christmas is your favorite season, you will enjoy the 18 deco-rated Christmas trees at Edgewood.

Smoking is allowed outside and in the kitchen only.

Edgewood Plantation is about halfway between Williamsburg and Richmond, along sce-nic Route 5.

FIFE AND DRUM INN $$–$$$$
411 Prince George St.
(757) 345-1776, (888) 838-1783
www.fifeanddruminn.com

The building that houses the Fife and Drum—one block off Merchants Square—has been in the Hitchens family for three generations, ever since A.W. Hitchens built it to replace the general store and pasture he sold to what became the Colonial Williamsburg Foundation in 1933.

Granddaughter Sharon Skruggs and her husband, Billy, talked for years about turning it into a small inn—and in 1999, they got their chance.

Their inn—seven rooms, two suites, and a nearby guest cottage that sleeps up to six—is tucked into one of the best locations in Williamsburg. It is less than 100 yards to the Merchants Square entrance to the colonial area, and only steps from some of the best restaurants and shopping.

The inn is also packed with historical bric-a-brac, collected into a theme for each room. The William and Mary Room (overlooking the college) has Civil War artifacts like a preserved musket; the Cedars Room, named after the post-war Cedarcrest tourist house, has that home's actual 1950s registration book.

Fife and Drum also comes with "two innkeepers who grew up here," as Sharon says. Guests get more than just insider recommendations of shops and restaurants—they get local color and stories. Like the time the Skruggs' sons (then 8 and 9) dug up shards of pottery and other things that didn't look like the usual backyard "treasure." Turns out they'd discovered remnants of the Richneck Plantation, which has been part of ongoing CW archaeological research ever since.

For all the history, the inn has the amenities of a hotel—high-speed Internet access in the common room, phones and cable TV in each room. The inn welcomes children over age six; children under 14 must stay in a room with an adult (two of the rooms sleep three). The inn is nonsmoking, and pets are not permitted.

FOX & GRAPE BED & BREAKFAST $$
701 Monumental Ave.
(757) 229-6914, (888) 229-8289
www.foxandgrapebb.com

Hosts Brandy and Lorene Christin offer two guest rooms, each with a private bath. Both rooms have queen-size beds; one can sleep a third guest in an additional single bed. Breakfast includes juices, coffee, tea, fresh fruit cups with whipped topping or yogurt, freshly-baked turnovers with sausage, egg casseroles, and croissants, served in the Tudor dining room, or have your coffee on the spacious wraparound porch. A minimum stay of two nights is required on weekends. There is off-street parking for guests. Smoking is prohibited.

GOVERNOR'S TRACE $$
303 Capitol Landing Rd.
(757) 229-7552, (800) 303-7552
www.governorstrace.com

Conveniently located just steps from the eastern end of the Historic Area, this Georgian brick house was built during the restoration of Colonial Williamsburg and occupies more than a half-acre of a former peanut plantation that extended the length of what is now Capitol Landing Road. Nearby, 13 of Blackbeard's pirates were hanged. Today's visitors receive a much more cordial welcome than the pirates did. Hosts Sue and Dick Lake are happy to tailor a touring itinerary to help you make the best use of your time.

Shuttered windows, brass candlelight lanterns, and a fireplace are featured in one room with a waist-high, four-poster king-size bed. Another room offers a private screened porch, four-poster colonial-style canopy bed, gingham, country florals, and pastels against a background of family antiques. Private baths adjoin the rooms, which are air-conditioned.

One guest room can be combined with the adjacent room to turn the entire second floor into a suite for two couples traveling together. It offers a queen-size antique-brass bed. The bathroom, done in brass, features a large glass shower enclosure.

Governor's Trace serves breakfast in the rooms and provides cozy robes so guests need not "dress" for breakfast. A leisurely candlelight breakfast in your room might be just the perfect unusual touch to make your stay memorable. This is a nonsmoking accommodation. It offers off-street parking. No pets are allowed.

> **i** In true southern hospitality, when bed-and-breakfasts are booked up, many of the innkeepers will refer you to one of their "competitors." To make it even easier for visitors, 20 of the Williamsburg area bed-and-breakfasts have formed a network to help you find a place to stay. Just click on the network's Web site at www.bandbwilliamsburg.com and find up-to-date information on lodging and room availability.

THE INN AT 802 $$$
802 Jamestown Rd.
(757) 345-3316, (888) 757-3316
www.innat802.com

Innkeepers Joe and Cathy Bradley renovated this brick Cape Cod in 2005, creating a lovely in-town bed-and-breakfast where relaxation and charm are the order of the day. Located next to the College of William and Mary, the inn is just a 12-minute walk from Colonial Williamsburg and a leisurely drive away from Jamestown, Yorktown, and Busch Gardens.

Each of the four carefully appointed rooms comes with a private bath. The King George Room, located on the first floor, features a king-size, rice-carved four-poster with goose-down comforter and full private bath with tub and shower. The Duke of Gloucester Room, also located on the first floor, has a pencil-post queen-size bed with goose-down comforter and a full bath. The Lafayette, located on the second floor, is a spacious guest room with a queen-size, rice-carved bed and a full-size bed, as well as a full private bath with tub and shower. This room can easily accommodate three guests. The Francis Nicholson, also located on the second floor, is the largest guest room in the inn. It features a

king-size walnut bed with a feather mattress and goose-down comforter, and a twin bed. In addition to free wireless Internet and central heat and air-conditioning, each guest room has a ceiling fan, radio, TV, and DVD player.

Common areas include a large living room and well-stocked library, both with fireplaces; a formal dining room; a glass-enclosed sunroom that overlooks a manicured garden, and a full guest kitchen stocked with complimentary beverages. Breakfast is served in the formal dining room, where the table is set with fine crystal, china, and silver to set off the sumptuous home-made fare. Prepared daily and served by candlelight, the morning meal includes fresh fruit, juice, coffee, tea, hot chocolate, assorted entrees, bacon, sausage or ham, and homemade pastries. The dining room can be closed off and used as conference room accommodating 10 people.

Children older than six are welcome. This is a nonsmoking inn.

THE LEGACY OF WILLIAMSBURG
BED AND BREAKFAST $$–$$$
930 Jamestown Rd.
(757) 220-0524, (800) 962-4722
www.legacyofwilliamsburgbb.com

From the crown molding lining the ceiling to the wooden and brick floors, the Legacy has the feel of an 18th-century inn. Throughout the house, candlelight adds a soft glow, and six fireplaces keep the atmosphere cozy in the cooler months. Those who know inns, know this one is special— The Legacy has been named a Worldwide Inn of the Year and listed as one of the top romantic inns in the United States by *Arrington's Bed & Breakfast*.

Each of the three suites and one guest room features a queen-size poster bed with canopy and a private bath complete with comfy terry-cloth robes. Wingback chairs face the oval fireplace in the Williamsburg Suite, while a love seat sits opposite the taller brick fireplace in the Nicholson Suite. The Grand Suite has its own selection of books above the elegant wooden mantel. The Brush Everard Room also offers a curtained canopy bed with chairs and window dressings in matching shades of colonial blue.

If you fancy a game of chance before you retire, stop by the "tavern room" for board games. Innkeepers Joan and Art Ricker keep the library stocked with books for leisure reading. Guests also have access to modern amenities, including a TV, an iron and ironing board, and a hair dryer.

Breakfast by candlelight in the Keeping Room includes homemade baked goods.

The Legacy is less than five blocks from the Historic Area. Cars can be parked in private, off-street spaces.

This nonsmoking bed-and-breakfast does not allow pets or children younger than 12.

LIBERTY ROSE BED
AND BREAKFAST $$$–$$$$
1022 Jamestown Rd.
(757) 253-1260, (800) 545-1825
www.libertyrose.com

This elegant inn has held a four-diamond rating from AAA and prides itself on creating the kind of romantic atmosphere perfect for honeymoons or couples celebrating an anniversary. (American Historic Inns has had the Liberty Rose on its top-10 "most romantic" list for years.)

Owners Sandra and Brad Hirz renovated a 1920s house made from Jamestown brick and white clapboard. Situated on a hillside covered with beautiful old trees, the inn is one mile from the Historic Area. The backyard gardens feature courtyards, and old-fashioned swings hang from oak trees.

Inside you'll find English, Victorian, French country, and colonial antiques. Rich fabrics and wallpapers contribute to the mood. A grand piano and fireplace in the salon and complimentary soft drinks, chocolates, and chocolate-chip cookies in the glassed-in breakfast porch are particularly inviting. All rooms offer telephones, TVs, VCRs, movies, lush bathrobes, bubble bath, alarm clocks, and gold miniature flashlights.

If decorating is a hobby for you, consult your hosts, as they did all of the professional-quality sewing, papering, sawing, hanging, and refinishing on the inn.

Breakfast includes such delicacies as stuffed French toast with marmalade and cream cheese, fruit, juices, and everything from apple-cinnamon pecan pancakes to eggs, toast, and the like.

Liberty Rose does not accept pets or children. Smoking is prohibited.

NEWPORT HOUSE $$$
710 South Henry St.
(757) 229-1775, (877) 565-1775
www.newporthousebb.com

A five-minute walk from the Historic Area, the Newport House is a reproduction from a 1756 design by colonial architect Peter Harrison, whose buildings spanned the British empire from America to India and who was the architect of the Williamsburg Statehouse rebuilding in 1749. The building is furnished entirely with English and American period antiques and reproductions—even guests' blankets are historically authentic. Each air-conditioned bedroom has a private bathroom and contains two four-poster canopy beds (an extra-long queen-size and a single).

Breakfast is based on 18th-century recipes and includes Rhode Island johnnycakes, a 1650s bread, scuppernong jelly, baked goodies, and more. Pancakes and waffles are served with honey from the owners' own beehive, and fresh berries and apples—when in season—come straight from the property's garden. The morning meal is also usually accompanied by a historical lecture from host John Fitzhugh Millar. He is a former museum director and captain of a full-rigged ship, as well as author and publisher of many books of history. His wife, Cathy Millar, is a registered nurse whose hobbies include gardening, needlework, and making reproduction 18th-century clothing.

On Tuesdays at 8 p.m., you may participate in colonial country dancing in the ballroom of the house. Beginners are welcome to join in or watch during these occasions. A harpsichord is available for guests' enjoyment, and with a few days' advance notice guests may rent colonial clothing either for their entire stay or for dinner at one of the colonial taverns. Newport House accepts no pets and is a nonsmoking house. With advance notice, it may be possible for your hosts to pick you up at Williamsburg's train/bus station or at the Newport News/Williamsburg International Airport.

Although credit cards cannot be used for payment, they can be used to hold a reservation.

NORTH BEND PLANTATION   **$$**
12200 Weyanoke Rd.
Charles City County
(804) 829-5176
www.northbendplantation.com

One of the truly old bed-and-breakfast structures in the area (built ca. 1819 and enlarged in 1853), North Bend Plantation is on the National Register of Historic Places and also is designated a Virginia Historic Landmark. The National Park Service features it on its Civil War and birding trails. Your hosts here are Ridgely and George Copland, the fifth generation of the family to own the home, which was built for Sarah Harrison, George's great-great-aunt and sister of William Henry Harrison, the ninth president of the United States.

The main house's Greek Revival design will meet your expectations of a plantation house and educate you concerning the changes in architecture on antebellum plantations. It is situated on 500 acres just east of Charles City Court House and one mile off Route 5 on Weyanoke Road, about a 25-minute drive west of Williamsburg.

The Civil War has close associations with this residence. In 1864, Union General Phil Sheridan headquartered at North Bend, as you will see upon examining the plantation desk he used at that time. Union breastworks from the war still exist intact on the grounds.

Possessions treasured and displayed by the family include old and rare books, colonial antiques from related plantation families, and an antique doll collection. Modern fun is to be had, as well: a fine swimming pool, billiards room, croquet, horseshoes, volleyball, and a full country breakfast including fresh fruit, juices, waffles, omelets, bacon, sausage, and biscuits.

Accommodations include varying combinations of bed sizes and styles, and all rooms feature private baths and TVs. The Magnolia Room features a canopied queen-size rice bed and a shower. The Sheridan Room features a high queen-size tester bed (ca. 1810–40) that belonged to Edmund Ruffin, George Copland's great-great-grandfather. The headboard was shot out in the Civil War. General Sheridan's desk and a sitting area are in the room. The Federal Room features an iron-and-brass queen-size bed. The Rose Room has a queen-size canopy bed, a fireplace, and a sitting area. The Maids Quarters connects to the Magnolia Room and has a double bed. An upstairs sun porch (one of three) is available for guests' enjoyment.

Guests are treated with refreshments on arrival: cookies and lemonade or hot cider, depending on the season. A choice example of southern cooking in a pleasant historic setting is available nearby at Charles City Tavern (see our Restaurants chapter); reservations can be made for you at North Bend. Children six and older are welcome, but pets are not. Smoking is restricted to certain areas. Senior citizens receive a 10 percent discount.

PINEY GROVE AT
SOUTHALL'S PLANTATION   **$$–$$$$**
16920 Southall Plantation Lane
Charles City County
(804) 829-2480, (804) 829-2196
www.pineygrove.com

A 12-mile drive west of Williamsburg, off the Route 5 Scenic Byway, is Piney Grove at Southall's Plantation. Three generations of the Gordineer family welcome travelers to their home, which is a Virginia Historic Landmark and is listed on the National Register of Historic Places.

Built circa 1790 on 300 acres first occupied by the Chickahominy Indians, Piney Grove is the oldest existing example of log architecture in Tidewater Virginia. Another home on the property, the Ladysmith, is a modest Greek Revival plantation house built in 1857. Both houses have been meticulously restored to their original appearances and include every modern convenience for guests.

Six spacious guest rooms—each with a private bath, working fireplace, small refrigerator, and coffeemaker—are tastefully appointed with family heirlooms as well as antiques and artifacts that chronicle four centuries of Virginia home life. Suites are available for parties of up to 4 guests.

The parlor library boasts a collection of books on Virginia history. A nature trail, garden walk, and pool invite outdoor activity. Mint juleps, hot toddies, cider, and nightcaps of brandy are offered in every season. A candlelight plantation breakfast is served in the 1790 Log Room.

No pets or smoking is permitted. Children are welcome, and young guests will particularly enjoy the barnyard animals. Credit cards are not accepted. The inn takes checks, cash, or traveler's checks.

WAR HILL INN $$
4560 Longhill Rd.
(757) 565-0248, (800) 743-0248
www.warhillinn.com
Set on a bucolic 32-acre estate four miles from downtown Williamsburg, this house was built in 1968 for hosts Shirley and Bill Lee under the guidance of a Colonial Williamsburg architect. Crickets, frogs, owls, and Angus cattle are the closest neighbors, and it is easy, upon awakening, to imagine yourself having traveled 200 years back to a peaceful setting in the colonial period.

Among War Hill's attractions is a reproduction colonial cottage, the Washington Cottage. It offers a canopy bed for a comfortable rest, a private bath, and a whirlpool tub for your relaxation and enjoyment. The Jefferson Cottage also features a fireplace, whirlpool bath, and kitchenette. Four other rooms in the main house all have private baths, antique furnishings, and TVs. Inquire whether the accommodation you are considering has queen-size, double, or single beds, as all are offered. Children are welcome here. Smoking is not allowed in the house.

WEDMORE PLACE $$$-$$$$
At the Williamsburg Winery
5310 Wessex Hundred
(757) 941-0310, (866) 933-6673
www.wedmoreplace.com
The luxury accommodations offered on the manicured grounds of the Williamsburg Winery are styled as a "European Country Hotel." All 28 rooms have king-size beds and wood-burning fireplaces. Two conference rooms are suitable for private functions or executive retreats. An outdoor pool with sundeck, a well-stocked library, and fine dining on the premises (Café Provencal) make this a full-service retreat for those in need of some upscale escape. The winery, located just steps away, offers tours and another dining option at Gabriel Archer's Tavern. There are four room styles ranging from traditional to suites. Special offers are outlined on the Web site, which also offers photographs of the well-appointed rooms and gorgeous grounds.

WILLIAMSBURG MANOR BED
AND BREAKFAST $$-$$$
600 Richmond Rd.
(757) 220-8011, (800) 422-8011
www.williamsburg-manor.com
This 1929 Georgian brick Colonial Revival house is just a five-minute walk from Merchants Square and steps away from the College of William and Mary. Innkeepers Laura and Craig Reeves opened it to guests in 1992 and offer a wealth of experience and expertise about the area.

The interior spaces and gardens of the Williamsburg Manor have been updated to combine the spirit of Colonial Williamsburg with modern amenities. All rooms feature queen-size beds with private full baths, 32-inch flat panel TVs, iPod docking stations, and free wireless Internet.

The innkeepers are also professional caterers and take pride in preparing a delicious array of southern breakfast favorites. The menu is always different, but they can accommodate special diets and allergies. The Manor is available for weddings, family reunions, private parties, and other special occasions. More information about the Reeves' catering business, The Catering Company, can be found at www.williamsburg occasions.com.

Well-behaved children and pets are welcome. It is a nonsmoking house. Off-street parking is available to guests.

WILLIAMSBURG SAMPLER BED AND BREAKFAST $$–$$$

922 Jamestown Rd.
(757) 253-0398, (800) 722-1169
www.williamsburgsampler.com

Across the street from the College of William and Mary and within a 10-minute walk of Merchants Square, this stately brick home in the style of an 18th-century plantation manor house is decorated throughout with antiques, books, a magnificent pewter collection, other Americana, and—how did you guess?—a host of wonderful samplers that innkeeper Ike Sisane has collected.

Excellence is a hallmark of the Sampler, and it has been noted as having the "Best Breakfast" by *Arrington's Bed & Breakfast Journal*, featured on CBS TV, and singled out for accolades by former Gov. George Allen. A wealth of authentic colonial details includes a "keeping room," graceful wooden staircases, and pegged hardwood planked floors. A welcome non-colonial touch is central air-conditioning.

Four of the guest accommodations offer fireplaces. King-size, rice-carved four-poster beds are available, and Thomasville furnishings, a private bath, and a comfortable sitting area with wing chairs or daybed are features of every guest room. Two, two-room suites open to a rooftop garden overlooking the gardens and woods below. Television with premium cable is offered in each room.

The morning meal at the Sampler has been dubbed the "Skip Lunch" breakfast. A hearty meal including fresh muffins and "the best waffles in the USA"—a German guest's comment—is served fireside.

Beautiful grounds at the rear invite a stroll just downhill from a replica of Colonial Williamsburg's 18th-century Coke-Garrett Carriage House. Or you can work off that breakfast in the fitness center in the carriage house. Off-street parking is provided at this nonsmoking house. Children 13 and older are welcome. No pets, please. The Sampler accepts MasterCard and Visa.

A WILLIAMSBURG WHITE HOUSE $$–$$$

718 Jamestown Rd.
(757) 229-8580, (866) 229-8580
www.awilliamsburgwhitehouse.com

This unique bed-and-breakfast, located four blocks from the Historic Area, does everything but play "Hail to the Chief" for visitors. Innkeepers Deborah and John Keane have remodeled a three-story, 105-year-old Colonial in presidential style. There are five suites, one of which has two bedrooms, all with private baths. Each is named for a former president and decorated in a style befitting his taste. The Roosevelt Suite, for instance, celebrates Teddy's love of train travel with a queen-size railroad–like berth.

Guests awake to made-to-order breakfasts, served on fine china in the Reagan Dining Room or at a table for two in the JFK Library, where they can peruse the extensive collection of historical and political books. Afternoon sweets, wines, ports, and sherry are served in the Diplomatic Reception Room.

Partisan politics extends even to the parking lot where spaces bear "Democrats only" and "Republicans only" designations.

There is free wireless Internet access, and the inn offers its one-and-a-half acre lawn for weddings. Special elopement and vow renewal packages are also available.

Private Guest Homes

Over the past decade there has been an enormous amount of hotel construction in Williamsburg, one factor that has accounted for the collapse of what was once a thriving niche—the rental of guest rooms in private homes. Just a few remain, but they do offer an affordable option.

Most guest homes do not accept credit cards but do take personal checks or cash.

HUGHES GUEST HOME $

106 Newport Ave.
(757) 229-3493

Across Newport Avenue from the Williamsburg Lodge, Genevieve O. Hughes offers three rooms for you to enjoy in her large two-story home decorated with family antiques. One double-bed room features a private bath, and a suite with one double and two twin beds has a shared bath. It is a two-minute walk to the restored area. This is a nonsmoking home, and pets cannot be accommodated.

JOHNSON'S GUEST HOME $
101 Thomas Nelson Lane
(757) 229-3909
Your host, Mrs. Wallace C. Johnson, has opened her home to guests for more than three decades. Located in a close-in subdivision known as Skipwith Farms, the house is about two miles from the Historic Area, and convenient to the College of William and Mary.

Canopy beds grace two of the three guest rooms (one has a fireplace); twin beds are in the third. Private and semiprivate bath arrangements are offered, along with televisions. Combinations of rooms upstairs can be arranged for families or other groups. No pets or smoking but well-behaved children over the age of five are welcome.

THOMPSON GUEST HOME $
1007 Lafayette St.
(757) 229-3455
Off-street parking and private baths are available for guests to use here. There are three guest rooms offering double or twin beds, and the location is convenient to shopping and the Historic Area.

REGIONAL CUISINE
AND RESTAURANTS

Williamsburg has been feeding visitors for several hundred years. The original public establishments here were the taverns you now will find in the city's Historic Area.

Since then, the variety of cuisines offered locally has expanded quite a bit so that you can now get fine Vietnamese food, down-home Southern cooking, and everything in-between. You can order grits at a pancake house, but you'll also see them at the most expensive restaurants in town—often served with shrimp.

Arguably the best thing to happen on the Williamsburg restaurant scene has nothing to do with the food. In 2009, a new state law went into effect prohibiting smoking in restaurants that did not have a separate ventilation system for their smoking areas. As a result, nearly every restaurant in Virginia, a state that relied on tobacco as its primary cash crop and economic bulwark for hundreds of years, is now nonsmoking.

Two beverage notes: Iced tea is the drink of choice to accompany all southern meals, but it is served sweetened. Those folks in Boston may have thrown their tea into the harbor, but southern colonials and their progeny maintain that sugar, not salt water, is the best companion. Ask for your tea unsweetened if that is your preference.

If you are looking for places that serve or sell adult beverages, the designation is "ABC," short for the Commonwealth's Alcoholic Beverage Control, the agency that regulates the sale of beer, wine, or spirits. Beer and wine are sold in supermarkets, but liquor is sold by the state in ABC stores.

We start off this chapter on restaurants for the uninitiated and the adventurous—those who travel and want to know, "what can I get to eat here that's unique to the place?" The regional specialties in Williamsburg evolved from the early bounty of Virginia's fields and rivers; many are still heartily consumed in the Historic Triangle today. After that we move on to a general listing of restaurants in alphabetical order.

Price Code

Area restaurants almost universally accept Visa and MasterCard, so we only note exceptions. The state charges a tax on meals, and localities charge a minimal meals tax.

The following code indicates the average price of two entrees only—without appetizer, dessert, beverages, tax, or gratuity.

$	Less than $20
$$	$21 to $35
$$$	$36 to $50
$$$$	More than $50

REGIONAL CUISINE

BRUNSWICK STEW

Local restaurants serve this hearty mixture by the gallon. While the original version of this savory dish called for a couple of freshly shot squirrels and rabbits, the meat you find in today's dishes typically is chicken, with a little beef or ham tossed in for good measure. Onions, celery, corn, okra (if it's available), lots of tomatoes, potatoes, butter beans, and generally whatever else is ripe in the garden are added, as are vinegar, sugar, salt and pepper, even ketchup. To get it just right, this thick concoction must be simmered all day in a big iron pot. By the way, you may have heard some apocryphal tales about the true origins of Brunswick stew. Brunswick County, North Carolina, claims it, along with several other East Coast Brunswicks. We believe Virginia lore, which says intrepid hunters back in the early 1700s created the dish in the Old Dominion's Brunswick County, relying on resourcefulness and whatever happened to cross their paths out in the wilds. In other words, squirrels and rabbits were all the game they bagged that day.

Frequently, you can find Brunswick stew on sale at any number of outdoor festivals or church bazaars. To assure yourself of getting a stew of the highest quality, check out the Old Chickahominy House (see listing later in this chapter).

Ham

Pigs do not stand a chance around here. Can a state have a "most famous meat"? If it can, then Virginia's candidate is certainly ham. Its popularity dates from colonial times, when hog and hominy were an essential part of the early settlers' diets. Ham was easy to preserve—an important quality in a time before refrigeration. After slaughter, pig meat was smoked, dried, sugar-cured, even pickled. Virginia ham became so well known that it was soon being exported to the North and even abroad.

Before we go any further, let's clear up the great ham confusion. On local menus you may see entrees prepared with Virginia ham, Smithfield ham, Williamsburg ham, or sometimes simply country ham. While all of these pork products are similar in that they are salt-cured, there are some important differences among them. The one basic difference between Virginia hams and other cured hams is that Virginia hams are dry salt-cured before smoking. Technically, only hams cured in Smithfield, a small town across the James River from Williamsburg, can be called Smithfield hams. These hams, left in the skin and aged for up to a year, have a stronger, smokier taste than younger Virginia hams, sometimes known as Williamsburg or country hams. Smithfield hams are coated with pepper

during the curing process, which enhances the hams' flavor. You may see these hams hanging in burlap sacks in local stores. They require overnight soaking before cooking, but don't make the mistake one Pennsylvania woman did upon her first encounter with a Smithfield ham. After years of preparing only the sugar-cured variety, she received a Smithfield ham from a generous son-in-law and proceeded to boil it hour after hour "to tone down the salty taste." The result: a stringy, inedible addition to the trash pile and a very dismayed son-in-law.

Once your Smithfield ham is prepared correctly (those knowledgeable recommend soaking it for at least 24 hours, simmering it for about 20 minutes per pound, then baking it in a 350-degree oven for 20 to 25 minutes, basting frequently), it should be consumed sparingly, thinly sliced. Typically, it is nestled in a buttermilk biscuit, but like its Italian sibling prosciutto, Smithfield ham works well as an appetizer, wrapped around melon, for example.

Bar-B-Que

Those who are not native to the American South may not know or care about the finer distinctions between varieties of this pit-cooked, chopped-pork delight, but Bar-B-Que aficionados will tell you Virginia barbecue tends to have a delicate, smoky flavor. The sauce adds a tang, not a kick. Down in the Carolinas, they make their barbecue with a stronger vinegar base, and you'll sometimes see references to pulled barbecue, which is more strip-like than chopped.

Here in the Tidewater area of Virginia, there's plenty of debate over who makes the best barbecue. We've listed a few of our favorite purveyors so you can try them all and cast your vote.

COUNTY GRILL & SMOKEHOUSE $
1215-A George Washington
Memorial Hwy, York County
(757) 591-0600
www.countrygrilladsmokehouse.ccom
The beef and pork varieties available in sandwiches and platters. Tables are decked out in butcher paper and equipped with half a dozen

different barbecue sauces. You can wash it all down with one of the microbrews you'll find on tap. Daily specials are available. This spot has been a favorite of *Daily Press* readers for several years running. It's open seven days a week.

PIERCE'S PITT BAR-B-QUE $
447 East Rochambeau Dr.
(757) 565-2955
www.pierces.com

Here's a bit of local history: When highway construction on I-64 restricted access to Pierce's, barbecue fans parked their semis, cars, and vans on the new highway's shoulders in order to get their "cue." The highway department put up a fence. No problem. What's a little ol' fence to a determined barbecue connoisseur? It was knocked down and scrambled over more than once by folks determined to get to Pierce's. In fact, no matter when you come, you are almost certain to have at least a short wait in line, because people are still clamoring to get at Pierce's pulled-pork barbecue, made right on the premises (you can follow your nose to Pierce's on a clear day). Just ask beachgoers and other travelers from all over the state who make the pilgrimage regularly. In addition to pork, which is slightly sweeter than most Carolina-style barbecue, but still packs plenty of spice on the back side, Pierce's now serves BBQ chicken, which is equally excellent. They also have all the sides you'd expect—slaw, beans, collard greens, onion rings—plus home-baked cookies and cakes. They sell most items by the pint and quart, packed to go if you need to be on your way.

When the trees are bare, you can see Pierce's through the woods along I-64—it's between exits 234 and 238. From exit 238, turn left at the stop sign at the top of the ramp, then right at the first traffic light. That's Rochambeau Drive. Pierce's is three miles west. From exit 234, make a right at the top of the ramp onto Route 199. Travel one mile to the East Mooretown Road exit, then turn left at Lowe's onto Rochambeau Drive. Pierce's is two miles east. Open 10 a.m. to 9 p.m. daily except Thanksgiving, Christmas, and New Year's Day.

QUEEN ANNE DAIRY SNACK $
7127 Merrimac Trail (Route 143)
(757) 229-3051

Pulling up to this establishment is a retro visit to the 1950s era of walk-up window service. Though the building has seen better days and only has a couple of old outside picnic tables and benches on which to sit, don't be put off. This little place serves some of the best barbecue in this part of Virginia. If you're in the mood for takeout, pick up a pint of this popular Carolina-style barbecue to take home with you. Chopped barbecue sandwiches also are available if you're ready to eat. To top it off, order one of their old-fashioned shakes, sundaes, or malts. No credit cards. Open 11 a.m. to 4:30 p.m. Mon to Fri.

ROCKY MOUNT BAR-B-Q HOUSE $
10113 Jefferson Ave., Newport News
(757) 596-0243
www.rockymountbbq.com

In the restaurant business longevity pretty much says it all. Rocky Mount has been cooking North Carolina–style barbecue for more than 40 years. The shredded or sliced pork here has a vinegar tang, a perfect contrast to the warm, sweet hush puppies which accompany your meal. Platters and sandwiches are served with a wide variety of sides—coleslaw, baked beans (made with ground beef), lima beans, collards, sweet potato casserole, onion rings, and more. (They offer the side dishes as a meal itself—the four-veggie platter.) Kids eat free on Tues. (One child per paying adult, please.) Save room for the delicious banana pudding. Takeout and catering are available. The restaurant also stocks many of the products its kitchen uses—Atkinson's corn bread and hush puppy mix, their own special vinegar sauce, and Hub's Peanuts. Open Mon through Sat 11 a.m. to 8:30 p.m. Closed Sun.

From the Water

Virginia's rivers were so full of fish in colonial days that in 1614 John Smith recorded in his diary that he could have walked across the Chesapeake Bay on the backs of its inhabitants—rockfish, blue crabs, sturgeon, herring, shad and shad roe, mussels, oysters, and clams. Sadly, over the centuries development has so polluted Virginia's waterways that some species are highly endangered. Sturgeon are hard to find now, and oyster beds are disappearing. But area fishermen still reel in plenty of blues, croakers, shad, spot, pike, bass, crappie, and other varieties of freshwater and saltwater fish.

On local piers you're likely to see weekend anglers patiently baiting their lines for crabs. Virginia's most common crab is the blue crab, or *Callinectes sapidus*, which translates as "savory, beautiful swimmer." This ornery-looking creature lives two or three years and periodically molts, shucking off its exoskeleton. For a short stretch of time after molting, the blue crab is soft and vulnerable, but a new, hard shell quickly forms. Commercial crabbers harvest this tender prey to sell as soft-shell crab, considered a delicacy locally but apt to make the noninitiate ask, "You mean I'm supposed to eat it legs and all?" Hard crabs are harvested too, of course, and come in a variety of stages and forms. Stopping off at area fishing docks you may overhear talk about peelers, jimmies, sooks, sponge crabs, busters, and doublers.

While commercial fishermen work from their boats, dropping large baited crab pots made of specially treated steel wire into area waterways, the simple way to catch a crustacean dinner is to tie chicken necks or fish heads to kite string, grab a dip net, and head for the shallows. The trick to this method of crabbing is to gently lure a nibbling crab close enough to net him from underneath. Crabs are smart enough to be frightened by abrupt movements or a sudden play of shadows on the water, such as a body blocking the sun. But they're not smart enough to stop coming back for more, so don't give up. You also can buy small crab pots for use from piers in local sporting goods stores. Crabbing is a time-honored way to spend a leisurely morning in eastern Virginia.

Naturally this quirky crustacean, so important to the culture and economy of the Hampton Roads area, long ago captured the imagination of cooks and consumers, spawning an endless variety of recipes from the humble crab cake to Crab Imperial. Backfin crabmeat is considered the tastiest and is often served simply—sautéed with butter or chilled with mayonnaise. You'll also see crabmeat served chilled, as a stuffing for avocados, tomatoes, or mushrooms. Heated, it combines with shrimp, lobster, and other seafood for a variety of baked dishes and casseroles.

Local cooks spar to create the best crab cakes, with feuds developing over whether cornmeal, cracker crumbs, or bread and eggs provide the most suitable base. Fresh soft-shell-crab season runs roughly from May to early fall. If you see the dish offered at other times of the year, you're probably getting a frozen product, which is not recommended.

Crab bisques, soups, and gumbos (both hot and chilled) are perennial favorites around here as well. Hampton crab bisque is made with cream, Tabasco, and sherry. Crab soups are sometimes based on fish stock, sometimes tomato broth. She-crab soup, which combines sauterne or sherry with whipping cream, butter, and lots of crab, including the roe, is just too good to miss.

Some popular local eateries that serve up delicious crab cakes and other crab dishes are noted here.

CHARLES CITY TAVERN
9220 John Tyler Memorial Hwy. (Route 5)
Charles City County
(804) 829-5004

For a Sunday brunch with regional flair, check out the crab cakes Harrison at this historic tavern. This dish features two crab cakes served over grilled Smithfield ham and toasted Sally Lunn bread topped off with hollandaise sauce. The brunch menu also features crab cakes Chesapeake, a dish that closely resembles eggs Benedict, with crab cakes served in the place of the traditional Canadian bacon. Dinner fare, served seven evenings a week, includes both the crab cakes Harrison and an excellent surf and turf, featuring filet mignon and (what else) crab cakes.

CRAB SHACK ON THE JAMES $$
7601 River Rd., foot of the James
River Fishing Pier
Newport News
(757) 245-2722
www.crabshackonthejames.com

For the ultimate crab dinner, you might want to wander down I-64 to drop anchor at the Crab Shack in Newport News. As popular with locals as it is with tourists, the Crab Shack serves up some of the best hard-shell crabs, crab cakes, oysters, shrimp, and even calamari, on the peninsula. It would be a shame to miss this place even if seafood is not your thing because the setting—a long closed-in porch jutting out over the James—makes the trip from Williamsburg worthwhile. Open daily for lunch and dinner.

THE DINING ROOM AT FORD'S COLONY
240 Ford's Colony Dr., Williamsburg
(757) 258-4107, (800) 334-6033

This extremely posh restaurant serves outstanding seafood. Although menu selections may vary, Ford's Colony has featured such delights as crab cakes topped with shiitake mushrooms and a delicious bisque that pairs roasted red peppers and crabmeat. Open Tues through Sat, 5:30 to 9 p.m., and for Sunday brunch, 11:30 a.m. to 3 p.m.

Peanuts

Don't leave town without sampling Virginia's crunchy, roasted peanuts. After all, in 2007 Suffolk and Isle of Wight counties, just south of Williamsburg, accounted for 35 percent of the state's peanut production—you are in Peanut Country, people. Noted here are two of the best places in Williamsburg to stock up.

THE PEANUT SHOP
414 Prince George St. (Merchants Square)
(757) 229-3908

Crunchy home-style peanuts prepared in a mind-boggling variety of ways, including our favorite: chocolate-covered. Not sure what you want? The Peanut Shop regularly offers samples!

WHITLEY'S VIRGINIA PEANUTS AND PEANUT FACTORY
1351 Richmond Rd.
(757) 229-4056

You'll find delicious "home-cooked" Virginia peanuts, Virginia hams, gift baskets, and other goods from the Commonwealth, all available for you to carry out or mail order back home.

RESTAURANTS

An alphabetical listing of neighborhood haunts, favorite delis, out-of-the-mainstream locations follows. With visitors and tourists comprising the majority of diners, casual dress is appropriate. Where there are exceptions, we indicate such.

ABERDEEN BARN $$
1601 Richmond Rd.
(757) 229-6661
www.aberdeen-barn.com

Best known for its aged steaks, this restaurant opens at 5 p.m. for dinner. The decor is rustic, subdued, and candlelit—think old-fashioned steakhouse. This is not the place to start a diet—a popular starter is a basket of sesame sticks accompanied by a crock of cheese spread. Guests rave about the prime rib, but also praise the seafood. A kids' menu adds appeal for families. Be sure to save room for "The Mother Lode," a dessert for two consisting of a chocolate chip brownie, topped with ice cream and hot fudge. Reservations are recommended.

AROMA'S COFFEEHOUSE, CAFÉ AND BAKE SHOP $
431 Prince George St.
(757) 221-6676
www.aromasworld.com

Take a quick glance around the room at Aroma's: A business meeting at one table; a group of William and Mary students cramming at another, a pair of retirees jabbering about their golf game at a third. Some days it seems as if all of Williamsburg is at Aroma's, the coffee spot of choice in what passes for downtown, one block off Merchants Square. Whether you want a quick blast of caffeine, a snack, or a full meal, it's hard to go wrong.

The decor is charmingly casual, as is the service (order at the counter, pick it up yourself). The menu features a mix of standard, but fresh, sandwiches and wraps (roast beef on focaccia, garden veggie wrap), soups and salads. Breakfast is served through 10:30 a.m. daily (until noon on Sun), and dinner specials are available after 5 p.m.

The kids' menu was obviously designed by the parent of a picky eater. Actual sandwich description: "Turkey and cheese on white break—Plain, Plain, Plain, that means no fixins'." The nachos are fixed "how kids like 'em, PLAIN with cheese as the only topping."

The deserts are decadent (especially the apple pie), and a full range of specialty coffees and loose-leaf teas are available. Several nights a week, a band will wedge itself into the corner for live music, and the drink of choice will shift from coffee to wine or beer.

Because of its popularity, grabbing a table can be tricky at peak times. Most days, even in the winter, the outside tables are a great option. Free Wi-Fi is available, too.

A second location opened in Newport News' City Center development in 2007.

artcafé26 $$$
5107-2 Center St.
New Town
(757) 565-7788
www.artcafe26.com

Exceptional cuisine blends with elegant design at this one-of-a-kind cafe, which opens at a leisurely hour for breakfast (10:30 a.m.) and lunch, serving dinner just two nights a week. (Translation: make dinner reservations as far as possible in advance.) The woman in charge is owner Sibilla Dengs a native of Aachen, a city in Germany's Rhine valley near the Belgian and Dutch borders. The German architect Mies van der Rohe famously once said, "God is in the details." Not here. Here, Sibilla is in the details. An art historian by training, her careful crafting of culinary and fine art has created a truly unique fine-dining experience.

A row of suede couches face a long wall of framed art—"People drink their coffee and read the newspaper there," Dengs says, but they must also admire the subtle art lessons she builds into her exhibits, hanging works by the same artist side by side, one artfully framed, the other not.

Her visiting chefs, all trained in Europe, make no such gaffes when it comes to presenting the food. "Too pretty to eat," is the phrase these plates call to mind, but we do anyway. At dinner, the amuse bouche one night is a parchment paper cone of popcorn aerated in, of all things, truffle oil. It is accompanied by a basil emulsification, served in a shot glass, with a straw. Sipping it produces a sensation close to inhaling it. It is nearly intoxicating.

The restaurant showcases molecular gastronomy—the branch of science that studies the physical and chemical processes of cooking, and how the interplay of different senses affects enjoyment. In the hands of a skilled chef, it turns chemistry into art. That intensity and adventurousness carry through the entire meal. When it comes time to order wine, Sibilla pulls out three bottles to do a quick compare-and-contrast tableside. An entree might put a fresh twist on a fish-and-scallops dish by including a side of hand-spun cotton candy with an eyedropper of an artisan vinegar (for those who ducked organic chemistry: the acidic vinegar breaks the bonds of the long carbon chains in the sugar). The arctic char arrives covered in foam—the effect is to make one think this fish is so fresh it has just washed ashore. Delightful!

The menu changes frequently (see the Web site for current details), emphasizing seasonal organic ingredients. Like most nouvelle cuisine restaurants, portions are small—the focus is on freshness and the intensity of the flavors, not volume. And while artcafé26 does offer a small children's menu, this probably isn't the place for kids at dinner—unless they are laid-back, budding foodies.

You should also allow plenty of time—the pace is deliberately leisurely, and Sibilla and her staff like to engage in educational conversation along the way. You can complete a lovely dinner in an hour—but you'll feel disappointed that you didn't allow two hours instead.

Open from 10:30 a.m. to 5 p.m. Tues through Thurs; 10:30 a.m. to 9:30 p.m. on Fri; Sat 8:30 a.m. to 3 p.m., then 6 p.m. to 9:30 p.m. for dinner; and 10 a.m. to 2 p.m. on Sun.

Oh, and that name? The "art" part is obvious, but the "26?" "That is my little secret," Sibilla says.

THE BACKFIN SEAFOOD RESTAURANT $$$
New Town
3701 Strawberry Plains Rd.
(757) 565-5430
www.backfinrestaurant.com

This is among the most popular local restaurants for a lot of reasons. The comfortable, come-as-you-are atmosphere enhances the experience. Open daily for lunch and dinner, the menu features a variety of baskets, sandwiches, salads, soups, and appetizers, as well as low-cost children's entrees. Insiders love the crab cakes (offered as a sandwich at lunch or on a platter at dinner), the Backfin skins (potato skins stuffed with crabmeat and topped with melted cheddar and bacon), the hot crab dip, and the raw bar selection of steamed shrimp, oysters, clams, and crab legs. Like pasta? They'll add shrimp, scallops, or crabmeat (or all three, if you prefer) to a basic linguine in Alfredo sauce. Don't eat seafood? Fear not, the burgers here are among the best in town. The good news is that anything you order will please. Be sure to check the chalkboard for daily lunch and dinner specials. A final word: Save room for a slice of their homemade key lime pie. You'll be glad you did. Lunch is served from 11 a.m. to 3 p.m. with dinner from 4:30 to 9:30 p.m.

BAKER'S CRUST $
Settler's Market at New Town
5234 Monticello Ave.
(757) 253-2787
www.bakerscrust.com

This local chain has six Virginia locations (including two in the Richmond and three in Norfolk/Virginia Beach). The newest is a welcome addition to New Town, offering affordable and delicious food in an inviting setting. High-backed leather booths ring the dining room; a separate bar area is a popular spot for a glass of wine during happy hour. The real draw here is, however, the fresh-baked breads, salads (full and half portions), burgers, soups, and crepes—prepared both as entrees (shrimp and jumbo lump crab or steak and mushroom) and desserts (the "Wimbledon" version contains fresh strawberries and whipped cream). Several varieties of Mediterranean flatbread pizzas work as appetizers for the table; the roasted tomato and house-made mozzarella panini is warm, gooey, and full of iron-rich baby spinach leaves. Don't limit yourself to trying just one thing—the most popular items on the menu are the soup/salad/sandwich combos. Steam rises from the liquid center of the chocolate lava mini-bundt cake—cool it off with the scoop of vanilla bean ice cream served alongside. Children are welcomed with a menu they can color and seven smaller-plate options—pasta, burger, chicken fingers—each $4.99.

During the winter months, one daily special is an appetizer and entree for $10.99. Bottles of wine are half-price every Wednesday. Customers who dine-in get a 25 percent discount on whole loaves bought to take home, but that means you will have to stop at the bakery case—just try to get out of there without a lemon square or a double chocolate chunk cookie to go. Takeout and catering menus are available.

Open at 11 a.m. for lunch and dinner Mon through Fri; open at 8 a.m. for breakfast on Sat and Sun every day. Dinner is served until 9 p.m. every day; until 10 p.m. on Fri and Sat.

BERRET'S SEAFOOD RESTAURANT AND TAPHOUSE GRILL $$$
Merchants Square
199 South Boundary St.
(757) 253-1847
www.berrets.com

Berret's location on Merchants Square is popular with young professionals as well as tourists and college students. In addition to the usual raw-bar fare, it offers grilled steaks, chicken, and fish. Inside you'll find tasty, fresh Chesapeake Bay seafood and a wide selection of other choices served in a pleasant, upbeat atmosphere. The seafood chowders and fresh soups of the day are always wonderful. Ask for the specials of the day, as they are usually based on what is available locally. A children's menu is available. Reservations are recommended.

i The Indians taught the Jamestown colonists the secret behind the famous Virginia cured ham. Their methods of salting, smoking, and aging venison were adapted by the Europeans. Today, the distinctive taste of salt-cured ham is achieved by following essentially the same process used by the early settlers.

BLACK ANGUS GRILLE $$
1433 Richmond Rd.
(757) 229-6823
www.blackangusgrille.com

Chef Bobby Mageras, trained at the Culinary Institute of America in Hyde Park, New York, offers an imaginative selection of prime rib and other specialties including veal, chicken, lobster, shrimp, and Eastern Shore seafood. He welcomes vegetarians, and offers them original entrees using locally available, seasonal ingredients. The dessert list is equally tantalizing, so save room. This is a popular, locally owned and operated restaurant, which seats 200. Dinner reservations are recommended.

BLUE TALON BISTRO $$$
420 Prince George St.
(757) 476-2583
www.bluetalonbistro.com

Any short list of Williamsburg's best restaurants would include this charming, French-inflected bistro, which has a unique menu and a great location one block off Merchants Square. (Returning visitors in search of The Cheese Shop, which moved to Duke of Gloucester Street in 2003, may turn up here at its former location and happily discover the Blue Talon instead.)

Cafe tables on the sidewalk and the fare—"Champagne, sausages, fromages"—stenciled on large-pane storefront windows lend a Parisian air. Inside, the space evokes early 20th-century elegance—hammered tin ceiling, tile floor with inlaid mosaics, light wood and rattan furniture. It's a nice change from the pervasive colonial motif.

Owner/chef David Everett's focus is "serious comfort food," but his menu is European and traditional. French onion soup, sautéed calves liver, foie gras, paté, escargot, sweetbreads, braised goat, lamb steak, cassoulet, potpies, and all manner of crepe are standards. The wine list is extensive. The chocolate mousse, a rich cloud of flavor scooped tableside from a lion's head into a bowl of sliced strawberries drizzled with powdered sugar and chocolate sauce, could feed a small nation. Cappuccino, made with Italian Illy coffee, is prepared with the precise amount of microbubbles in the milk so as to leave a heart-shaped inset of foam—the so-called "Illy apple"—on the surface.

An excellent Web site allows guests to take a behind-the-scenes tour, book a reservation, check current menus, and learn about upcoming events, including the weekly wine night with all bottles half-price.

Traveling alone? An especially nice place to dine is at the stainless steel bar, within easy reach of a selection of newspapers hanging from hooks on a half-wall that separates the bar area from the front dining room. Bar seating is always first-come, first-served, and don't ask them to change the channel to ESPN. The bar TV runs a perpetual spool of Julia Child reruns.

One note: Vegetarian entree options are limited to the macaroni and cheese (a huge, yummy portion) and a white bean crepe with grilled vegetables.

Open for breakfast, lunch, and dinner from 8 a.m. to 9 p.m. Reservations are recommended for dinner.

CAFÉ PROVENCAL $$$
At the Williamsburg Winery
5810 Wessex Hundred
(757) 941-0310
www.williamsburgwinery.com

One of the best-kept secrets in Williamsburg, this lovely Country French-inflected restaurant is located inside Wedmore Place, the luxury hotel on the grounds of the Williamsburg Winery. The kitchen emphasis is on "house-made," beginning with a produce garden on the property that provides fresh vegetables and herbs. Fish, seafood, and steaks are all of the highest quality, accompanied by inventive side dishes like roasted wild mushrooms, mascarpone polenta and butternut squash ravioli. An extensive wine list includes bottled reserves from the winery, adjacent to the hotel. Arrive in daylight, if possible, to enjoy the picturesque property, or make a reservation for dinner following the winery tour. A unique evening out.

CAPTAIN GEORGE'S
SEAFOOD RESTAURANT $$$
5363 Richmond Rd.
(757) 565-2323
www.captaingeorges.com

Don't be startled by the tall ship splitting this restaurant. It's your landmark from the highway. The all-you-can-eat buffet inside is a sight to see and a challenge to even the hungriest members of your party. Dozens of baked, broiled, and fried seafood entrees are complemented by separate salad and dessert bars. The full menu offers more than 70 items, including seafood and beef. A children's menu is available, and there are banquet rooms for large parties. The line moves quickly, so don't anticipate a long wait. Dinner is served Mon through Fri beginning at 4:30 p.m., Sat beginning at 4 p.m., and Sun, when doors open at noon. Throughout the summer, a production of the Haunted Dinner Theater is offered at Captain George's on various evenings. For more information, turn to our Nightlife chapter.

CARROT TREE KITCHENS $
1782 Jamestown Rd.
(757) 229-0957
www.carrottreekitchens.com

Yes, the building that houses this local favorite was once a motel and, yes, some people still think of the Carrot Tree as a bakery, which is how it began. But owner Debi Helseth has branched out—converting the former motel into a 40-seat breakfast and lunch spot, and adding a second location in Yorktown. (See our chapter on Jamestown and Yorktown for details.)

In 1990, challenged by a restaurant manager to produce a better carrot cake, Helseth called her grandmother at midnight for a recipe and baked through the night. The delicious result not only wowed her boss, she began selling the cakes wholesale out of her garage. In 1995, she opened Carrot Tree Kitchens on Jamestown Road, just a few miles northeast of the ferry terminus and the Jamestown historic area.

Helseth still sells a delectable array of baked goods from glass cases at the entrance (you have a stronger will than we do if you get away without a sweet treat to go), but the breakfast and lunch menus have made this more than just a place to pick up dessert. The house specialties are Brunswick stew, ham biscuits, and crab cakes. There is always a freshly made quiche of the day and a wide variety of sandwiches and wraps. In the summer months, the gazpacho made from fresh tomatoes is a must. (It and many other menu items are sold for takeout by the pint and quart.) The only complaint we have is that the food here deserves better than the plasticware it is served on.

Open Tues through Fri from 8 a.m. to 5:30 p.m. Sat and Mon from 8 a.m. to 4 p.m. Sun brunch and lunch is served 10 a.m. to 4 p.m.

CENTER STREET GRILL $$–$$$
5101 Center St.
New Town
(757) 220-4600
www.centerstreetgrill.com

A gathering place for locals who like the raw bar and the convivial atmosphere after the end of the business day, this restaurant attempts to offer something for everyone. The most popular items among the appetizers are the fried calamari (appropriately spicy), duck tacos, and Philly roll (fried egg roll stuffed with rib eye steak, onions, and American cheese!). Menu favorites among the entrees include the mahi-mahi, the smoked beef brisket, North Carolina barbecue, and shrimp and grits. All meats are smoked in-house. Other restaurants are sleepy (or closed) on Monday nights; the Center Street Grill packs 'em in with half-price burgers. Kids under eight can choose among hamburgers, chicken tenders, corn dog, or mac and cheese. A drink is included for $5. In warmer weather, dine alfresco on the outdoor patio. Open daily for lunch and dinner from 11 a.m. Sunday brunch begins at 10 a.m. Reservations are required for parties of six or more.

CHARLES CITY TAVERN $$
9220 John Tyler Memorial Hwy. (Route 5)
Charles City County
(804) 829-5004
Halfway between Williamsburg and Richmond is this superb restaurant in a remodeled, late-19th-century farmhouse. You can dine inside or outside, in favorable weather. The menu is varied, and specials are offered daily. This place is known for its lump crab cakes. Open for lunch and dinner Tues through Sat, and on Sun for brunch and dinner. This is a superb choice when you're touring the Route 5 plantations, as it is just minutes from Sherwood Forest, Berkeley, and Shirley Plantations. Reservations are strongly recommended, particularly for dinner.

CHARLY'S $
Williamsburg-Jamestown Airport
100 Marclay Rd.
(757) 258-0034
This airport cafe takes the title of Williamsburg's quirkiest place to eat. You would never find it unless you fly directly into Williamsburg's privately owned airport, which most people don't. Even getting to Charly's is a little odd—you'll pass a landfill on Marclay Road before reaching the humble airport terminal which houses the ground-floor restaurant. Open only for lunch, the hot and cold sandwiches are served on fresh-baked bread. The seafood bisque is a local favorite, as are the desserts, which are also made from scratch. But the reason to come here is for the unusual view. The restaurant and its patio have a clear view of the runway, and it's fascinating to

watch the takeoffs and landings while dining. Of course, there are no scheduled flights in or out of this facility, so if you're coming for the view, pick a clear day on which a private pilot might decide to take a spin. (There are 60-plus airplanes based here, plus a flight school, the Colonial Air Center.) Open daily from 11 a.m. until 3 p.m., until 4 p.m. on weekends. On Sun, a prime rib special is offered for $14.95.

THE CHEESE SHOP $
Merchants Square
410 Duke of Gloucester St.
(757) 220-0298
www.cheeseshopwilliamsburg.com
If you ask where to get a quick lunch in the Historic Area, chances are good you will be directed to The Cheese Shop. Its well-deserved reputation for super sandwiches was built on an outstanding freshly sliced roast beef special, served on fresh-baked French bread with a "top secret" house dressing. The other offerings—which include Virginia ham, smoked turkey, provolone and prosciutto on ciabatta—are equally as satisfying. Moreover, everything you need to make a meal—side salads, beverages, chips, and desserts—is of top-notch quality and readily available on the counter or in cases surrounding the counter at the rear of the store where lunch orders are placed.

In 2003, the Cheese Shop moved from its longtime home on Prince George to Duke of Gloucester street, expanding the number of specialty and gourmet food products it could offer, and quadrupling the number of wine bottles it could stock with the addition of basement-level wine cellar.

There is (limited) seating in the storefront and on a patio fronting Merchants Square, but the Power family—Mary Ellen, Tom, and their three adult children—would need another building entirely to seat the crowds that stop in for a reasonably priced, yummy lunch during high season. One tip is to call in your order for pickup at the outdoor window, which opens onto the breezeway between the Cheese Shop and Wythe Candy. The window is open for the

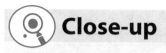# Close-up

A Chef's Kitchen

(501 Prince George St., 757-564-8500; www.achefskitchen.biz)

This unique combination cooking school and fine dining experience leaves visitors with a happy but awkward conundrum: Should I shout about this place from the highest rooftop? Or keep it to myself, fearing that once word gets out, a difficult reservation will become impossible?

Owners John and Wanda Gonzales had long wanted to open a teaching kitchen where guests could learn about food while being entertained and served inspired dishes and great wines. John Gonzales (pronounce it GON-zales, with two syllables rather than the Hispanic version with three), a self-described "CW Brat," grew up in a Colonial Williamsburg house next to the Governor's Palace. (His father, Donald, was a senior CW executive.) After training at the Culinary Institute of America in Hyde Park, New York, and stints at the Watergate Hotel, the Jockey Club, and Ritz Carlton in Washington, D.C., Gonzales was lured home by Colonial Williamsburg to redesign the menus at their taverns.

That done, **A Chef's Kitchen** was his next project. Located in a brick building two blocks off Merchants Square, the restaurant/school opened in 2005.

The dinner class is offered once a night, Wed through Sat, beginning promptly at 6:30 p.m. A seating lasts about three hours and begins with champagne and hors d'oeuvres served at the marble countertop where Gonzales and sous chef Sam Hall are preparing a five-course meal for 26. *You* might be frazzled; *they* are totally at ease, happy to chat about what they're making while guests munch on figs stuffed with goat cheese and rolled in toasted almonds, or nibble at the pastry pinwheels rolled with thinly shaved local ham, grated Emmental and Gruyère, chives, and bits of Asian pear. "It's basically ham and cheese," Gonzales deadpans in his appealing, down-to-earth manner.

For the meal, guests are seated at three long tables, arranged lecture hall–style, with a large television monitor positioned so that everyone can see the cooktop. During the five courses that follow—soup, salad, pasta, an entree and dessert—Gonzales and Hall keep up a steady, affable banter, offering user-friendly tips about cooking and food. Over an evening, you might learn about the true shelf life of baking soda, the importance of emulsification, why Eggbeaters beat fresh eggs in a Caesar salad. ("One of our rules is 'Do NOT give the customers salmonella poisoning,'" Gonzales says.) When buying fish, he suggests you ask if it is chemical-free and if it is wild-caught. "If they say they don't know, tell them, 'It's supposed to be on your clipboard back there.'"

The younger Hall holds his own. Mindful that he is sampling an awful lot of the risotto which he'll serve with wild gulf shrimp, he explains, "I'm constantly tasting this risotto because . . . I'm hungry."

Menus change monthly. The fixed price dinner is $74.50, which includes champagne and three wine flights, and copies of the recipes for that night's menu. No tips are accepted. Before doors open, guests linger in the lobby, a specialty foods and kitchen goods shop. Fine wines (all rated 87 points or higher by the professional wine magazines) are bargain priced at $10 a bottle. Many of the ingredients Gonzales and Hall will introduce during the evening—chestnut puree, Celtic sea salt, locally milled cornmeal—are on sale here, as are Gonzales's two cookbooks—*Holiday Fare: Favorite Williamsburg Recipes* and *The Colonial Williamsburg Tavern Cookbook*.

A credit card is required to hold your reservation, and it is not unreasonable to think MONTHS ahead to secure one of the 26 seats available each night. The chefs can accommodate almost any dietary restriction except Kosher or vegan with advance notice. There is no children's menu or reduced price for teetotalers. Cooking classes on a wide variety of cuisines are offered at 6 p.m. on Tuesday nights. All classes are $39.50 per person except the "wine pairings" classes which are $45 per person.

lunch crush—11 a.m. to 3 p.m. daily. The entire sandwich menu can be viewed online at the Web site listed above.

William and Mary alumni will admit that during their college days many an undergrad lived on "bread ends" ($1 for a huge bag) and house dressing (various sizes beginning at 50 cents), the continued sale of which ensures the endearment of each successive generation of students. "We bake the bread every day in the store. Sometimes those bread ends are still hot when we put them in the bag," said Mary Ellen Power Jr. "We don't have any plans to stop doing it because I think there would be a mutiny if we did."

CHEZ TRINH $$
157 Monticello Ave.
(757) 253-1888
www.chez-trinh.com
Tucked on the back side of the Williamsburg Shopping Center (enter on Monticello Avenue near Marshalls) is this lovely Vietnamese restaurant, which specializes in fresh Asian cuisine, including a nearly endless variety of stir-fry, rice paper rolls, crispy stuffed crepes, seafood dishes, and many vegetarian options. The "winning combination" is a huge serving of Vietnamese noodle soup (Pho) with two different types of noodles, chicken, pork, and shrimp served in a beautiful china bowl. Music is offered several nights a week when William and Mary is in session—oldies, gospel, and Korean songs on Tues, Thurs, and Fri beginning at 7 p.m. College students provide the music on Sat.

Open daily for lunch from 11:30 a.m. to 2:30 p.m., except Sun when they open at 12 p.m. Dinner is served every night from 5 p.m. to 9:30 p.m. Takeout is available..

CITIES GRILLE AND WINE SHOP $$–$$$
Governor's Green
4511C John Tyler Hwy
(757) 564-3955
www.citiesgrilles.com
This was once a pioneer in fine dining in Williamsburg—one of only a handful of places in the mid-1990s you could get a good meal with a great bottle of wine. The menu sticks to its original conceit: a "tour" of different American regional cuisines, based on the city of origin—New York, say, or Richmond or Seattle. While the cleverness wears off with time, the menu still has reliable favorites, like the Memphis-style (or is that Elvis-style?) meatloaf, or the chicken salad, based on the recipe from the regionally famous (now closed) Thalhimer's department store. The wine list has won the *Wine Spectator* magazine's Award of Excellence. The location is a tad out of the way, southwest of town, at the intersection of Route 5 and Ironbound Road. Hours are 11:30 a.m. to 3 p.m. for lunch, 5 p.m. to 8:30 p.m. weekdays, until 9:30 p.m. on weekends.

THE COFFEEHOUSE $
Williamsburg Shopping Center
Route 5 at Route 199
(757) 229-9791
www.gocoffeehouse.com
Are you a coffee or tea connoisseur? If so, this coffee shop and bakery is reason enough to turn in to the Williamsburg Crossing Shopping Center—a retail development whose fortunes have suffered a bit since the opening of New Town (see Close-up, p. 81), a few miles away.

The shop offers 24 varieties of coffee and 22 types of loose tea. Regional and estate coffee beans, many organic and most Free Trade, from the Americas, Africa, Southeast Asia, and the Pacific are roasted on the premises, ensuring java lovers the freshest brew. Check the daily specials on the blackboard—the "Snicker" blend is like dessert in a cup. All manner of specialty coffees are available, too—espresso, macchiato, cappuccino, cafe mocha, cafe latte, and cafe au lait. On a hot day, Italian sodas and cream sodas are alternatives. French pastries, cakes, brownies, muffins, and other sweet treats are baked on premises, as well as French and multigrain breads for sandwiches which are mainstays of a lunch menu that includes quiche and soups of the day. Bring your laptop: there's free wi-fi on-site. Open from 7 a.m. to 6 p.m. Mon through Fri, 8 a.m. to 5 p.m. Sat.

COLLEGE DELLY $
336 Richmond Rd.
(757) 229-6627

Directly across from the William and Mary campus, this sandwich shop is a longtime favorite with students, locals, and tourists looking for a quick, tasty meal. Reading the sandwich ingredients—all made with Boars Head brand meats—will certainly fire up your appetite. There's also the freshly made Italian and Greek dishes (especially the souvlaki and shish kebab), homemade soups, and stews to consider. There's a friendly competition between this establishment and Paul's Deli, just across the parking lot, as to who makes the best Hot Holly, a sub sandwich of roast beef, cheese, turkey, bacon, lettuce, tomato, and pickle on a toasted roll. You'll have to try both on successive days and decide for yourself. Desserts are by the Carrot Tree (see the full listing above). The College Delly offers limited delivery service in the evenings until 1 a.m., and the hungry night owls will appreciate that the restaurant is open from 10:30 a.m. until 2 a.m. weeknights and Sat, and until midnight on Sun.

THE CORNER POCKET $$
4805 Courthouse St.
(757) 220-0808
www.thecornerpocket.us

This isn't a pool hall that serves food; it's a great restaurant that happens to have pool tables.

Now located in New Town (see our Close-up, p. 81), a mixed-use development west of downtown, the Corner Pocket features creative takes on pub food in a smoke-free environment. Meals are graced with little touches that show a well-trained chef (Jason Wade, formerly of The *) working with fresh ingredients—sprigs of fragrant rosemary on the Guinness-infused pot roast, sweet corn in the salsa accompanying the black bean nachos. The roasted fish tacos, Reuben, and jambalaya also get raves (the latter is so popular it's known to run out). Kids are welcomed with their own menu and crayons.

When the weather cooperates, which is most of the year in mild southern Virginia, food and drinks are served outdoors on a covered patio that wraps around two sides of the building.

And the pool? Thirteen tables including three nine-foot professional tables with great lighting and plenty of room. In addition to billiards tournaments, the Corner Pocket also has a thing for the blues, frequently offering live music.

Opens at 11:30 Mon through Fri, 4 p.m. on Sat and Sun. Dinner is served till midnight, making this one of latest places to get a full tasty meal. Closing time is 1 a.m. Sun through Tues; 2 a.m. Wed through Sat.

THE DINING ROOM AT
FORD'S COLONY $$$$
240 Ford's Colony Dr.
(757) 258-4107, (800) 334-6033
www.fordscolonycc.com

This award-winning dining room has an intimate feel, with windows that offer impressive views of the grounds. Contemporary American creations and innovative variations on classic American and European dishes are carefully prepared for discerning diners, with the menu changing seasonally, sometimes nightly. The extensive wine list (more than 1,000 entries) has been honored with an award from *Wine Spectator* magazine. The quiet, formal elegance of the room is matched by the equally quiet, efficient service of the staff. The chef works magic with just about everything he prepares, but his variations on salmon are among the best. Reservations are a must. Open for dinner only, Tues through Sat.

DORALDO'S $$
1915 Pocahontas Trail
The Village Shops at Kingsmill
(757) 220-0795

This friendly Italian restaurant offers a traditional menu and serves up tasty, authentic cuisine. Chef and owner Frank Alosa's extensive menu features a combination of northern and southern Italian dishes—including veal, fish, eggplant, chicken, seafood, beef, and an array of pastas and, of course, pizzas. A basket of delicious garlic knots is presented, gratis, to begin the meal. The mozzarella sticks are uncommonly yummy as is the house salad—a fresh mix of tomato, onion, cucumber, and red cabbage served with a red-

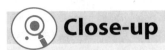

Close-up

18th-Century Eating for 21st-Century Tastes

Many people feel their visit to Williamsburg would be incomplete without the experience of being served by a waitress in a mobcap, serenaded by a strolling balladeer, or having the origins of their Sally Lunn bread explained. These are the special features of the meals served at Colonial Williamsburg's restored taverns, which serve 18th-century favorites adapted for 21st-century tastes. (Somehow children survived 250 years ago without chicken nuggets; no such dire circumstances exist now—each of the taverns has something for the kids. They also take MasterCard and Visa.)

All of the taverns are located in the Historic Area and are open to the public. (You do not need a Colonial Williamsburg ticket to eat at the taverns.) Free parking is available for tavern patrons.

A centralized number, (757) 229-2141 or (800) TAVERNS, handles reservations for the taverns, as well as Colonial Williamsburg's other restaurants—the Williamsburg Inn's Regency Room and Golden Horseshoe, and the Williamsburg Lodge (see our listings for those restaurants in this chapter). Dinner reservations, in season, are a must. You can also peruse all the restaurants' menus at www.colonialwilliamsburg.com.

Chowning's Tavern (100 East Duke of Gloucester St.; $). Josiah Chowning opened his tavern in 1766 and appealing to the "ordinary sort." The restored building which re-creates his once popular eatery is located right in the center of the Historic Area, serving soups, stews, sandwiches, and of course, cheeseburgers, from 11:30 a.m. to 3 p.m.

Beginning at 5 p.m. Chowning's becomes a popular spot for fun lovers, with music and colonial games of Gambols. Light fare—rib bites, barbeque sandwiches, a crock of cheese with "sippets"—is available. As the evening wears on, the atmosphere might get a little rowdier, as Chowning's also has a fine selection of ales, rum punches, and wine to wash down the fresh-roasted Virginia peanuts delivered to every table.

Christiana Campbell's Tavern (101 South Waller St.; $$$). George Washington favored meals at this establishment, opposite the eastern end of the capitol building, and one of unique pleasures here is listening to servers recount his favorable critiques of the place, taken from his diary. The cuisine these days focuses on traditional seafood dishes—chowder, oyster

---

wine vinaigrette. Children are welcome, and there is plenty of kid-friendly food on the regular menu and the one designed just for them. Close to Busch Gardens, you can't see Doraldo's from US 60. Turn into the Village Shops shopping center—it's on the eastern end. Open 11 a.m. to 2:30 p.m. for lunch and 5 to 9 p.m. for dinner.

EMERALD THAI $
264G McLaws Circle
(757) 645-2511

Despite its strip mall setting, Emerald Thai is a delight. The usual Thai standards are done

exceptionally well here. Small touches make the difference—chunks of pineapple in the cashew chicken; a hint of heat in the peanut salad dressing. The acid test for Thai fare, of course, is pad thai noodles—and Emerald's passes, nicely.

Let's remember that this is Thai cuisine in Williamsburg, not San Francisco or New York. The dishes are kept on the mild side (you can request more spice), but still taste authentic.

The location, near the Kingsmill Resort and Busch Gardens, makes this spot more convenient to those attractions' visitors than to guests staying near the Historic Area. Prepare salad, crab ragout, crab cakes and the like. The entrees are complemented by longtime tavern favorites of cabbage slaw, spoon bread, and sweet potato muffins. During the holiday season, the tavern hosts tea with Mrs. Campbell, who entertains guests with accounts of her 18th-century contemporaries and the quaint customs of the period.

Dinner is served from 5 p.m. Tues through Sat. Reservations are required, and parking is available behind the tavern.

King's Arms Tavern (416 East Duke of Gloucester St.; $$$). In its decor and its menu, this restaurant reflects the refined tastes of the colonial gentry who dined here. The house specialties include fried chicken, peanut soup, prime rib, and Sally Lunn bread. The bar offers specialty drinks such as "rummer" and punch royal. After your meal, try the 18th-century favorite, syllabub, a concoction of cream, white wine, sherry, sugar, and lemon that separates into a meringue-like topping with the wine and sherry at the bottom of the glass. Open Thurs through Mon for lunch from 11:30 a.m. to 2:30 p.m. and for dinner from 5 p.m. until closing.

In conjunction with CW's "Revolutionary City" programming, the tavern offers "Breakfast with Citizens of the Revolution" Fri through Sun, in season. Guests enjoy engaging conversation with the people who shaped our country.

Shields Tavern (422 East Duke of Gloucester St.; $$$). Operated by James Shields in the 1740s, this tavern has been carefully appointed to serve visitors colonial Virginia foods in a setting that predates the other taverns by 25 years. Menu selections are inspired by the food served to the period's "middle class"—lesser gentry and traveling merchants. Southern favorites such as seafood gumbo and cornmeal-battered fried oysters supplement barbecued ribs and Welsh rarebit. A selection of sandwiches ranges from Virginia ham and cheddar to pulled pork or hot turkey. Dessert offerings include peanut butter pie and wild berry crumble pie among the tempting treats.

Shields also features a full bar menu, with specialty drinks such as apple cider, rum punch, champagne cocktails, and spiced wine; beers and ales; and favorites such as Chowning's root beer and King's Arms Tavern ginger ale. Strolling balladeers and character interpreters welcome guests. Open for lunch and dinner Tues through Sat. Dinner reservations are required.

to hunt a bit: McLaws Circle is on the southern side of US 60; Emerald Thai is in the eastern portion of a two-building retail cluster. Open for lunch and dinner Mon through Sat, dinner only on Sun.

FAT CANARY $$$$
410 West Duke of Gloucester St.
(757) 229-3333
www.fatcanarywilliamsburg.com
Recipient of a four diamond designation from AAA every year since it opened, this upscale restaurant has a lot of things going for it beginning with its fine pedigree—the owners, the Powers family, have a long history in Williamsburg, having operated the adjacent Cheese Shop for decades. The restaurant also occupies prime real estate in Merchants Square. To top it off, the food is exceptional.

The name comes from a line in a colonial-era poem, "Oh for a bowl of fat Canary," a reference to the slang word for wine, a provision picked up by ships sailing to the New World that stopped off in the Canary Islands to load up on "essentials."

The fare offered is a mix of carefully crafted seafood and meat dishes with special attention paid to local favorites—crispy Rappahannock Oysters or fricassee of rabbit with mushrooms, leeks, sage, and a buttermilk biscuit. Steaks are tender, the fish is fresh. The graces that accompany each entree are well thought out and creative.

There is no children's menu, and given the price of the entrees—$25 and up—this is the night you'll want to spring for a babysitter.

The wine list is extensive, drawn from a wine cellar, open the public, on the basement floor. Dinner is served from 5 p.m. to 10 p.m. daily. Reservations are encouraged, especially in season. Dinner is also served at the bar, but seating is on a first-come, first-served basis.

FOOD FOR THOUGHT $$
1647 Richmond Rd.
(757) 645-4665
www.foodforthoughtrestaurant.com

Conveniently located on Restaurant Row about equidistant from Prime Outlets and Colonial Williamsburg, Food for Thought offers sustenance to mind and body. Famous quotations stenciled on the milk-pail blue walls and trivia cards on each table reinforce the impression left by the menu—somebody's been thinking. The fare is eclectic, offering both American comfort food and select dishes from a variety of ethnic cuisines—Jamaican Jerk Chicken, Thai One On, Baked Eggplant Marinara. Vegetarians will find plenty to choose from here and so will kids—here's a rare children's menu that offers more than grilled cheese and chicken tenders. There's pot roast, meatloaf, ribs, and a vegetarian option. The soups are made on the premises—if you like a little heat, try the Spicey Dicey Black-eyed Pea Soup—and the complimentary bread is freshly baked.

Open at 11:30 daily serving lunch and dinner, reservations are taken for parties of three or more. A line can form, but you can save yourself some time by getting your name on the call-ahead list by phoning in before you arrive.

GABRIEL ARCHER TAVERN AT THE WILLIAMSBURG WINERY $
5800 Wessex Hundred
(757) 229-0999, ext. 117
www.williamsburgwinery.com

If you're looking for a quiet, inexpensive lunch in a wholly pleasant setting where a glass of wine is proffered along with made-to-order entrees, drive out to the Williamsburg Winery. The menu is limited—smoked salmon, selected pâtés, Italian prosciutto, a wonderful fresh mozzarella and roasted red pepper sandwich on basil focaccia, and the like—but it is tastefully, carefully prepared and nicely served. You'll dine in a quiet setting amid grape orchards. Gentle breezes keep you cool on the veranda, or you can opt for the air-conditioned dining room. The service is attentive but low-key—and since this place is a little off the beaten track, it's rarely noisy or busy. Along with your meal, enjoy a glass of Governor's White or John Adlum Chardonnay. Other wines are offered as well. Top off your meal with a tour of the winery and a visit to the gift shop across the lane from the tavern.

(For more on the winery, see our Attractions chapter.) The tavern is open for lunch 11 a.m. to 4 p.m. Mon through Sat and for dinner 6 to 9 p.m. Thurs through Mon, Apr through Dec.

GIUSEPPE'S ITALIAN CAFE $-$$
5525 Olde Towne Rd.
(757) 565-1977
www.giuseppes.com

The enticing aroma of delicately blended olive oil and fresh garlic tells you immediately that this is real Italian food at its finest. Owner Joe Scordo offers a pleasing blend of carefully prepared fine food, a comfortable, upbeat dining room, and friendly service in their trattoria, with alfresco dining in season. An unusual and varied menu with a wide variety of prices offers such treats as several vegetarian entrees, an outstanding lentil and sausage soup (featured in *Bon Appétit* magazine), and contemporary versions of old Italian standby desserts such as spumoni and cannoli. Everything is made to order; yet the small kitchen churns out meals quickly, so there's no waiting between courses. Because of the fine quality of the food, this is an extremely popular restaurant for both lunch and dinner. Open 11:30 to 2 p.m., Mon through Sat. Open from 5 p.m. to 9 p.m. for dinner Mon through Thurs, until 9:30 p.m. Fri and Sat. Closed Sun.

GOLDEN HORSESHOE
CLUBHOUSE GRILLE $$
401 South England St.
(757) 229-2141, (800) TAVERNS
There are two restaurants serving the Williamsburg Inn's golf course, one facing the famous Gold Course fairways; the other overlooking the Green Course. Light lunches are available from 11 a.m. until 4 p.m. daily, dinners from 6 to 9 p.m. Wed through Sun, in season. A favorite lunch spot of the city's business class, the burgers here are excellent, as are the sandwiches, soups, and salads. Reservations are recommended for dinner.

GREEN LEAFE CAFE $$
765 Scotland St.
(757) 220-3405

4345 New Town Ave.
(757) 221-9582
www.greenleafe.com
This friendly watering hole is the unofficial bar of the College of William and Mary, located across the street from campus. A second location in New Town attracts young professionals, i.e., Tribe grads who have never left town. Ask the affable bartender at the college location about the best thing on the menu and he will likely tell you not only what beer is on special, but what the price for a pitcher is, including tax. You can tell he's used to dealing with patrons who may not have enough for a tip. Of course, they take their beer *very* seriously at the Green Leafe, carrying a large selection of unusual drafts (including some from Williamsburg's own Aleworks (see our listing at the end of the Attractions chapter). Themed beer nights occur each week: microbrews for $3 on Mondays, East Coast drafts with $8 entrees on Tuesday, West Coast draft nights with $8 pasta

entrees on Wednesday, etc. They'll even fill your growler to go. Oh, and they serve food here, too. There are terrific burgers and sandwiches. The crunchy, slightly spicy French fries have few equals in these parts. As a result of this combination of top-notch beverages and tasty grub, along with multiple TVs showing sports events (New Town) or live music and dancing (college area), this is probably not the best choice for quiet conversation over dinner. The cafe serves food from 11 a.m. until 1:30 a.m.; the bar is open until everyone is happy or 2 a.m., whichever comes first.

HARBOUR COFFEE $
4260-105 Casey Blvd.
Williamsburg, 23188
(757) 220-2334
www.harbourcoffee.com
Tucked at the far back corner of the New Town development is this fine coffee shop. It has all the basics—tables and floppy chairs for relaxing, free Wi-Fi to get some work done (or goofing off), the normal selection of hyper-caffeinated specialty drinks.

A couple notable twists: Harbour is dedicated to sustainability and green living. It strives to select and roast coffees grown in a sustainable and eco-friendly fashion (leaving the shade trees in place to provide habitat for birds, for example), often stretching beyond the standards of Fair Trade organizations. On the menu: selections of muffins, oatmeal, bagels, and quiche for breakfast; salads, wraps, quesadillas, and paninis for lunch and dinner. Open 8 a.m. to 5 p.m. Mon to Thurs, 8 a.m. to 3 p.m. Fri and Sat. Closed Sun.

HAYASHI JAPANESE RESTAURANT &
SUSHI BAR $$
5601 Richmond Rd.
(757) 253-0282
www.hayashijapanese.com
Hayashi offers traditional Japanese cuisine as well as a full sushi bar. The decor is understated, making for a serene meal. Open for lunch and dinner Mon through Sat, dinner only beginning at 3 p.m. Sun.

JAMESTOWN PIE COMPANY $
1804 Jamestown Rd.
(757) 229-7775
www.buyapie.com

A local favorite, the slogan of this small, takeout-only, establishment is "round food is good food." Accordingly, they serve pizza, open-top potpies, and 24 varieties of dessert pies. (They have salads and sandwiches, too. These are not round.) This is pretty much the last chance for picnic fare before you reach Jamestown Island—if you time it right you can pack a wonderful lunch (or dessert) from the Pie Company and have your picnic before touring either the Settlement or the National Park site. Another idea is to pick up something delicious here before you begin a leisurely drive along the scenic Colonial Parkway, which has its western terminus between Jamestown Settlement and the National Park site. There are many turnouts and places to picnic along the parkway.

The specialty of the house is pecan pie, but a unique alternative is the Virginia Peanut Pie (also available in chocolate). The Pie Company makes 16 different types of fruit pies, but some are not available off-season. All pies are available in sugar-free versions, but you must order in advance. Prices range from $13.99 to $16.99.

One thing the Pie Company does not have is indoor seating—except at its Newport News location. See our chapter on Hampton and Newport News for details.

THE JEFFERSON RESTAURANT $$
1453 Richmond Rd.
(757) 229-2296

Since 1956, this restaurant has been delighting patrons with delicious steaks, fresh seafood, and other choices from the wide variety on the menu. With waiters dressed in colonial attire, The Jefferson's charming English country decor invites a leisurely meal with cocktails and a selection from the wine list. We recommend reservations—and dessert. It's open daily 3 to 10 p.m.

JIMMY'S OVEN AND GRILL $
7201 Richmond Rd.
(757) 565-1465

Locals pack this place on weekends and often on weeknights, testimony to the fact that the pizza is authentic and the pastas are made to order. This small eatery is known for super pizzas (any style) with standard toppings, as well as traditional pasta entrees. The menu also features seafood and steaks. The restaurant is open daily from 11 a.m. to 10 p.m.

J. M. RANDALLS CLASSIC AMERICAN GRILL & TAVERN $$
4854-16 Longhill Rd. (Old Towne Shopping Center)
(757) 259-0406
www.jmrandalls.com

The food gets raves from regulars but what brings people here is the live music and convivial atmosphere. Acoustic, blues, jazz—the place swings until 2 a.m. seven days a week. Owner Randall Plaxa will tell you without much prompting that the stage here has hosted 69 Grammy winners. There are daily specials, including tapas (small plates). The bar offers 75 varieties of wine (Thursdays they offer half-price bottled wine with dinner), and 80 different kinds of beer, including 13 drafts. There's a cover charge when live music is offered, usually ranging from $3 to $15 (for big-name acts). Sunday brunch features NFL football on five screens, and the same screens get another workout for Monday Night Football. Also featured are interactive trivia, video games, open mic events, and Texas Hold 'em tournaments. Believe it or not, there is a kids' menu! And breakfast! The only hours this place is closed are between 2 a.m. and 7 a.m, when the kitchen switches gears to serve the early morning crowd.

KINGSMILL RESTAURANTS $$–$$$
1010 Kingsmill Rd.
(757) 253-3900
www.kingsmill.com

The restaurants of this resort offer everything from aged steaks to specialty pizzas to fresh-made ice cream. You will have to pass through the guard gate at the entrance, but all restaurants are open to the public, although hours vary seasonally so check the Web site or call before you go. Reservations are recommended for dinner or Sunday brunch. Smoking is not permitted in any of these establishments.

The Bray Bistro, on the main level of the Conference Center, is very popular for its Friday night Chesapeake Seafood Buffet and Sunday buffet brunch.

Eagles is Kingsmill's upscale interpretation of a traditional steak house, serving beechwood-smoked steaks, beer-infused creations, and exquisite salads and side dishes. Open for breakfast, lunch, and dinner until 10 p.m.

Regatta's Café cooks its pizzas in a wood-burning oven. They also offer Italian specialties like paninis and pastas. Open for lunch and dinner most nights until 9 p.m.

When the weather is warm, the **Marina Bar & Grille** offers guests a chance sit outdoors with a beautiful view of the James while enjoying light fare and live entertainment. The outdoor fireplace is particularly cozy if a brief chill sneaks in.

The Mill is Kingsmill's on-site bakery featuring coffees, lattes, mochas, and espressos made from organic and fair-trade beans roasted in Virginia. Its ice-cream menu offers locally made flavors that change each season. True to its name, The Mill features one of the area's widest selections of freshly baked breads. Open at 7 a.m. daily; until 5 p.m. Mon through Thurs, until 7 p.m. Fri and Sat.

For drinks in a casual setting, try **Moody's Tavern** on the top level of the Conference Center, which specializes in Anheuser-Busch products and cocktails.

THE KITCHEN AT POWHATAN PLANTATION $$$
3601 Ironbound Rd.
(757) 253-7893

If you're in the mood for a special night out and a superb dining experience in an atmosphere unlike any other in the area, this is the place to go. Located in a small outbuilding in the shadow of the restored, 18th-century Powhatan Plantation house, this restaurant is quaint but exquisite. Enjoy a limited but excellent menu featuring fresh seafood, wild game, and regional favorites in a colonial setting. An extensive wine list and excellent desserts and specials are offered nightly. The dining room is very small, so reservations are a must.

KYOTO JAPANESE STEAK & SEAFOOD HOUSE & SUSHI BAR $$–$$$
1621 Richmond Rd.
(757) 220-8888
www.kyoto2.com

In a town where family dining is a major draw, this restaurant has hit on a combination sure to entertain youngsters and delight their parents as well. This attractive eatery offers typical Japanese steak house fare as well as sushi and other entrees that have been prepared to please American palates. After you select your entree, watch the teppan showman chef prepare it. Things get downright fun if you're willing to applaud your chef, who is spurred on by appreciative guests. All meals come with soup, salad, hibachi shrimp appetizer, vegetables, rice, and hot tea. Entrees include teriyaki chicken, hibachi shrimp or steak, bonsai scallops, sukiyaki steak, or teppanyaki filet mignon. Delicious house specialties feature specially prepared combinations of meat, poultry, and seafood—even a surf and turf of steak and lobster called the Kobe King Special. Vegetarian and children's meals are also offered. Reservations are recommended. pen 4 to 11 p.m. daily.

LA TOLTECA $
3048 Richmond Rd.
(757) 253-2939

135 Second St.
(757) 259-0958

This popular, locally run Mexican restaurant has two locations, one on either side of town. Both offer tasty tamales, chiles rellenos, chalupas, chimichangas, enchiladas, and burritos. A lengthy list of vegetarian selections makes this a good choice for those who don't eat meat. Specials include fajita night on Wednesday (buy one, get the second half price) and a $9.95 Sunday brunch buffet (at the Richmond Road location only). The bar serves an impressive variety of Mexican beers, 12 types of tequila, and margaritas in every possible variation, including mango and peach. For dessert, try the Mexican fried ice cream. Kids have their own menu of Mexican specialties. Both restaurants are small, so don't be surprised to find a line at the Richmond Road location, a problem that is less common at the Second Street restaurant.

LE YACA $$$$
The Village Shops at Kingsmill
1915 Pocahontas Trail
(757) 220-3616
www.leyacawilliamsburg.com
This is one of the area's finest restaurants, offering creative cuisine in a country French atmosphere. Whether you opt for a five-course dinner or something lighter, do not miss the delicious onion soup—a puree of onions in a rich stock, nicely spiced and served with grated cheese and house-made croutons. (We tell you this even though we are not really fond of most French onion soup.) House specialties include garlic- and herb-crusted lamb loin roast, and inventively prepared shrimp and scallop dishes. At least once you must order the Marquis au Chocolate for dessert. Reservations are recommended. (Ask to be seated in the rooms on either side of the lovely fireplace. There are some other less inviting rooms and, inscrutably, you may get seated there even when there are plenty of seats in the main dining room. This gets what should be a wonderful experience off on the wrong foot.) Lunch is served 11:30 a.m. to 2:30 p.m. Mon through Fri. Dinner is available from 5:45 to 9:30 p.m. Mon through Sat. A $25 four-course table service brunch is about the most decadent way you can possibly start a week—or end a weekend.

MANHATTAN BAGEL $
1437 Richmond Rd.
(757) 259-9221

Perhaps we have not been able to convince you that everybody here eats pancakes and waffles for breakfast, as one might surmise from driving along Williamsburg's commercial streets. If you instead crave an authentic New York bagel, this is the place. Choose from 24 different flavors, including the hard-to-find-in-the-south "salt" bagel, baked continuously throughout the day, and offered with myriad accompaniments. (Popular selections include the deli sandwiches.) Also available are gourmet coffees, espresso, and cappuccino. Jumbo muffins, cinnamon rolls, pastries, and other sweets are featured as well. The atmosphere is casual yet inviting, and this place is always impeccably clean. Open daily from 6:30 a.m. to 3 p.m.

MAURIZIO'S $$
Festival Marketplace
264 McLaws Circle
(757) 229-0337
This authentically Italian restaurant (Owner Maurizio Fiorello hails from Palermo, Sicily) offers deliciously prepared food in a setting that makes the most of its shopping center location, a stone's throw from Busch Gardens. The service here is friendlier and more attentive than most places—everybody is family. All dishes are made to order from scratch. The kitchen prides itself on using fresh ingredients. The variety is a notch above typical Italian restaurant fare—there are not too many other places in town one can get Carciofi Adriana, marinated artichokes and fresh mozzarella wrapped in proscuitto de parma, drizzled with herb-infused olive oil. The tender osso buco is served over saffron rice. For dessert, try the Tronchetto Limone, a cheesecake-filled pastry dusted with cinnamon and sugar served in a pool of lemon-flavored crème brûlée and drizzled with milk chocolate. Crunchy garlic knots dripping with melted butter are so good you must remind yourself not to fill up. A children's menu offers kid-friendly options like ravioli and chicken tenders. Pizza and subs are available for those (perhaps your teens) with less adventurous taste buds. The tomato sauce is so popular, customers have demanded it be bottled for takeout—three

generations of Fiorellos—Maurizio, his father, and his son—smile from the label.

Dark wood furniture and attractive lighting give the room an elegant feel. During the warmer months outdoor seating is available. The staff is happy to accommodate large parties.

Open daily from 11 a.m. to 10 p.m., until 11 p.m. on Fri and Sat.

i We enjoy our Virginia peanuts—any style, any time. If a restaurant's menu offers a selection with peanuts, try it! Local favorites include peanut soup and yummy peanut pie.

MIYAKO JAPANESE RESTAURANT $$
153 Monticello Ave.
(757) 564-0800

This charming restaurant offers diners the unique opportunity to sample authentic Japanese cuisine—from sushi to sashimi—in a casual, upbeat atmosphere. The list of appetizers, entrees, and yes, even desserts, includes traditional favorites such as shrimp or vegetable tempura, steamed or fried dumplings, teriyaki steak and seafood, and much more. There is sushi for beginners and those accustomed to the vinegar rice rolls. The restaurant's smoke-free regulation enhances the experience. Beer and wine are served on the premises. Miyako is open for lunch 11 a.m. to 2:30 p.m., and dinner 5 to 10 p.m. Mon through Sat; it is closed on Sun.

MR. LIU'S CHINESE RESTAURANT & LOUNGE $$
The Village Shops at Kingsmill
1915 Pocahontas Trail
(757) 253-0990

Rick Liu and his staff present excellent Hunan, Szechuan, Mandarin, and Cantonese cuisine in a quiet, modern setting accented by beautiful examples of Chinese art. The preparation and presentation of every dish, whether traditional or a house specialty, are attended to with great care. Beef with broccoli, for example, a carefully arranged ring of broccoli filled with tender,

meticulously seasoned beef. If you are in a hurry or would prefer to take your meals with you, carryout orders are welcome. There is also limited delivery service available.

NAWAB INDIAN CUISINE $$
204 Monticello Ave.
(757) 565-3200
www.nawabonline.com

The dining room is small, but crisp white linens, ceiling fans, and nicely attired, attentive waiters set the stage for your East Indian meal at this excellent restaurant. The extensive menu offers something to please everyone—from the seasoned diner to those who've come to taste Indian cuisine for the first time. The menu is so extensive that making a choice is the most difficult thing you'll face here. In addition to appetizers, soups, and salads, the menu offers a variety of tandoori specialties—all cooked in a clay pit oven fueled by charcoal—including chicken, lamb, beef, shrimp, and fish options. As you would expect, there are curries galore—with the temperature adjusted to your preference. Indian staples, such as raita, mango chutney, and specialty breads including naan, roti, and pratha are featured. First-timers might want to order the Nawab Special, a sampler of Indian foods that includes soup, tandoori chicken, lamb kabob, a choice of lamb, beef, or chicken curry, vegetable korma, basmati rice, and naan bread. Open daily for lunch and dinner.

NEW YORK DELI $
6572 Richmond Rd., Lightfoot
(757) 564-9258

The name of this popular deli should pay tribute to the delicious Greek food available here. Yes, you can get the standard New York deli fare: good corned beef and Swiss on rye, piled-high roast beef, pastrami, kosher dills, smoked turkey and ham, coleslaw, assorted beverages, and more—but try some of the Greek specialties if you want a taste treat. This place is informal, but the food is something special. No credit cards.

OLD CHICKAHOMINY HOUSE
RESTAURANT & ANTIQUES $
1211 Jamestown Rd.
(757) 229-4689
www.oldchickahominy.com

First established in 1955 as a one-room house on the banks of the Chickahominy River, this popular restaurant moved to its current location a few miles from the Historic Area in 1962. The recipient of the *Gazette's* 2007 "Best Kept Secret" Award, word has gotten out. Locals keep the Chickahominy hopping during the off-season. The rest of the year the place is packed with visitors who remember a good thing and return again and again. Luckily, not only are there chairs on the porch to rock in while you wait, there are three floors of antiques, jewelry, handbags, Virginiana, and seasonal decorative items to browse.

The restaurant, which has a fixed menu, is decorated in the style of a colonial tavern, but the real attraction is the reasonably priced breakfasts and lunches. They include fresh chicken and dumplings, a delicious traditional Virginia ham biscuit, and hearty Brunswick stew. Miss Melinda's Special is a sampler plate perfect for first-time guests. (Miss Melinda is the cat. Be careful not to let her slip out as you enter through the colonial-style louvered doors.) Save room for a slice of homemade pies. Try the buttermilk—it is excellent and not commonly found in this area. The restaurant is open for breakfast and lunch only—but everything on the menu can be packaged for takeout. Fully cooked hams are available for shipping. Open 8:30 to 10:30 a.m. for breakfast, and 11:30 a.m. to 2:30 p.m. for lunch each day.

OPUS 9
5143 Main St.
(757) 645-4779
http://opus9steakhouse.com

Located in New Town, the shopping and dining district (see our Close-up, page 81) Opus 9 is arguably Williamsburg's premier steakhouse, winning the title of "Best Steakhouse" in the *Virginia Gazette's* competition in just its second year of operation, and among a crowded field. Prime, aged steaks highlight the entree selections, including Steak

"Oscar 9", New York Strip Au Poivre, and a unique Bone-In Filet Mignon, but there are delicious seafood options including Maine lobster, crab cakes, and nightly fresh fish specials. House made desserts are a standout—save room for the tiramisu, crème brulee, or Bananas Foster Cheesecake.

This is one of the pricier places to dine out, but in response to the economic recession, in 2009 the restaurant instituted a limited lunch menu—"10 under $10"—that proved to be a very popular option for its value. Open every day for lunch from 11 a.m. to 2:30 p.m. and for dinner from 4:30 p.m. until close.

PAPILLON: A BISTRO $$
Williamsburg Hospitality House
415 Richmond Rd.
(757) 229-4020

The comfortable decor in this room provides a relaxed but elegant setting in which to enjoy a meal. This is an upscale but comfortable restaurant with an excellent menu for breakfast and lunch. The breakfast buffet is especially good. Breakfast is served from 6:30 to 11 a.m., except Sun, when the hours are 7 a.m. to noon. Papillon is located in the same building as 415 Grill.

PAUL'S DELI RESTAURANT & PIZZA $
761 Scotland St.
(757) 229-8976

Fresh "New England–style" pizza is this deli's featured dish, but you will also find Greek and Italian dishes on the menu. A large selection of imported and domestic beers and wines is available to complement your choice or to help you cheer as you follow the action on one of the nine televisions located throughout the place. Just off Richmond Road across from William and Mary's football stadium, this is a popular spot with students. It's open for lunch and dinner daily until 2 a.m., and delivery to area lodgings is available.

PEKING AND MONGOLIAN GRILL $–$$
Kingsgate Greene Shopping Center
122 Waller Mill Rd.
(757) 229-2288
www.peking-va.com

Three popular local restaurants have merged to form one great dining venue. Here you'll find one kind of barbecue that's news, even in the South! If you wish, you can order from the traditional Chinese menu. Or you can opt for the Mongolian barbecue or Japanese hibachi and sushi. After enjoying one of the wonderful soups, move to the curved buffet line and select the ingredients for a fresh salad. Try the peanut dressing. After your salad, return to the buffet and fill a bowl with Chinese noodles and fresh-cut vegetables, meats, chicken, lamb, or seafood and top off your selections from a variety of sauces and herbed oils. At that point, the show begins. Hand your bowl to the cook behind the curved buffet and watch as he sizzles it, walking slowly in a circle around the huge round grill, stirring your meal with what have to be the world's largest chopsticks. There is a tasty dessert section at the buffet if you have any room left.

PIERCE'S PITT BAR-B-QUE $
447 East Rochambeau Dr.
(757) 565-2955
See our full description of this Williamsburg institution, one of the best places to eat in town since 1971, in the barbecue section at the beginning of this chapter.

RETRO'S $
435 Prince George St.
(757) 253-8816
www.retrosgoodeats.com
A chalkboard the length of one wall immediately signals "kids are welcome here," and Retro's combination of yummy dogs, burgers, and frozen custard can make this place busier than the mall on the day after Thanksgiving if you happen to hit it when a school field trip descends. Timing is everything because for cheap eats, you can't do much better in Williamsburg. Retro's serves its Black Angus beef dogs anyway you want 'em—cheese, relish, slaw, sauerkraut, three kinds of mustard, jalapeños, onions, Carolina BBQ. If people dress their dogs with it, they've got it here. The burgers are similarly tasty. When the weather warms up, the pull here is the frozen custard, a dense, creamy concoction served in a cone with sprinkles, dipped in chocolate, or made into a shake, float, banana split, or sundae. Just reading the dessert menu has been known to add calories. Bud Light is available, but the best thing on draft is the root beer.

Takeout is available; phoned-in orders are welcomed. Open every day from 11 a.m. to 6 p.m. in the winter, until 8 p.m. in spring, and until 9 p.m. May through Dec.

SAL'S BY VICTOR $$
Williamsburg Shopping Center
1242 Richmond Rd.
(757) 220-2641
www.salsbyvictor.com
A 2009 fire shut this popular eatery, which reopened temporarily in a new location at 1452 Richmond Rd. Repairs to the original building were underway, and by August 2010 Sal's by Victor was scheduled to be back in its home in the Williamsburg Shopping Center.

The proximity to the William and Mary campus and a reputation for delicious pizza make this restaurant, run by Vittorio Minichiello, popular with students and faculty.

The veal dishes here are particularly good, as is the fresh pasta. The espresso creations pair well with the homemade cannoli. Be sure to check the chalkboard or ask your server about daily dinner specials, because they often are too good to pass up. This is truly a family restaurant, and children are not only welcome, they have a section of the menu devoted especially to them. FYI: Sal's delivers after 5 p.m., for free. After a busy day of touring or playing, the pizza here cannot be beat—especially when it is delivered freshly made and hot. This Sal's is open 11 a.m. to 11 p.m. with a midnight close on Fri and Sat.

SAL'S RISTORANTE ITALIANO $
835 Capitol Landing Rd.
(757) 221-0443
www.salsristoranteitaliano.com
This restaurant offers a Greek twist on Italian favorites. Excellent hot and cold appetizers and

"the largest sandwiches in town" complement a wide selection of pastas and pizzas. Pastas and breads are fired in the brick hearth, which imports a special, smoky flavor that is unmistakable. Located across from the International Village, it is often busy with European students who come to Williamsburg in season to work at Busch Gardens and Water Country USA. Children are welcome.

THE SEAFARE OF WILLIAMSBURG $$$
1632 Richmond Rd.
(757) 229-0099

Lobster, served any number of ways, is a specialty here. But look beyond lobster for some other delicious options. The seafood is very well prepared as you would expect. For dry-land diners, options include milk-fed veal, prime beef dishes, and tableside gourmet preparations. A wine steward will help you select a vintage to enjoy with your meal, and cocktails also are available. You might select one of the flambé desserts to top off a pleasant dinner. The restaurant is open for lunch on Sun and dinner daily until 11 p.m.

SEASONS CAFE RESTAURANT $$
Merchants Square
110 South Henry St.
(757) 259-0018

Seasons has captured a loyal audience since its opening in the old post office on Merchants Square in 1993. The restaurant seats 350, with nearly one-third on an awning-covered patio outside. But the restaurant is divided into several rooms and small areas to provide a sense of intimacy. The theme is most definitely southern (check out the plantation mural), but the cuisine is varied and delicious: Linguine with spicy peanut sauce and fresh swordfish are favorites. Don't overlook the salad bar with its creative seafood and other salads, or the grilled sandwiches on sourdough bread. The smoked barbecued ribs are national-award winners. A terrific Sunday brunch offers seafood Newburg, beef Burgundy, and breakfast items such as flavored waffles. Flavored cappuccinos from the bar will round out an enjoyable meal.

THE TRELLIS
Merchants Square
403 Duke of Gloucester St.
(757) 229-8610
www.thetrellis.com

The Trellis, a fine-dining fixture on Duke of Gloucester Street, reopened in April 2010 after a $1.5 million renovation that began in January 2010. The new owner, David Everett, is a star graduate of the Culinary Institute of America.

Everett already runs the Blue Talon Bistro, an exceptional restaurant, on Prince George Street. Though he holds the title of Executive Chef at The Trellis, he hired a *chef de cuisine* to overhaul the menu with an emphasis on the highest-quality meats, fish, and produce from trusted local and regional purveyors.

"We tried at first to do a menu that was 100 percent American, but it got to be too much," said Adam Steely, one of the many Blue Talon executives who helped remake The Trellis. "We can get coffee from Hawaii, but it costs $30 a pound." Instead, they chose Harbour Coffee, a shop in New Town dedicated to sustainable agro-production, as their supplier. "We want to support local farmers and businesses by showing off their stuff here."

Some things they didn't change: Former owner Marcel Desaulnier's famous Death by Chocolate remains, but Steely envisions more. "We're planning to have an *entire* chocolate menu."

The new restaurant has been totally remodeled in warm earth tones, a palette chosen to bring the garden suggested by the restaurant's name, inside the building. A serpentine path of riverbed stones, set in tile, meanders from the entrance to the bar, which will offer 10 to 15 seats and a cocktail lounge.

"The one thing that's lacking on Duke of Gloucester Street is a bar," Steely said. "The Fat Canary has just 11 seats and you have to know judo to get one."

The former "barrel room" behind the bar is being converted into a room for private parties. One long, butcher-block table will seat 10, with a view through a wall of glass of the wine storage.

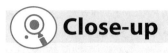 **Close-up**

The Pancake Tour

A Williamsburg fact that is just a little less well-known than its historic origins is that it has the world's highest per capita ratio of pancake and waffle houses. There are only something like 7,000 year-round residents in the 'Burg. Driving along Richmond Road and Pocahontas Trail you being to wonder if the pancake houses actually outnumber the people. Could tourists really need this many flapjacks? Is it the William & Mary undergrads who are scarfing down all these waffles?

Sadly, now that this claim to fame has been brought to light a rather sinister trend must also be mentioned. The tremendous influx of chain hotels offering "free" continental breakfasts may spell the demise of Williamsburg's pancake and waffle industry. Already, several have closed. So please. Help Williamsburg keep its carbo-loading tradition alive by ladling some syrup onto a stack of silver dollars before you leave town. We've rounded up our favorites here:

The Astronomical Pancake House $
5437 Richmond Rd.
(757) 253–6565

Astronomical is right. The pancakes are the size of dinner plates and come in a wide variety of fruit flavors or reliable old buttermilk. The breakfast potatoes, too, are very well done.

The Colonial Pancake House $
100 Page St. at Penniman Road
(757) 253-5852

Established in 1955, local businesspeople and college faculty have made this family-owned restaurant an informal clubhouse. Open daily for breakfast and lunch, the traditional southern cooking includes fried chicken worth writing home about.

The Gazebo House of Pancakes and Waffles $
409 Bypass Rd.
(757) 220-0883

There are 21 pancake and waffle dishes and complete Virginia country breakfasts offered all day. A variety of specials and fresh sandwiches are available at lunchtime Mon through Fri, when area businesspeople join tourists to relax while enjoying the indoor garden environment. Open daily from 6 a.m. to 2 p.m. daily.

Mama Steve's House of Pancakes $

1509 Richmond Rd.
(757) 229-7613

A landmark along Richmond Road, many of the people you see eating here are locals, which speaks volumes about the price, service, and food quality. Open daily from 7 a.m. to 2 p.m.

National Pancake House $
Festival Marketplace
264 McLaws Circle
(757) 220-9433

This restaurant features homemade Belgian waffles, pancakes, country fresh eggs, and healthy alternatives, as well as a soup and sandwich lunch menu. Open 7 a.m. to 2 p.m. daily.

Old Mill House of Pancakes & Waffles $
2005 Richmond Rd.
(757) 229-3613

Locals really like this inviting little place, perhaps because they are greeted by the charming smile of Miss Irene, a local celebrity. Open for breakfast and lunch daily, this restaurant presents 20 varieties of pancakes and waffles in an airy, cheerful atmosphere. Particularly good are the French strawberry pancakes and cheese blintzes, which are unlike any you'll find anywhere else in the world. There are also club sandwiches and burgers for the lunch crowd. The Plantation Breakfast is a must for hearty eaters.

Outside, patio seats will have a view of the new "trellis," the signature entryway feature that originally gave the restaurant its name. Steely says the new owners never considered changing the name. "It's a landmark."

VICTORIA'S $-$$
Williamsburg Crossing Shopping Center
5251 John Tyler Hwy
(757) 253-2233

This cafe with a relaxed atmosphere has a small dining room that is often packed—evidence that the food and service are excellent. While casual in demeanor, the restaurant serves very fine grilled and baked entrees, with fresh fish, meats, and pastas, as well as burgers, a creative children's menu, and super desserts from the Carrot Tree Kitchens, a popular local bake shop. Note that it is a favorite of those coming or going to the seven movie theaters around the corner. Open for lunch and dinner Mon through Sat, it is usually busiest just before and after the evening movies. Insiders know not to leave without inquiring what freshly baked goodies are on the dessert list for the day.

THE WILLIAMSBURG INN
REGENCY ROOM $$$$
136 East Francis St.
(757) 229-2141, (800) TAVERNS

One of the finest restaurants in the Tidewater area, the Regency Room is consistently recognized with fine-dining awards—and with good reason. Listed as a Mobil Four-Star and AAA Four-Diamond facility, the Regency is featured in the Guide to Distinguished Restaurants of North America and is the recipient of *Wine Spectator's* Award of Excellence for its wine list.

Executive Chef Calvin Belknap and his staff offer a rare and pleasant experience with classic continental dishes and regional specialties. Elegant appointments surround you while an attentive service staff works unobtrusively to provide your requirements. Breakfast, lunch, and dinner seatings are available. Gentlemen are required to wear a jacket and tie. Dinner reservations are the only way to ensure seating at your preferred time.

THE WILLIAMSBURG LODGE BAY
ROOM AND CAFE $$$
310 South England St.
(757) 229-2141, (800) TAVERNS

Fine breakfasts, lunches, and dinners are available in the Bay Room every day of the week, but two meals are worthy of special acclaim. Williamsburg insiders return again and again to the brunch on Sunday, which offers made-to-order omelets and a buffet with fine breads, pastries, fruits, and hot dishes. Every Friday and Saturday evening, the Chesapeake Bay Seafood Feast offers a bounty of fresh seafood consistently favored by residents of the area. We recommend reservations for all Bay Room dinners, but especially for these two meals.

The cafe provides quick, excellent meals also. The setting, menu, and price are scaled down somewhat from the Bay Room, and the mood is less formal. But the food is well prepared, well served, and tasty. You must at least consider the desserts.

NIGHTLIFE

rammy Award–winner Bruce Hornsby is, without a doubt, one of Williamsburg's favorite sons. But if your timing isn't right to catch Hornsby on a Williamsburg stage, don't despair. Although this isn't a rowdy, rocking kind of town, there is enough variety for just about everyone to find something fun to do once the sun goes down.

While now and then you still can find DJs who spin loud, throbbing dance music, the local bar scene these days is decidedly more low-key. Rock 'n' roll has taken a backseat to the jazz and blues, and taverns that offer a quiet, restful place to sip microbrews and enjoy friendly conversations have elbowed out nightclubs. Fewer nightspots have live music, but there are sports bars and other unusual diversions—from candlelit walking tours to rowdy dinner theaters to18th-century-style concerts.

If you're in the mood for Broadway or opera and have the whole night to spare, you might plan a trip to Norfolk, about an hour's drive east on I-64. Or, if you're looking for big-name musical acts, check out the schedules at the coliseums in Hampton and Richmond or the Verizon Wireless Amphitheater in Virginia Beach. We give you the information you need to map out your itinerary in our Out-of-Town Nightspots section near the end of this chapter. For ticket information and availability, call the numbers listed or contact Ticketmaster at (757) 872-8100 or visit www.ticketmaster.com.

The best way to find out what's happening in and around Williamsburg is to check the *Virginia Gazette* (published Wed and Sat) or the *Daily Press* (particularly Friday's "Ticket Weekend," featuring entertainment news, and the "Sunday Ticket" section, which offers a guide to arts and leisure activities). Or you can visit the *Daily Press's* entertainment Web site at www.hrticket.com.

Other sources for entertainment news include *Williamsburg Magazine* (a free monthly publication you can pick up just about anywhere) and *Colonial Guide* (a seasonal publication available free at numerous locations around the greater Williamsburg area). The *Richmond Times-Dispatch* (published daily) lists happenings and entertainment in the greater Richmond area. To find out what a particular evening's offerings include in and around the Historic Area, consult *Colonial Williamsburg This Week,* available at the visitor center.

WHERE'S THE PARTY?

When people want to have fun and socialize in Williamsburg, these are the spots they visit:

THE CORNER POCKET
4805 Courthouse St.
(757) 220-0808
www.thecornerpocket.us
This upscale billiards parlor has terrific food (see our description in the Restaurants chapter) and a great atmosphere. Thirteen tables including three nine-foot professional tables with great lighting and plenty of room offer the best facility for billiards around, making the Corner Pocket a frequent host to area tournaments.

Occasionally, however, they cover the tables and install a stage, bringing in blues, jazz, and zydeco acts for live performances. Check the Web site for more upcoming shows.

Dinner is served here till midnight, making this one of latest places to get a full tasty meal.

Closing time is 1 a.m. Sun through Tues, 2 a.m. Wed through Sat.

GREEN LEAFE CAFE (TWO LOCATIONS)
765 Scotland St. at Richmond Rd.
(757) 220-3405

Green Leafe—New Town
4345 New Town Ave.

(757) 221-9582
www.greenleafe.com
Open since 1974, this is—without question—the most enduring nightspot in town. (It even says so in the *New York Times* review framed and hanging on the wall.) See our full description of these two delightful watering holes in the Restaurant chapter. Suffice to say, if you like beer, you'll find something to satisfy here—they offer 64 drafts and over 150 different bottled beers. (They'll even refill your growler to go.) There's also a wide variety of single-malt Scotches and a number of single-barrel bourbons and high-end tequilas. Is it a surprise *USA Today* named Green Leafe to its "Top 10 Bar" list? Themed beer nights, specials on "shakers and 'tinis," live music (college area) and sports viewing (New Town) occur weekly. Tasty food served from 11 a.m. until 1:30 a.m.; the bar is open until everyone is happy or 2 a.m., whichever comes first.

J. M. RANDALLS RESTAURANT & TAVERN
4854 Longhill Rd. (Old Towne Square)
(757) 259-0406
www.jmrandalls.com
Since opening in 1995, this nightspot has developed quite a reputation for its blues and jazz offerings, hosting 69 Grammy winners. Open until 2 a.m. seven days a week, J. M. Randalls features regional, national, and international acts Tues through Sun. An occasional informal jam session provides aspiring musicians with an opportunity to play with the pros. Big-screen football is a popular Sunday- and Monday-night option, and NTN interactive trivia has really caught on in recent years. The kitchen turns out favorites like bourbon-marinated steak, honey molasses barbecue ribs, and pierogies. If our description

conjures up an image of a smoky blues joint in your mind, erase it. Randalls is a popular family spot where kids are encouraged to listen to the first set and cultivate their love of music.

PAUL'S DELI RESTAURANT & PIZZA
761 Scotland St.
(757) 229-8976
A popular destination of the college crowd, Paul's occasionally offers a variety of progressive, alternative, and acoustical music on Wednesday nights. Call ahead to find out who's on the agenda when you're in town. For those who like a little armchair (or barstool) quarterbacking, nine television screens will take you to the action. This lively spot is open until 2 a.m. and serves some of the best pizza in the 'Burg.

WILLIAMSBURG REGIONAL LIBRARY
515 Scotland St.
(757) 259-4070
www.wrl.org
If you think of a library as a place where the noise level never rises above a whisper, you're in for a surprise. At the regional library, the fall through spring evening concert series is crammed full of entertaining sounds. Although the lineup varies, you can count on a diverse array of performers: In its Dewey Decibel Concert Series, music runs the gamut from folk, bluegrass, and country to traditional and jazz. Past performances have included Robin and Linda Williams, Tommy Emmanuel, and Stephen Bennett, as well as a free concert by the Langley Winds (a woodwind quintet from the U.S. Air Force's Heritage of America Band). And if you're wondering about the seating arrangements and acoustics, we're happy to inform you that the regional library has a full 266-seat theater complete with stage lights and an excellent sound system. The *Daily Press* named the theater "Best Small Venue" in its Musical Achievement Awards.

Concert dates vary, but most start at 8 p.m. Some concerts are free, but for the most part ticket prices are $15 or less and usually half-price for those younger than 16. Call ahead to have tickets held at the door. Tickets can be reserved as far as two months in advance with advance payment either by telephone with a credit card or in person with cash, check, or credit card.

DINNER THEATER

Two popular (if campy) dinner theaters entertain visitors while filling their bellies.

HAUNTED DINNER THEATER
Captain George's Seafood Restaurant
5363 Richmond Rd.
(757) 258-2500, (888) 426-3746
www.haunteddinnertheater.com
Offered from June through the end of December, this two-and-a-half-hour hair-raising experience combines an all-you-can-eat buffet dinner of snow crab legs, prime rib, broiled chicken, manicotti, fried shrimp, seafood casserole, BBQ ribs, and clams with a full-length play complete with music and special effects. The 2010 show is titled "Shipwrecked in Williamsburg." Even though this dinner theater bills itself as "haunted," its low-key spookiness is family friendly. Tickets cost $44.50 for adults and $28.95 for children ages 5 through 12. Tickets may be purchased online at the Web site. Shows start at 7 p.m. on various dates.

MYSTERY DINNER PLAYHOUSE
Clarion Inn & Suites
5351 Richmond Rd., Williamsburg, VA 23188
(888) 471-4802
www.mysterydinner.com
If you're a sleuth at heart and are in the mood for a good "whodunit," check out this lively dinner theater option. While enjoying a delicious meal, audiences can chat with the play's characters and look for clues to solve the mystery. At the end of the show, everyone gets a chance to take a "stab" at fingering the bad guy. Those who guess right win a prize. Performances are Wed, Fri, and Sat at 7:30 p.m., with Monday and Thurs shows added sometimes during the busy summer months. Tickets for dinner and the show cost $41.95 or $31.95 for children 12 and under. Senior citizen and group discounts are offered.

THE ORIGINAL GHOSTS OF WILLIAMSBURG CANDLELIGHT TOURS
Historic Area
(877) 62-GHOST
www.theghosttour.com
When can the past make you gasp? At 8 and 8:45 p.m. every night Mar through Dec, if you choose to participate in a "ghosts" tour offered by a local tour company. Based on the book by L. B. Taylor Jr., the one-and-a-half-hour tour introduces you to legendary ghosts, folklore, and legends of the colonial capital. It actually is great fun and a nice alternative to the club scene. Cost of the tour is $11; free to children six and younger. Group rates are available, and reservations are required. Tickets can be purchased online at the Web site listed above.

MOVIES

Williamsburg has three very different choices for filmgoers: an art house, a cinema that offers full meals, and a multiplex in the New Town area.

KIMBALL THEATRE
428 Duke of Gloucester St.
(757) 565-8588, (800) HISTORY
www.kimballtheatre.com
This restored, 583-seat theater, owned by the Colonial Williamsburg Foundation, has a full schedule—lectures, concerts, and art films and documentaries. Current offerings can be heard by calling the local number listed above; advance tickets can be purchased by calling the toll-free Colonial Williamsburg reservation line. A second, 35-seat theater inside the building—dubbed the screening room—shows films, too.

MOVIE TAVERN
1430 Richmond Rd., High St. Shopping Center
(757) 941-5361 (recorded movie listings)
(757) 941-5362 (box office)
Sure you can get popcorn here, but you can also have a burger, a beer, or a sandwich wrap and a glass of wine brought to your table as you watch first-run films. At 9 a.m. Sat, "Flapjacks and a flick" offers all-you-can-eat pancakes and a kid-

friendly film. Some of the screens are reserved for art house films and documentaries. Call the recorded movie line listed above for current movies and showtimes, or visit the Web site.

NEW TOWN CINEMAS 12
4911 Courthouse St.
New Town
(757) 645-0440 (recorded movie listings)
The 12 screens at this Regal Cinema offer first-run movies in a shopping and entertainment district.

OUT-OF-TOWN NIGHTSPOTS

Hampton

HAMPTON COLISEUM
1000 Coliseum Dr.
(757) 838-4203 (Event Information)
www.hamptoncoliseum.org
When big acts come to the peninsula, this is where they play, in a spaceship-looking arena about 40 minutes east of Williamsburg on I-64 (exit 263). To find out what's happening for the dates you plan to be in town, call the box office, or visit the Web site listed above.

Norfolk

HARRISON OPERA HOUSE
160 East Virginia Beach Blvd.
(757) 877-2550, (866) OPERA-VA
www.vaopera.org
The Harrison is home to the Norfolk-based Virginia Opera, which was formed in 1975 and performs regular series in Norfolk, Richmond, and northern Virginia. Recent Norfolk operas have included *La Bohème*, *Don Giovanni*, and *Porgy & Bess*. Check the Web site for current offerings and ticket information.

NORFOLK SCOPE AND CHRYSLER HALL
415 St. Pauls Blvd.
(757) 664-6464
www.sevenvenues.com
When big acts come to Southside Hampton Roads, these two venues are where you'll find them. Just a few blocks from the waterfront, the 13,800-seat dome-shaped Scope (it sort of looks like an alien spaceship, too) houses sporting events (home ice of the Admirals hockey team) and big-name musicians. The more majestic Chrysler Hall is home to the Virginia Symphony (www.virginiasymphony.org), and the Broadway Touring Company productions, usually beginning in October. Norfolk has aggregated schedule and ticket information for all its cultural attractions at one Web site, called "Seven Venues." To see the full listing, visit the Web site listed above.

THE NORVA
317 Monticello Ave.
(757) 627-4547
www.thenorva.com
Housed in a restored vaudeville theater, the Norva consistently draws excellent touring rock, country, R&B, and hip-hop acts. It's locally owned, and promoter Bill Reid competes (successfully) with larger corporate-owned venues by luring the musicians with all sorts of perks, including a plush backstage area and a Jacuzzi.

Almost all shows are general admission; the main floor is generally left open, without seats, for standing and dancing. At those shows, there's limited table seating—first come, first served, on the main floor and the second-floor balcony. (Tip: Make a reservation to eat at the attached Kelly's Tavern and you get early entry to shows to grab the best locations.) Parking is available at a number of nearby garages, including the MacArthur Center mall. Tickets are available at the Norva's Web site or through Ticketmaster.

Virginia Beach

VIRGINIA BEACH AMPHITHEATER
3550 Cellar Door Way
(757) 368-3000
www.livenation.com
It may be a bit of a drive (at least 90 minutes when traffic cooperates, which it usually does not, given all the tunnels and bridges between Williamsburg and the ocean), but this amphitheater is a regular stop on the outdoor summer

music tours of many popular acts. There's seating under the pavilion or on the lawn—but go early if you're sitting on the grass and be prepared to brave whatever elements are in play at the time. The amphitheater has 7,500 reserved seats, with room for about 12,500 on the lawn. Two giant screens on either side of the stage provide a view for those in the back. Refreshments are available at every show. To purchase tickets call (877) 598-8698 or visit the Live Nation Web site listed above.

i Southeastern Virginia can lay claim to some landmark places and occasions in rock 'n' roll history. Did you know, for instance, that Fort Monroe was the birthplace of country-rock renegade Steve Earle, or that rockabilly giant Gene Vincent (think "Be-Bop-A-Lula") hails from Norfolk? How about the fact that Missy "Misdemeanor" Elliott, one of America's hip-hop princesses, was born in Portsmouth and recorded her solo debut album at Master Sound Studio in Virginia Beach?

SHOPPING

While it may be history that brings visitors to the Historic Triangle, once they get here they want to shop. This is nothing new: Merchants Square dates to 1935 and bills itself as one of the oldest shopping malls in the country. West of town, the granddaddy of outlet shopping, The Williamsburg Pottery Factory, started drawing visitors in 1938 and has spawned many an imitator along Richmond Road, including some upscale competition.

What follows is a list of where to find what, beginning with the Historic Area. In general, you'll find specialty shops offering unique fine-quality items grouped near Merchants Square. If you're looking for manufacturers' outlet stores, head westward out Richmond Road (US Route 60), where shopping centers give way to outlet malls and finally to the Pottery Factory.

For shopping specialists, we've broken out those places where you can browse book-shelves, shop for Christmas decorations, or pick up a unique item of Virginiana.

Turn to our close-up in this chapter to learn more about New Town, which became Williamsburg's second city center and its first of the 21st century.

THE HISTORIC AREA

Along Duke of Gloucester Street are many restored shops where you can buy items crafted on the premises by artisans you can observe at work. (You do not need to hve a CW ticket in order to shop here.)

The Golden Ball Shop offers metalcraft items, including ladies', gentlemen's, and children's fine jewelry in silver and gold, which can be engraved to order.

The Colonial Post Office, a functioning branch of the U.S. Post Office, carries handmade papers, leather-bound books, maps, marbled paper, prints, and cartoons.

The Raleigh Tavern Bakery has counter service. Pick up some Sally Lunn bread, sweet potato muffins, or ginger cake for a quick snack.

M. Dubois Grocer's Shop offers Smithfield hams, jams, relishes, and other colonial fare.

General merchandise shops include **Prentis Store, Tarpley's Store,** and **Greenhow Store,** carrying pottery, hats, games, toys, baskets, candles, pipes, handwoven linens, leather and wooden crafts, jewelry, and many more items.

These shops are open year-round and are the places to find a memento of your visit or a unique gift.

The Colonial Nursery, an open-air market across from Bruton Parish Church sells 18th-century plants, seeds, bulbs, and some pottery. An interpreter will be on hand to answer questions about 18th-century gardening.

MERCHANTS SQUARE

Centered on the western end of Duke of Gloucester Street, Merchants Square was established in 1935 expressly to create a shopping center for the redeveloping Williamsburg community. Businesses formerly scattered throughout the Historic Area were relocated here, primarily to cater to residents since the tourist trade at that time was humble. The architecture synthesized colonial and early 19th-century design, a deliberate choice made so that the business district would blend as seamlessly as possible with the Historic Area.

As Williamsburg and the surrounding counties grew, more businesses opened elsewhere, leaving Merchants Square to focus on providing goods and services demanded by tourists. In a way, this also protected Merchants Square from market forces that have afflicted many American downtowns. Business here is very much alive and flourishing. The ambience is charming without feeling fake. The buildings are human-scale, the brick walkways dotted with benches, the main block closed to all but pedestrian traffic. All in all, a few hours on Merchants Square are a very pleasant way to spend some free time. Many others have recognized this—in 2005, Merchants Square was added to the National Register of Historic Places. In 2009, the American Planning Association recognized Duke of Gloucester as one of its "10 Great Streets."

Though there are about 40 stores in a two-to-three block area—a combination of specialty shops, fine restaurants, and upscale chain stores—we have listed a few favorites below. Places to eat are detailed in our Restaurant chapter

A word about parking: If you can, leave your car wherever you're lodging and take the CW bus, the city trolley, or walk. Parking behind the shops is free, and there are a paid lot on Francis Street and a city parking garage (enter on North Henry Street), but time limits are strictly enforced and tickets are regularly issued. Parking costs $1 an hour. (The first 30 minutes are free, and the maximum charge is $8 a day.) Credit cards are accepted, and payment is fully automated. The garage is open daily from 6 a.m. to midnight and staffed to assist patrons. Overnight parking is not allowed.

Clothing

BINN'S
435 Duke of Gloucester St.
(757) 229-3391
Women's clothing including sportswear, dresses, apparel for special occasions, shoes, accessories, cosmetics, and luxury gift boutique.

THE CAMPUS SHOP
425 Prince George St.
(757) 229-4301
Gifts and apparel featuring the logo of the College of William and Mary.

CAROUSEL CHILDREN'S CLOTHIER
420 Duke of Gloucester St.
(757) 229-1710
Unique children's clothing and accessories, including colonial dresses for girls and a 3-piece boys' vest and pant set, handmade exclusively for the Carousel.

CLASSIC CRAVATS
110-D S. Henry St.
(757) 229-0055
Quality neckwear, including long ties, bow ties, pocket handkerchiefs, silk squares, and men's jewelry and accessories.

R. BRYANT LTD.
429 Duke of Gloucester St.
(757) 253-0055
Traditional men's and boys' clothing with a flair for fresh designs in classic items. On-premise tailor.

Food

SMITHFIELD HAM SHOPPE
421 Prince George St.
(757) 258-8604
Virginia's most famous ham—salt-cured, cooked, uncooked, whole hams, or biscuit slices—can be bought here and shipped home. Also on sale are all the things you might serve with your ham—wine, cheese, mustards, dressings. There's also an extensive menu of sandwiches, salads, soups (including peanut), and sweets for carryout.

WYTHE CANDY AND GOURMET SHOP
414 Duke of Gloucester St.
(757) 229-4406
A perennial favorite for all visitors with a sweet tooth. The homemade fudge is excellent, but there are too many other choices to just settle on one thing. Can't eat sugar? The shop has a wonderful selection of sugar-free goodies, too.

Gifts and Accessories

THE CHRISTMAS SHOP
415 Duke of Gloucester St.
(757) 229-2514

The vast array of decorations offered for the tree and home includes many that are uniquely Williamsburg—pineapples, fifers, drummers, painted images of the Governor's Palace and the like.

EVERYTHING WILLIAMSBURG
110 N. Henry St.
(757) 565-8476
From tees to tavernware, a broad selection of exclusive Colonial Williamsburg logo products.

G. BATES STUDIO WORKSHOP
413 W. Duke of Gloucester St.
(757) 229-5400
A tasteful collection of hard-to-find gifts and home accessories, the seven rooms here feature Vera Bradley products, stylish jewelry, and accents for home and garden.

I MUST SAY
425 Prince George St.
(757) 229-2755
Antiques, gifts, cards and home accessories.

J. FENTON GALLERY
110-B S. Henry St.
(757) 221-8200
Contemporary American-crafted items including clothing, handbags, watches, jewelry and jewelry boxes, pottery, games, metal wall sculptures, and whimsical and humorous gifts in all price ranges. The emphasis is on unusual individual pieces by American artists, many from Virginia. Selected stained-glass, hand-blown glass and glass fountains, kaleidoscopes, puzzle boxes, and an extensive collection of Judaica.

NANCY THOMAS GALLERY
407 W. Duke of Gloucester St.
(757) 259-1938
Features the work of folk artist Nancy Thomas of Yorktown. (A second location in Yorktown is detailed in the Jamestown and Yorktown chapter.)

QUILTS UNLIMITED
110-E South Henry St.
(757) 253-8700
Antique and contemporary quilts, high-quality traditional handcrafts, fabrics, and quilting supplies. You'll also find a selection of Colonial Clothing and Virginia handicrafts and handbags by Donna Sharp & Lesportsac.

SCOTLAND HOUSE LTD.
430 Duke of Gloucester St.
(757) 229-7800
Stop by Scotland House Ltd. for imported ladies' and gentlemen's apparel, tartan, heraldry, and gifts.

SHIRLEY PEWTER SHOP
417 Duke of Gloucester St.
(757) 229-3668
One of the oldest businesses on Merchants Square, many of the pewter handicrafts on sale here are made by hand in Williamsburg at their workshop on Jamestown Road. Engraving is done on the premises and often can be done the same day.

THE TOYMAKER OF WILLIAMSBURG
415 W. Duke of Gloucester St.
(757) 229-5660
Unusual toys, dolls, puzzles, and games for kids of all ages, including hard-to-find imported goods. Especially popular is the wide variety of toy soldiers and figurines, wooden trains and construction sets.

WILLIAMSBURG AT HOME
439 W. Duke of Gloucester St.
(757) 220-7749
Home furnishings and accessories, featuring WILLIAMSBURG® furniture, bedding, rugs, lighting, fixtures, prints, fabrics, and wallpapers.

WILLIAMSBURG CRAFT HOUSE
402 W. Duke of Gloucester St.
(757) 220-7747
Dinnerware, flatware, glassware, pewter, silver, delft, fine ceramic giftware, and jewelry.

Jewelry

THE PRECIOUS GEM
423 W. Duke of Gloucester St.
(757) 220-1115

Owner and master craftsman Reggie Akdogan, trained in Turkey, is known for his exquisite jewelry designs featuring diamonds, sapphires, and rubies in solid gold and platinum.

Alice's Adventures in Wonderland, if it's still there, and it might be since the asking price is $20,000.) The staff can appraise prints, maps, and books for insurance, estate, or tax purposes. They can also assist those with an interest in beginning collections of their own. Annually, the store doubles as a gallery with a themed art exhibition, a nice match for there large collection of original art, antique prints, photographs, and maps. Open 10 a.m. to 6 p.m. daily except Thanksgiving and Christmas.

SILVER VAULT LTD.
416 Duke of Gloucester St.
(757) 220-3777

Sterling jewelry, silver hollowware and frames, sterling and silverplate gifts for babies, plus colorful tabletop accessories.

ANTIQUES

ATTIC COLLECTIONS
2229 Richmond Rd.
(757) 229-0032

This minimall in a single building includes several individual shops. Don't let the size of the building fool you. More than 4,000 square feet of treasures reside here, including the useful and the whimsical, the elegant and the amusing. The largest items are furniture pieces, but there is glassware from the 18th century forward (including Depression glassware), buttons, marbles, books, postcards, prints, paintings, posters, lamps, kitchenware, toys, vintage clothing, accessories, and jewelry. Upstairs, you'll find Forget-Me-Nots and Sugar and Spice, which carry consignment clothing for adults and children, respectively. Closed Tues and Wed.

CHARLIE'S ANTIQUES AND AMAZING STONES
7766 Richmond Rd.
Toano
(757) 566-8300

To give you an idea of the size of Charlie and Susie Crawford's collection of antiques, reproduction furniture, Asian art and decoratives, bric-and-brac, marble and bronze sculpture and statuary, ornamental iron and outdoor furniture, please note that Charlie's has its own speed limit: 8 miles per hour. Enter the sprawling property, 20 minutes from Williamsburg, and slow down—so you can catch a glimpse of the ferocious bears (sculptures) lining either side of the rutted driveway. Many an hour could be wiled away strolling through the goods here, especially for those looking for unique furnishings and souvenirs. There's also a large collection of natural stones and pavers for landscaping needs—decorative pebbles, garden stones, large boulders, field stones for water gardens, pathways, and walls. Sold by the pound or ton. (A sign warns: "No returns on rocks.") Closed Tues and Wed in the winter months, except by appointment.

LIGHTFOOT ANTIQUES MALL & COUNTRY GENERAL STORE
7003 Richmond Rd.
(757) 229-8759

The masked pumps out front indicate that this once was the site of a small gas station. Today the building, located adjacent to the Colonial Town Plaza Shops, is home to myriad antiques, collectibles, and assorted attic treasures. The showroom is packed with lots of goodies, from used skis and old furniture to mantelpieces, lanterns, musical instruments, picture frames, weathervanes, glassware, needlework, and old-timey telephones. If you have a couple of hours to spend digging through the stacks, you just might find that special something you've been looking for but couldn't find elsewhere.

WILLIAMSBURG ANTIQUE MALL
500 Lightfoot Rd.
(757) 565-3422
www.antiqueswilliamsburg.com
Tucked away off US 60 in Lightfoot (but visible from Route 199) is this collection of 300-plus dealers of antiques and collectibles. This place is unique in that you wander freely, picking up goodies you wish to buy (they supply handy baskets to hold your newly found treasures), and then you leave via a central checkout area. You'll find just about anything from furniture, jewelry, glass, old photos, clocks, pottery, frames, clothing and decorative textiles, boxes, toys, cameras, and more. Open seven days a week.

ART GALLERIES AND CRAFTS

BERTRAM & WILLIAMS BOOKS
AND FINE ART
1459 Richmond Rd.
(757) 564-9670
www.bertbook.com
This bookstore stages annual art exhibitions and carries a large inventory of books, original art, antique prints, photographs, and maps. See our complete description in the Bookstore category.

KINKS, QUIRKS AND CAFFEINE
113-A Colony Square Shopping Center
1303 Jamestown Rd.
(757) 229-5889
www.kinksandquirks.com
Drop in for a latte and find yourself surrounded by funky and original works by a variety of American artisans. From fine jewelry by artists such as Island Cowgirl, Patricia Locke, Bianca Zoie, Watchcraft, and Olga Ganoudis to beautiful art furniture by STICKS, Shoestring Creations, Avner Zabari, Studio 78, and Dtales, this place offers an eclectic collection of fine crafts and art from around the country. Need a unique souvenir, or something special for a gift or your home? Ask the owner, Jennifer Raines, who goes by the honorific "chick-in-charge." Open 10 a.m. to 6 p.m. Mon through Sat and noon to 5 p.m. Sun. A second location, along Riverwalk Landing, is detailed in our chapter on Yorktown.

PRINCE GEORGE ART AND FRAME
Colony Square Shopping Center
107 Jamestown Rd.
(757) 229-7644
Beautiful prints, graphics and posters from this longtime Williamsburg business grace local homes and offices. Custom framing done here is of the highest quality.

THIS CENTURY GALLERY
219 North Boundary St.
(757) 229-4949
In a city devoted to its past, this gallery bucks the trend with contemporary crafts and art pieces. Frequent shows feature new artists' works. Gallery openings are an occasion for the city's art lovers to meet, socialize, and enjoy the featured artists' works.

A TOUCH OF EARTH
The Gallery Shops at Lightfoot
6580 Richmond Rd.
(757) 565-0425
www.atouchofearthgallery.com
Located twenty minutes west of Williamsburg on US Route 60, this unique space is the oldest American crafts gallery in the area, offering highly prized American craft work by fine artists in many media. Their "Gloom Chaser" makes a memorable souvenir. Open 10 a.m. to 5:45 p.m. Mon through Sat, 11 a.m. to 5 p.m. Sun.

VERNON WOOTEN STUDIO & GALLERY
1315 Jamestown Rd., Suite 204
(757) 253-1953
www.huntprints.com
This small studio features Wooten's original paintings of foxhunts in oil, watercolor, and acrylic. Framed and unframed limited editions are available. Open 9 a.m. to 5 p.m. Mon through Sat, noon to 5 p.m. Sun.

BOOKSTORES

Williamsburg is a college town, after all, and so has a higher number of bookstores than a city of 13,000 might otherwise command. The big chains are here, but there are some good deals and quirky finds to be had in the city's rare and used independents. An alphabetical listing follows.

BARNES & NOBLE
345 Duke of Gloucester St.
(757) 253-4900
wm.bncollege.com

Located less than a block from the western entrance to the Historic Area, the monthly schedule at this B&N is chockablock with events, including Open Mic night, Irish music sessions, knitting circles, and scholarly readings by heavy hitters from the college faculty. This store also doubles as William and Mary's official bookstore, so in addition to The Campus Shop on Prince George Street, this is a good place to pick up an official green and gold hoodie. Open Mon through Sat 9 a.m. to 9 p.m., Sun 9 a.m. to 8 p.m.

BARNES & NOBLE
5101 Main St.
(757) 564-0687

Located in the New Town development just west of Monticello Avenue, this store anchors the central shopping district. The store has regular story hours for kids, frequent book signings, and school book fairs. Open Mon through Sat 10 a.m. to 10 p.m.; Sun until 9 p.m.

BERTRAM & WILLIAMS BOOKS AND FINE ART
1459 Richmond Rd.
(757) 564-9670
www.bertbook.com

Amid the pancake houses and the hamburger joints along Richmond Road is this oasis of cerebral calm. Opened in 1998, this bookstore looks deceptively small from the road. Inside, you'll find room after room of collectibles. The store specializes in modern first editions and autographed books. (Ask to see their signed copy of *Alice's Adventures in Wonderland,* if it's still there, and it might be since the asking price is $20,000.) The staff can appraise prints, maps, and books for insurance, estate, or tax purposes. They can also assist those with an inter-

est in beginning collections of their own. Annually, the store doubles as a gallery with a themed art exhibition, a nice match for there large collection of original art, antique prints, photographs, and maps. Open 10 a.m. to 6 p.m. daily except Thanksgiving and Christmas.

BOOK EXCHANGE
Colony Square Shopping Center
1303 Jamestown Rd.
(757) 220-3778

Tucked a few doors down from the Fresh Market (a great place to pick up lunch, a sweet, or a bottle of fine wine to go, by the way) is this book swap service, which sells books for 50 percent off the publisher's cover price. The inventory comes from Williamsburg's readers—customers trade in their own paperbacks, audiobooks, and select hardcovers for a store credit equal to 25 percent of the book's cover price.(A paperback with a $8 cover price, would garner a $2 credit.) Store credit remains on file and expires only if your account is inactive for more than a year. Books are accepted based on their condition and the store's stock needs. Take your new purchases to the other end of the shopping center, where the Coffee Beanery welcomes those who want a cup o' joe or an iced chai while they read. Book Exchange is open Mon through Fri, 10 a.m. to 7 p.m., Sat until 5 p.m., Sun noon to 5 p.m.

THE BOOKPRESS LTD.
1304 Jamestown Rd.
(757) 229-1260
www.bookpress.com

Specializing in antiquarian books, old prints, and maps, the staff here can help locate and obtain rare books. They also issue regularly printed catalogues featuring books on architecture, fine and applied arts, gardening, the book arts (including the history of printing), colonial Americana and Virginiana, wine, and horticulture, as well as rare books in other subject areas. (Visit their Web site to request a catalogue by mail or be added to their e-newsletter.) Leave ample time to browse and enjoy. Open 10 a.m. to 5 p.m., Mon through Fri, and at other times by appointment.

BOOKS-A-MILLION
Williamsburg Shopping Center
1252 Richmond Rd.
(757) 259-9193

Close to campus housing, the tables at the Joe Muggs coffee shop here are always crammed with students and covered with laptops and textbooks. Local newspapers, including the *Virginia Gazette*, are on sale, as well as periodicals and books. Open 9 a.m. to 10 p.m. Mon through Thurs, until 11 p.m. Fri and Sat and until 9 p.m. Sun.

COMIC CUBICLE
4809-2 Courthouse St.
(757) 229-5299

A Williamsburg fixture since 1992, owner Mark Welch moved his store from the Williamsburg Crossing Shopping Center to New Town in 2006. The big day of the week here is Wednesday when Welch receives the latest issues in popular serials—Green Lantern, Ironman, Spider-Man. Welch also carries collectible comics, graphic novels for kids and adults, collector cards, and related merchandise. Kids, if you're in town, the first Saturday in May is always free comic book day. Open 11 a.m. to 7 p.m. Mon through Sat, except Wed when he opens at 12 in order to get the latest issues on sale; 1 p.m. to 5 p.m. Sun.

MERMAID BOOKS
421-a Prince George St. (Downstairs)
(757) 229-2603
www.mermaidbookswilliamsburg.com

To find this hidden gem, look on the *side* of the Smithfield Ham Shoppe—an arrow painted on the building points you down the stairs to this basement bookstore, a good choice for browsers looking for new and used books, antiques, collectibles, ephemera, and gifts. On a rainy day, you could let a cloud pass while reading all the old New Yorker cartoons thumb-tacked the bookshelves. Hatley Mason is just the third owner in 30 years, having bought the shop in part to "preserve this wonderful space," and to showcase his collection of Williamsburg memorabilia that dates to the beginning of the Rockefeller restoration. He has some of the earliest maps and original guidebooks from the 1930s. Open daily 10 a.m. to 5 p.m., Sun noon to 5 p.m.

CHRISTMAS ALL YEAR

BASSETT'S CHRISTMAS SHOP
207 Bypass Rd.
(757) 229-7648

Fans of the holiday season find Bassett's an excellent store to hunt for ornaments, trees, Madame Alexander dolls, and other fine gift items. They carry many well-known designer brands—Jim Shore ornaments and figurines, Christopher Radko ornaments, snow globes and garland, Department 56 lighted houses, and exclusive items from Cat's Meow. Open daily 10 a.m. to 9 p.m. Mar through Dec; in winter months, they close at 5 p.m. weekdays, regular hours on the weekend.

CHRISTMAS MOUSE
1991 Richmond Rd.
(757) 221-0357

Through the windows you'll see dozens of trees lighted and decorated with unique items. Inside you'll find more things associated with the holidays than you ever imagined possible. A second store is located west on US 60 in Norge. Open year-round.

THE CHRISTMAS SHOP
See the listing under Merchants Square.

i Ring, ring . . . Santa's calling! If you plan on visiting Williamsburg around Christmas, a call from Santa might make the young ones feel better about not being home for the holidays. The James City County Parks and Recreation Department offers a Santa Calling Program. Parents must fill out a form explaining what they would like Santa to say, and then Santa calls. To obtain a form, dial (757) 259-3200.

COOKE'S CHRISTMAS
1820 Jamestown Rd.
(757) 220-0099

The Schell family has operated a garden center from this site for 20 years, but vacationers who like to pick up a special item for the tree while traveling will be most interested in the facility adjacent to the nursery, which sells a wide array of seasonal decorating items. "Themed" trees boast special ornaments for the teacher, the bride and groom, musicians, you name it. There's a whole tree of dog ornaments, if you want to pick out something resembling your own pup. A wide variety of Mark Roberts Santas and fairies are available, and there's an entire section of the store devoted to wreath making, with ribbons and all the necessary items to fashion your own. Beginning on the Sunday after Thanksgiving each year, Santa stops by to take requests from those who would like an audience with the big man. Bring your camera.

Open 9 a.m. to 6 p.m. Mon through Sat, noon to 5 p.m. Sun. (Hours are somewhat shortened in Jan and Feb, so call before you come to make sure they are open in the winter months.)

GROCERIES AND SPECIALTY FOODS

THE CANDY STORE
6623 Richmond Rd.
(757) 565-1151

You might be able to drive past this barn-shaped building, but if there are any kids in your car, they likely won't let you. The Wythe-Will Distributing Company has stocked the shelves of this specialty shop with many of the fine chocolates that it sells at the Wythe Candy and Gourmet Shop in Merchants Square. There's everything from saltwater taffy to Ghirardelli chocolates. (It will be hard to leave without a sample of the homemade fudge.) The Candy Store also carries a line of Virginia-made products, including wines, peanuts, hams, jellies, and apple butter. Open daily 10 a.m. to 6 p.m.

EDWARDS' VIRGINIA HAM SHOPPE
OF WILLIAMSBURG
1814 Richmond Rd.
(757) 220-6618
www.virginiatraditions.com

This mouthwatering shop sells Surry hickory-smoked hams and bacon direct from the family smokehouse, plus a variety of Virginian specialty foods, including jellies, jams, flours, cake and pie mixes, and more. They'll ship, too. Open 9 a.m. to 9 p.m. May through Dec, 10 a.m. to 6 p.m. the rest of the year.

FRESH MARKET
Colony Square Shopping Center
1303 Jamestown Rd.
(757) 565-1661

Classical music, ambient lighting, bins of fresh flowers, artfully displayed—wait. This is a grocery store? Indeed it is. This upscale North Carolina–based chain makes grocery shopping seem like something more than a chore. Top-of-the-line meat, seafood and produce, fresh herbs, hard-to-fine spices, small-label packaged good are attractively arranged in wide aisles, which are necessary because this place can get packed with hungry locals. Tourists take note, the deli counter makes terrific sandwiches and side salads, and the baked goods are, um, to die for. Pick a bottle from their impressive wine section and you've got the makings of a deluxe picnic. Open Mon through Sat, 8 a.m. to 9 p.m., Sun, 10 a.m. to 8 p.m.

HOME FURNISHINGS

THE SHOPS AT CAROLINA FURNITURE OF WILLIAMSBURG
5425 Richmond Rd.
(757) 565-3000
www.carolina-furniture.com

Eight separate shops representing 400 different manufacturers of furniture and carpet are collected on this retail "campus." You can park your car and walk among the offerings which include Ralph Lauren furniture, Martha Stewart Signature, Colonial Craftsmen, and Williamsburg Brass, Gifts and Lighting. The Carolina Carpets store is the Williamsburg outlet for Karastan goods, offered at discounts of 40 to 60 percent. Broadloom carpeting and one-of-a-kind Oriental rugs also are discounted. Countrywide shipping service makes this store convenient to your home, wherever you live.

SUTER'S HANDCRAFTED FURNITURE
800 Richmond Rd.
(757) 564-8812, (800) 252-2131
www.suters.com
Suter's has been making furniture for Virginia homeowners since 1839. At the factory in Harrisonburg, they create beds, tables, chairs, and chests in classic 17th- and 18th-century styles—Chippendale, Queen Anne, Hepplewhite, and Sheraton—using the finest cherry, mahogany, and walnut. The Williamsburg location (only their third) opened in 2005. They routinely ship furniture all over the United States.

TK ASIAN ANTIQUES
1654 Jamestown Rd.
(757) 229-7720
www.tkasianantiquities.com
This unique business collects and sells ancient Chinese artifacts such as bronze and pottery ritual vessels and sculpture. Other inventory includes a selection of 18th- and 19th- century Chinese furniture and rare Chinese art deco furniture (ca 1930). Prices range from hundreds of dollars to millions per piece. Restoration services are also provided.

TREVILLIAN FURNITURE AND INTERIORS
3301 Venture Lane
(757) 229-9505
If you're looking for home furnishings and accessories, Trevillian offers fine furnishings and interior decorating services as well as a popular moving and transport service (they are especially skilled with antiques and prized items). Open 10 a.m. to 5:30 p.m. Mon through Fri and 10 a.m. to 5 p.m. Sat. Closed Sun.

IN NORGE

WILLIAMSBURG WICKER AND RATTAN
7422 Richmond Rd.
(757) 565-3620
A charming Victorian house shop features many fine lines of wicker and rattan, including Henry Link, Lane Venture, Lloyd Flanders, and Ficks Reed. Shipping is provided. Open 9:30a.m. to 5 p.m. Mon through Sat

IN TOANO

CHARLIE'S ANTIQUES AND AMAZING STONES
7766 Richmond Rd.
(757) 566-8300
See our complete description in the Antiques section of this chapter.

THE FARMHOUSE
7787 Richmond Rd.
(757) 566-8344
You can't miss this store—there's a ladder-back chair big enough for Shrek on the front lawn, along with a lot of outdoor furniture, which is for sale (unlike the giant chair). Inside, you'll have to thread your way through the two floors of finished and unfinished bookcases, dressers, desks, tables, and beds in pine, maple, oak, and cherry. The Farmhouse will also make custom furniture in any size. Closed Sun.

JEWELRY

MASTER CRAFTSMEN
221 North Boundary St.
(757) 253-2993
www.mastercraftsmenshop.com
This fine artisan's shop offers high-quality, handcrafted jewelry, hand-spun pewter, and a variety of beautiful keepsakes in silver, made on the premises since 1982. Each year since 1985 they have designed a new angel ornament for the Christmas tree; recently they started a second line of Christmas keepsakes, introducing pewter Santa ornaments. But the top reason people shop here is the array of bracelets—bangle, cuff, charm—made by local silversmiths. Pewter cups, plates, and bowls are made in-house, too. Hand- and machine-engraving are offered.

THE PRECIOUS GEM
See our description under Merchants Square.

SILVER VAULT
See our description under Merchants Square.

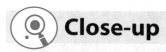

Close-up

New Town

Perhaps unique to an American city that's been around as long as Williamsburg has, there really is no "downtown" here. Merchants Square was organized in the 1930s to bring scattered businesses to a central location. Though many residents shop and dine here, in the summer especially, it's given over to the tourist trade. Moreover, government offices are located elsewhere; the majority of the people who live in what would pass as Williamsburg's downtown are college kids studying at William and Mary.

All of that was part of the impetus for **New Town,** a 365-acre, mixed-use community, on the drawing boards since 1997. Designed according to the architectural and planning principles of the "New Urbanism" school, this area along both sides of Monticello Avenue west of the historic district was jointly developed by the College of William and Mary and the C.C. Casey Company. Though the project, like everything else, took a few hits during the economic downtown at the end of 21st century's first decade, New Town has mostly fulfilled its promise of creating a second city center for Billsburg.

There are more than 300,000 square feet of shops, restaurants, and business space in New Town, including a **Barnes & Noble,** which anchors the main retail street, and a 12-screen **movie theater.** Unique businesses like the Corner Pocket, an upscale billiards hall, and the **Comic Cubicle,** which brings fans of Ironman and the Green Lantern to New Town for the latest issues, make this an appealing destination for tourist and local alike. New Town has all the amenities you'd expect in a small town—doctor's office, hair salons, fitness centers, banks, courthouse, and post office.

"The thing I love about New Town is that it's such a good mix," said Mark Welch, who moved his comic book store, Comic Cubicle, from the Williamsburg Crossing Shopping Center to New Town in 2006. "There's a really healthy combination of owner-occupied businesses and national chains."

The residential component includes about 500 households, a mix of garden apartments, town houses, and traditional homes, many with front porches. There are also live/work loft apartments above some storefronts. Walking and biking trails link the whole community, part of an effort to design a place where it's impossible not to know your neighbors. For a complete list of New Town businesses, visit www.newtownwilliamsburg.com.

OUTLET SHOPPING

PIANO-ORGAN OUTLET
6316 Richmond Rd.
(757) 564-9592

This freestanding shop is very visible on the north side of the highway as you approach Lightfoot. The keyboard selection in this store is extensive, and prices are very reasonable. Open Mon through Fri 10 a.m. to 5 p.m. Sat 10 a.m. to 5 p.m., Sun 1 to 5 p.m.

PRIME OUTLETS AT WILLIAMSBURG
5699 Richmond Rd.
(757) 565-0702
www.primeoutlets.com

If a town's outlet shopping area can have a crown jewel, this is it. You could spend days trying to sample all of this sprawling, ever-expanding outdoor mall's shops and still not get to everything. All of the top-of-the-line brands are represented here. In fact, the tenant list is too long to include everybody, but some of the biggest draws are Coach, Lacoste, Tommy

Bahama, Chico's, True Religion Jeans, adidas, J. Crew, and Hugo Boss. In Spring 2010, Levi's and New Balance opened storefronts here. As with all outlet shopping, you may have to hunt for true bargains, but savings can range from 20 to 70 percent off the original retail price. When you arrive, stop by the Guest Services booth located in the food court, to pick up a coupon book—a good idea is to flip through the coupons first and make a list of must-stop stores before you begin to wander. The truly organized bargain hunters may want to sign up for Prime Outlets e-mails while they are still planning their Williamsburg trip—the loyalty club sends out regular postings with coupons and information about special offers. Visit PrimeOutlets.com to join, or to see a full list of tenants.

WILLIAMSBURG DOLL FACTORY
7441 Richmond Rd.
(757) 564-9703
www.dollfactory.com
A special pleasure here is to watch artists put the finishing touches on Lady Anne Porcelain Dolls. You can pick one out to join your doll family, load up on supplies of all kinds, dolls from other major manufacturers and fine stuffed animals. Open 10 a.m. to 5 p.m. Mon through Sat; 11 a.m. to 4 p.m. Sun.

WILLIAMSBURG OUTLET MALL
6401 Richmond Rd.
(757) 565-3378, (800) SHOP-333
www.williamsburgoutletmall.com
This is the place to shop on a rainy day—the factory outlet stores here are part of Williamsburg's only enclosed mall. The single-story structure is arranged in a cross shape, with food courts in the center and the long portion extending away from the highway frontage. The shops offer from 20 to 70 percent off regular retail prices.

For a full list of tenants, check the Web site listed above. Mall hours vary, so check the Web site or call for those too.

WILLIAMSBURG POTTERY FACTORY AND OUTLETS
US 60 West
Lightfoot
(757) 564-3326
www.williamsburgpottery.com
In the summer, shoppers arrive at "The Pottery," as it's known locally, by the busload and in recent years many have left wondering why. This vast collection of ramshackle buildings—1 million square feet of stuff on sale—is dear to Williamsburg's heart, but as retail experiences go, time may have passed it by.

To understand why the Pottery has such a firm hold on the shopper's imagination, you have to know its history. In 1938, a local potter named James Maloney bought some factory seconds, laid them out on a table in front of his home seven miles west of Colonial Williamsburg, and sold out quickly. He bought more and added his own salt-glazed ware, made using 18th-century methods, to the mix. The original Pottery Factory sold distinctive, artisan-made goods. Maloney had a hit.

Over time, the roadside stand evolved from a one-man operation into one of the largest bargain centers on the East Coast, growing into a no-frills retail complex where rock-bottom prices could be offered because nothing was spent on the backdrop and small factories on the premises made cement gardenware, wood items, painted plasterware, and floral arrangements, cutting the middlemen out of the equation. To this day, nothing is spent on packaging—purchases are wrapped in newspaper sealed with masking tape.

But as the Pottery grew, so did the retail choices elsewhere. Outlet shopping is now commonplace. What made the Pottery unique is now ho-hum. And the place looks tired. The barbed-wire fence surrounding the complex gives it the air of a minimum security prison.

That said, there are still plenty of people willing to spend a day wandering the vast offerings here, and if you invest the time, you can find bargains. The complex is split into two parts, bisected by the CSX railroad tracks. On one side is the Pottery, with its ceramic factory, the Solar Shops, greenhouses, Buildings 21, 22, and 23. (There are maps of the complex available at the entrance gate.) Building 21 is where you will find a fresh bakery, gourmet foods, wine and spirits, kitchenware, a cheese shop, brass, candles, cushions, clocks, ceramics, linens, and other decorator items. On the other side, along US Route 60, are the factory outlet stores, which include Atlantic Dominion Cigarettes, King Neptune's Treasures, Pepperidge Farm, Lens Cleaners/Pens Plus, and Knives, Swords & Leather.

The Pottery has a restaurant, a cafe, and a snack bar on the premises. The drive from downtown Williamsburg is about 10 to 15 minutes west via US Route 60. An alternate route is to take I-64 to the Lightfoot exit (234A) and go south on Route 199. Turn left on Richmond Road (US Route 60). The Pottery is approximately one mile down on the right. Summer hours are 9 a.m. to 6:30 p.m. daily, until 7 p.m. Sat. (It closes at 5:30 p.m. in winter.)

VIRGINIANA

CIVIL WAR AND NATIVE AMERICAN STORE AND GALLERY
1441 Richmond Rd.
(757) 253-1155
Unique items related to the Civil War and Virginia Indian culture, including a large selection of lim-

ited edition prints by artists Mort Kunstler, Don Troiani, John Paul Strain, and others. Replica rifles, pistols, swords, and buckles are available, as are handmade craft items include pottery, kachinas, flutes, dolls, and jewelry. Open daily.

OLD CHICKAHOMINY HOUSE RESTAURANTS & ANTIQUES
1211 Jamestown Rd.
(757) 229-4689
The eatery half of this establishment is covered in our Restaurant chapter, but the gift shop is worth investigating even if you're not hungry. Antique furniture, 18th-century clocks, Dresden china, prints and oils, a Christmas shop with antique ornaments, and other gift items all are available in several quaint showrooms.

SHIRLEY METALCRAFT
1205 Jamestown Rd.
(757) 229-1378
Looking for many of the same wonderful, handcrafted wares sold at Shirley Pewter Shop on Merchants Square, but don't want to hassle with the parking? This shop is where the items are made! You'll see pewter and other fine materials worked into lovely objects to be treasured as keepsakes or as gifts. The Shirley mark is noted nationally for fine craftsmanship and elegant, creative design.

ATTRACTIONS

Years ago, *the* reason people came to Williamsburg was the extraordinary restoration of colonial life on the eve of the American Revolution. These days, there are many more magnets: the roller coasters at Busch Gardens, the cool pull of the Hubba Hubba Highway at Water Country USA, the shopping at Prime Outlets.

So we've broken down the things to do in Williamsburg into two camps. The first is historic attractions, including plantations for those who want to further immerse themselves in the past, and the excellent programs and sights to see at Jamestown and Yorktown.

The second half is modern diversions—those for the young, the young at heart, and a few adult-only pleasures, like an afternoon at the Williamsburg winery or a tour of Williamsburg's only microbrewery.

We begin with the project that put Williamsburg back on the map.

COLONIAL WILLIAMSBURG

The massively ambitious restoration project that began here in the early 20th century was a hymn to democracy, a way of honoring and ensuring the memory of the birth of a nation. Over the decades it has morphed into something else. It's one thing to restore buildings. Quite another to hobnob with Thomas Jefferson, or share tea with Martha Washington. Colonial Williamsburg realized that no matter what the original mission, if they wanted the story of America's beginnings to continue to be told it had to be about more than buildings; it had to be about people.

That's why, strolling down Duke of Gloucester Street, you are meant to eavesdrop. Listen to the talk of taxes, politics, and religious freedom. A visit to Colonial Williamsburg is much more than leafing through the pages of a history book—it's a chance to put yourself, at least momentarily, in the shoes of British citizens who had the temerity, the guts even, to think about overthrowing the king. Imagine! After all, when all this discourse about independence was brewing, do you think most Virginians believed they could win?

The historical interpreters here emphasize the political and social history of the day. Because of the restoration, you get to experience that in

a way that allows you to employ all your senses. There is probably nowhere else in the United States where the sights, sounds, tastes, and even smells of the past come alive in the present as they do in Williamsburg, including the occasional waft of horse manure.

Colonial Williamsburg offers 301 acres of 18th-century history along with a full slate of lectures, concerts, theatrical performances, and militia exhibits year-round. The city is portrayed on the brink of revolution, when the air is tense with rumors of rebellion, espionage, and possible war. Throughout the Historic Area, costumed interpreters toil at their trades without modern conveniences like, say, electricity. In colonial taverns, balladeers serenade their audiences with the bawdy tales that were popular with previous generations while learned gentlemen of the time discuss the political issues that were at the forefront of everyone's mind.

With 88 original structures, 300 major reconstructions, 40 exhibition buildings, and 90 acres of gardens and greens, Williamsburg isn't a city you can see in a day—or even two. Allow enough time to listen to an evening reveille, dance in the candlelit House of Burgesses, and participate in a military drill. The memories you'll come away with are unlikely to be duplicated anywhere else. To start you on your trip to another era, we begin with a comprehensive look back at how it all began.

Historical Overview

Williamsburg served as the English colonial capital from 1699 to 1780 and, during that time, grew from a small settlement to a thriving, sophisticated urban center, reflecting the city's prominent role. By the mid-18th century, the population was nearing 2,000; slaves accounted for roughly half of that number. When courts convened, Williamsburg's population more than doubled, with citizens from the far reaches of the vast Virginia Colony arriving to participate in the fairs, festivities, and fancy dress balls of Publick Times.

American ideals of democracy and liberty took root here in the 1700s, as colonists began to question, and finally repudiate, British rule. Patrick Henry inveighed against taxation without representation in the House of Burgesses in 1765. The First Continental Congress was called from Williamsburg in 1774. The Declaration of Rights, soon to become the foundation for the first 10 amendments to the Constitution, was penned here by George Mason. Thousands of Continental Army soldiers were billeted in Williamsburg, which bustled with revolutionary fervor. In 1780, however, Thomas Jefferson's campaign to move the capital to Richmond succeeded, and Williamsburg, no longer the heart of social, political, and economic life in Virginia, entered an era of sleepy decline. Its population waned, and businesses were forced to close. While it continued to function as the county seat, 19th-century Williamsburg was mostly a market town for area farmers, disturbed only by Union General George McClellan's 1862 Peninsula Campaign during the Civil War.

The College of William and Mary and the Public Hospital remained the only institutions of much size or importance. Some public buildings fell into neglect and burned (the Palace in 1781), but most of the 18th-century homes and structures continued to be used simply because there

was little reason to build anew. While interim uses were at times less than noble (Prentis Store survived in the early 20th century as a gas station; the Magazine once served as a stable), the structures were saved from destruction.

Two Men and a Dream

Williamsburg might still be a sedate spot on the map if not for the actions of two men who conceived of a grander future for the once-great city. The Rev. W. A. R. Goodwin, rector of Bruton Parish Church, dreamed of reviving Virginia's colonial capital. He was successful in raising enough money to restore his own church, but in 1908 he left Williamsburg to become rector of a Rochester, New York, church. In 1923, however, he returned as professor of religion at the College of William and Mary. As luck would have it, the college chose Goodwin as its representative at a 1924 Phi Beta Kappa dinner in New York. Also attending the dinner was John D. Rockefeller Jr., heir to the Standard Oil fortune.

This meeting led to the Rockefellers' 1926 visit to Williamsburg, during which negotiations for the restoration of certain 18th-century buildings began. Planning was carried out in a highly secretive manner. Measurements of buildings were taken under cover of darkness. Rockefeller insisted on signing documents pseudonymously as "Mr. David." Town residents felt understandably apprehensive and mystified as they watched their rector buying up land. Rumors spread, and real estate values took off. Soon it was necessary to reveal to Williamsburg citizens the nature of the restoration plan. Initially, not all were pleased; some balked at the idea of their town being "sold." Others were skeptical about the practicality of such a scheme. As the restoration process began, however, the economic benefits of the project became clear. Tenancy agreements allowed most residents of 18th-century buildings to occupy their homes for life.

A Reconstruction Frenzy

Though Rockefeller at first intended to subsidize the restoration of a small number of structures, his enthusiasm and ambitions grew as research turned up more and more pertinent data. Drawings, maps, and records culled from libraries and museums in Europe and America revealed a trove of historical details. Teams of architects, led by William Graves Perry, restored original 18th-century sites and reconstructed others on original foundations. Hundreds of more modern buildings were razed or removed. Eighteenth-century building and brick-making techniques were painstakingly researched so that a restorations and reconstructions would resemble the originals as closely as possible.

The success of Goodwin's and Rockefeller's grand vision is well documented today. More than a half-million tour Colonial Williamsburg (CW, for short) each year. The Historic Area contains hundreds of restored public buildings, residences, outbuildings, dependencies, shops, and hostelries, plus acres of formal and informal gardens, pastures, and lanes.

While in one sense the restoration Goodwin and Rockefeller envisioned is complete, the Colonial Williamsburg Foundation continues to pursue its vision—or perhaps revision—of the past. In recent years, Colonial Williamsburg has redirected its focus somewhat. Previously, programs concentrated on the lives of an elite group—colonial governors, revolutionary leaders, and prominent citizens. There was critical backlash, perhaps most notably from the scholar Ada Louise Huxtable, whose 1997 book, *The Unreal America*, condemned historical restorations like Williamsburg as a "prettification of pioneer life." Today you will find more space given to the 18th-century community as a whole. Slaves, indentured servants, women, tradespeople, the typical family of the period, and other "middling" folk are increasingly featured in interpretive programs that more accurately reflect the complexities of 18th-century history.

One program, for instance, explores the paradoxical issue of freedom in a society that fought to win its independence from the British Crown while practicing and condoning slavery. Colonial Williamsburg also has used grant monies to improve and more fully assimilate interpretation

of the 18th-century African-American experience into its presentations. The role religion played in the daily lives of colonists is being more fully explored and interpreted for the benefit of visitors through lectures, tours, and concerts. Each year, black history, women's history, music, and religion are observed with special programming. Reenactments and re-creations of historical events—from a day of fasting, humiliation, and prayer in response to the Boston Tea Party to a mock trial and burning of Britain's chief minister, Lord North—occur on a regular basis throughout the Historic Area.

Costumed tradespeople at nearly 20 sites around the Historic Area also invite visitors to roll up their sleeves and assist them with their 18th-century trades, whether shoemaking, basket weaving, or silversmithing. In addition, Thomas Jefferson, Patrick Henry, and other Founding Fathers now engage visitors with compelling discourse on such topics as democracy, slavery, marriage, and the "Mother Country" of England.

The best way to find out what's on tap when you're in town is to consult *Colonial Williamsburg This Week*, a full-color map and program guide available at the Visitor Center or wherever CW tickets are sold. It contains up-to-date information on sites, special programs, shopping, and dining.

Modern Realities

In recent years the winds of change have begun blowing a little more forcefully down the dusty streets of Williamsburg. The bid for tourists' time and money is a competitive business, and paid admissions, which regularly hit the 1.2 million mark in the 1980s, dipped to the 660,000 in 2009, a 47-year low.

A new marketing campaign, "Be Part of the Story," and an emphasis on retooling programs to make them kid-friendly are part of the strategy to bring visitors back. Youngsters have more opportunities than ever to see, touch, smell, and hear about the 18th century. Children are able to make stitch books, play hoops, master a colonial ball-and-cup game, polish silver with the silversmiths, and tread mud with the brick makers. "Revolutionary City," street theater that allows visitors to eavesdrop on the imagined conversations of military leaders, merchants and other townspeople on the eve of war with England, is in its fifth year, with new dramas scheduled throughout the day. (Consult *This Week* for specific programs, times and locations.)

CW is also hoping its first "new" building on Duke of Gloucester Street in more than 50 years, R. Charlton's Coffeehouse, will capitalize on America's love of java. The coffeehouse was built on its original foundation using mostly 18th-century techniques. Richard Charlton opened his coffeehouse adjacent to the Capitol in 1760 as a stylish retreat from the humdrum activities of governing. Visitors to the coffeehouse will experience an interpretive tour that reveals the significance of the establishment—a gathering place for the political elite, and as such, a hotbed for discussion and debate, before concluding with a sample tasting of period coffeehouse beverages—coffee, tea, or chocolate.

i Children get a different perspective on history when they wear colonial costumes. Girls can don an elegant white 18th-century lawn dress with a colored sash and boys can sport a hunting shirt, haversack, and imitation rifle. Costumes can be rented at Market Square in Colonial Williamsburg's Historic Area or at WILLIAMSBURG Revolutions at the Visitor Center. The program is recommended for youth between the ages of 5–10.

Hands-on History

During your stroll through colonial times, get involved in what is happening around you. The teaching of history is a primary goal in Colonial Williamsburg, and the best people here embrace their mission with the passion of a great classroom teacher. To engage visitors as fully as possible, there are a variety of lively, hands-on learning presentations. Interactive programs allow visitors to be in the moment. Walking along Duke of

Gloucester Street, you might run into Patrick Henry or George Washington—ask them a question! When are you going to get another chance?

Getting Started
Visitor Center

Once you've committed yourself to a day at Williamsburg, head straight to the Visitor Center (follow the red-white-and-blue signs around town) to purchase tickets and obtain sightseeing information, maps, guidebooks, and advice about touring the colonial capital. Parking in the lot is ample and free.

Reservations for special tours and presentations, for meals in Colonial Williamsburg's several taverns and restaurants, and for lodging at its hotel facilities can be arranged here as well. There is also a bookstore, gift shop, and benches here, if you need to pick a place to rest (in air-conditioning) or meet up with the rest of your party.

The Visitor Center is open from 8:45 a.m. to 5:15 p.m. daily during the summer. Hours are shortened during the fall and winter months. Any and all questions you have about visiting Colonial Williamsburg attractions can be answered here, or by calling (800) 246-2099, (800) HISTORY, or (757) 229-1000. You can also log on to the CW Web site, at www.colonialwilliamsburg.com.

Tickets

You can feel transported back to the 18th century just by roaming the historic streets of Colonial Williamsburg free of charge, but visitors need a ticket to enter exhibition buildings and historic trade shops, ride the buses provided by CW, or take part in guided walking tours.

Tickets can be purchased at the Visitor Center, and at several sites around the Historic Area including the Lumber House ticket office on Duke of Gloucester Street. Shopping online is your best option, allowing you to see the range of choices and take advantage of specials and discounts which are offered, especially in the off-season. The CW Web site is www.colonialwilliamsburg.com.

A one-day pass is $36 for adults and $18 for children ages 6 to 17. Children 5 and under are admitted free. There are also two-day, annual passes, and a special rate for students and for Williamsburg residents. Guests staying at Colonial Williamsburg lodgings receive a substantial discount—$30 per adult for the length of your stay, $15 for children.

Every CW ticket includes admission to all exhibition buildings, daytime programs, and museums. Separate museum tickets are also available.

Hours of Operation

Colonial Williamsburg is open 365 days a year, but its hours and the availability of certain buildings and attractions vary. During the summer months, the Visitor Center is open from 8:45 a.m. to 5:15 p.m., and most buildings in the Historic Area are open from 9 a.m. to 5 p.m. with some variations. In the winter, open hours are generally shortened to 9:30 a.m. to 4:30 p.m. Double check your *Colonial Williamsburg This Week* guide before you make specific plans.

Transportation

A fleet of Colonial Williamsburg buses circulates through and around the Historic Area, stopping at major points of interest. They carry visitors to and from the Visitor Center continuously from morning until about 10 p.m. (this may change seasonally), and ticket holders may board at any stop. Special assistance and shuttle bus service are available to visitors with disabilities. If you need these services, inquire at the Visitor Center, Lumber House ticket office, or Merchants Square Information Center. As we mentioned in our Getting Here, Getting Around chapter, cars are more bother than they're worth when touring the Historic Area. Parking around the Historic Area is limited, and the streets are typically closed to vehicles from 8 a.m. to 10 p.m. Parking at the Visitor Center is free.

All guests at Colonial Williamsburg hotels can rent bikes and strollers at the Tazewell Fitness Center in the Williamsburg Lodge if the weather is nice. Strollers rent for $10.50 a day. Bikes can be rented by the hour for $5, for a half-day (four hours) for $11, or for a full day for $18. Call (757) 220-7690 for more information.

Historic Area Attractions

While it's impossible to absorb everything Colonial Williamsburg has to offer in a day or two, some visitors can't stay much longer. Even a short visit will be memorable if you take the time to plan your tour in advance. Before you visit, check out www.colonialwilliamsburg.com to get a general idea of what is happening during the time you plan to be in the area, or call (800) HISTORY for a free vacation planner. When you arrive in Williamsburg, ask hotel personnel or staff at the Colonial Williamsburg Visitor Center for a copy of *This Week*, a daily calendar and schedule that gives operating hours for Historic Area buildings, restaurants, tours, and events. This publication, without which we personally wouldn't step foot in Williamsburg, can help you decide on an agenda for each day.

Below, we highlight the major buildings and exhibits you won't want to miss, no matter how brief your stay. We recommend the escorted half-hour introductory tour Colonial Williamsburg offers as orientation for a leisurely self-touring vacation, or just as a very pleasant—if short—excursion into the world of 18th-century Williamsburg. You also will want to read through the *Official Colonial Williamsburg Guidebook and Map* (available at the Visitor Center), an excellent introduction to the diverse and sometimes complex experiences in store for you as you travel back in time. While we mention which buildings and exhibits require special reservations, it's always best to check at the Visitor Center the day you plan to tour a specific site, as hours of operation vary, and buildings occasionally are closed to the public.

The Buildings
Bruton Parish Church

On Duke of Gloucester Street west of the Palace Green, Bruton Parish Church is one of America's oldest Episcopal churches, in use since 1715. While Bruton Parish is owned not by Colonial Williamsburg but by congregation members, the public is welcome to tour the church from 9 a.m. to 5 p.m. Mon through Sat and from 1 to 5 p.m.

Sun. The church was fully restored in 1940. Walls and windows are original. The stone baptismal font, according to legend, was brought from an earlier Jamestown church. The churchyard holds many 18th-century graves. Buried inside the church is Francis Fauquier, one of Virginia's royal governors. Evening organ recitals, chamber music performances, and choral concerts frequently are presented at the church.

Capitol

Prior to the Revolutionary War, the House of Burgesses and a 12-member council met in this ornate structure at the east end of Duke of Gloucester Street. Many important political events that involved Virginia in the Revolutionary War took place here. The most significant was on May 15, 1776, when Virginia's legislators adopted a resolution declaring independence from England, two months before the Continental Congress adopted the Declaration of Independence in Philadelphia. Once war began, and until 1780 when the capital was moved to Richmond, it housed the state government. Foundations were laid in 1701 for the H-shaped building, designed with two wings to hold the bicameral legislative bodies that made up colonial government. Like the Governor's Palace, the original Capitol building suffered fire damage, burning in 1747. Its replacement, neglected after the capital moved to Richmond in 1780, eventually burned also. What you see today is a reconstruction of the first Capitol, about which more architectural evidence was found. Here, you can tour the House of Burgesses, Council Chambers, and General Courtroom and join in a number of special evening programs. These include *Cry Witch*, a re-creation of the dramatic trial of Grace Sherwood, the "Virginia Witch."

George Wythe House

Together with outbuildings and gardens, this spacious original Georgian-style home affords an understanding of gracious living in 18th-century Williamsburg. The house, featuring two great chimneys and large central halls, was used as George Washington's headquarters before the Battle of Yorktown. Owner George Wythe was the nation's first law professor and an influential teacher of Thomas Jefferson. During the last several years, the environmental and security systems were upgraded at the Wythe House and a $750,000 redecorating project was completed. The changes involved replacing marble fireplace mantels with more authentic ones of red sandstone and installing custom hand-printed wallpaper after a painstaking analysis revealed that the Wythe House most likely was wallpapered during Wythe's lifetime (1726–1806).

Behind the house you'll find symmetrical gardens, tree box topiaries, and an arbor of shady hornbeam. In reconstructed outbuildings, including a stable, smokehouse, laundry, kitchen, and lumber house, interpreters periodically demonstrate domestic activities such as cooking a batch of apple fritters over the kitchen's open hearth.

Governor's Palace

Set on 10 acres of restored gardens, this elegant mansion housed a series of royal governors and the Commonwealth of Virginia's first two governors, Patrick Henry and Thomas Jefferson. The original construction began in 1706 and took 17 years to complete; alterations and redecoration continued until the Dec. 22, 1781, fire that left only the foundation. At the north end of the Palace Green, the reconstructed mansion, with its entrance hall, parlor, ballroom, dining rooms, bedchambers, waiting areas, and even a wine cellar, is opulently furnished from an inventory of more than 12,000 items dating to the period of Lord Dunmore, Virginia's last royal governor. Lord Dunmore and his family lived in Governor's Palace in the early 1770s.

Children delight in trying to count the muskets mounted in a circle on the entrance hall ceiling. (We know how many are up there, but it's more fun if you guess before asking your guide.) Check out the incredible crown moldings and wall coverings (that's leather on the walls in the upstairs meeting room), and don't miss all the interesting details throughout the Palace. The chairs in Lady Dunmore's upstairs bedchamber are made to simulate bamboo, there really were

Venetian blinds on the windows, and the small statues lining the dining room mantel are the actual figurines representing the costumed characters from the masquerade ball commemorating King George III's 21st birthday.

In the 18th century the Governor's Palace was the scene of many get-togethers of early America's well-to-do. Dances, for example, were held about every three months in the palace ballroom, each typically lasting up to 18 hours, since many visitors had journeyed three or more days on horseback to reach Williamsburg and it would have been exceedingly impolite to send them home too soon.

On the palace grounds you will find a stable and carriage house, kitchen, scullery, laundry, and hexagonal "bagnio" or bathhouse, a real frill in colonial times. Take the time to stroll through the formal gardens, similar to early-18th-century English gardens, which lead to informal terraces and a fishpond. Children love running and playing hide-and-seek in the boxwood maze. The palace, which opened to the public in 1934, is one of Colonial Williamsburg's most popular attractions, drawing 650,000 visitors annually.

Magazine and Guardhouse

Across Duke of Gloucester from the popular Chowning's Tavern is the octagonal Magazine, which was built in 1715, by order of Lieutenant Governor Alexander Spotswood, to store arms for the protection of the colony and for trade with the Indians, and a Guardhouse, reconstructed in 1949. The Magazine played an important role during the French and Indian War (1754–63), when it became evident that the wooden stockade surrounding it served as woefully inadequate protection from enemies. In 1755 Peyton Randolph, Carter Burwell, John Chiswell, Benjamin Waller, and James Power were named as directors to hire workmen to build both a brick wall around the Magazine and a Guardhouse to protect this valuable weaponry storehouse. Although no one knows who actually erected the first Guardhouse and what it looked like, the original structure most likely consisted of a room for the officers, another for the men, and a piazza or porch for the sentry. It is believed that the reconstructed Guardhouse, following that formula, closely resembles the original.

Perhaps the biggest conflict surrounding the Magazine occurred before dawn on April 21, 1775, when British soldiers removed 15 half-barrels of gunpowder from the storehouse, stirring a protest from Williamsburg's angry citizenry and fanning the fires that led to the Revolution. (Other arms and ammunition stored in the Magazine at the time included shot, flints, and military equipment such as tents.) After the Revolution the Magazine housed a market, meetinghouse, dance school, and livery stable. Humble as they seem, these interim uses probably saved the original building from abandonment and destruction.

Peyton Randolph House

The Peyton Randolph House at Nicholson and North England Streets is among Williamsburg's oldest and finest 18th-century homes. The west wing of the house has stood at its current location since about 1715, sheltering the likes of General Rochambeau, the Marquis de Lafayette, and its namesake, the first president of the Continental Congress. Sir John Randolph purchased the west wing in 1721. A few years later he bought the adjacent one-and-a-half-story house that later became the structure's east wing. Sir John's son, Peyton, Speaker of the Virginia House of Burgesses in the years leading to the Revolution, built a spacious and well-appointed two-story central section that connected the two houses via a hall and magnificent stairway. Today this well-preserved center section contains some of the best surviving paneling in Williamsburg as well as much of the original edge-cut pine flooring. The parlor doors have unusually fine brass hinges and locks. In addition to the three sections of the house, there was a full complement of outbuildings in back, including a coach house, stable, dairy, and two-story brick kitchen.

Colonial Williamsburg began restoring the Peyton Randolph House in late 1939 and finished a few months later. Further restoration was completed in the late '60s. The center and west portions of the house opened for visitors in 1968. In recent years the house once again has been painstakingly restored. All of the work that was done was based on two decades of research and a remarkable room-by-room inventory of the house taken at the time of Peyton Randolph's death in 1775. Many of the outbuildings—including a smokehouse, dairy, storehouse, and 2,000-square-foot kitchen and covered way that attached it to the house—recently were reconstructed. These structures not only restore the historic site, but they also provide the opportunity to interpret the lives of the 27 slaves who lived and worked here.

i Guests of Colonial Williamsburg can leave their car keys in their hotel room and tour Duke of Gloucester Street the 18th-century way in one of CW's horse-drawn coaches. The coach and livestock program has been operating these unique tours continuously since 1947. Today, more than 50,000 guests embark on the 15- or 30-minute journey through Colonial Williamsburg annually. There are seven carriages reserved for the use of guests and visiting dignitaries. Space is limited. Tickets can be purchased at any ticket sales location.

Public Gaol

Behind the Capitol on Nicholson Street is the Public Gaol (pronounced "jail"), with partially original walls and wholly authentic grimness. Shackles that were excavated while the gaol was under restoration are on display. Take a look in the small, dank cells hung with leg irons, and consider spending a winter night in such a place with only a thin blanket for cover. Among the 18th-century inhabitants of these cells were Blackbeard's pirate crew, runaway slaves, Indians, insolvent debtors, and, occasionally, mentally ill persons. During the Revolution, British captives, accused spies, and Tory sympathizers were cordially allowed to use the gaol facilities. Part of the gaol has been refurbished to reflect its other

function—home to the gaol keeper and his family. Furnishings are representative of those owned by a typical family of the period.

Raleigh Tavern

Revolutionary heroes like Patrick Henry and Thomas Jefferson gathered to discuss politics and reach important conclusions in this famous Duke of Gloucester Street tavern, the first of Colonial Williamsburg's reconstructed buildings to open for public viewing. Built around 1717, the tavern was the axis around which 18th-century Virginia society, business, and politics revolved. George Washington dined here often and mentions the tavern in his diary. The Phi Beta Kappa Society was founded here in 1776. The tavern burned in 1859, but original foundations and drawings aided architects in the 1930s reconstruction. We were impressed by the billiard table: Its 6-foot-by-12-foot dimensions required that a room large enough to hold it be added onto the tavern. Behind the tavern is the Bake Shop, where visitors line up for Sally Lunn bread, sweet potato muffins, and ginger cake.

The Gardens

While the one-of-a-kind buildings of Colonial Williamsburg intrigue the mind, the Historic Area's 100 or so gardens are balm for the spirit. Luckily, you will stumble upon them just about everywhere you turn. Rest assured, in addition to its beauty, each garden has been meticulously researched for style and accuracy in the Dutch, English, and southern traditions of the 17th and 18th centuries. Archaeological digs conducted on many sites often revealed the remains of walkways, brick walls, and fence lines, which served as blueprints for the gardens and outbuildings eventually erected on each lot.

Most of Colonial Williamsburg's gardens were planted from the 1930s through the 1950s and reflect the Colonial Revival style, which tends to be rather refined and elegant. Ongoing research suggests that this interpretation of our nation's colonial gardens may not be accurate; thus Colonial Williamsburg gradually is reworking its gardens in a simpler form.

As you stroll through these gardens, you will enjoy a profusion of greens, including English boxwood, hollyhock, and Yaupon holly. Seasonal flowers—everything from the wandering phlox to the purple crocus—provide a wash of color that changes with the passing months. Kitchen and vegetable gardens are yet another part of the Historic Area landscape. While corn, tobacco, wheat, cotton, and flax were grown in the fields, it was the much smaller kitchen gardens that provided the fruits and vegetables used at the table and for preserving.

As part of its regular programming, Colonial Williamsburg offers a guided Garden History Walk through its restored grounds. Consult *This Week* for tour availability.

i Some people think no visit to Williamsburg is complete without sampling the fare in one of the popular restored taverns. See our Restaurants chapter for details about the fare at Chowning's, the King's Arms, Christiana Campbell's (where Washington dined) and Shields Tavern.

Trade Shops and Demonstrations

Scattered throughout the Historic Area are costumed craftspeople, journeymen, and apprentices practicing the various old trades that were part of life in the 18th century. At the Printing Office on Duke of Gloucester Street, visitors can see newspapers printed on an 18th-century press, learn about bookbinding, and watch periodic demonstrations of typesetting, papermaking, and decorating. At the James Anderson Blacksmith Shop, seven reconstructed forges operate, and smithing techniques are demonstrated. Silversmiths craft mote spoons—decoratively perforated and good for straining tea—at The Golden Ball, where you can also buy gold and silver jewelry. The Margaret Hunter Shop recreates the atmosphere and activity of an 18th-century milliner's, with hats, gloves, purses, shoes, and embroidery pieces on the shelves.

Next door to the King's Arms Tavern, a wigmaker uses goat, horse, yak, and human hair to conjure up a few curls. (A few years ago, the wigmaker shop began an apprentice program that for the first time in CW history admits women.) Out on North England Street, you can visit Robertson's Windmill, where wind-driven sails power stones that grind corn. Nearby, coopers shape and assemble staves to form casks, piggins, and other wooden containers. In addition, harness and saddle makers, shoemakers, cabinetmakers, brass founders, gunsmiths, wheelwrights, carpenters, cooks, and basket makers go about their business in Historic Area sites.

Mercantile Shops

While some of the historic trade shops sell crafted items, several operating mercantile shops accurately re-create 18th-century business premises, offering wares and services representative of colonial times. Finest among these is Prentis Store, an original building dating from 1740 that features reproductions of 18th-century wares. Tarpley's Store sells pottery, educational toys, and soaps, while the Greenhow Store's inventory includes candy, three-cornered hats, and fifes. These stores, along with the Mary Dickinson Store, which sells jewelry, toiletries, and women's accessories, and the M. Dubois Grocer's Shop, where you can pick up a bottle of tavern sparkling cider, can all be visited on Duke of Gloucester Street. At the Colonial Post Office you'll find an extensive collection of 18th-century prints and maps as well as postcards that can be hand-canceled using the original 18th-century Williamsburg postmark, while behind the Secretary's Office is Tickets, Treasures and Books, which sells Colonial Williamsburg tickets, children's items, and books relating to early American history. (For more details on many of these shops, see our Shopping chapter.)

Other Buildings and Exhibits

If you have time to explore more restored or reconstructed sites in the Historic Area, here are a few we particularly recommend.

Courthouse

With its cupola, weather vane, and round-headed windows, the Courthouse is visible up and down

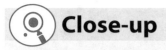 **Close-up**

Christmas in Colonial Williamsburg

In colonial times feasts and celebrations were the highlights of the Christmas season. Families and neighbors gathered together to celebrate with the best their tables could offer. In the 18th century, the holiday season began on December 24 and culminated with a large celebration on the Twelfth Night, January 6.

These days, the holiday season is still one of the most popular times to visit Colonial Williamsburg. The first Christmas celebration organized for visitors took place in 1936, and the celebrations have gotten even grander in recent decades, adding modern touches to time-honored colonial traditions. It's a perfect time to see the village decked out in 17th-century holiday decor, take in a holiday concert, and taste some traditional Yuletide dishes.

The Christmas season is officially ushered in on the first Sunday in December with the **Grand Illumination**. Candles and cressets are lit around the Historic Area, and musical and theatrical performances are held in several areas. Finally, three impressive fireworks displays take place over the Governor's Palace, the Magazine, and the Capitol.

Colonial Williamsburg guides will lead visitors through the streets to see decorations on all the buildings. Just outside the Historic Area, the **Green Spring Garden Club** hosts an annual Christmas homes tour of private residences that have been beautifully decorated as well.

And look for **concerts** of music played on 18th-century or reproduction instruments at the candlelit House of Burgesses or the Governor's Palace. In addition, the Fifes & Drums offer an annual concert of international military music and Christmas tunes.

Just be sure to make reservations early, as many hotels and restaurants book up weeks in advance. For more information, visit the Colonial Williamsburg Web site, www.history.org/Christmas, or call (800) HISTORY.

Duke of Gloucester Street. It is one of three courthouses in Williamsburg, and the first to be built here. A series of special programs allows visitors to experience the day-to-day functioning of early American jurisprudence. Costumed interpreters and guides lead visitors through participatory scenes, such as trials and impromptu dialogues. Interesting furnishings include the chief magistrate's throne-like chair and clothbound docket books used by colonial clerks and sheriffs.

Great Hopes Plantation

The original Great Hopes was in York County, Virginia. This re-creation, on the edge of the Historic Area (near the Visitor Center) is a representation of the "middling" plantations that existed around the colonial capital. Those plantations were the homes of most of the rural middle class, the ones who weren't shop and tavern keepers or tradespeople in town.

Only 5 percent of the colonial population was what Patrick Henry would have called "well-born." About a third or more were lower class, or "lesser sort," depending on where you lived. The rest of the people were "middling;" that is, hardworking, honest people who owned one hundred acres or more, and ten or so slaves.

At Great Hopes Plantation, guests watch the re-creation and evolution of an 18th-century plantation, learn about enslaved African Virginians and their masters, and learn how they lived and worked on a typical middle-sized rural Virginia farm. Programs include **Workin' the Soil, Healing the Soul** during which guests follow an interpreter through the reconstructed 18th-century rural kitchen, slave quarters, and agricultural and livestock fields for a look at day-to-day living for rural enslaved families.

James Geddy House and Foundry

The James Geddy House and Foundry, on Duke of Gloucester Street just across the Palace Green from Bruton Parish Church, was home to a family of artisans who worked in bronze, brass, pewter, and silver. Visitors to the house can learn about the life of an 18th-century tradesman and his children by helping out at the foundry or assisting Grandma Geddy (mother of eight) with the laundry.

Thomas Everard House

The Thomas Everard House on the Palace Green is known for its carved woodwork. The yard is paved with original bricks found during excavation, and the smokehouse and kitchen are original restored structures. The Thomas Everard House was one of three buildings included in a $2.5 million renovation project that included state-of-the-art air-conditioning and heating, fire detectors, security systems, and computerized humidity and temperature controls. While the restoration work was going on, historians had a rare opportunity to explore much of the building and readjust their thinking about its history. The house was built by John Brush, then occupied by Henry Cary, who extensively renovated it between 1730 and 1740. Thomas Everard moved in around 1770 and added wallpaper in the dining room and chamber. The Colonial Williamsburg tour focuses on the life of Everard, an immigrant and mayor of Williamsburg, and the lives of his family and 19 slaves.

Wetherburn's Tavern

Wetherburn's Tavern, an original building, was carefully refurnished using information gleaned from a detailed inventory left of Henry Wetherburn's estate and from artifacts uncovered during excavation at the site. Tours spotlight the lives of Wetherburn's family and slaves. The house is on Duke of Gloucester Street next to Tarpley's Store.

Beyond the Historic Area

Visitors with more than a few days to spend in the area, on return trips, or with special interests can enhance their appreciation of 18th-century history, arts, and related phenomena by visiting some of the properties operated by Colonial Williamsburg outside the Historic Area. Entry to all of these attractions is included in a Colonial Williamsburg pass. A separate ticket for the museums also is available.

ABBY ALDRICH ROCKEFELLER FOLK ART MUSEUM

(Entrance to the museum is through the Public Hospital of 1773 at 326 W. Francis St. between Nassau and South Henry Streets) (757) 220-7724

This museum, the oldest institution in the United States dedicated solely to the collection and preservation of American folk art, reopened in February 2007 in new quarters adjacent to the DeWitt Wallace Decorative Arts Museum. Exhibits feature paintings, drawings, furniture, ceramics, whirligigs, weather vanes, carvings, toys, quilts, musical instruments, and other folk works representing many diverse cultural traditions and geographic regions. John D. Rockefeller Jr. established the museum in 1957 in honor of his wife, Abby, who began collecting folk art early in the 20th century. In 1939, she gave her core collection of 425 objects to the Colonial Williamsburg Foundation, which formed the basis for the museum's collection. Today the collection of more than 5,000 objects includes items dating from the 1720s to the present shown in 11 galleries constituting 11,000 square feet of exhibition space.

BASSETT HALL

Off Francis St. (757) 220-7724

Bassett Hall is the two-story, 18th-century frame house that was the Williamsburg home of John D. Rockefeller Jr. and his wife, Abby Aldrich Rockefeller. While earlier tours of the home focused on Mrs. Rockefeller's folk art collection, visitors now learn about the Rockefellers themselves and about their contribution to the creation of Colonial Williamsburg. Bequeathed to the foundation in 1979, the house is set on a 585-acre tract of woodlands, and the property includes a teahouse, called the Orangerie, and three original outbuildings: a smokehouse, kitchen, and dairy. Bassett Hall reopened in 2002 after undergoing renovations that include a new exhibition of the history of the Rockefellers at Bassett Hall and a return of the extensive gardens to their 1940s appearance. Open seasonally 9 a.m. to 5 p.m. daily except Wed.

DEWITT WALLACE DECORATIVE ARTS MUSEUM
Corner of Francis and South Henry Streets
(757) 220-7724

Adjacent to the Public Hospital is a fascinating museum devoted to British and American decorative arts from 1600 through 1830. The contemporary two-tiered building, designed by internationally known architect I. M. Pei and completed in 1985, features exhibits of metal, ceramics, glass, prints, textiles, costumes, and other decorative objects from Colonial Williamsburg's permanent collections. The collection of Virginia furniture is the largest of its type in the world, and the collection of English pottery is more vast than any other on this side of the Atlantic. The museum features 11 galleries and 27,500 square feet of exhibition space, where more than 8,000 objects and works of art are on display. Among the finest pieces are a full-length portrait of George III, painted by English artist Allan Ramsay; a burled-walnut and gilt Tompion clock, which is among a handful of the most important pieces of English furniture in the United States; and a 1735 mahogany tea table, which had been owned by the Galt family for more than 200 years.

Changing exhibits have included *Identifying Ceramics: The Who, What, and Ware* and *Ordering the Wilderness*, which explores Virginians' relationship to both the land and the instruments used to survey and map it.

It would be easy to spend the better part of a day browsing through the illuminating museum or lingering in the comforting natural light of the museum's glass-roofed courtyards. Fortunately, a cafe on the gallery's lower level serves lunch, tea, and light refreshments. A gift shop selling reproductions and decorative arts journals is also on the premises. The museum is generally open from 11 a.m. to 6 p.m. daily, but hours vary seasonally and are subject to change without notice. Admission is included in any Colonial Williamsburg ticket or a separate museums ticket. Call the gallery for information on tours and exhibits.

PUBLIC HOSPITAL OF 1773
326 W. Francis St.
(757) 220-7724

The somber building at the corner of Francis and South Henry Streets is a reconstruction of the first public institution for the mentally ill to be built in colonial America. Opened in 1773 and known as the Hospital for Lunaticks, this facility first treated its inmates more as prisoners than patients, as the early small cells indicate. Nineteenth-century scientific and medical advances improved methods of treatment, which the hospital's interpretive exhibits chronicle, but also on display are a number of devices used to treat patients, some of which resemble implements of torture. The hospital is open from 11 a.m. to 6 p.m. daily.

Family Programs

If you think a historical site is not a place to take children—and still have a good time—think again. Colonial Williamsburg offers a growing number of special programs designed to enrich every family's exploration of the past. Although there are literally dozens of programs designed specifically for family enjoyment and participation, we have highlighted a handful we're sure you will enjoy. There are some exceptions, but the majority of family programs are offered beginning in mid-June and continuing through the summer. During their visit children also have the opportunity to don colonial garb (available for rent in a tent next to the Powder Magazine on Market Square) and play with 18th-century toys and games. Since activities not only vary from day to day, but also from hour to hour, check that indispensable *This Week* for specific times and locations.

The African American Experience—Colonial Williamsburg offers two historic sites to explore the day-to-day lives of enslaved Virginians. The Peyton Randolph House and outbuildings provide hands-on activities that represent the daily life of Peyton and Elizabeth Randolph and their relationship to slaves during the American Revolution. Great Hopes Plantation represents a middling planter family with a workforce of approximately seven enslaved people. Great Hopes is a hands-on site where interpreters perform a variety of daily work activities that represent slave history, culture, agriculture, and carpentry on an 18th-century plantation.

Brickyard—Colonial Williamsburg's brickyard is one of several trade sites where young guests can get involved. Children can jump in feet first and experience how 18th-century bricks were made by assisting tradespeople tread or walk through clay to smooth it. They also might get the chance to "offbear," a child's job in an 18th-century brickyard of helping carry the filled brick-mold to the drying beds and lay the bricks out to dry in the sun. Junior interpreters are on-site on a seasonal basis to help children get the most out of their visit.

Family Life at the Benjamin Powell Site—Children try their hand at a variety of 18th-century household tasks in a setting where you are encouraged to help with the daily activities like gardening and food preparation. Special emphasis is given to interpreting 18th-century childhood and exploring how varied seasons and times of day affect the family's activities. Seasonal.

Family Life at the Geddy Site—Kids learn about the family life of an 18th-century tradesman and children's daily activities. Hands-on activities and/or games are offered outside, weather permitting. At the Geddy Foundry, just behind the Geddy House, tradesmen craft brass, bronze, silver, and pewter castings.

Military Life at the Magazine—Young guests can participate in hands-on activities and interactive discussions about 18th-century military life.

Order in the Court—Guests take part in reenactments of a local court session and learn the ways men, women, and children took part in the colonial legal system.

People of the Past—Guests chat with residents of Williamsburg's 18th-century community about their lives, hopes, and challenges and meet Thomas Jefferson, Patrick Henry, enslaved preacher Gowan Pamphlet, and other Williamsburg residents.

Rare Breeds of Livestock—Children may see many of the new rare breeds of livestock that are similar to the types that lived in 18th-century Williamsburg, including Leicester Longwool sheep, Hog Island sheep, American milking Devon cattle, Randall cattle, Milking Shorthorn cattle, American Cream draft horses, Canadian horses, Ossabaw Hogs, and several varieties of poultry. During the spring and early summer months, pastures around town are often filled with new arrivals. Tours also are offered of Colonial Williamsburg's stables.

Theater for the Young—Young guests can join the troupe of professional actors and take the stage in a fun, fast-paced play about a Virginia patriot and the adventure he shares with his friends and countrymen.

Evening Events

Evening performances require a separate $12 ticket ($6 for annual pass holders). Check *This Week* for specific dates, times, and locations during the week you are visiting. As we noted earlier, programming changes frequently, so selections may be different during the time you are in town.

African-American Music—Through a combination of observed and participatory experiences, guests will have the opportunity to explore the diverse nature of African-American musical culture in colonial Virginia. Weather permitting.

Cry Witch—One of the most enduring of Colonial Williamsburg's programs, this is a highly enjoyable presentation of an early-18th-century witch trial, but it is not suitable for young children. Audience members may question the witnesses, weigh the evidence, and determine the guilt or innocence of the "Virginia witch," Grace Sherwood, who was tried for witchcraft in 1706. The location of this program sometimes varies, but it is typically held at the Capitol.

Dance, Our Dearest Diversion—"Virginians will dance or die" wrote an 18th-century diarist. What better time than the 21st century to learn a few new dance steps in the candlelit Capitol? The Hall of the House of Burgesses comes to life as guests experience one of the most favorite pastimes of colonial Virginians during this audience participatory program. The dancers discuss various types of 18th-century dances, from country dances to minuets, and demonstrate them for the audience. At various intervals throughout the program, the audience members will be asked to participate in the fun.

18th-Century Play Series: Polly Honeycombe—Young Polly is looking for a man to sweep her off her feet in the dashing, heroic fashion of the romance novels she reads. Polly finds such a man in Scribble, a poor, aspiring writer, but her father has arranged a sensible and profitable marriage to Mr. Ledger, a dull broker. Enacting scenes of excitement, adventure and intrigue found in her beloved books, Polly tries to outwit her practical father and her distracted mother with the help of her trusted nurse. Guests are sure to be entertained by this classic farce of mistaken identities and surprise revelations.

A Grand Medley of Entertainments—This 18th-century "variety show," a forerunner of modern circuses and vaudeville, includes music, magic, feats of strength, and other amusements guaranteed to please audiences young and old.

Listen My Children: Legends, Myths, and Fables for Families—This 45-minute gathering offers fun and interesting stories the whole family will enjoy. Storytellers share their tales by firelight as young and old hear some of the same legends that entertained families of centuries past.

Papa Said, Mama Said—Through this interactive program, guests explore the significance of stories passed down from their elders.

Other Programs and Events

THE COLONIAL WILLIAMSBURG FIFES & DRUMS

Beating drums or trilling fifes, this colorful group makes regular marches down Duke of Gloucester Street throughout much of the year. On various dates, visitors can enjoy the 18th-century ceremony of reveille in the morning at Market Square Green. In the early evening the corps does its retreat, a time when pickets are posted, flags lowered, and the soldiers relieved of their daily duties. All told, the corps performs in and around Colonial Williamsburg nearly 500 times during the year, in daily programs from April through October and during special programs on major holidays. In the spring and summer, the corps usually marches at 5 p.m. on Wed and 1 p.m. on Sat, weather permitting.

Founded in 1958, the corps traditionally has been made up of boys ages 10 through 18. In 1999 the Colonial Williamsburg Foundation opened the corps to female applicants for the first time. Typically, applicants for this extremely popular program are placed on a waiting list around age 5 and must participate in the required training before they can become active members of the corps. Nearly 100 youths perform as members of the corps' two units: a junior corps and a senior corps. Over the years the corps has served as Colonial Williamsburg's musical ambassadors across the nation, performing at Macy's Thanksgiving Day Parade in New York, the Pentagon in Washington, D.C., Independence Hall in Philadelphia, and the Art Institute of Chicago.

For specific Colonial Williamsburg Fifes & Drums performance times during your visit, consult *Colonial Williamsburg This Week,* the free program guide available at Colonial Williamsburg ticket offices and many other places around town.

i Over the last six decades, many of our nation's leaders have strolled down CW streets. Whether you know it or not, you are following in the footsteps of Presidents Franklin Roosevelt, Harry Truman, Dwight Eisenhower, Lyndon Johnson, Richard Nixon, Gerald Ford, Jimmy Carter, Ronald Reagan, and Bill Clinton.

Annual Events

There are a number of celebrations that take place in the restored area throughout the year.

Perhaps the most well known—and certainly the most spectacular—is the Grand Illumination, which marks the beginning of the Christmas holiday season in Colonial Williamsburg. This decades-old tradition attracts thousands of revelers to the Historic Area the first Sunday of December to hear the cannon sound, see the thousands of candles that illuminate the windows in public buildings, and view the colorful explosion of fireworks. Other annual events include a February Colonial Williamsburg Antiques Forum; a Garden Symposium each April; Memorial Day ceremonies; Independence Day festivities with fireworks on July 4; and military reenactments held at various times throughout the year. For a complete and detailed rundown of these events and other yearly festivals and celebrations, please turn to our chapter on Annual Events.

More History

Churches

BRUTON PARISH CHURCH
Duke of Gloucester St., Williamsburg
(757) 229-2891
www.brutonparish.org
If not for Bruton Parish Church, there might be no restored Colonial Williamsburg, as it was this historic church's rector, Dr. W. A. R. Goodwin, who persuaded John D. Rockefeller to commit his attention and his millions to bringing the forgotten capital back to life. Goodwin's church, in use since 1715, is one of America's oldest Episcopal churches with a rich history of its own. Its architectural features include the 1769 tower; high box pews dedicated to Presidents Washington, Jefferson, Monroe, and Tyler, all of whom worshipped here; and a bronze lectern donated by Theodore Roosevelt. Fully restored in 1940, the church also boasts original walls and windows and a stone baptismal font said to have come from an earlier Jamestown church. The churchyard holds hundreds of 18th-century graves. Church tours are offered from 9 a.m. to 5 p.m. Mon to Sat. No admission is charged for church tours, but donations are welcome. Bruton Parish holds services every Sunday, with noonday

prayers on Monday. It also is a popular venue for choral concerts and small chamber ensembles. The **Bruton Parish Book & Gift Shop** (757) 220-1489, also is on Duke of Gloucester Street. Open 10 a.m. to 5 p.m. Mon through Sat and 1 to 5 p.m. Sun, it stocks not only religious books but also jewelry, stuffed animals, and other gifts.

THE FIRST BAPTIST CHURCH
727 West Scotland St., Williamsburg
(757) 229-1952
One of the earliest Baptist congregations in the country, it is more importantly one of the first African-American churches in America, organized in 1776. Blacks had been allowed to worship in Bruton Parish Church, where they were seated in the North Gallery. Because they were not included in the worship service, they left the parish and built Brush Harbor on the Greensprings Plantation west of town, where they worshipped early in the morning, late at night, and sometimes in secret. This site was remote from the city, so they built a second Brush Harbor at Raccoon Chase, nearer Williamsburg, and sought spiritual fellowship there. A resident of Williamsburg, Jesse Coles, heard of these communities and made his carriage house available to blacks in the city. The group that met there organized in 1776 as the First Baptist Church. The church applied for admission into the Dover Association in 1791 and was accepted two years later.

For more than a century, the congregation worshipped in a brick church building built in 1855 on Nassau Street, now gone. In 1956, the congregation moved into its present structure at 727 West Scotland St. In the lower level of this church is a fascinating display tracing the history of this important congregation; furnishings of the earlier church are used in various parts of the current edifice. Worship service at First Baptist is at 11 a.m. Sun.

HICKORY NECK EPISCOPAL CHURCH
8300 Richmond Rd., Toano
(757) 566-0276
www.hickoryneck.org
The Virginia landscape is dotted with small brick churches dating from the colonial period, many

associated with plantations, others with small communities that vanished in the ensuing years. One worship site of historic interest is Hickory Neck Church on the western side of Toano. The edifice was built about 1740 and continues to be the worship place of an active Episcopal parish. On April 21, 1781, it housed militia opposing the British army. Later that year the militiamen fought in the siege of Yorktown. Standing with your back to busy US 60, it is still possible here to glimpse a vista without 21st-century encroachments. If you're interested in attending worship services, they are held at 8, 9, and 11:15 a.m. on Sun. Although there are no official tours, the church is always open.

i On Easter Sunday a consortium of religious leaders representing various faiths leads a "sunrise service," usually beginning at 7 a.m., at the historic cross on Jamestown Island. Check the religion pages of the *Virginia Gazette* to get specifics each Easter.

Plantations

While Virginia's Historic Triangle offers visitors plenty to see and do, it also provides easy access to myriad attractions just a short drive outside the immediate Williamsburg area. Of particular interest to history and architecture buffs are the historic James River plantations in James City and Charles City Counties. For many whose vision of the south has been shaped by *Gone with the Wind*, these structures will be a surprise. Predating the era of Greek Revival columns and other such adornments, the refined Georgian architecture of the buildings, executed in rich redbrick or in white wood, is understated and takes its elegance from simplicity and tasteful detail. These were among the first mansions in the country, and their history is, in a sense, ours. These magnificent estates are located along the James River because that was the area's main artery when they were built. Luckily, many are open to the public. In cases where the houses are not open, visitors usually are welcome to tour the grounds. The trip on Route 5 from Williamsburg to Richmond to visit the plantations is gorgeous, passing through thick, overarching forests and wide open farmlands. It was colonial Virginia's premier land route and remains a favorite route west, especially in autumn.

There is a Progressive Plantation Tour for groups, which includes guided tours of the grounds and houses at Piney Grove, North Bend, Edgewood, and sometimes other plantations. (Westover only offers home tours twice a year.) Give them plenty of advance notice and you might just be treated to homemade cookies and lemonade. For more details on the Progressive Tour, call (804) 829-2480.

BELLE AIRE PLANTATION
11800 John Tyler Hwy
(Route 5), Charles City County
(804) 829-2431
Just off Virginia's scenic byway, Route 5, east of the Charles City County courthouse complex, this charming and deceptively large mid-17th-century frame house—the only one known to still stand in the Commonwealth—was built around 1670. While it was open to the public for many years, unfortunately today it is not, though the owners do open their doors to group tours of 20 or more, provided they make reservations well in advance. There is an admission fee. The tour includes a peek at four first-floor rooms, three upstairs bedchambers, and the grounds. (Belle Aire also is open during Historic Garden Week, near the end of April each year.) Call for group rates.

BERKELEY PLANTATION
12602 Harrison Landing Rd.,
off Route 5, Charles City
(804) 829-6018, (888) 466-6018
www.berkeleyplantation.com
This was the site of the first official Thanksgiving in North America, celebrated by English settlers on December 4, 1619. It is on Route 5, halfway between Williamsburg and Richmond. Berkeley is one of Virginia's most historic plantations, as it was the birthplace of Benjamin Harrison, a signer

of the Declaration of Independence, and his third son, William Henry Harrison, who was the ninth president of the United States. The plantation was patented in 1618, and the stately Georgian mansion, overlooking the James River, was built in 1726 of brick fired on the site. It is said to be the oldest three-story brick house in Virginia and the first with a pediment roof. The handsome Adam woodwork and double arches in the Great Rooms were installed by Benjamin Harrison VI in 1790 at the direction of Thomas Jefferson. The rooms in the house are furnished with period antiques. As you approach the site along Route 5 in Charles City County, you'll have to follow a sharp curve onto a side road that leads to the plantation drive.

Two tidbits of Berkeley history deserve particular attention. "Taps" was composed here by U.S. General Daniel Butterfield in 1862 during the Civil War while Union troops were encamped on the site. And the first bourbon whiskey in America was distilled here in 1621. Allow about 90 minutes for your visit.

The plantation is open daily from 9 a.m. to 4:30 p.m. (off-season 10:30 a.m. to 3:30 p.m.; closed Thanksgiving and Christmas day). Tickets for a garden and house tour cost $11 for adults, $7.50 for students ages 13 to 16, and $6 for children ages 6 to 12. Discounted tickets are offered for senior citizens, military, and AAA members.

EDGEWOOD PLANTATION
4800 John Tyler Hwy.
(Route 5), Charles City County
(804) 829-2962
www.edgewoodplantation.com
You will enjoy the section of the historic plantation trail (Route 5 west from Williamsburg) that leads through forests past this superb Gothic Revival house (ca. 1849) in Charles City County. With only a minimum of imagination, you might envision Edgar Allan Poe passing in a carriage in the other direction. (Indeed, the house is reputed to have a ghost in residence!) In a countryside filled with the formalities of Georgian and Colonial Revival architecture, this is a truly refreshing structure. Today the plantation is operated as an opulent bed-and-breakfast inn, which we have profiled in our Bed-and-Breakfasts and Guest Homes chapter. Even if you choose not to go in, you will see it clearly from the highway.

Edgewood arranges group tours with advance notice of at least a week or two. Luncheon and candlelight tours are the most popular. Check the home's Web site for details.

NORTH BEND PLANTATION
12200 Weyanoke Rd.
Charles City County
(804) 829-5176
www.northbendplantation.com
The original plantation house was built in 1819 for Sarah Harrison, the wife of wealthy landowner John Minge and a sister to William Henry Harrison, our ninth president. In 1853 the house was doubled in size, and a total renovation was completed in 1982 by the Copland family, descendants of noted agriculturist Edmund Ruffin and current owners of the house. Even after all the changes, North Bend's main house survives as the best-preserved example of the academic Greek Revival style of architecture in Charles City County. Of special historic note is the plantation's 1864 occupancy by General Phillip Sheridan and his 30,000 Union troops.

Today, the plantation operates as a bed-and-breakfast (see our chapter on Bed-and-Breakfasts for lodging information). Day and evening tours for groups of 10 or more are offered by appointment. If you just happen to be in the neighborhood, the 500-acre grounds are open daily from 9 a.m. to 5 p.m. for a self-guided tour. To begin your tour, simply stop in at the grounds kiosk and pick up a bright yellow brochure. Points of interest include the smokehouse and dairy house, both built around 1819, a slave quarters, and the site of the 1853 cookhouse. The tour ends just outside the house, where tables and chairs have been set up to give visitors an opportunity to sit awhile and take in the view. North Bend is about 25 minutes west of Williamsburg. To reach the plantation, take Route 5 to Highway 619, then travel about 1 mile to Weyanoke Road.

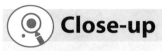 **Close-up**

Presidents Park

Know the names of all the U.S. presidents, but not their faces? Presidents Park, which opened in 2004, features much-larger-than-life busts of all 43 U.S. presidents. The "big heads," as they are affectionately known locally, are by sculptor David Adickes, whose work has been shown in art museums across the country and internationally.

Located across Route 199 from Water Country USA, the park's directors hope the indoor and outdoor exhibits here will complement Williamsburg's rich colonial history with lessons that begin with George Washington's inauguration in 1789 and bring visitors to modern times. Plaques adjacent to each bust, which range in height from 16 to 18 feet high, highlight facts about each president. The only president missing is Barack Obama. There is a small bust inside the museum and a replica of the Oval Office with cardboard cutouts of Barack and Michelle Obama behind the desk. Copies of some of Michelle Obama's stylish dresses, as well as the inauguration gowns of other first ladies, are also on display.

While the park is self-guided, tours on special topics such as the Constitution and Bill of Rights, religion, civil rights and slavery, and protecting the nation may be arranged for groups. The park also hosts special days for students who are home-schooled.

A museum building houses classrooms, meeting rooms, a gift shop, cafe, banquet room, and other amenities. Open daily, except Christmas and New Year's Day, from 10 a.m. The museum closes at 8 p.m. from Apr through Aug and at 4 p.m. from Sept through Mar. Admission is $9.75 for adults, $8.75 for seniors 55 and older and military, and $6.50 for children ages 6 to 17. Group tours are available. For more information, go to www.presidentspark.org, or call (800) 588-4327.

PINEY GROVE AT SOUTHALL'S PLANTATION
16920 Southall Plantation Lane
Charles City County
(804) 829-2480
www.pineygrove.com

Piney Grove was built around the year 1800 on the 300-acre Southall's Plantation, a property that was first occupied by the Chickahominy Indians, and survives as the oldest and best-preserved example of log architecture in southeastern Virginia. In recent years Piney Grove, 8 miles north of Route 5 on Route 623 (which eventually becomes Route 615), has served the public as a beautifully appointed bed-and-breakfast inn. In 1994 the owners introduced a self-guided tour of the plantation grounds, which takes visitors along a splendid nature trail that begins beneath a century-old cedar, meanders around a swimming hole and past a gazebo, and then winds along the edge of a ravine where the trail is canopied by beech, hickory, and white oak trees. A short path leads down into the ravine to Piney Springs, where constantly flowing water eventually funnels into the Chickahominy River. Past the ravine the trail skirts a horse corral and pasture, offering a scenic view of Piney Grove, as well as a view of Moss Side Barn, once part of Southall's Plantation. The trail ends at Glebe Lane, originally called "The Old Main Road from Barret's Ferry to Charles City Court House."

A self-guided grounds tour is offered daily from 9 a.m. to 5 p.m. for a small donation. Guided tours are offered for groups only, with advance reservation. To find out more about Piney Grove's operations as a bed-and-breakfast inn, consult our Bed-and-Breakfasts chapter.

SHERWOOD FOREST PLANTATION
14501 John Tyler Hwy. (Route 5)
Charles City County
(804) 829-5377
www.sherwoodforest.org
Without a doubt, this is one of the loveliest homesteads in this part of Virginia. Sherwood Forest Plantation was the home of President John Tyler. It is about a 30-minute drive west of Williamsburg. Considered the longest frame house in America, it measures 300 feet along its front facade. Built about 1730, the original structure was altered and renovated by President Tyler in 1844. The house today looks very much like it did when Tyler retired here from the White House in 1845. He brought with him his new bride, Julia Gardiner of Gardiner's Island, New York. Since then, the plantation has been continuously occupied by members of the Tyler family and has been a working plantation for more than 240 years.

The house features a private ballroom 68 feet in length and is furnished with an extensive collection of 18th- and 19th-century family heirlooms. President Tyler's china, porcelain, silver, mirrors, tables, chairs, and other furnishings are still in use here. In the library are the books of Governor Tyler (President Tyler's father), John Tyler, and his son, Dr. Lyon Gardiner Tyler, who served as president of the College of William and Mary.

The grounds are open daily, except Thanksgiving and Christmas, from 9 a.m. until 5 p.m. House tours are by reservation only. Tours of the grounds are $10. Senior citizen, military, and AAA discounts are offered.

SHIRLEY PLANTATION
501 Shirley Plantation Rd.
Charles City County
(804) 829-5121, (800) 232-1613
www.shirleyplantation.com
This fine plantation, off Route 5 on the banks of the James River about 35 miles from Williamsburg, is perhaps the most famous of Virginia's plantations. Designated a National Historic Landmark, Shirley was founded in 1613 and granted to Edward Hill in 1660. The present mansion house was begun in 1723 by the third Edward Hill, a member of the House of Burgesses in the Virginia Colony, for his daughter Elizabeth, who married John Carter, son of King Carter. It was finished in 1738 and is largely in its original state.

The house is a recognized architectural treasure. Its famous walnut-railed staircase rises three stories without visible means of support and is the only one of its kind in America. The mansion is filled with family portraits, furniture, crested silver, and other family heirlooms. George Washington, Thomas Jefferson, John Tyler, Teddy Roosevelt, and John Rockefeller were all guests at Shirley. Robert E. Lee's mother, Anne Hill Carter, was married to "Light Horse" Harry Lee in the parlor.

The house opens at 9:30 a.m. daily, except Thanksgiving and Christmas, and the last tour begins promptly at 4:30 p.m. The grounds remain open until 6 p.m. or sunset, whichever comes first. Admission is $11 for adults, $7.50 for ages 6 to 18. Seniors, military, and AAA members are offered discounts. Children younger than 6 get in free.

WESTOVER PLANTATION
7000 Westover Rd.
Charles City County
(804) 829-2882
www.jamesriverplantations.org/westover
During the colonial period, this exquisite plantation was the property of William Byrd, who owned extensive properties that stretched for many miles in each direction. Off Route 5 in Charles City County, it is adjacent to Berkeley Plantation. Situated on the banks of the James River, this palatial early Georgian house is sometimes described as the most elegant Georgian structure in the United States. The plantation features an outstanding Georgian boxwood garden and 150-year-old giant tulip poplars. William Byrd's tomb is also on the property. The gardens and grounds are open to visitors from 9 a.m. to 6 p.m. daily, but the house is not open to the public. The plantation house is open twice a year for tours, including the Garden Club of Virginia's Historic Garden Week, held in late April each year.

MODERN ATTRACTIONS

Even the most studious kid's patience might be tested by day after day of museums, historical exhibits, plantation visits, and peering into old churches? Adult's, too! Fortunately, there are many other ways to pass the days in Williamsburg, some perfect for kids and their adult chaperones. And after the roller coasters and the waterslides, we round out the chapter with tours better suited for just the grown-ups.

AMUSEMENT PARKS

BUSCH GARDENS
One Busch Gardens Blvd.
(Off I-64 at exit 243A)
(757) 253-3369, (800) 343-7946
www.buschgardens.com/va
When Busch Gardens opened in the mid-1970s, it was a secondary diversion: Tourists would come to Williamsburg for the history, then spend a day or so at the theme park.

Today, it's the opposite—more than three million visitors a year pass through the turnstiles at Busch Gardens, many making a special trip *just* for its renowned roller coasters. They may, or may not, take in some of the history while they're here.

Located on US Route 60 three miles east of Williamsburg, Busch Gardens turns 35 in 2010. In that time, it has carved a reputation for beauty— its 350-plus acres set among hills, trees, and streams has been voted "Most Beautiful Theme Park" by the National Amusement Park Historical Association for 20 years running—and also thrills. Among its 50 rides are five major roller coasters (six if you count a kiddie coaster)—two of which have opened since 2005. The park also relaunched its children's ride area in 2009, built around Sesame Street characters.

Increasingly, Busch Gardens is using special events to encourage repeat visitors or attract those who might not otherwise come to the park. Starting in the mid-2000s, the park began offering weekend concert series featuring music acts from the' 60s through the '80s. Added to that in 2010 are a contemporary Christian music series, and the ASA Action Sports World Tour, featuring three weekends of competition in skateboarding, BMX bicycling, and in-line skating.

The other major change for the park: New ownership. As part of the 2009 takeover of Anheuser-Busch by the Belgian beer conglomerate InBev, the Busch Entertainment theme parks division—including Busch Gardens Williamsburg and nearby Water Country USA—was sold to the Blackstone Group private-equity firm. Blackstone now owns 10 theme parks under the SeaWorld Parks & Entertainment corporate name.

For all the changes, however, Busch Gardens remains at its core a theme park—one built around the notion that you're traveling throughout 17th-century Europe. We'll use that as a convenient way to organize the description of the park.

Getting There

The park opens for the season in late March— mostly weekends only, but some daily operation around Easter to catch spring breakers and school vacations. From Memorial Day through Labor Day, it operates daily. In September and October, it's back to weekend-only operations for the Howl-O-Scream season. Starting in 2009, the park added a holiday-season schedule, Christmas Town, weekends only from Thanksgiving through mid-September, then daily through the school holidays.

Opening times are staggered, from 9:15 a.m. at Sesame Street Forest to as late as 10 a.m. for most of the park. Closing times vary, from as early as 8 p.m. early in the season to as late as 11 p.m. some holiday weekends. The park's Web site has an updated calendar for each day of the season, including schedules of different entertainment shows and special events.

Getting to Busch Gardens is easy: Take I-64 to the Busch Gardens exit (exit 243A). The exit leads directly to the park entrance. If you're coming from the Historic Area or the western part of the Williamsburg area, take US 60 south, past Kingsmill and the Budweiser brewery; the park entrance will be on your right. Parking is $12—

but the closest lots are reserved for season-pass holders, or for those who pay extra. Lots can fill up quickly; trams are used to shuttle people from the most-distant ones.

Single-day tickets are $61.95, or $51.95 for children aged 3 to 9—but any number of discount programs are available: active-duty military discounts, multi-day ticket packages, combo tickets with sister park Water Country USA, and season passes. Check the Web site for details; also look on Internet search engines for Busch Gardens discounts. Tickets get you unlimited rides, admission to the park's regular show lineup, in-park transportation, and other entertainment, but fees may be charged for arcade games, carnival games, and certain special events. The admission price does not include food and drink.

Getting Around Inside

The park sprawls over 350 acres and has a number of significant hills that surround its central waterway, the Rhine River (actually a pond formed by a dam across a branch of Grove Creek). The park's main entrance places you at England—roughly at 5 o'clock if you imagine the park as the face of a clock. Continuing clockwise, you pass through Italy, Germany, France, Ireland, and Scotland.

A variety of paved walkways and bridges link the different sections of the park—but the hills can be a killer, especially after a long, hot day or when you have a group of kids in tow. The park's internal transportation systems can be a savior at those times.

The Aeronaut Skyride's triangular route connects England to France to Germany and back on aerial cars. They offer terrific views of the park and surrounding woods. Three steam locomotives circle the park clockwise, with stops at Scotland, Italy, and France.

Still, plan to do plenty of walking, wear sensible shoes, and grab a park map on your way in. Strollers and wheelchairs (including electric wheelchairs) can be rented near the ticket booths, but the numbers are limited.

The Big Thrills

The major rides at Busch Gardens include:

Alpengeist—A floorless steel roller coaster that hurtles passengers (and their lunches) at nearly 70 mph. Located in Germany.

Apollo's Chariot—The tall, humpbacked coaster you see from the interstate, Apollo's Chariot has the biggest drop (210 feet) and fastest speeds (73 mph) of Busch Garden's coasters. In Italy.

The Battering Ram—A swooping pendulum ride. In Italy.

Curse of DarKastle—A sleigh ride through the interior of a mysterious castle. In Germany.

Da Vinci's Cradle—A stomach-lurching—yet flat—midway ride. In Italy.

Escape from Pompeii—One part boat ride, one part volcanic eruption. In Italy.

Europe in the Air—New in 2010, this simulator "flies" guests over the continent's major landmarks. In Ireland.

Griffon—Opened in 2007 to rave reviews. Imagine falling 200 feet straight down. At 70 mph. With nothing beneath your feet but the sky. That's the *start*. In France.

Le Scoot—A log flume. In France.

Loch Ness Monster—The park's oldest coaster, dating to 1978, features interlocking loops and a long, dark helix tunnel. In Scotland, where else?

Roman Rapids—A gentle, serene raft ride—for at least 10 feet. Then it's neither gentle nor serene. Bring a towel. In Italy.

The Countries

Busch Gardens groups its attractions into six "countries," each occupying its own portion of the park. They needn't be explored in any particular order (in fact, many park regulars have their own definite—and often contradictory—opinions on the "best" way to maximize fun and avoid crowds).

Each of the nations has various dining and shopping options, some (but not all) themed to the cuisine and wares of that country. For convenience, we'll take them clockwise from the main entrance.

England

This area, just inside the park's main entrance, is designed to evoke an English village. It's home to a Big Ben–like clock tower (it makes for a great meeting place if your party plans to split up) and a replica of Shakespeare's Globe Theatre. The show, new as of early 2010, is "Sesame Street Presents Lights, Camera, Imagination!" featuring Elmo, Cookie Monster, and Big Bird.

To the left is "Sesame Street: Forest of Fun," a collection of many of the park's "Kid-siderate" child rides. Among them: Grover's Alpine Express (a kid-friendly roller coaster), Bert and Ernie's Loch Adventure (a miniature log flume), and wet and dry play areas.

Italy

This village is dominated by two thrill rides— Escape from Pompeii and Apollo's Chariot.

Think of Escape from Pompeii as a boat ride to the edge of Hades. What starts as a pleasant, gentle float becomes a simulated trip through a volcano, complete with bursts of flame, ending with a long, flume-like drop. (Stand back: Spectators usually end up wetter than the riders.)

Apollo's Chariot is one of the park's signature coasters—a hypercoaster to aficionados, with a height of 170 feet, and a 210-foot drop. (How? Those hills—it takes advantage of a small valley. Not that you'll be able to tell as you top out at 73 mph.)

Between them are a set of rides intended as an homage to Leonard da Vinci, plus a handful of the Kid-siderate children's rides.

Also in Italy: Roman Rapids, a raft expedition that sends riders swirling past ruins, through fog, and down the rapids. Obey the warnings on this one: You'll get wet. That doesn't mean you *might* get wet, or *could* get splashed. You'll be doused, then soaked. Leave the phone with someone for safekeeping, OK?

Germany

Clockwise from Italy, across a long footbridge, is Germany. It's home to the park's excellent bumper-car arena ("Das Autobahn"), kid's airplane ride ("Der Red Baron"), a lovely restored antique carousel ("Kinder Karussel"), and the large Festhaus dining area and Oktoberfest show hall.

The two thrill rides here are Curse of DarKastle and Alpengeist. DarKastle simulates a sleigh ride through a mountain castle—one that just might be haunted. Music, 3-D visuals, and other special effects heighten the frights.

If DarKastle is about simulating fear, Alpengeist generates it for real—it shows up on many Top 10 lists for steel roller coasters. Imagine a ski lift gone horribly wrong. Your feet dangle in midair as the coaster twists you through six inversions at speeds up to 67 mph.

Where's the Wolf?

Frequent visitors may wonder about the Big Bad Wolf, an aggressive steel coaster that featured a 99-foot drop toward the surface of the Rhine waterway. Alas, it closed at the end of the 2009 summer season. After 25 years of operation, it had reached the end of its designed service life. Rather than refurbish the ride, park management choose to retire it. No word yet on what will replace it.

France

At the "top" of the park's imagined clock face, France has the requisite log flume ("Le Scoot"), the Trappers Smokehouse dining area, and the Royal Palace Theater, home to the weekend summer concert series.

It also has the park's newest thriller, a dive-style roller coaster called Griffon that opened in 2007. It's named for the mythical beast (half eagle, half lion), and the weak-stomached might prefer to be eaten by a griffin rather than ride this one. You're hauled in a floorless car up 205 feet, dangled over a precipice—then dropped, straight down (it takes almost four seconds). Before your stomach can catch up, you're yanked up into an inverted Immelmann loop (named after a WWI German fighter pilot). Not enough? You do it *again* on a smaller (130-foot) drop into a second Immelmann before scrubbing off the speed in a shallow splash pool. Best not to do this one right after a big lunch.

Ireland

This newest village, at roughly 2 o'clock on the clockface, features most of the park's wildlife shows. Jack Hanna's Wild Reserve features Wolf Valley, home to a small pack of grey wolves; the Eagle Ridge preserve for injured bald eagles; and other animals in the Conservation Station.

Ireland also is the site of the park's newest motion ride, Europe in the Air, which opened in 2010 and simulates a low, diving aerial ride over landmarks like Stonehenge, a German castle, and the European landscape.

Also new, in the Abbey Stone Theatre: an Irish-themed live show, featuring Celtic musicians, singers, and dancing.

Scotland

The faux-Scottish village occupies the rough center of the park. There's nothing faux about the wildlife here, though. The exhibit features a variety of Scottish animals—border collies, blackface sheep, and majestic Clydesdale horses.

Also wild in Scotland: the Loch Ness Monster coaster. In some ways, it's tame compared to its cousins elsewhere in the park—it *only* reaches 60 mph and drops 100 feet. But it's a sentimental favorite for many aficionados—it opened in 1978, and was the first coaster in the world with interlocking loops.

WATER PARKS

WATER COUNTRY USA
176 Water Country Parkway
(800) 343-7946
www.watercountryusa.com

i Busch Gardens is a big park, and its staff doesn't page for lost persons. Your best bet is to prearrange a central meeting place should members of your party get separated. Some suggestions: the Big Ben clock in England, in front of Das Festhaus in Germany, or in front of the Royal Palace Theatre in France.

This wild and wet place to cool off during Virginia's mostly muggy summers sits on 40 acres of wooded land three miles east of Colonial Williamsburg on Route 199. The largest water theme park in Virginia, Water Country now offers more than a dozen water rides as well as a pool, sunbathing, live shows, a variety of restaurants, arcades, and, of course, bathhouse facilities.

The theme at Water Country is 1950s and '60s cool. Like Busch Gardens, this is a beautifully maintained facility, landscaped with palms, ornamental grasses, pines, and bold, bright flowers like hibiscus, hot pink geraniums, and blazing yellow marigolds. Bare feet abound, but swim shoes or waterproof sandals will protect from hot pavement and stubbed toes. If you don't want to wear shoes on some of the rides, there are "sneaker keepers" at the base of many attractions. Some strollers, shaped like dolphins, of course, are available near the main concession area.

This family-friendly place boasts rides suited to all ages and all levels of swimming ability. Pools and rides are temperature-controlled, a feature especially helpful for early-season splashing. And while thrills are the main business of this attraction, relaxation hasn't been forgotten. Beach bums can catch a wave at Surfers' Bay, then grab a few rays on the four-tiered sundeck. Parents can sit on deck chairs while the kids splash around in the supervised play area. All ages will appreciate "Aquabatics!" a dive show featuring acrobats and rhythmic gymnasts at the Caban-A-Rama Theater. And visitors who are a tad anxious about all that water will be pleased to know Water Country USA has been rated among America's safest theme parks by Barclay & Associates, an independent risk-management firm.

Getting Inside

Water Country USA opens in mid-May and closes in early September. From mid-June through mid-August hours generally are 10 a.m. to 8 p.m., although the park typically closes at 6 p.m. both earlier and later in the season and at 7 p.m. in late August. On hot summer days we like to start early to get in as much water action as we can before the park gets really packed.

To reach the park from I-64, take exit 243A and follow Route 199 for a quarter-mile to the entrance. Parking is $12, although free parking is included in some of the special passes—the 1-Park pass which offers unlimited season-long admission, for instance, costs $99.95, but parking is included.

One-day admission is $42.95 for adults, $35.95 for children ages three to nine. Children two and younger enter free.

If you plan on also touring Busch Gardens, a better value is the 2-Park Discovery Ticket which provides unlimited admission to both parks for seven consecutive days from the first day of use for $79.95. There are more options if you're going to be in the area for a while. Check the Web site for detailed information.

Unless a member of your group is staying dry for the whole day, you should consider renting a locker for your valuables (cash, car keys, identification) and dry clothes for the ride home. Leave as much as possible in your car but if you must carry cash with you, your best bet is to store it in one of those plastic cylinders that hangs from a cord around the neck. If you're like us and can't get by without sunglasses, they, too, should be worn on some type of head-hugging cord. One last word of advice: Take towels with you, and park them on lawn chairs at Surfers' Bay or one of the children's play areas. That way you'll have a home base to return to when you just want to sit awhile or test the waters in the wave pool.

The park has a fairly large supply of free life vests for nonswimmers and small children. Because you can find them on racks throughout the park, many people pick them up and drop them off as needed. We have found that after 2 p.m. it's hard to locate one of the smaller children's vests—it might be a good idea to hold on to one for your entire visit. Plastic swim diapers, required throughout the park, can also be purchased.

i When lightning strikes—hang on to your ticket! Water Country USA prides itself on its safety record, one element of which is closing all water rides if lightning is seen in the area. The park may re-open within as little as 30 minutes if the clouds pass quickly, but if the park closes, you can use your ticket to gain entry another day.

Water Attractions

Now that you've stashed your valuables and suited up, it's time for the main event. What follows are individual descriptions of each of the water rides and play areas.

Aquazoid

If you like special effects, you'll love this 864-foot ride. Named for a 1950s mutant movie monster, Aquazoid's big black tubes have enough space for a family of four to pile in together and zip through curtains of water into a pitch-dark tunnel before splashing through yet another curtain of water at the speed of 11 feet per second. On your journey your senses will be assaulted by beams of light and howling sound effects as you escape from the Aquazoid's lair and plunge 78 feet into a splash pool.

Big Daddy Falls

Get the whole family together and climb into a humongous inner tube for a wet and wild river-rafting adventure. This 670-foot water ride splashes through twists and turns, slips into a dark tunnel, then plunges into a slow-moving river alive with waterfalls before racing around the bend to a final splashdown. (The first time we tried this ride we thought the waterfall effect was a little overdone until we realized it had started to rain buckets as we slid through the tunnel.)

Cow-A-Bunga

This children's play area features a 4,500-square-foot heated pool, an interactive speedboat with a water-skiing cow (what "udder" silliness), a curving water flume, a short but slick triple slide, and several fountains. There is plenty of deck seating for parents who want to watch the action from the sidelines.

H2O UFO

The park's newest and largest interactive children's play area has a sci-fi theme and features a fun combination of slides and spray jets. There's even a fairly long, scaled-down waterslide for kids (and their parents) who aren't quite ready to take a walk on the wilder side. Park your gear on one of the many lawn chairs and make a splash.

Hubba Hubba Highway

Covering 3.5 acres, Hubba Hubba Highway features a winding jet stream with a 2,000-square-foot lagoon entrance.

Jet Scream

Everybody loves flume rides, and Water Country USA's is one of the longest and most exciting in the nation at 415 feet. Start 50 feet off the ground and streak down one of four twisting waterslides at 25 mph into a splashdown pool.

Kritter Koral

Splash fun for the tiniest of tots, complete with scaled-down waterslides, play equipment, and fountains. A word to tweens and teens who want to relive their youth—the lifeguards will shoo you out of there immediately to keep the pool safe for the little ones.

Malibu Pipeline

A twisting, two-person tube ride through enclosed double flumes, complete with strobe lighting, waterfalls, and a splash pool at the bottom.

Meltdown

This attraction is the fastest and steepest of all Water Country USA rides. This zoom-flume carries four people at a time along its icy waters.

Grab three of your closest friends, get in the surf 'boggan raft, and you are ready for a high-speed glide through 180-degree turns. It will only take you 35 seconds to travel 701 feet, thanks to the 76-foot vertical drop. That's averaging about 22 feet per second!

Nitro Racer

If you like a little competition with your fun, this super-fast, slippery drag race is for you. After climbing to the top, six contestants (a great opportunity to grab bragging rights in a big family) race down a 320-foot-long slide to see who can reach the finish line first. Prepare your little ones before the drop: Big guys definitely have the advantage on Nitro!

Rampage

Grab your surf 'boggan, and speed down 75 feet of steep, slick Teflon slide. Then shoot across the long landing pool, and try to catch your breath. This is one of the shortest and perhaps scariest rides in the park. The view from the top is not for those who suffer from vertigo.

Rock 'n' Roll Island's Jammin' Jukebox

This slide tower is situated in the park's newest area, Rock 'n' Roll Island, featuring music from the 1950s and '60s. Three body slides, The Twist, The Hully Gully, and The Funky Chicken, shoot from the top of this 33-foot-tall slide tower. In addition, there are nearly 600 feet of twisting and turning tubes, and a 700-foot "lazy river" surrounds the 9,000-square foot pool.

Surfers' Bay

This is Virginia's largest wave pool, though it seems more like an ocean with its 650,000 gallons of water. Periods of mechanically produced 4-foot waves alternate with times of smooth surf for relaxation. Want to really chill out?

Stretch out in one of more than 1,000 lounge chairs on the wood sundeck surrounding the bay. Or, if you're looking for a little shelter from the elements, head for one of the bright canopied cabanas found poolside. Grab your seats early as they go fast.

Wild Thang

Take another walk on the wild side—with a companion—on this popular 500-foot-long double inner-tube ride past jungle scenes, under waterfalls, and through tunnels before splashing down.

Extras

Caban-A-Rama Theatre

This is your site for daily shows. "Aquabatics," a combination high-dive and gymnastics show, brings some of the world's best athletes to the park. The dives made from an 85-foot tower into a small, 11-foot-deep pool are truly breathtaking. Schedules are posted at the theater's entrance.

Dining

There are seven eateries offering hot dogs, smoked sausages, chicken, pizza, pretzels, subs, fries, funnel cakes, ice cream, lemonade, sports drinks, and beer. Snack bars are situated around the park and open for business as crowds dictate. Guests can eat at shaded outdoor tables, and a catering facility may be reserved in advance for groups of 20 or more. Food is pricey, lines can be long on the busiest days, and service can make kids, who just want to get back in line for another ride, fidgety. If you can, pack a picnic in a cooler and eat at the tables on grassy areas in the parking lot (no food or beverages may be brought into the park). The tables are on grassy median strips and most are shaded by umbrellas, so it's both a cheap and pleasant alternative. There's also a shaded pavilion for picnicking off to the right of the park entrance. Make sure to have your hand stamped at the gate so you can get back inside the park.

Shopping

Swimwear, gifts, souvenirs, sunglasses, and sunscreen are for sale at on-site surf and gift shops.

Safety Features

Water Country USA has an excellent reputation as a safe, fun place to enjoy water without hitting the beach. The park employs more than 80 certified lifeguards and stations supervisors at each ride and attraction. Lifeguards are trained in CPR, first aid, and accident prevention, and they participate in ongoing training programs and drills. Life vests and inner tubes are provided for free for anyone who would like one. Each year American Red Cross–certified volunteers offer swim lessons to area residents.

A first-aid station is open during all operating hours, paths are treated with salt to prevent falls, pool depths are clearly marked, and individual safety rules are posted at each ride. Children younger than eight must always be in the company of a parent or other adult. Bad weather? One component of safety policy is to close the park immediately if there is lightning. This combination of rules and features at Water Country USA set the standards for safety among the nation's water parks. Precisely because the park is so safety-conscious, visitors can truly relax and enjoy a wet and wild adventure.

WINES AND OTHER ADULT ATTRACTIONS

WILLIAMSBURG ALEWERKS
189-B Ewell Rd.
(757) 220-3670
www.williamsburgalewerks.com
Lovers of beer can be as passionate, even obsessive, as lovers of great wine or terrific restaurants. And for decades, beer lovers in Williamsburg were bereft of anything they could call their hometown beer. (Do not speak to this kind of beer lovers about that massive Budweiser plant at the south end of town—it's like recommending McDonald's to a foodie.)

Williamsburg Alewerks fixed that. Since it opened in 2006, it has produced small volumes of colonial-style ales, porters, and stouts to growing appreciation of craft-beer lovers.

In an era when seemingly every city and ski lodge in American has a microbrewery, the lack of one in Williamsburg struck managing partner Chuck Haines as an opportunity.

The quality of brewmaster Geoff Logan's beers quickly caught on locally. Now his six year-round brews and variety of seasonal and special reserve beers are available on tap at dozens of area bars and restaurants, and in bottles at grocery stores.

Production is modest compared to national brands—about 2,500 barrels per year, compared to as many as 9 million barrels per year at the Anheuser-Busch plant. But the quality of the microbrews, from a beer lover's perspective, is beyond comparison to the national brands. The Drake Tail India pale ale and Washington's Porter get particularly good reviews.

Hour-long tours are held daily (except Sun) at 3 p.m. For $5, adults 21 and over get a tour of the brewery, tastings of the current varieties in a souvenir glass—and education on the history of beer, both worldwide and in the American colonies. (People under 21 can take the tour for free—but, sorry, no tastings.)

You'll need to hunt for the Alewerks: Its retail shop is tucked just inside an industrial park, and the brewhouse itself is in an adjacent building. Both are off Mooretown Road on the northwest side of town. From the Historic Area, take US Route 60/Richmond Road north to Airport Road. Take a right on Airport Road, then a quick left onto Mooretown, and continue north to the first right, Ewell Road. The Alewerks is about a half-mile ahead on the right, near where Ewell circles back to Mooretown. From the north, take Route 199 to the Mooretown Road exit; continue south on Mooretown about three-quarters of a mile, then turn left on Ewell. The Alewerks will be immediately on your left.

If you're a beer lover (or are looking for a gift for one), it's worth the trip.

THE WILLIAMSBURG WINERY
5800 Wessex Hundred
(757) 229-0999
www.williamsburgwinery.com
A 320-acre farm owned by Patrick and Peggy Duffeler and known as the Wessex Hundred (the same name it had in colonial times) is the site of the state's largest winery (the Williamsburg Winery produces more than 60,000 cases a year). The first Chardonnay vines were planted in spring 1985. Two years later, the first wines were bottled. One of their very first wines, the 1988 Chardon-

nay, won the Virginia's Governor's Cup, the top prize in the prestigious Virginia wine competition. Today more than 50 acres are in cultivation.

Tours and Tastings

Guided tours begin in the retail store and lead to the 18th-century-style brick building that holds a banquet room, underground cellars, a bottling room, warehousing space, and offices. Tour guides explain the winemaking process and point out interesting objects associated with the winery, including pictures of a 17th-century skeleton found here during a dig and founder Patrick Duffeler's collection of more than 300 18th-century wine bottles dating as far back as 1710. Duffeler (who was born in Belgium, and organized car races before becoming a vintner) takes an approach to viticulture that combines traditional winemaking methods with modern technology. Currently the winery makes a number of different varietals aged in oak barrels you'll see lined up in the temperature-controlled cellar where the woody aroma of fermentation greets guests. Stainless-steel fermenters also are used here, mostly in the creation of blends.

By Virginia law, varietals—wines named after the grape from which they are produced—must contain at least 75 percent of that particular grape, such as the Chardonnay, Merlot, Cabernet Sauvignon, or Riesling. However, the Williamsburg Winery uses 100 percent varietal grape in its Chardonnays, including the John Adlum regular bottling; the Acte 12 Chardonnay, named for the Virginia House of Burgesses 1619 act calling for the planting of vines by settlers; a Vintage Reserve Chardonnay, entirely barrel-fermented; and Ratcliff Vineyard Chardonnay. An altogether different bottling, the Gabriel Archer Reserve, is a Bordeaux-style blend of Cabernet Franc, Cabernet Sauvignon, and Merlot. The winery also makes two Cabernet Sauvignons and a Cabernet Sauvignon Reserve, a Merlot and Merlot Reserve, and James River White, a blend of Chardonnay and Seyval. The Governor's White, a mix of Riesling and Vidal grapes, is the best-selling wine made in Virginia. Other blends include Two Shilling Red, a light-bodied blend of Ruby Cabernet and Merlot meant to be served lightly chilled, and Plantation Blush, made from Riesling and Seyval.

Since 1996 the company has released a half-dozen labels made at its Dominion Wine Cellars, a former wine cooperative in Culpeper that was purchased by the Williamsburg Winery a few years back. These include Johannisberg Riesling, Lord Culpeper Seyval Blanc, and Filippo Mazzeo Reserve, a Cabernet Sauvignon and Nebbiolo mix. Some wonderful dessert wines—a raspberry Merlot, a blackberry Merlot, and a Late Harves Vidal—round out the Dominion label offerings.

After your tour, you will be invited to participate in a tasting, which will include samples of seven of the wines mentioned above. The tour and tasting also include a short film and a souvenir wine glass.

The winery is open daily except Thanksgiving, Christmas, and New Year's Day. From Apr through Oct, hours are 10 a.m. to 6 p.m. Mon through Sat, 11 a.m. to 6 p.m. Sun. They close at 5 p.m. Nov through Mar. Regular tours are $8. Reserve Wine Tastings are available by appointment only for $30 per person in the private wine cellar. A country sampler of assorted cheese and crackers will complement your personalized tasting and an oversized etched reserve wine glass is included in the price. There is also an online special tour and tasting with lunch at the Gabriel Archer Tavern for $28. Make a reservation

online at the Web site listed above. Guests keep an engraved tasting glass, and lunch includes a glass of wine, main course, dessert, and coffee or tea. (See our full description of the Gabriel Archer Tavern in the Restaurants chapter.)

After the tour, you can browse through the retail store, which sells winery products, international wines, replicas of 18th-century wine bottles that were hand-blown in the traditional manner by artisans who work at Jamestown Glasshouse, fancy corkscrews, and other accessories for the wine connoisseur. The winery also offers a collection of authentic salt-glazed pottery—coasters, pitchers, wine cups, and coolers—designed with a grape motif by Duffeler. Discounts are offered on purchases of six or more bottles of wine, and shipping is available within Virginia.

Getting There

To reach the winery from I-64, take exit 242 onto Route 199 and take a left turn onto Brookwood Lane. Turn left again onto Lake Powell Road and you'll soon see the winery sign. From Colonial Williamsburg, travel Route 132 south (North Henry Street) through the Historic Area until you reach the junction with Route 199. Take a left onto Route 199 going west and take the next right onto Brookwood Lane. At Lake Powell Road, turn left and follow the signs. (The state's highway sign for vineyards, a cluster of grapes, will help guide you to the winery, too.)

JAMESTOWN AND YORKTOWN

In a sense, America was born twice on this narrow peninsula bordered by the James and York rivers—once, in 1607, when Capt. Christopher Newport and his men stepped ashore on the banks of the river they named for their king and founded James Towne; again, in 1781, when the Continental Army defeated the British at Yorktown in the decisive battle of the American Revolution. That's a lot of history to pack into one 23-mile stretch. Thanks to forward-thinking preservationists who marked these sites as off-limits to development centuries ago, you can get a real sense of what happened here in a one- or two-day visit.

Jamestown marked its quadricentennial in 2007—400 years since English colonists first debarked from their three wooden ships after a four-month journey across the Atlantic and struggled, mightily, to establish a life here. Though largely abandoned as a settlement by 1750, this marshy island is thoroughly enmeshed in the American historical imagination, entangled with the legend of Pocahontas and John Smith, two figures who have come to represent the meeting of minds and clash of cultures between the colonists and the Virginia Indians who inhabited this region first that followed.

To mark the anniversary, both of Jamestown's major attractions—the Jamestown Settlement, which re-creates life in 17th-century America, and the Jamestown National Historic Site, run by the U.S. Park Service, experienced major makeovers. Even Yorktown, where the National Park Service maintains the battlefields, got an overhaul, in anticipation of the surge of visitors. The result is that both areas look better than ever and, though devoted to the past, bring it to life in thoroughly modern ways. In Yorktown, new county administration buildings, including an eye-grabbing courthouse, have spruced up Ballard Street near the waterfront, which itself has been thoroughly spiffed up and renamed the Riverwalk, with a brick-paved path that connects the Yorktown Victory Center to the restaurants and shops along Water Street. (See our close-up on Riverwalk.)

Jamestown and Yorktown—two of the Historic Triangle's crown jewels—continue to reinvent themselves while making strides to enhance the authenticity of each visitor's journey back in time. Read on and learn all the details in this tale of two towns that are such an integral part of American heritage.

JAMESTOWN

History

Imagine leaving your home and country with little more than the possessions you could carry in a small chest. Imagine boarding a vessel powered only by breezes (or gales for the more unfortunate) to cross the wild Atlantic Ocean. Imagine months at sea with no privacy, little fresh food, no heat or comfort of any kind, all in order to reach a land said to be inhabited by fierce native tribes where previous attempts at settlement had ended in disaster. Who would undertake such a journey? But imagine, too, dreaming of a fertile and bounteous land. Imagine dreaming of being free—from debt, from lack of opportunity, from city squalor, from whatever mistakes or burdens were part of your past. Imagine holding in your mind simultaneously the alternating hopes and forebodings of such an enterprise, and you can begin to fathom the experience of the Jamestown settlers.

In December 1606 three wooden ships sailed from London for the New World. Southerly winds blew the 105 adventuresome members of the expedition to the Caribbean, where one of the men died. Here they obtained fresh provisions before voyaging again, this time up North America's eastern coast. Some four months and 6,000 miles after their departure from England they found a swampy wilderness on the banks of the James River and pronounced it fit for settlement. Thus began the long and fascinating story of our country's beginnings.

The early years were difficult ones for the settlers of Jamestown, the New World's first permanent English-speaking colony. The climate proved hot and humid, the land marshy and mosquito-ridden. Several of the colonists' attempts at industry, including glass-making, failed to create a solid economy. And the large native population of Indians, ruled by Powhatan, was understandably distrustful of these invaders from across the seas. The winter of 1609–10, known as the "Starving Time," was especially terrible for the colony. Only about 90 gaunt settlers were still alive when supplies and reinforcements finally arrived. Indeed, more than half of the colonists who came to Virginia in the colony's first seven years died. Ultimately, tobacco cultivation succeeded where all else had failed, ensuring survival. More and more settlers arrived, attracted by cash crop opportunities as well as the desire for a better life than that afforded by the rigidly hierarchical societies of Europe. Soon the Virginia Colony was flourishing; plantation society took firm root in its rich, sandy soils and lush woodlands.

In recent decades, Spanish documents have been uncovered that discuss the arrival of 20 or so Africans in Virginia in the summer of 1619. These written accounts suggest that the Africans first reached Virginia aboard the Portuguese ship *San Juan Bautista*, which had sailed from Luanda, Angola, bound for Mexico. Further research suggests that most of the Africans who came to Virginia during the first half of the 17th century

hailed from Angola. These men and women more than likely knew how to farm and had been acquainted with both Europeans and Christianity. About a third of these early arrivals and their children were or became free, and some acquired their own land. The number of Africans in Virginia remained relatively small throughout the 17th century, accounting for only 2 to 3 percent of the non-Indian population in 1650, and about 10 percent by the turn of the century.

On July 30, 1619, the first representative legislative assembly in British America met at Jamestown. The community continued to thrive as the Virginia Colony's first capital until 1699 when, after the burning of the Statehouse, the seat of government was moved inland to Williamsburg for reasons involving health problems caused by insects in this low-lying marshland location. No longer a vital political and economic hub, by 1750 Jamestown ceased to exist as an actual community. Fortunately, much of the Jamestown story has been restored to us. Some genuine remnants of the famous settlement survive, including the bell tower of the church the colonists built and foundations of their simple homes. Archaeological discoveries (the highly acclaimed Jamestown Rediscovery Project, an ongoing archaeological dig, began in 1994), scholarly research, and a number of organizations' dedication to understanding our nation's past have combined to produce the Jamestown historic experience today.

There are two separate experiences for tourists and students in Jamestown: the Jamestown National Historic Site, coadministered by the National Park Service and Preservation Virginia, and Jamestown Settlement, operated by Virginia's Jamestown-Yorktown Foundation. While these two attractions operate separately, they are just a mile apart and can be easily visited in the course of the same day.

Getting There

To get to Jamestown from I-64, take exit 242A, Route 199, which brings you to the Colonial Parkway, where signs will lead you to Jamestown. If you're coming from Williamsburg, simply take Jamestown Road (Route 31) and follow signs from there. Visitors arriving from the south on Route 31 will cross the James River on the Jamestown Ferry, a pleasant (and free) excursion we profile in our chapter on Day Trips. Jamestown Settlement lies at the intersection of Route 31 and the Colonial Parkway, just up from the Jamestown Ferry docks.

A note on the Colonial Parkway: This scenic, 23-mile roadway was built specifically to connect Jamestown and Yorktown, marking the beginning and the end of the British colonial experience in America. There are no gas stations or amenities, but leave time to stop at the many roadside historical markers. (See our Close-up in the Getting There chapter.)

NOTE: The western end of the road was closed in 2009 following an accident in which a barge hit a piling seriously damaging the bridge crossing Powhatan Creek. Scheduled to reopen by summer 2010, work is running behind mostly due to uncooperative weather. From Williamsburg, the Parkway remains open to traffic headed east to Yorktown and as far west as the intersection with Route 199. A marked detour utilizing Route 199 and Jamestown Road (Route 31) will guide you to Jamestown if the Parkway has not yet reopened in its entirety.

Attractions

JAMESTOWN NATIONAL HISTORIC SITE
Western end of Colonial Parkway
(757) 229-1733
www.nps.gov/colo
In the beginning, all America was Virginia, wrote William Byrd in 1732, and this scruffy island on the banks of the James is where Virginia, named for Queen Elizabeth I, the so-called "Virgin Queen," began.

The programs offered here are coadministered by the National Park Service, which bought 1,500 acres of the island in 1934, but it was Preservation Virginia (formerly the Association for the Preservation of Virginia Antiquities) whose leaders first saw the need to ensure this spot be maintained. They bought, and continue to hold, 22.5 acres of the island in 1893.

In time for the quadricentennial, a new visitor center opened in 2007, a little farther inland than the old one, and offering an interpretive introduction to the island. There is an extensive collection of 17th-century Jamestown artifacts on display and a new, 18-minute orientation film. Here is where you pay your admission fee, hook up with one of the rangers leading a tour, or pick up a self-guiding leaflet if you prefer to go at your own pace. A new feature on the historic site itself is the interactive "virtual viewer," a panoramic camera that superimposes images onto the existing, vacant land to show visitors where buildings stood, where objects were recovered and what the fort looked like 400 years ago. With the press of a button, monitors then show short films, re-creating pivotal events from Jamestown history that occurred at these sites, like the burning of Swann's Tavern during the Bacon Rebellion, or the 1635 meeting of the Virginia Assembly at which Governor John Harvey was arrested for treason. Way cool.

Guided tours for groups are available, on a reservation basis, in spring, winter, and fall.

Begin your tour of the Old Towne Site at the Tercentenary Monument, a 103-foot shaft of New Hampshire granite that was erected in 1907 to mark the 300th anniversary of Jamestown's founding. River tides have washed away part of this early town site, but on your walking tour of Jamestown you can explore the 1639 Church Tower, the sole 17th-century structure still standing, and view ruins of the original settlement made visible by archaeological exploration. These include foundations of some of the early statehouses and ruins of the original glass furnaces built in 1608. Near the Church Tower along the James River waterfront is the Jamestown Rediscovery archaeological excavation site, where you can watch researchers sift through the remains of the James Fort, once believed lost forever, and talk to interpreters about the latest dig finds.

Excavation on the site began in 1994 after archaeologist William Kelso led the team that discovered that the fort was not lost under the James River, as was formerly believed. It is estimated that about 85 percent of the fort still exists on land. Of that, about 20 percent has been uncovered so far.

You'll also see statues of John Smith and Pocahontas as well as the Dale House, which sits near the seawall, just beyond the Confederate earthwork. The Dale House serves as a snack bar, now that its former tenants—the archaeologists—have moved into a beautiful building of their own, called the Archearium.

Further progress was made in 2001, allowing visitors to get a feel for what the settlers would have seen inside or outside the walls of the fort. Partial sections of the south and east palisade walls, the southeast bulwark, an eastern extension, and gates were built last winter. Construction of the frame of a longhouse building discovered inside the fort area helps visitors understand the dimensions and shape of the structures.

Next, a pause at the Memorial Cross is in order. The cross marks some 300 shallow graves that were dug by the settlers during the so-called "Starving Time," the dismal winter of 1609–10. Walk to the other side of the visitor center, and you will find the New Towne Site, which contains reproductions of ruins built over original foundations, including those of the Ambler Mansion, a two-story home built in the mid-1700s. Also in New Towne is the Manufacturing Site, where a number of commercial endeavors—including brick making, pottery making, and brewing—occurred in the mid-1600s.

After you've toured the town site, take one of the loop drives around **Jamestown Island.** These 3- and 5-mile self-guided automobile tours through a wilderness of pine and swamp will bring you close to the vision early colonists must have beheld when they set foot in America—a natural environment at once beautiful and frightening. Herds of deer still roam the forested ridges of the island, sometimes coming close to the ruins under cover of dusk. Muskrats hide in the Jamestown marshes; you might glimpse one paddling leisurely through the swamp. A profusion of waterfowl, including ospreys, herons, and mallards, makes seasonal stops. Roll down your windows, listen to the music of songbirds, feel the stillness all around you. If time permits, pull over to read the markers inscribed with interesting historical and botanical data.

Save time to visit the reconstructed **Glasshouse,** which is actually located on the mainland, across the bridge that brings you to the island, but included in your park admission fee. Costumed craftspeople demonstrate 400-year-old techniques, making glassware much like that created and used by settlers. While hard woods such as hickory and oak fueled the kilns in 1608, today natural gas heats the fiery furnace. The products, which register a red-hot 2,000 degrees when first pulled from the heat, are lovely. Clear and green goblets, bell jars, flasks, wineglasses, pitchers, and the like can be purchased here. A display case also shows off some of the glassblowers' after-hours work—the vases and such they make to perfect their skills long after the tourists have gone home.

You may want to return to the visitor center for souvenirs before leaving. Reproductions of colonial stoneware, glassware made at the Glasshouse, a vast selection of books, videotapes, toys, games, and other keepsakes are for sale.

Admission to Jamestown Island is $10 per adult, age 16 or older, and covers reentry for up to a week, as well as entry to the Yorktown battlefield. Children 15 and younger are admitted free. Interagency Annual, Senior, and Access passes are accepted. Educational groups are admitted free of charge with advance notice and a written fee waiver. Jamestown is open from 9 a.m. to 5 p.m. every day of the year except Thanksgiving and Christmas. Parking is free.

Interpretive Programs

To truly get a feel for the place and the era, children may participate in a number of special programs. These include the Pinch Pot program during the summer months, in which children can make their own pot out of clay, and the Colonial Junior Ranger programs, in which children 12 and younger can learn about Jamestown while enjoying a series of activities with their families. The Junior Ranger program, which is designed for family groups only, provides each child with a chance to earn a patch and a certificate. Other interpretive programs are offered seasonally, including ranger-led tours of the town site and living-history character tours. Preregistration is not required. Most programs are either free with admission or have a small materials cost per child.

JAMESTOWN SETTLEMENT
Route 31 and Colonial Parkway
(757) 253-4838, (888) 593-4682
www.historyisfun.org
Opened in 1957 in time for the 350th anniversary, Jamestown Settlement underwent major renovations in 2006, in time for the quadricentennial. New museum galleries doubled the size of the exhibition space, added classrooms, and expanded the cafe, with indoor and outdoor seating for 300. Combined with the outdoor living-history exhibits, the programs offered here re-create both the early colonists and the Virginia Indians habitats and customs in a lively manner without sacrificing historical authenticity. Museumgoers can board replicas of the ships that brought the English settlers to the New World in 1607, which are docked along the James River; grind corn; play quoits; and watch as tools are made and muskets are fired. If you are traveling with kids, especially young children, and have time to visit just one of the two Jamestown sites, the settlement is likelier to offer a richer experience for all.

Tickets are available in the high-ceiled lobby. Start your visit by watching an introductory film, *1607: A Nation Takes Root*, shown approximately every 30 minutes, that presents a dramatic overview of the first decades of the British colonial experience in the Virginia colony. After the film, make your way through the Great Hall, where exhibits use artifacts, maps, and full-scale dioramas to illustrate a chronological journey of life in Virginia from 1600 to 1699, with a special emphasis on the native Powhatans and the West Africans who began arriving here in large numbers

when tobacco cultivation became the dominant economic enterprise.

A short walk from the galleries, the outdoor exhibits offer a hands-on way of learning about American history. Costumed interpreters reenact the quotidian details of life in colonial Virginia. Here is a museum where visitors are actually *encouraged* to touch and use the items on display—climb into a dugout canoe, play ninepins, lie down in a bunk aboard the *Susan Constant*.

At the Powhatan Village, visit the Virginia Indian houses (the British called them longhouses but the Algonquian word is *yahekin*) made of sapling frames covered with reed mats. These dwellings are re-creations based on archaeological findings and eyewitness drawings made by a New World explorer. Walk around the ceremonial circle made up of seven carved wooden poles created by an Indian artist and her husband. Historical interpreters dressed as Powhatans make tools from bone or smoke fish over a fire and cook it on a baking stone. Children can play cob darts, a game of pitching dried corn ears through a hanging vine hoop.

Three Ships

Follow the path down from the village to the pier, where full-size replica ships of the *Susan Constant*, *Godspeed*, and *Discovery* are docked. The *Susan Constant* replica, built at the settlement from 1989 to 1991, is brightly painted and fully rigged. Exploration of shipwrecked vessels of similar make and period provided clues as to the appearance and construction of this remarkable craft. Go on board the 116-foot-long ship and imagine calling it home for nearly five months with an estimated 143 other men and boys. You can climb down to the 'tween deck, where passengers were quartered, for an idea of just how cramped conditions were. (And remember during the voyage from England, the 'tween deck probably was loaded with cargo waist high.)

Take note that the *Susan Constant*, *Godspeed*, and *Discovery* are functional ships, which occasionally sail from Jamestown Settlement to participate in a maritime event or take part in an educational demonstration. (Visitors always have access to at least one of the ships.) Costumed crew members describe life at sea, unfurling sails, dropping anchor, posting colors, and letting hardy souls try their hand at steering with a shipstaff or nautical knot tying. Children learn the role of 17th-century ship's boys and may be asked to ring the ship's bell or read directions on the compass. Other demonstrations may include raising sails or operating a pulley (to show how simple machines work). A 20-by-50-foot pier shelter near the three ships is designed to resemble a waterfront building and is used for demonstrations, such as piloting and navigation.

James Fort

When you're ready to stand on solid ground again, debark and head up to James Fort. Enter these stockade walls, and you'll experience the rough-and-ready life of the settlers from 1610–14—thatched roof, wattle-and-daub houses with rudimentary furnishings, the smell of wood smoke, the ceaseless worry and toil of survival. Inspect a cannon, try on armor, help a colonist tend the garden. Children might be interested in learning to fetch water the old-fashioned way—with a pole draped over their shoulders and heavy buckets attached to either end. Historical interpreters may be engaged in early Virginia industries, manufacturing lumber, blacksmithing, or doing chores such as daubing a house or preparing food.

In addition to regular exhibits and activities, Jamestown Settlement sponsors a number of special programs throughout the year. These include a public lecture series; children's programs, always featuring hands-on learning activities; a November Foods and Feasts presentation that demonstrates how the early colonists prepared and preserved food; and "A Colonial Christmas" in December. (For more details, see our Annual Events chapter.)

Cafe and Gift Shop

The cafe is open from 9 a.m. to 5 p.m. and serves a variety of sandwiches, salads, and snacks. The gift shop carries everything from reproductions

of 17th-century glassware and pottery to a variety of souvenirs, trinkets, and toys. Other items available include publications, reproductions, jewelry, and gift items.

Jamestown Settlement is open from 9 a.m. to 5 p.m. daily, with hours extended to 6 p.m. from June 15 to August 15. It is closed Christmas and New Year's Day. Ask about the guided tours that are offered throughout the day. It's best to visit when skies are clear, but even on a rainy day, the film and the museum's expansive exhibits are worth seeing. In the summer, river breezes help make all but the hottest of days tolerable. Allow at least three hours for a thorough exploration.

Admission to Jamestown Settlement is $14 for adults, $6.50 for children ages 6 to 12, and free to children under 6. A combination ticket for both the settlement and the Yorktown Victory Center, a Museum of the American Revolution, costs $19.25 for adults and $9.25 for children ages 6 to 12. Residents of York and James City Counties and Williamsburg are admitted free.

i Jamestown is not only a drawing card for history buffs. Best-selling mystery writer Patricia Cornwell visited the island in the summer of 1999 to gather material for a novel. *The Last Precinct* was published in October 2000 and picked up where the heroine, Dr. Kay Scarpetta, left off in *Black Notice*. Cornwell also has donated $50,000 from the proceeds of the novel *Black Notice* to the Jamestown Rediscovery Project.

Restaurants and Shopping

After the 1699 fire that devastated Jamestown and forced the colonial capital to move inland to Williamsburg, Jamestown went into a ghostly decline. By 1750, it ceased to exist as a town. It wasn't until the late 19th century, and Preservation Virginia's 1889 purchase of a portion of Jamestown Island, that redevelopment—designed to preserve and protect the historic site—began in the area.

There are now many housing subdivisions lining either side of Jamestown Road, and a popular, free ferry to Surry County at its terminus with the river, but there is still not much in the way of commerce. The exceptions are worth noting since once you get to Jamestown proper, the only places to eat or shop are at the two major attractions—the National Park Site and Jamestown Settlement.

In our Restaurants chapter, see our complete descriptions of **The Carrot Tree** and the **Jamestown Pie Company.** Both of these establishments are located close to the Jamestown attractions. The Carrot Tree has table service and carryout, including baked goods so renown they supply some of the best restaurants in town. The Jamestown Pie Company is takeout only, although there are a few picnic tables in a stand of shady trees. It's a good place to stop for picnic fixings if you plan to tour the Colonial Parkway beginning at its eastern terminus.

One other commercial entity of note is **Cooke's Christmas,** a barnlike store adjacent to Cooke's Nursery, that specializes in holiday decorating. Worth a stop if you are looking to pick up something special for your tree or someone else's. See our full description in the Christmas section of our Shopping chapter.

YORKTOWN

Every October 19, Yorktown throws a parade and sets off fireworks, all the sorts of things that most places break out for the 4th of July.

The reason, of course, is that was the day the Battle of Yorktown was won, the day the Revolutionary Army of George Washington and the French army under Comte de Rochambeau defeated the British.

The funny thing? In 1781, the locals didn't celebrate much. Their town had just been almost obliterated by a six-week siege and eight-day bombardment, in which more than 15,000 shells were fired. Moreover, at the time no one really knew the war was over. While the surrender of Cornwallis's army was a major loss, the British still held New York and several important ports.

But politically, the British parliament had seen enough. The British had been fighting (and paying for) wars in America off and on since the French and Indian War began in 1754. On the Continent and throughout the West Indies, they were skirmishing with the French and Spanish.

Faced with too many enemies and not enough cash, the British government chose to negotiate peace and grant independence to the colonies (which took almost two more years).

All that complexity isn't easily condensed into a fireworks show. The beauty of Yorktown, from a visitor's perspective, is that you can take in as much as you want—the pomp of simple "victory," or the minutiae of history, right down to walking the very grounds where that victory was won.

Getting There

By far the most-scenic way to Yorktown from Williamsburg is along the Colonial Parkway, a 23-mile roadway that bisects the peninsula from Jamestown to Yorktown, figuratively tracing the history of British colonial rule in America. (See our Close-up in the Getting There chapter.)

Turnouts on both sides of the three-lane road (the middle lane is for passing) provide stopping places to read historical markers or simply view the scenery. Along the Yorktown end of the parkway, that scenery can occasionally include close-up views of today's military: The roadway passes through the Yorktown Naval Weapons Station, the depot for all ammunition used by the U.S. Navy's Atlantic Fleet, headquartered at Norfolk.

If the parkway isn't your speed (literally: the limit is 45 mph), the next best approach from Williamsburg is eastbound I-64. Take the Yorktown Naval Weapons Station exit (exit 247); turn left on Jefferson Avenue (Route 143), then left again on Yorktown Road (Route 238).

From Norfolk or Newport News, exit I-64 at Fort Eustis Boulevard (exit 250). At the traffic light at the bottom of the ramp, turn left onto Jefferson Avenue (Route 143), and then quickly right at the next light onto Fort Eustis Blvd. (Route 105). Travel three miles to US 17, turn left. Watch carefully for signs as you near Yorktown. To get to the park service visitor center, take the Colonial Parkway exit to the right. For direct access to the downtown waterfront and the Yorktown Victory Center, you can either turn left, across oncoming traffic, to approach the town from the river bottoms—or from the uphill side by turning right onto Alexander Hamilton Boulevard at the York County government center. Miss your turn and you'll end up crossing the York River on the Coleman toll bridge.

The Town

For all the historic markers labeled 1600-something, Yorktown's history dates back even further. The original settlers along this stretch of the York River were the Kiskiack Indians, who called the water the Pamunkey.

Captain John Smith explored the area in 1607, but it was nearly 20 years before any large numbers of English settlers began to cultivate the rich land. The town itself was founded in 1691 by the "Act for Ports and Towns" passed by the Virginia General Assembly for the transport of the colony's lucrative tobacco crop to Europe via England. This was also, in part, an attempt to force urban growth in the colony and centralize the water traffic among the numerous plantations spreading up the Chesapeake Bay. Taking advantage of the deep channel of the York, British ships could pull far enough upriver for shelter from the storms of the Atlantic Ocean and the Chesapeake Bay. The network of creeks that crisscrosses the Virginia Peninsula allowed access from the James River side as well.

The town takes its name from surrounding York County and the York River, which were renamed around 1643 to honor the Duke of York, later King James II. (Before that, they river was called the Charles in honor of James's father, the first Duke of York and later King Charles I. He lost his crown—not to mention his head—in the English Civil War.) Fifty acres of land on the plantation of Benjamin Read—including a wharf, ferry, store, and well—were set aside for a county seat that was intended to grow and prosper in commerce. Sheltered by the bluff, with a wide beach to hold the storehouses and other businesses of the sea trade, the site became busy and flourished throughout the colonial period.

The oldest house in the town is the Sessions House, built in 1692 by Thomas Sessions and a survivor of the siege of 1781 and later the Civil War. A courthouse has stood on the same site since 1697, and a new church for York Parish was built in the same year. After their construction the town's growth accelerated. By the mid-18th century, as many as 50 large trading ships would be in the vicinity of Yorktown at any given time, and the town had grown relatively prosperous.

In the latter half of the 1700s, however, the tobacco trade had shifted to the inland Piedmont region, and the shipping patterns changed accordingly. A slow process of decline began, and by 1776 the port was less important in Commonwealth affairs. The Battle of Yorktown hastened the decline of the community. The intense barrage of cannon fire from the Allied siege line and the fighting during the battle destroyed more than half of the town, and it never fully recovered.

Although there is little evidence remaining, the Civil War brought renewed activity to the town. During the Peninsula Campaign of that conflict, Yorktown was one anchor of the Confederate defenses crossing the Peninsula to block Union progress toward Williamsburg; the fortifications of the Revolutionary War were renovated for that purpose.

i If bicycling is your preferred way to travel, you can try a trail that begins at Washington's Headquarters (in the encampment part of the Yorktown battlefield tour) and connects with a 5-mile bicycle loop in adjoining Newport News Park. Bring your helmet and remember to ride single file on the far right side of the road.

Historic Buildings

Structures dating from the colonial period attest to the wealth citizens gained from Yorktown's prominence. Some of the most notable are listed here.

ARCHER COTTAGE
Water St.
(757) 890-0916

This former waterfront tavern, originally built in the early 1700s, and all but the stone foundation reconstructed after an 1814 fire, probably played a key role in Yorktown's early days as a bustling, hard-drinking port. The building belongs to the National Park Service and is used as an office. It is not open to the public.

THE AUGUSTINE MOORE HOUSE
Moore House Rd., near the
Coast Guard Station
(757) 898-2410

This is the historic home where the terms of surrender were drawn in 1781. It has been restored and furnished to its 18th-century appearance. A living-history program tells the interesting story of the arguments that took place during the negotiations. The house is open from spring through fall. For specific dates and times, contact the National Park Service.

GRACE EPISCOPAL CHURCH
Church St.
(757) 898-3261
www.gracechurchyorktown.org

In colonial times this church was known as the York-Hampton Church, which dates to at least 1642. The church has been damaged several times by war and fire, but the original walls have been standing since 1697 and have been incorporated into a number of reconstructions. It remains the place of worship for an active Episcopal parish. A bookshop on-site offers theological and devotional literature, selected gifts, and cards. The church is open for viewing from 9 a.m. to 5 p.m. Mon through Sat.

THE NELSON HOUSE
Main St.
(757) 898-2410

With its Georgian design, glazed Flemish bond brickwork, and lovely formal gardens, the Nelson House was home to one of the wealthiest of the town's families. The most notable scion of the Nelson family was Thomas Nelson Jr., a governor of Virginia, commander of the Virginia militia, and signer of the Declaration of Independence. It was this home that Cornwallis used as headquarters during the siege, and colonial cannonballs still are lodged in the wall facing the American siege line. Legend has it that Thomas Nelson Jr. himself gave the order to fire those cannons, even though it might have meant the destruction of his home and possibly his fortune, an act putting literal force behind his pledge in the Declaration of Independence. The Nelson House is open spring through fall. Admission is included in the $10 fee to the Yorktown Visitor Center and battlefield. The house is open in the summer from 10 a.m. to 4:30 p.m. and daily from 1 to 4 p.m. the rest of the year.

OLD CUSTOM HOUSE
410 Main St.
(757) 898-2410

Reputed to have been built by Richard Ambler in 1720 as his "large brick storehouse" and used by him while he served as customs collector, this sturdy monument to Yorktown commerce is administered by the Comte de Grasse Chapter of the Daughters of the American Revolution. Believed to be the oldest customhouse in the United States, the Yorktown structure was named to the Virginia Landmarks Register in the spring of 1999. The customhouse has an interesting history. Over the years it has been a dwelling, a store, the headquarters of Confederate General John B. Magruder during the Civil War, and the medical offices of African-American physician D. M. Norton. Its restoration—at the hands of the Daughters of the American Revolution, who staged tea parties, cake sales, and masked balls to raise needed funds—is considered a milestone in the historic preservation movement. It is open infrequently, summer Sundays by chance. Admission to the customhouse is free.

POOR POTTER SITE
Read St.
(757) 898-2410

The site of the largest-known pottery factory in colonial America tells the story of how this industry flourished in Yorktown during the early 1700s. Hours are seasonal, so call ahead before you visit. Until funding becomes available to restore this site, it will continue to be protected by an unsightly metal structure.

Celebrations

Each year Yorktown observes two major celebrations related to its military history. Independence Day is celebrated with the rest of the nation, and crowds of people gather in and about the town to enjoy the traditional Fourth of July parade and the individual observations, entertainments, and celebrations at the museums, homes, and centers. The day culminates in a spectacular fireworks display on the York River, visible for miles around. On October 19 Yorktown again pulls out all the stops with exhibits, reenactments of military life, "tall ship" visits, naval reenactments, music, and other celebrations as Virginians and visitors celebrate with appropriate enthusiasm Washington's—and the United States'—victory. (For more on yearly events in and around Yorktown, turn to our Annual Events chapter.)

Yorktown Today

In many ways, Yorktown today remains as it has been for hundreds of years—a small 'ville oriented toward the river that bears its name. The waters are still heavily used by commercial traffic—upstream to the naval station and the paper mill at West Point, 30 miles west, or to the Western Refining oil refinery just downstream from the town.

Downtown Yorktown today makes some bows to the modern world—it's still the seat of government for York County, largely a suburb of Newport News, Hampton, and even Williamsburg that is home to 60,000. But other than those working in government offices, most of Yorktown is devoted to the area's history.

The waterfront is dominated by the results of a $25 million renovation completed in 2005—a riverwalk, improved beach facilities (yes, the river has a beach—a bow in the channel has deposited a deep bank of sand), and a shopping area.

Attractions

As at Jamestown, the history of Yorktown is neatly captured in the complementary approaches of the federal government's National Park Service and the Yorktown Victory Center, operated by the state-chartered Jamestown-Yorktown Foundation.

The Park Service facilities focus on preservation; the foundation focuses on interpretation through historic re-creations.

NATIONAL PARK SERVICE YORKTOWN BATTLEFIELD VISITOR CENTER
Eastern end of Colonial Parkway
(757) 898-2410
www.nps.gov/york
The Park Service's visitor center is a small brick building nearly hidden by the 10-foot high earth works. The center has an interesting set of indoor exhibits (including the actual tents George Washington used as his field headquarters), and a concise '70s-era film using re-creations to give some sense of the siege.

In other words, the visitor center is intentionally understated and serves to keep the attention where it's due—the acres of open fields and earthen fortifications. To truly appreciate the scale of the battle, you need only walk the fields, or drive the seven-mile self-guided tour of the sprawling battlegrounds.

You can view samples of the types of cannon and mortar the siege forces used, tucked behind earthworks a half-mile south of the visitor center. You can stare across the fields—just as Washington, Rochambeau, and Cornwallis did—to gauge the distances and effect of the artillery.

Most evocative, however, is Redoubt 9—one of two earthen fortifications that were linchpins of the British defensive line. (Nearby Redoubt 10 is fenced off—the meandering banks of the York River have washed out chunks of the river bluffs over the past 200-plus years, leaving the redoubt teetering at the edge of a cliff.)

In a few bloody minutes one moonless night, a few hundred British, French, Americans and German mercenaries fought hand to hand. The

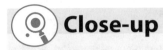

Close-up

How to Besiege a Town

The phrase **"Battle of Yorktown"** conjures images of climatic pitched combat between closely packed ground troops. There were moments of that at Yorktown, of course—but the confrontation is more accurately described as a siege, stretching out over weeks, conducted by troops largely hidden from each other by giant earthen walls. Some of the most critical moments happened miles away, at the mouth of the Chesapeake Bay and at British headquarters in New York.

The war in the summer of 1781 was at stalemate. The British held New York and other strategic points in the north—but had no hope of seizing control of the countryside. In the South, a British army commanded by Gen. Charles Lord Cornwallis had won key victories throughout the Carolinas and Virginia (nearly capturing Virginia Gov. Thomas Jefferson in the process). But by the late summer, Cornwallis's troops were badly in need of rest and reinforcements. He marched them toward Yorktown.

It seemed a perfect stronghold: Port facilities on the York River, barely a mile from the Chesapeake Bay, and only 30 miles from the bay's entrance to the Atlantic. Marshes, creeks, and dense hardwood forests made a close approach to Yorktown difficult. Cornwallis immediately constructed earthen barriers to provide a defensive line for his nearly 10,000 men.

In reality, however, what Cornwallis built was a perfect trap—for himself.

His commander, Gen. Henry Clinton, sent word that the British fleet would sail from New York to resupply and replenish Cornwallis's tired troops. But French spies had spotted Cornwallis's work, and sent word themselves to the Marquis de Lafayette and Gen. George Washington. The French fleet hurried to blockade the Chesapeake; Washington and the Comte de Rochambeau led their 7,000 troops on a four-week, largely secret, march from their base in Rhode Island to Virginia.

On September 5, the British fleet arrived at the bay—only to discover the French blockade. The two fleets pounded each other for three hours, neither able to win decisively. But the French didn't need to win—they simply needed to keep the British from reaching Cornwallis. The British, their ships badly damaged, withdrew to New York.

A week later, Washington and Rochambeau arrived in Williamsburg. Within the month, they were joined by thousands more French, who brought artillery and siege tools. Washington and his allied army, now more than 19,000 strong, headed to Yorktown.

Franco-American allies prevailed. Within a few hours, their artillery was firing into town at almost point-blank range; within three days, British Gen. Charles Lord Cornwallis surrendered.

There is no single preferred way to view the battlefield. The 15-minute film *The Siege at Yorktown* provides excellent context (the actor portraying Cornwallis lays on arrogance to the verge of campiness), and a re-creation of a Revolutionary-era warship gives a glimpse of life aboard (hint: duck).

Outside, park service rangers lead 30-minute guided walking tours that describe the historical context and the allies' siege tactics. To get a broader view (including some insight into the difficulties of marching massive troop numbers through a marshy, heavily forested region), pick up a free map at the visitor center and take the self-guided driving tour through the fortifications or the slightly longer nine-mile tour that includes the troop encampments.

Many visitors, however, simply choose to walk the grounds, taking in the sweep and imag-

Cornwallis, still confident that reinforcements were on the way, pulled his troops back from their outer line of defenses so he could concentrate them more tightly to repulse an attack. Washington and Rochambeau didn't attack directly, though—they seized the British outer defenses and set up to batter and starve the British into submission.

On October 6, in just a few hours, the allied troops built an earthen siege line—essentially a mile-long trench and berm. It allowed them to bombard the town while being protected from British fire. The cannon and mortar steadily pounded the town and wore down the supplies and morale of the British. Clinton, from New York, promised to arrive soon to break the siege—but Cornwallis was starting to worry that help wouldn't come in time.

On October 11, Washington ordered the digging of a second siege line, a quarter-mile closer. From there, they could dominate the British position with fire from three sides. All that prevented the completion of that line was two forward British strongholds, the earthen forts known as Redoubts 9 and 10.

On the moonless night of October 14, two groups of French and Americans (commanded by Alexander Hamilton) sneaked toward those forts. They carried their muskets—but left the weapons unloaded, lest an accidental shot give them away.

Standing inside **Redoubt 9,** you can vividly imagine the chaos and carnage of more than 400 men—British, Scots, German mercenaries, French, and Americans—clashing. With little time to reload their guns, the fights devolved to hand combat with bayonets and axes. The defenders were forced to give up in less than a half-hour.

Now the allies could rain down shells at near-point-blank range. On October 16–17, Cornwallis, still hoping for reinforcements, tried a bold counterattack to buy time. It failed. That night, he began to retreat across the York River in a desperate attempt to flee northward. His first flotilla of small boats made it—but when they returned for another load, a sudden squall churned the river so violently that escape was impossible.

The British fate was sealed. Out of food, and suffering terrible casualties, Cornwallis sent out an officer holding a white flag. After a day and a half of negotiations, Cornwallis's army—fully one-third of the British forces in colonial America—surrendered.

At the surrender ceremony on October 19, however, Cornwallis was not to be found. Humiliated, he complained of illness and remained in his quarters. His second-in-command led the 8,000 British troops to the place now called **Surrender Field.**

ining the epic events that occurred on these quiet, wide fields.

Admission to the park is $10, good over a seven-day period for both Yorktown Battlefield and Historic Jamestown. An annual pass is available for $40.

For $83.75, you can purchase a five-day combination ticket, good for both the park service facilities; Colonial Williamsburg; and the state's Jamestown Settlement and Yorktown Victory Center.

VICTORY MONUMENT
Historic Main St.
(757) 898-2410

On Oct. 29, 1781, a resolution of the Continental Congress made a call for a Yorktown Monument to the Alliance and Victory. It was to be a century, however, before the cornerstone was laid on Oct. 18, 1881. The monument is the record of the centennial celebration that took place in the town that year. The stirring inscriptions around its base are worth investigating, and there is a convenient parking lot across the street so you may walk over to do so. For information contact the Park Service.

THE WATERMEN'S MUSEUM
309 Water St.
(757) 887-2641
www.watermens.org

Right on the York River, The Watermen's Museum preserves and interprets the long history of Tidewater Virginians' relationship with the water and its bounties. It features artifacts, literature, exhibits, and photographs depicting crabbers, oyster harvesters, and clammers at work on the Chesapeake Bay and its tributaries, from the original Virginia Indians fishermen to present-day harvesters of the water's bounty.

On the grounds you can see traditional watermen's equipment, a modified skipjack, and a dugout canoe that was hand-fashioned by a local high school senior as a classroom project and donated to the museum. Programs, seminars, activities, and special events are available to the public throughout the museum's season, which runs from early April through mid-December.

The main building of the museum is a 1935 Colonial Revival house, a masterpiece of engineering that was floated 3 miles across the York River from its original site in Gloucester County in 1987. The house now is a handsome and fitting tribute to the generations of men and women in the area who gained their livelihood from the water. An expansion has added a second building overlooking the river, designed for additional exhibits, public lectures, and educational programming. The renovated Carriage House, which also was brought from Gloucester to Yorktown and features an expansive riverside dock, can be rented for wedding receptions, private parties, and meetings. The well-stocked gift shop is worth a visit by itself. At $4 for adults and $1 for students, admission to the Watermen's Museum is a bargain. Groups of 15 or more may make arrangements to visit anytime—even during the off-season—by calling in advance. Discounted rates are offered for group tours. The museum is open to the general public from Apr through Dec

15. Hours are 10 a.m. to 4 p.m. Tues through Sat and 1 to 4 p.m. Sun.

YORKTOWN VICTORY CENTER
Old Virginia Route 238
(757) 887-1776
www.historyisfun.org

If the national park is a place to imagine the horrors of war through the stillness of the battlefield, the nearby Yorktown Victory Center is a place to experience colonial life—and, yes, life in the Revolutionary Army—through a series of canny re-creations.

The museum at the Victory Center features several exhibits. The Witnesses of Revolution gallery uses sculptures and recorded readings to tell the stories of ten people caught up in the war—patriots and loyalists, African slaves and Native Americans, soldiers and the families they left behind.

Other exhibits include a rare copy of the Declaration of Independence—not a handwritten version like the one on display at the National Archives, but a hastily produced, mass-market edition printed in Boston in 1776. The Converging on Yorktown exhibit includes muskets, rifles, swords, and other artifacts from the battle. Another gallery traces the aftermath of the war through the people from a variety of cultures who created a new, free Virginia.

If that sounds like standard, if well-done, museum stuff, you're right. For many, the real fun will be outside.

The Revolutionary War encampment gives a tiny glimpse into life in Washington's Army. You'll learn how many soldiers shared a tent (too many), peek into a field hospital for a look at colonial-era medicine (and learn why if wounds didn't kill you, disease or the "medicine" might). You'll see colonial-era laptops (yep, they called 'em that) to understand why the quartermaster had the hardest job—and less frightening—but no less revealing—is the colonial-era farm up the hill. Costumed docents will proudly show off the farmhouse—this is the home of a rising middle-class family. You can tell because of its sheer size (one room, almost 200 square feet, plus an upstairs loft for the children to sleep)—and because it has a separate kitchen/smokehouse to keep the open cooking fire away from the living quarters. (Only the poor would think to cook and sleep in the same place!)

At other outbuildings, you'll learn how to break flax to make linen, and how tobacco—the king of the post-Revolutionary economy—wasn't just a cash crop; it was *cash*.

Watch out for the chickens, turkeys, and guinea fowl, though. Just as in the colonial era, they walk around freely.

Admission is $9.50 for adults, $5.25 for children ages 6 through 12. A combination ticket with the Jamestown Settlement is $19.25 for adults, $9.25 for children 6-12. Annual passes are available for $35 for adults, $17.50 for children.

i For a small town, the various attractions at Yorktown actually sprawl across a large, hilly area. It's a mile-plus walk from the Park Service visitor center to the Yorktown Victory Center museum, for example. On holidays and weekends, parking can be at a premium, too. One you've parked somewhere, use the free Yorktown trolley to shuttle to the various places. From mid-March through October, It runs a continuous loop every 20 to 25 minutes, from 10 a.m. to 6 p.m., stopping at all the key locations—the park service center, the Yorktown Victory Monument, the beach, Riverwalk, the Waterman's Museum, the Yorktown Victory Center, the county historical museum and county government center. For more information, call the York County government at (757) 890-3500.

Restaurants

Price Code (Dinner for 2)

$ . . . . Less than $20
$$ . . . . $20 to $40
$$$ . . . . More than $40

Credit cards are accepted at these restaurants unless otherwise noted.

CARROT TREE
411 Main St.
(757) 988-1999

Located inside the Cole Digges House, Yorktown's oldest home (built in 1720), is this second outpost of the popular Jamestown restaurant and bakery. Here you'll find the same fresh, homey foods with an emphasis on regional favorites—Brunswick stew, crab cakes, chowders—and wraps, salads, and sandwiches. Save room for dessert. The carrot cake might not even be the yummiest among the offerings although it is exceptional. Open daily for lunch 11 a.m. to 3:30 p.m., for dinner 4:30 to 8:30 p.m. Thurs through Sat and for High Tea at 4 p.m. on Tues and Wed.

NICK'S RIVERWALK RESTAURANT AND RIVAH CAFÉ $$$
323 Water St.
(757) 875-1522
www.riverwalkrestaurant.net

The centerpiece of the project is Nick's Riverwalk Restaurant and the Rivah Café, whose spacious rooms have terrific views of the water and passing boats. The restaurant kept the name—but little else—with the quirky, kitschy Nick's Seafood Pavilion, a 50-year landmark on Water Street. (The menu, and much of the staff, of the old Nick's has moved down street to the River Room and Island Café, inside the Duke of York Hotel.)

Nick's Riverwalk is actually operated by the same group that owns Berret's (CQ) Seafood Restaurant and Taphouse Grill on Merchants Square in Williamsburg; like Berret's, the new Nick's focuses on local seafood and a wide variety of wines and beers.

The Blue Plate is a terrific example—she-crab soup, crab cakes, crab imperial (baked crabmeat in puff pastry) served with shrimp or oysters. Scallops, lobster, and salmon also earn places on the menu, along with the usual salads, steaks, and sandwiches.

The two rooms largely share a lunch menu; at dinner, the Riverwalk stays with full-course offerings while the cafe offers a lighter, less-expensive mix of sandwiches and pizza. The cafe also has a courtyard well suited for outdoor dining in all but the coldest months.

Trivia: The inlaid mosaic in the Riverwalk entrance was transplanted from the original Nick's, as were the mosaics in the bathrooms; the original restaurant was demolished to make room for the parking garage.

Reservations are accepted for the dining room, but not the cafe. The Riverwalk also has a Sunday brunch that frequently tops local "best of" lists. Open seven days most of the year, but closed on Mon in Jan and Feb. A private room is available for functions.

RIVER ROOM $$$
Duke of York Hotel
508 Water St.
Yorktown, VA 23690
(757) 898-3232
www.dukeofyorkmotel.com
After the original Nick's Seafood Pavilion closed, much of the staff—including longtime chef and general manager Jimmy Kirkales—moved to the River Room, at the urging of owner Cole Crockett.

Many of the old faves are on the menu: shrimp and scallops Grecian; the seafood shish kebab (lobster, shrimp, scallops, tomato, onion, mushrooms, and brown butter); and lobster Dien Bien (lobster over rice, tomatoes, mushrooms, garlic, scallions, and brown butter).

The restaurant is open for dinner Wed through Sun, 4:30 to 9 p.m. in season; during the winter months, it's open Fri, Sat, and Sun only.

The restaurant has simpler fare for breakfast and lunch as well, and is open 7:30 a.m. to 2 p.m. seven days a week most of the year; it's closed Tues during the winter.

YORKTOWN PUB $$
540 Water St.
(757) 886-9964
www.yorktownpub.com
If you want good, basic pub food in a rollicking, even raucous, atmosphere, the Yorktown Pub is the place. The menu features the usual array of burgers, sandwiches, and local seafood.

As a watering hole, the pub has an eclectic mix of locals, tourists, and the many military people stationed nearby. As you'd expect of a beach pub, it's very casual, with plenty of jeans in evidence, knotty pine walls, and worn wooden booths.

Accommodations
DUKE OF YORK MOTOR HOTEL
508 Water St.
(757) 898-3232
www.dukeofyorkmotel.com
This three-story motel is the only one you'll find with rooms facing the beautiful York River. There's a nice swimming pool in the cool courtyard on the side away from the river. Connecting rooms can be provided upon advance request. In July the rate for a basic double is $70 to $140, very reasonable considering that you have a water view, beach access, all of Yorktown history to explore, and proximity to the beautiful Colonial Parkway with its scenic 20-minute drive to Williamsburg and Jamestown.

MARL INN $$
220 Church St.
(757) 898-3859
marlinnbandb.com
This charming bed-and-breakfast, just 20 minutes from Colonial Williamsburg, adds another layer of experience to your tour of the Historic Triangle—owner Tom Nelson is a descendant of Thomas Nelson, signer of the Declaration of Independence. Nelson operates this bed and breakfast with his wife, Poppet. There are four guest rooms, and a full breakfast is provided—unless you don't want one. The Nelsons will take $20 off the room rate if you'd prefer the continental breakfast they lay out in the dining room. (Poppet Nelson reports 80 percent of the guests take the continental breakfast option!)

The Marl Inn is child- and pet-friendly (The Nelsons have two dogs of their own). There is no smoking.

MOSS COTTAGE $$
224 Nelson St.
(757) 715-2007
www.mossguestcottage.com
A charming one-bedroom colonial cottage is only a short walk to the beach and Riverwalk's restaurants, gift shops, antiques shops, art galleries, and historic attractions. Fully furnished with complete kitchen, living area, dining area, breakfast nook, and private brick patio, this makes a lovely setting for a honeymoon, anniversary, or romantic getaway. No smoking or pets are allowed.

YORK RIVER INN BED & BREAKFAST $$
209 Ambler St., Yorktown
(757) 887-8800, (800) 884-7003
www.yorkriverinn.com
Discriminating visitors will enjoy the colonial ambience of this inn, the only Williamsburg-area B&B with a waterfront location. This charming lodge overlooks the York River and Coleman Bridge. Innkeeper William Cole thinks of his inn as "a home with frequent guests," and he carries out that philosophy in every detail, from the warm greeting you receive to the elaborate breakfast.

The inn provides cable TV in each room, fresh flowers, plush bathrobes, fax services, and other amenities for guests' enjoyment and comfort. Your host's experience in the museum field, including 19 years with Colonial Williamsburg and four as director of the Waterman's Museum, and his detailed knowledge of the area will help you spend your time here wisely and enjoyably.

The first-floor public area has a panoramic view of the York River and Coleman Bridge, augmented by a deck. Virginia antiques from the innkeeper's family and his own collection of Virginia furnishings are features of the dining and living areas.

Upstairs are guest rooms. The Presidents' Room on the second floor features an open deck overlooking the river. The queen-size bed and two comfortable lounge chairs are accented by the interesting display of items associated with seven Virginia-born presidents. The Pocahontas Room offers a queen-size bed and other amenities.

On the third floor, the Washington Room is the inn's largest, graced with a Victorian bedroom suite from the innkeeper's family. There are two seating areas, one overlooking the river. The Jacuzzi is a special treat after a day of touring.

Cole prides himself on serving a hearty breakfast, which is offered in the dining area overlooking the river. Goodies can include a clam casserole, three-cheese quiche, or fresh honeydew-pineapple-kiwi salad.

This is a nonsmoking inn, and neither pets nor children can be accommodated.

To reach the inn from US Route 17, turn onto Route 1001 (Mathews Street) and then immediately right onto Ambler Street. Proceed 1 block to the inn, which will be directly ahead of you.

Shopping

FOUNDING FATHERS
Riverwalk Landing
(757) 875-1776
This shop, owned by the same folks as Stars and Stripes Forever across the plaza, features an array of historically themed home decor and furnishings; a year-round Christmas shop; regional foods for gifts; and a collection of books covering the area's history. Hours are 10 a.m. to 6 p.m. daily.

GIN TAIL ANTIQUES
114 Ballard St.
(757) 890-1335
Antiques lovers will enjoy this shop's gallery of Americana and folk art. It specializes in 18th- and 19th-century furniture and accessories, including rugs, ceramics, and animal art. Gin Tail is open 10 a.m. to 5 p.m. Wed through Sat and noon to 4 p.m. Sun.

KINKS & QUIRKS CONTEMPORARY HANDCRAFTS
327 Water St.
(757) 877-8787
www.kinksandquirks.com
This second location of the popular Williamsburg gallery-and-gift shop carries equally funky, arty, and unique art, jewelry, home furnishings, and

Riverwalk Landing

Yorktown's historical waterfront, Riverwalk Landing, is a shopping and dining complex on the beach side of Water Street. Riverwalk gives the town something of a center—a place to host a weekly farmer's market (May through Dec), several concert series (outdoors in the summer, indoors at the old Freight Shed in the winter), and other seasonal events like a Civil War weekend (Memorial Day), an annual wine festival (October), and Christmas celebration.

Oh, yes—the riverfront is also a centerpiece of events on July 4 and October 19 to commemorate the unpleasantness that ended in the siege here.

Most of the events are hosted on Riverwalk Plaza—an open area with a small bandstand that stretches eastward toward the beach. Next door is the restored Freight Shed, variously used since the 1930s as a ferry terminal and U.S. Post Office. It was renovated and moved a few hundred yards as part of the revitalization; it's now available for receptions and meetings.

A word to the wise: While the 270-space parking terrace across from Riverwalk is convenient, it fills quickly on weekends and during special events. Other surface parking lots are available throughout town; park elsewhere, then take the free Yorktown trolley, which runs every 20 minutes.

more. See details about the Williamsburg location in our Shopping chapter.

NANCY THOMAS GALLERY
145 Ballard St.
(757) 898-0738, (877) 645-0601
www.nancythomas.com

A master folk artist with a national reputation (Whoopi Goldberg once commissioned a set of 12 monthly plaques) and a presence in museums and films (her work can be seen in Jessica Lange's apartment in *Tootsie*), Nancy Thomas calls Yorktown her home. This fascinating shop is where you will find her nationally acclaimed works on display: paintings, wood plaques and sculptures, freestanding whimsical animals, angels, trees, wreaths, Christmas decorations, and a variety of textiles and ceramics. The gallery also carries primitive antiques and a line of custom-upholstered furniture. A second Nancy Thomas Gallery is in Williamsburg's Merchants Square. The Yorktown store is open 10 a.m. to 5 p.m. Mon through Sat, and noon to 5:00 p.m. Sun.

PERIOD DESIGNS
401 Main St.
(757) 886-9482
www.perioddesigns.com

Stop in and check out the wide variety of reproductions of 17th- and 18th-century decorative arts as well as some high-quality antiques from the same period. The shop—housed in the restored circa 1710 Mungo Somerwell House—was started by three friends, all William and Mary graduates. Michelle Erickson creates historically accurate ceramics for museums, while Virginia Lascara makes period frame moldings and floor cloths. Robert Hunter is an antiques dealer who also designs historical products. This shop carries fine floor coverings, ceramics, and furniture as well as items in tin, brass, leather, iron, and glass. Its framing service is museum quality. Period Designs is open Tues through Sat 10 a.m. to 5 p.m. and Sun noon to 5 p.m.

STARS AND STRIPES FOREVER
Riverwalk Landing
(757) 898-0288
You can't have as much patriotic history in an area without having a patriotic gift shop, right? Stars and Stripes, on the water side of Riverwalk Landing, has the gamut of patriotic and government-themed gifts. Memorabilia and souvenirs from various military branches? Check. Tongue-in-cheek commentary on today's politics? Got it. Braying donkeys and trumpeting elephants? That, too (the stuffed kind—not members of Congress).

SWAN TAVERN ANTIQUES
300 Main St.
(757) 898-3033
This fine shop, housed in a charming re-created structure, offers one of the finest collections of antiques in the area. The collection concentrates on 18th-century English items and furniture, candlesticks, prints, and accessories. The items are of the highest quality, and each is a prize find. Swan Tavern also has a wide selection of miniatures that the owner has collected, plus boxwoods that he grew at his Lisburne home. Open 10 a.m. to 5 p.m. Mon through Sat, Sun 12:30 to 5 p.m.

THE WATERMEN'S MUSEUM GIFT SHOP
309 Water St.
(757) 888-2623
www.watermens.org
This excellent shop on the museum's grounds offers a variety of interesting and unusual items, showcasing local artists and artisans and featuring items related to the water. You will find many pieces in here to be cherished as high-quality souvenirs or as gifts for those to whom Yorktown and the Chesapeake Bay are important. The shop is open Tues through Sat from 10 a.m. to 4 p.m. and Sun from 1 to 4 p.m.; during winter months, the museum and shop are only open on weekends.

i In the summer of 1999, Period Designs of Yorktown had a brush with fame when its owners were commissioned to make nearly 500 reproductions for the Mel Gibson film *The Patriot*. The pieces ranged from charts, maps, and 18th-century prints to tea sets and blankets.

THE YORKTOWN SHOPPE
402 Main St.
(757) 898-2984
www.yorktownshoppe.com
In this small shop you will find a number of items appropriate to the setting and period to which Yorktown is a monument. There are fine carvings and paintings, replica and whimsical houses, pierced lanterns, Old World Santas, special clothes, a variety of wrought-iron items, and the extremely popular Old World balance toys, in which a figure balances on a horizontal bar. The Yorktown Shoppe is the exclusive holder of Marlene Whiting's series of Yorktown houses. Whiting's Brandywine Collectibles also includes the 16-piece Williamsburg set. The shop carries Linda Bennett's unique-buttoned dresses, plus pewter ornaments carved by local artists. Open 10 a.m. to 5 p.m. Mon through Sat, 1 to 5 p.m. Sun.

KIDSTUFF

With Busch Gardens and Water Country USA in your backyard, it's hard to imagine that there isn't enough for kids to do in Williamsburg, but some like less overwhelming diversions. (Some kids might like this, too.) It's also tough to justify the entrance fee at some attractions if you have less than a whole day to spend there. Here are some alternatives when have just a few hours to spare, or want a more unusual experience out of your time in Williamsburg.

ATTRACTIONS

GO-KARTS PLUS
6910 Richmond Rd.
(757) 564-7600
www.gokartsplus.com

This thrills-and-spills park, just west of the Williamsburg Pottery Factory on US Route 60, features waterfall minigolf, four stock-car tracks, super stock-cars, a crank 'n' roll train for little ones, Formula One racers, a figure-eight race track, bumper cars, bumper boats, and video games. (There are age and height requirements for some of the rides—6-year-olds can test-drive the rookie track, but you must be 12 to drive a super stock-car.) Most rides in Kiddie Land are geared for children ages 3 to 8.

Admission and parking are free. Rides are paid for with tickets purchased at a counter. Discount books, good for the season or as long as you're in town, can help reduce the cost of the rides. Open daily beginning in late Mar through Oct. Hours Memorial Day through Labor Day are generally 11 a.m. to 11 p.m., but spring and fall hours vary according to the weather, so call in advance to avoid disappointing the troops.

PIRATE'S COVE ADVENTURE GOLF
2001 Mooretown Rd.
(757) 259-4600
www.piratescove.com

You can't miss this spot—just look for the "mountain" rising up from the road next to the Big Kmart near Kingsgate Greene Shopping Center. This park features a pirate theme, with nautical accents—wooden walkways, rope fences, and ship's bow sticking out of the ground as if it had been sunk by Blackbeard himself. A waterfall flows down one side of the mountain, and two courses run through caves. Pirate's Cove has 36 holes on two courses. Try your hand at the Captain's Course or Blackbeard's Challenge—the cost is $7.95 for adults and $7.50 for children. Pirate's Cove is open Mar through Nov, 10 a.m. to 11 p.m. Call for hours before Memorial Day and after Labor Day.

RANGER RICK'S
301 Lightfoot Rd.
(757) 565-4653

Want to take a few swings? The lighted batting cage and golf range is open daily.

HORSEBACK RIDING

Horseback riding is a Virginia tradition dating back at least to George Washington, whose first real job was as a surveyor, exploring the then-uncharted wilds of the Old Dominion. The Historic Triangle has many stables that welcome children, who can take classes and, in some cases, sign up for summer riding camps. Generally, these places require children to be at least six or seven years old. Some require that the young equestrian be accompanied by an adult at all times; others provide adult supervision. Rules vary from place to place. Call ahead and find out what gear is required as well as days and hours of operation.

CARLTON FARMS
3516 Mott Lane
(757) 220-3553
Riding lessons beginning at age 7.

CEDAR VALLEY FARM
2016 Forge Rd., Toano
(757) 566-2621

LAKEWOOD TRAILS
(757) 566-9633

STONEHOUSE STABLES
2116-A Forge Rd., Toano
(757) 566-0666
www.stonehousestables.com

PARKS AND RECREATION

JAMES CITY COUNTY—WILLIAMSBURG COMMUNITY CENTER
5301 Longhill Rd.
(757) 259-4200
When it comes to offering kids active options for their free time, this place fills the bill. Preschool and youth classes are offered in art, dance, piano, and sports. The new "My Place" playground is wheelchair accessible and has adaptive equipment for handicapped children. There are also softball, baseball, and soccer fields.

Learn-to-swim classes are offered for those age six months and older, as well as classes in competitive racing skills for swimmers ages 5 to 9 and 10 to 15. Water aerobics, aqua arthritis, private lessons, basic water safety, lifesaving, scouting water safety, and water safety instructor classes are also available. Families and youth are welcome to use the pool and whirlpool when they're not occpied by aquatic classes. (The pool schedule is available at the front desk or online at www.jccEgov.com/recreation.)

The **Rec Connect Program** offers year-round fitness activities, creative crafts, interactive reading, team projects, drama, music, environmental education, swimming, and field trips to elementary and middle school youth, grades K–8.

Programs are available before and after school, and during school vacation periods.

Teens are also welcome. In addition to various sports, health and wellness, and special interest programs, numerous leadership and career development classes are offered year-round to middle and high school students, including the popular babysitting certification classes. During winter and spring break the center schedules fun trips for teens such as bowling, indoor rock climbing, skating, laser tag, and museums visits.

The center is open 6 a.m. to 9 p.m. Mon through Thurs; until 8 p.m. Fri. Sat hours are 9 a.m. to 6 p.m. and Sun 1 p.m. to 6 p.m. Resident members can choose between an annual, semi-annual, or quarterly membership fee. Although the center is primarily for people living in the community, nonresidents are permitted to use the facility for an $11 charge a day for adults, $4 for children ages 5 to 17. There are also nonresident annual and semiannual membership fees.

SKATE PARK
5301 Longhill Rd.
(757) 259-4200
Located directly across the street from the James City-Williamsburg Community Center is this bowl-style skate park which offers 10,000 square feet of concrete jumps and ramps. There are two movable ramps, a hand rail, and multiple grinding edges. Skateboards, in-line skates, and scooters are permitted to use the facility at the same time. Spectators are not permitted inside the fenced area. There is no fee for entry. Children under 12 must be accompanied by someone 16 or older. The skate park is open 9 a.m. till dark year-round.

KIDSBURG
Mid County Park, 3793 Ironbound Rd.
(757) 229-1232
In May 1994 more than 1,000 volunteers pitched in and turned an empty grassy site into a unique playground that challenges children's minds and physical skills. Today "Kidsburg" is maintained by James City County. Most days you'll find kids

swarming the replica of the ship *Susan Constant*, the James Fort Tot Lot, the George P. Coleman Memorial Bridge, and two theaters. Admission is free. Hours are from sunrise to dusk.

YORKTOWN WATERFRONT
Water St., Yorktown
(no phone)
A two-acre beach along the York River provides opportunities for boating, swimming, and fishing. A large picnic area is located east of the beach, so carrying lunch is an option. Several restaurants within walking distance also are open during the day should hunger strike. Public restrooms, with shower facilities, are available at the west end of the beach and are open (Apr through Oct) from dawn to dusk. Several trees can offer escape from the midday sun and a boardwalk, really a sidewalk, can take you from one end of the beach to the other. Be award: there are no lifeguards on duty.

ON A RAINY DAY

AMF WILLIAMSBURG LANES
5544 Olde Towne Rd.
(757) 565-3311
No bowler is too young to play the game here. Novices pull up the bumpers in the gutters so everyone has a good time—and a decent score at the end of a game. While the place is wildly popular and often crowded with league play, kids are welcome anytime. If you should experience a wait, visit the game room and snack bar. The cost before 5 p.m. is $3.50 a game for adults, $3 for children. After 5, each game is $4.50. Shoe rental is $3.40 for adults, $2.87 for children. The center also has summer and fall youth leagues.

MUSCARELLE MUSEUM OF ART
Jamestown Rd.
(757) 221-2703
www.wm.edu/muscarelle
Art is for everyone—especially children! And nowhere else in town are youngsters consid-

ered more enthusiastically during scheduled programs and workshops than at this wonderful small museum on the campus of the College of William and Mary.

The museum offers Gallery/Studio classes year-round for students in elementary through high school. Each class uses art on display in the museum as inspiration for its activities, many of which are hands-on. Under the supervision of artists and teachers, students are given the opportunity to experiment with various media and techniques.

One especially popular series is the Art Makes You Smart program for preschoolers. Once a month, children ages three to five, along with their adult companion, are invited to explore the museum with the assistance of an early childhood educator. They tour the facility, hear stories, sing songs, play games, and make art.

At various times of the year, the museum sponsors festivals that celebrate specific cultures and exhibits and offers performances, tours, and hands-on activities for children.

Call or visit the museum's Web site for currently scheduled programs and events for youngsters.

WILLIAMSBURG REGIONAL LIBRARY
515 Scotland St.
(757) 259-4070

7770 Croaker Rd.
(757) 295-4040
www.wrl.org
Both locations of the Williamsburg Regional Library provide services for children from birth through high school, including storytime for preschoolers and early elementary schoolchildren, author visits, children's theater groups, professional storytellers, puppet theaters, and assorted workshops. Older children can also get involved in several library events, including the popular Teen Volunteer Program. Most programs are offered free of charge. For more information call the numbers listed above.

VIRGINIA'S INDIAN CULTURE

In the early 17th century, the wilds of the mid-Atlantic coast represented a "New World" to English colonists but had been home to another population for generations: the Virginia Indians.

Nomadic hunters had occupied the region from as early as 17,000 BC. Around 1500 BC, Woodland Indians established more permanent settlements and began cultivating land. When European settlers came, they found Algonquian-speaking Indians, living in longhouses, hunting, fishing, and growing crops, notably corn. Some 32 different tribes, some of whom paid tribute to Powhatan, inhabited the area in the early 1600s.

Those tribes could not withstand the military and social forces that came with colonization. As the English settlers continued to arrive, the indigenous people were deprived of more of their ancestral land. Within 100 years of the English's arrival, the number of Virginia Indians had dropped by an estimated 85 percent.

Nonetheless, the influence of native tribes is present in the Historic Triangle today. The stories, some true and some legend, of Powhatan and his daughter Pocahontas are part of the region's lore. Place-names derived from the Indians are omnipresent; throughout southeastern Virginia, there are parkways, motels, condominiums, and stores named with Virginia Algonquian words. While the Virginia Algonquian language, never written, is no longer in active use, a number of its words—squash, succotash, opossum, moccasin—are now part of everyday American English.

Artifacts uncovered during archaeological digs have provided a mother lode of information about the lives of Virginia's earliest inhabitants. A dig at Governor's Land at Two Rivers, for instance, produced new data about the Paspahegh Indians, whose main town was one of the first to be destroyed by Jamestown settlers. Finds at the site, which may date from 1500, include ceramics and a burial pit containing copper beads. At Jamestown Island and Jamestown Settlement, there are statues, displays, and living-history programs that focus on the role of Virginia Indians in the settlement of the New World. Across the York River in Gloucester County, archaeologists from the College of William and Mary and other institutions have found what was likely the principal residence of Powhatan in 1607, along with evidence of a town that had been a place of leadership for hundreds of years before

Powhatan was born. The owners of a farm on the York River found artifacts and notified archaeologists, who after extensive digging discovered a massive concentration of material that indicates the site was a substantial settlement dating from around AD 1200.

But what about the descendants of these tribes who met, traded, fought, and were ultimately overpowered by the European settlers? In Virginia, eight different tribes dating from the time of European contact are recognized by the state. Data from the 2000 U.S. Census shows about 21,172 people living in Virginia call themselves American Indians. Several of the tribes descended from those who paid tribute to or were allies with Powhatan live within an hour or so of Williamsburg. Until very recently the lives of Virginia's contemporary Indians often seemed obscured by our fascination with history and myth, not to mention Hollywood stereotypes. While Virginia's Indians, including those living on two of the nation's oldest reservations, are largely assimilated into mainstream society, the preservation of heritage is of vital importance to them. The information we've listed below about the region's Indians and their programs, events, and ongoing traditions is proof that their culture is alive and thriving here today. You can call the phone numbers listed below to learn more about each tribe, or contact the **Virginia Council on Indians**. Call (804) 225-2084, or visit http://indians.vipnet.org.

TRIBES

CHICKAHOMINY
Charles City County
(804) 829-2027
Chief Stephen Adkins
The name Chickahominy means "coarse-ground corn people." Close to 1,000 Chickahominy Indians live in the United States, with the largest concentration in Charles City County. At the heart of their active community are the Samaria Baptist Church and Charles City Primary School.

While the Chickahominy are largely assimilated into mainstream American society, tribe members maintain strong ties with each other and work at passing on their traditions. The fourth Saturday and Sunday of every September, the Chickahominy Indian Fall Festival and Powwow is held on the tribal grounds, with activities including traditional dances and handmade jewelry exhibitions. Many of the traditional dances are performed by the Chickahominy Redman Dancers.

EASTERN CHICKAHOMINY
New Kent County
(804) 966-2760
Chief Gene Adkins
About 150 members of this division of the Chickahominy tribe became residents of New Kent County, 25 miles east of Richmond, in 1925. The tribe has about 140 members, and is especially proud of its 26 veterans with military service in the Armed Forces since WWI. The Eastern Chicka-

hominy purchased 41 acres in 2002, becoming one of the last of the state-recognized tribes to own their own land. Their church is Tsena Commocko Baptist in New Kent.

MATTAPONI RESERVATION
Off Route 30 at Route 626, West Point
(804) 769-4508
Chief Carl Custalow
The name Mattaponi is an Anglicized version of the original "Mattapanient," which early American linguists thought to mean "landing place." Of the 500 members of the tribe, some 63 Mattaponi Indians live on a 125-acre reservation established in 1658 north of the Pamunkey River. Today the members of this tribe are Southern Baptists who have made their church a center of their community's activities. The tribe is self-governed by a chief and council. A pottery now occupies the old reservation schoolhouse; potters fashion both traditional and nontraditional objects, using clays from the riverbanks and from commercial sources. Visitors may purchase these handmade pieces. The Wahunsunakah Drum Group, which performs traditional drumming, operates out of the reservation. The reservation—situated on the banks of the Mattaponi River—welcomes visitors from 2 to 5 p.m. Sat and Sun.

PAMUNKEY RESERVATION
Off Route 30,
King William County
(804) 843-4792
Chief Kevin Brown
While the Pamunkey were once one of the most powerful tribes in Eastern Virginia, today around 100 tribal members live on their 1,200-acre reservation in King William County, with other members living off the reservation. Evidence of Indian occupation on the Pamunkey reservation dates back around 12,000 years. The reservation located in King William County is now on the Virginia Landmarks Register. Pamunkey women founded a potters' guild in the 1930s, and today they are dedicated to preserving the traditional coil-and-pinch method of making pots, using clay collected from the banks of the Pamunkey

River. Etched bowls, vases, jugs, pipes, and other handcrafted items are sold at the reservation. The reservation is about 40 minutes from Williamsburg, along Route 633 off of Route 30. Visitors are welcome anytime.

UPPER MATTAPONI

Off Route 30, northwestern King William County
(804) 769-0041
Chief Kenneth Adams

The Upper Mattaponi Indians, an urban, non-reservation group who trace their origins to both the Mattaponi and Pamunkey reservations, reside in northwestern King William County and nearby communities. The tribe is developing a new cultural center across from its house of worship, the Indian View Baptist Church.

The Upper Mattaponi Tribal Center is on Route 30, about a mile southeast of Route 360. The tribe holds its meetings at the center. The tribal center is housed in a brick building that tribal forefathers helped build and that once was the Sharon Indian School, now on the Virginia Landmarks Register. The Upper Mattaponi tribe has its annual American Indian Powwow and Spring Festival on the Saturday and Sunday of Memorial Day weekend, held on the tribal grounds across the street from the tribal center. This event offers American Indian dancing and drumming, storytelling, arts and crafts, children's games, native food and refreshments, miniature-horse rides, and more. Cost is $5 for adults, free for children younger than 12. The Powwow runs from 10 a.m. to 5 p.m. Visitors are encouraged to bring lawn chairs. Write to the center for more information about the Upper Mattaponi, at P.O. Box 182, King William County, VA 23086, or go to www.uppermattaponi.org.

OTHER TRIBES

There are several other Indian tribes that are recognized by the Commonwealth of Virginia. They include the Monacan, whose 1,400 members primarily live in Amherst County, the westernmost of the state's eight recognized tribes. For information, call the **Monacan Indian Nation Headquarters** at (434) 946-0389, or go to www.monacannation.com.

The **Nansemond** have about 300 members living in the cities throughout South Hampton Roads, (757) 986-3354, or go to www.nansemond.org.

Approximately 250 members of the Rappahannock live in King, Queen, Caroline, and Essex Counties. Call the **Rappahannock Tribal Office** at (804) 769-0260.

MUSEUMS

HAMPTON UNIVERSITY MUSEUM
American Indian Collection
Huntington Building
Frissell Avenue, Hampton
(757) 727-5308
www.hamptonu.edu/museum

More than 1,600 art and artifact objects from 93 tribes constitute the large American Indian collection at Hampton University Museum. The collection became available for public viewing in October 1998, when its move to the Huntington Building from the now-closed Academy Building of 1881 was completed. Established in 1868, most of the collection was gathered between that year and 1923 by faculty, friends of the school, and American Indian students sent by the federal government to receive an education at Hampton University. Most artifacts are from Plains Indians, but some pieces of contemporary Pamunkey pottery are also part of the collection. By the way, the museum's central collection of 19th- and 20th-century African-American paintings, sculptures, and prints is one of the country's best. Museum hours are 8 a.m. to 5 p.m. Mon through Fri and noon to 4 p.m. on Sat, closed Sun and major holidays. Admission is free. To reach the museum from Williamsburg, take I-64 East to exit 267 in Hampton and follow the signs.

JAMESTOWN SETTLEMENT
Route 31 and
Colonial Parkway, Jamestown
(757) 229-1607, (888) 593-4682

At this popular museum, explored thoroughly in our Jamestown and Yorktown chapter, exhibits explore the daily life, religion, social structure, government, economy, and customs of the Powhatan tribes, who inhabited coastal Virginia when the English arrived in 1607. An outdoor Powhatan Indian exhibit—complete with costumed interpreters—gives kids and grown-ups alike a taste of life as it was lived by Virginia Indians. Admission to the settlement is $14 for adults and $6.50 for children ages 6 to 12.

The settlement is open from 9 a.m. to 5 p.m. daily (until 6 p.m. from mid-June to mid-Aug). Closed Christmas and New Year's Day.

MARINERS' MUSEUM
100 Museum Dr. (exit 258A off I-64)
Newport News

(757) 596-2222, (800) 581-SAIL
www.mariner.org
The Chesapeake Bay Gallery of this world-renowned museum, described in detail in our Newport News and Hampton chapter, features a dugout canoe from 1630, one of the few Indian vessels ever discovered. Admission is $14 for visitors 13 and older, $12 for senior citizens age 65 and older, $8 for children ages 6 to 12, and free to those younger than 6. AAA and active duty military discounts are available, with ID. The Mariners' Museum is open 10 a.m. to 5 p.m., Wed through Sat. Closed Mon, Tues, Christmas, and Thanksgiving.

MATTAPONI INDIAN MUSEUM AND MINNIE HA HA EDUCATIONAL TRADING POST
1409 Mattaponi Reservation Circle,
off Route 30
West Point
(804) 769-2194
The privately-owned Mattaponi Indian Museum, built here in 1954, features tribal artifacts, including a stone necklace said to have been worn by Pocahontas and a tomahawk said to have been used by Opechancanough in the 1622 attacks. Some ancient artifacts on display date from 5000 BC. Classes in Mattaponi history, beadwork, cooking, Indian medicine, crafts, dance, and lore are taught at the nearby trading post. The museum is open on Sat and Sun from 2 to 5 p.m. or by arrangement. Admission is $1. Arrangements must be made in advance for classes at the trading post. The fee for each two-hour program participant is $2.50.

PAMUNKEY INDIAN MUSEUM
Lay Landing Road off Route 30 and
Route 133, King William County
(804) 843-4792
On the Pamunkey Reservation is the Pamunkey Indian Museum, designed to resemble traditional Indian longhouse dwellings, with displays of artifacts, replicas of stone tools, and the ongoing tradition of pottery-making in the centuries-old manner of the Pamunkey women. Many of the pieces made at the museum can be purchased in the gift shop. Museum hours are 10 a.m. to 4 p.m. Tues through Sat and 1 to 4 p.m. on Sun. Admission is $2.50 for adults, $1.75 for seniors, and $1.25 for children. For groups of 10 or more, admission is $1 per person.

OUR MILITARY HERITAGE

The Hampton Roads region has been inextricably linked with the military from the moment European settlers landed here.

One of the Jamestown settlers' first activities was to build a fort. They weren't just worried about the Native Americans—the British rightly feared what the Spaniards would do if they found the nascent colony. The area's waterways and position at the mouth of the Chesapeake Bay are what attracted the British—and why the region was critical in three separate wars.

Today, the successors to those battlefield fortifications give the region one of the largest military concentrations in the United States, with major installations for all four military branches (plus the U.S. Coast Guard and—shh!—the CIA to boot). By extension, much of the region's industry serves the military—including the only place on the planet that builds nuclear aircraft carriers.

Whether it's artifacts, monuments, bases, or plants, the military presence is almost everywhere.

DIGGING INTO HISTORY

Historians long understood that Jamestown had military trappings to go with the stated purpose of the Virginia Company (making money). But the archaeological discoveries of the last 15 years have sharpened that picture.

Archaeologists have discovered most of the foundation of the original fort (parts have been washed away by the meandering James River) and more than a *million* artifacts. Among them are helmets, breastplates, fragments of armor, and parts of matchlock muskets.

There was a reason, after all, that Jamestown was set so far inland—roughly 20 miles from the Chesapeake Bay, and 10 more from the Atlantic. The Spanish had already established the first European settlement on mainland North America at Saint Augustine, Florida, and their ships ventured along the Eastern seaboard. The two nations were fighting for European supremacy; British ships still preyed on Spanish merchant vessels. (Virginia Company Capt. Christopher Newport, in fact, had spent nearly 20 years as one of those "privateers" who harassed the Spanish.)

After nearly five months at sea, the three ships of the Virginia Company initially stopped at Cape Henry, at the southern tip of the bay. But they understood the foolish danger of settling there in plain sight, so upriver they headed, deciding a few days later to establish themselves on a swampy spit of land.

They chose that site for Jamestown partly because no Native Americans lived there. The natives were nearby, though. A group of them attacked the new settlement within just a few days of its establishment, hastening the construction of the fort.

The relations between the colonists and the Powhatan Confederation were complex. There were moments of rapprochement, such as Capt. John Smith's account of how Pocahontas saved his life. But the introduction of tobacco as a cash crop required ever-expanding swaths of land. The natives fought back against the encroachment—a series of attacks in 1622 became known to the English as a massacre. But by the mid-1600s, English weapons and rampant European diseases had effectively shattered the Powhatan Confederation.

The archaeological artifacts from those wars are replete at both the national park's Jamestown—especially the Archearium—and at the nearby Jamestown Settlement re-creations and museum.

18TH-CENTURY MILITARY CULTURE

The military history of the next century is revealed throughout the area—but two places in particular serve as focal points.

There's Yorktown, of course, site of the last battle of the Revolutionary War. The exhibits and museums at both the major sites there show the state of the military technology—and capture the mixture of pomp and squalor that defined warfare then. (Find out more in our Jamestown and Yorktown chapter.)

But Colonial Williamsburg shows other important aspects of military culture in the emerging colonies.

If you want to understand the relationship of military power to political authority in colonial times, you'll find no starker display than the main entrance to the Governor's Palace. Festooned on the walls are dozens of muskets and swords. They may be neatly arranged—but they were kept there so the royal governor could muster power at almost a moment's notice.

A few blocks away, the Powder Magazine houses another large collection of 1700s militaria, with an emphasis on the muskets used by the colonial militia. In Market Square at Colonial Williamsburg, period cannon are fired daily in demonstrations of the drill required to load, aim, and discharge the pieces. The military uniforms of the era are worn by costumed interpreters and the members of The Colonial Williamsburg Fifes & Drums, who demonstrate the martial music of the period in frequent parades on Duke of Gloucester Street.

ENTRENCHED IN CIVIL WAR

The region's land and waters were the site of heavy fighting for a third time during the Civil War.

Throughout the war, the Union Army's strategy was simple: Capture the Confederate capital of Richmond; collapse the Confederacy. Despite the stalemate in Northern Virginia, the Union was well-positioned to do that in 1862: They held a stranglehold on the Chesapeake Bay and Hampton Roads harbor with the combination of Fort Monroe at the tip of Hampton and Fort Wool, a tiny, well-armed fort on a rock outcropping.

With those forts and a blockading fleet in the harbor, the Union could choke off supplies to both Norfolk and upriver to Richmond—and bring in troops and supplies for an attack from Richmond's eastern flank.

The result was not one, but two, significant battles.

The first, the Battle of Hampton Roads, occurred on Mar. 9, 1862, when the CSS *Virginia* (a scuttled Union warship, the *Merrimac* captured by the Confederacy and rebuilt as an ironclad) rumbled out of Norfolk and wreaked havoc on the wooden Union ships. The *Virginia* single-handedly could have broken the blockade—after just a few hours of battle, it destroyed two Unions ships and left a third aground before retiring at dark. Everyone expected the blockade to be shattered the next morning.

Overnight, however, the first Union ironclad, USS *Monitor*, arrived. With dawn commenced a daylong battle of blasting shells at each other at point-blank range. Neither could penetrate the other's armor—but the *Monitor* didn't need to win; it simply needed to keep *Virginia* from breaking the blockade. The Union's stranglehold on the harbor and peninsula was safe.

Less than two weeks later, McClellan landed the first of his 121,500 men at Fort Monroe to begin his assault up the peninsula.

On the Confederate side, Gen. John Magruder had prepared a defensive line using earthen fortifications (including some of the Revolutionary-era fortifications at Yorktown) and natural barriers like the Warwick River. They stalled the rapid advance McClelland had hoped for; a series of strategic Confederate retreats eventually set up the decisive Seven Days Battles on the outskirts of Richmond. There, a new Confederate commander, Gen. Robert E. Lee, fought him to a stalemate, and McClellan withdrew.

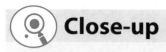

Close-up

Yorktown National Cemetery

Not far from Surrender Field lay the gravestones of more than 2,200 fallen American soldiers—but not from the Revolutionary battle fought at Yorktown. These dead gave their lives during the **Civil War** battle here.

Some 80 years after the siege that led to independence, Yorktown was the site of a second, smaller battle, triggered by the same strategic location alongside a deep-water river port.

In 1862, the North successfully blockaded Hampton Roads harbor and Norfolk, and held control of Fort Monroe at the harbor's mouth. Union Gen. Richard McClellan used the ability to bring in troops and supplies to Fort Monroe to launch an offensive up the Virginia Peninsula. His aim: End the war quickly by seizing the Confederate capital of Richmond.

The Confederates countered by building a defensive line along the natural obstacle of the Warwick River, supplementing it with earthen works and dams that strategically blocked other routes to Richmond with floodwaters. The Confederates choose Yorktown as the northern terminus because it still had leftover fortifications from the Revolutionary War.

McClellan's troops heavily outnumbered the Confederates—but instead of attacking, he chose to besiege and bombard Yorktown. McClellan may have been looking for a crushing blow, like Washington and Rochambeau before him. Instead, the delay caused by his fastidious preparations gave the Confederates time to slip away.

A few weeks later, as McClellan pushed to the outskirts of Richmond, the Confederate Army of Northern Virginia was turned over to a new commander—Gen. Robert E. Lee. He routed McClellan in the bloody Seven Days Battles of June and July, and sent the Union troops retreating back to the safety of Fort Monroe.

In the Civil War Battle of Yorktown, the remains of 632 Union dead were buried in the heart of the **Revolutionary War battlefield**—not far, in fact, from **Moore House**, the Yorktown home where Cornwallis's surrender was negotiated.

Later, the Yorktown cemetery was chosen to serve as a national cemetery for those killed in the Civil War throughout the region. More than 1,500 others were disinterred from their hastily made wartime graves, and reburied with military honors at Yorktown.

The maneuverings of the campaign and the day-to-day lives of its soldiers are memorialized in several area attractions—in particular, the Casemate Museum at Fort Monroe; the spectacular USS *Monitor* exhibit at the Mariner's Museum in Newport News; Endview Plantation and Lee Hall Mansion in northern Newport News; and Dam No. 1 in Newport News Park, site of a significant skirmish in Magruder's delaying action.

Farther afield, a number of important Civil War battles are within a day's drive of the Historic Triangle. The early battles at Manassas, Fredericksburg, and Richmond are to the northwest; due West, at Petersburg, is an excellent museum, operated by the National Parks Service, on the final siege and battle of the war. To simplify the process of planning your trip, consider picking up a copy of the *Insiders' Guide to Civil War Sites in the Eastern Theater*. It includes 21 tours, covering nearly the entire state of Virginia and portions of Maryland, Pennsylvania, and West Virginia, as well as maps, personality sketches of figures who played key roles in the war, and chapters on accommodations and restaurants.

THE 20TH CENTURY

The ironclad battle in the Civil War only hinted at the changes technology would cause in warfare.

A single morning's battle made obsolete thousands of years of wooden warship construction. A few decades later and 70 miles to the southeast, aviation began with the Wright Brothers' flights at Kitty Hawk, North Carolina.

Today, the state of military art can be seen throughout the Historic Triangle—in the F-22 Raptor stealth fighters that fly out of Langley Air Force Base, the F-18 Super Hornets at Virginia Beach's Oceana Naval Air Station, the nuclear aircraft carriers and submarines built at Northrop Grumman Newport News and based across the harbor at Naval Station Norfolk, and the sophisticated aeronautical research performed at NASA's Langley Research Center.

The region's military bases, combined, are home to nearly 100,000 active-duty soldiers, sailors, airmen, and Marines; tens of thousands of civilians work with them on base or at regional civilian contracting firms.

The biggest of those is Northrop Grumman Newport News, formerly Newport News Shipbuilding, which has been building America's mightiest warships since the Spanish-American War. Today, it's the only yard in the world that builds nuclear-powered aircraft carriers—in early 2010, it delivered to the Navy the USS *George H.W. Bush,* the last of the *Nimitz*-class carriers, and began work on the USS *Gerald Ford,* the first of a new class. Fittingly, the yard was also behind the last major maintenance of the USS *Enterprise,* the world's first nuclear aircraft carrier, which is scheduled to be taken out of service when the *Ford* enters it in 2015.

The shipyard does not offer tours to the public, so you'll have to be satisfied with the glimpses of the ships you can get from US 60 and various other locations in downtown Newport News.

The same is true at most of the region's military bases—public access is tightly limited, and what little is allowed can change quickly as security threats arise around the world. Check with the bases for up-to-date information.

CAMP PEARY

Off I-64 at exit 238

Nowhere is this "no access" rule more rigid than Camp Peary. Officially, it's known as the Armed Forces Experimental Training Activity, Department of Defense. That's a paper-thin ruse; everyone from locals to techno-thriller author Tom Clancy refers to it as The Farm, the CIA's major covert training center. Public tours? Sorry.

FORT EUSTIS/U.S. ARMY TRANSPORTATION MUSEUM

Upper Newport News, exit 250A off I-64 (757) 878-4920

Military leaders have a maxim: Amateurs study tactics; professionals study logistics. Nowhere is this more true than Fort Eustis, home to the army's command and training center for air, sea, rail, and land transportation. The base is scheduled to grow larger in coming years during a round of base closures and consolidations.

Most of the base is restricted to the public—but the excellent U.S. Army Transportation Museum, just inside the base gates, is open for tours. As prosaic as the topic may sound, the museum brings to life the lifeblood of military campaigns—the movement of food, munitions, and fuel to frontline troops. Visitors can explore more than 200 years of Army transportation history including miniatures, dioramas, experimental models, and exhibits focusing on the personal stories of Army personnel during Operations Desert Storm and Desert Shield. Kids will enjoy seeing a truck and a jeep that flies. There also are four outdoor parks where aircraft, trains, ships, land craft, and jeeps are on display.

The museum, located just 11 miles south of Williamsburg, is open daily from 9 a.m. to 4:30 p.m. It is closed Mon and federal holidays. Admission is free, but donations are accepted.

Also on the base is the **Matthew Jones House,** located on Harrison Road.

This restored Virginia Historic Landmark was originally designed as an architectural museum house exposing three historic periods. The Matthew Jones House boasts 90 architectural features that are labeled as teaching points. A tour booklet keyed to the numbers helps you identify each feature. In-house collections highlight the history of Mulberry Island and the Jones and Webb families, who lived there for a span of 275 years. It's generally open 1 to 4 p.m. Sat and Sun June through Labor Day and by arrangement for tours. Admission is free, but donations are accepted. For more information on visiting hours, your best bet is to contact the visitor center at (757) 886-7777.

FORT MONROE
**Old Point Comfort,
southeastern Hampton
(757) 788-2238**

Fort Monroe is situated at one of the most historic—and strategically important—places in Virginia, where the James River and Hampton Roadstead meet the Chesapeake Bay. The Jamestown settlers stopped here briefly on their way upstream, and Old Point Comfort has been the site of a military base since 1609, when the Virginia Company established Fort Algernourne to protect Jamestown from waterborne assault from other European nations.

But not for much longer: Fort Monroe (which in recent years was headquarters to the U.S. Army's training command) is scheduled to close by September 2011 as part of the military's most-recent round of base consolidations. Most of its functions will move to Fort Eustis. City and state officials are considering a number of plans, ranging from preservation to commercial development.

Of particular interest on the post is the **Casemate Museum** (757) 788-3391, which traces the history of the base through the centuries (including its role as a prison for Confederate President Jefferson Davis after the Civil War). A seawall surrounding much of the base offers a breathtaking view of boaters on the Chesapeake Bay.

To reach the base, follow Mercury Boulevard through Phoebus to its eastern tip at the Fort Monroe gate. For more information on the Casemate Museum, see Hampton's Attractions in our Newport News and Hampton chapter.

HAMPTON NATIONAL CEMETERY
**Cemetery Road,
Hampton University Campus
(757) 728-3131**

This cemetery dates from the Civil War, with many of the fallen from both sides interred here. Burials of veterans still are conducted in both the older and newer parts of the cemetery, and beautiful and fitting tributes to the servicemen and servicewomen interred here are presented each Memorial Day.

LANGLEY AIR FORCE BASE
**End of LaSalle Avenue
(757) 764-9990**

This base has a history of operation beginning as Langley Field in the days when the flight line consisted of biplanes; for a while, military dirigibles were housed here as well. Today it is home to the U.S. Air Force's most modern aircraft, the F-22 Raptor stealth fighters, frequently seen in training flights in the area's skies. Langley is also headquarters for the Air Combat Command, which oversees all Air Force combat commands. Sharing the base property is the 787-acre NASA Langley Research Center, where the Project Mercury missions were conceived and where air and space flight research is conducted. Although the base does not have exhibits open to the public, periodic open houses and air shows afford an opportunity to visit. For information on the air shows, call (757) 764-2018.

The base's official visitor center is the Virginia Air and Space Center, an outstanding aviation museum in downtown Hampton. For more information, see the VASC section of our Hampton chapter.

NAVAL STATION NORFOLK
**9079 Hampton Blvd.
Norfolk
(757) 444-0948
http://cnic.navy.mil/norfolksta/index.htm**

Naval Station Norfolk is the world's largest at 4,300 acres, and is home to five aircraft carriers (and 75 ships in all), and the U.S. Navy's Atlantic Fleet command.

You can get excellent views of the ships at their docks from either of the Hampton Roads bridge tunnels. But why settle for that? The Navy offers 45-minute guided tours of the base, conducted by naval personnel. Schedules vary with the season, from one a day in winter to up to nine per day in summer. Call the number above for up-to-date scheduling information.

NAVAL WEAPONS STATION YORKTOWN
Route 143, Yorktown
(757) 887-4939
As the title suggests, this installation is where ordnance used by the Atlantic Fleet is maintained and stored. On Route 143, just west of Lee Hall, it extends much of the length of the York River between Williamsburg and Yorktown. Ships being armed can be seen at the station's piers from pullouts on the Colonial Parkway near its Yorktown end. This view will have to do, as the weapons station is a closed base.

NAVY WEAPONS STATION, CHEATHAM ANNEX
York County
(757) 887-4939
This bulk storage facility in York County belongs to the Fleet and Industrial Supply Center in Norfolk. The center's loading piers in the York River are visible from the Colonial Parkway just where it turns inland from the river.

THE ARTS

The first performing arts theater in the Americas was located in Williamsburg on the edge of Palace Green. Long gone, that early theater has not been reconstructed but when it comes to the arts, the Historic Triangle offers plenty to see, hear, and do. There are museums and galleries devoted to the visual arts. Live concert performances are an almost weekly occurrence, and dance is alive and well here.

Travel a bit east to Newport News, Hampton, and points south of Hampton Roads, and you'll find museums with state-of-the-art IMAX movies, interactive exhibits, and other places to keep children as well as adults entertained for days. You'll also find performances by the Virginia Opera, Virginia Ballet Company, and other professional performing arts groups.

Two especially popular and longtime Williamsburg festivals include An Occasion for the Arts, held the first Sunday in October, and the Junior Women's Club Art Show, in the spring. Both are held on Merchants Square. Growing in popularity is a performing arts event called First Night, an alcohol-free New Year's Eve celebration of the arts, with performances staged at several venues around downtown Williamsburg. (For information on this and other events, check our Annual Events chapter.) Here, all venues are in Williamsburg unless otherwise stated.

VENUES

The majority of the fine performances produced in the city are staged at Phi Beta Kappa Memorial Hall, on the campus of the College of William and Mary, the Kimball Theatre in Merchants Square, or at the Williamsburg Regional Library, which hosts various musical performances throughout the year.

KIMBALL THEATRE
428 Duke of Gloucester St.
(757) 565-8588, (800) HISTORY
www.kimballtheatre.com
Extensively remodeled in 2001, this 583-seat chandelier-lit theater now looks essentially as it did when it opened in 1933 as the Williamsburg Theater. Owned by the Colonial Williamsburg Foundation, has a full schedule—lectures, concerts, and art films and documentaries. A very popular recurring performance is Dean Shostak's Crystal Concerts. Current offerings can be heard by calling the local number listed above; advance tickets can be purchased by calling the toll-free Colonial Williamsburg reservation line.

PHI BETA KAPPA MEMORIAL HALL
College of William and Mary
Jamestown Road
(757) 221-2655,
(757) 221-2674 (box office)
www.wm.edu/theatre
This air-conditioned 750-seat hall is venue for a variety of performances, lectures, and forums of the highest quality, with the College of William and Mary the most frequent sponsor. William and Mary's theater department—whose graduates include Glenn Close and Linda Lavin—offers a high-quality season of performances here during the academic year, and the music and dance departments provide concerts of equally fine caliber. The William and Mary Concert Series held in the hall is a subscription series of performances by nationally and internationally acclaimed performers and groups presenting symphonies, ballet, chamber music, theater, and solo performances. Ticket sales are publicized in the fall. Think ahead—tickets go very quickly. The hall is wheelchair accessible and has an electronic system for the hearing impaired.

WILLIAMSBURG REGIONAL LIBRARY ART CENTER
515 Scotland St.
(757) 259-4070
www.wrl.org

The library has done an extraordinary job of becoming, in effect, the community's cultural arts center. In the art center's lobby there are small ongoing exhibits by visual artists working in a variety of media. The auditorium, which seats 268, provides venue for lectures, debates, forums, and performances of all kinds, from symphonies, chamber concerts, and choral presentations to high school–band rock 'n' roll. The Art Center's emphasis is on providing enriching, educational programming for the community. Events held here are typically free, but occasionally an event organized by an outside group will charge a minimal fee. The library also hosts a number of national acts that require a cover charge ranging from free to $20. (See our Nightlife chapter for more information.)

PERFORMING ARTS

Music

Symphonic, operatic, and recital performances by touring professionals and virtuoso students from the College of William and Mary's music department are presented throughout the year at Phi Beta Kappa Memorial Hall. Williamsburg also is home to several professional and skilled amateur musical groups, each presenting a varied program throughout the season. The venues differ depending upon the performance. The best way to get timely information is to monitor the *Virginia Gazette*'s arts and performance sections.

SUMMER BREEZE CONCERT SERIES
Merchants Square
(757) 220-7751

A popular and informal arts offering is the Summer Breeze on the Square, which features performances of America's original art form on Thursday nights in July. Attendees are invited to bring folding chairs and blankets for these out-door performances, held on Merchants Square at 7 p.m. A temporary stage is set up in front of The Trellis restaurant and the whole spectrum of music, from folk to jazz, delights listeners. Summer Breeze on the Square is a joint effort of the Merchants Square Association, the City of Williamsburg, and James City County.

WILLIAMSBURG CHORAL GUILD
P.O. Box 1864, Williamsburg, VA 23187
(757) 220-1808
www.williamsburgchoralguild.org

The Williamsburg Choral Guild is an established and esteemed mixed choral group made up of about 100 area volunteer singers. Guild members rehearse from late August through early May, presenting three subscription concerts during that time. The Web site keeps a current list of upcoming performances.

i Community members can get on the William and Mary Cultural Events Calendar mailing list. For information about college-sponsored arts happenings, call (757) 221-4000, the college's general information number.

WILLIAMSBURG SYMPHONIA
312 Waller Mill Rd.
(757) 229-9857
www.williamsburgsymphonia.org

The Williamsburg Symphonia offers concerts by subscription in Williamsburg. In addition, the orchestra performs special holiday and family concerts annually. The Symphonia is noted throughout the region for the excellence of its programs. Janna Hymes directs the professional chamber orchestra, with whom a number of outstanding solo artists perform for specific programs. All Masterworks and Family concerts are performed at the Kimball Theatre in Merchants Square. Pops concerts take place in various Williamsburg locations. Check the Web site for more information.

WILLIAMSBURG WOMEN'S CHORUS
(757) 564-7875
www.williamsburgwomenschorus.org

The Williamsburg Women's Chorus is an all-volunteer group of 40 women who come together to sing in a variety of musical styles from Baroque to Broadway. The chorus performs two to four public concerts a year throughout the greater Williamsburg area. Auditions are required of aspiring new members. Check their Web site for upcoming concerts and more information.

i Musician and Grammy Award–winning pop artist Bruce Hornsby, who was born and raised in Williamsburg, still lives in town with his wife and two sons. He often can be seen at local sports events, restaurants, and simply walking about town with his family, taking in the sights like everyone else.

Theater

Williamsburg enjoys Shakespeare's plays during an annual summer festival held each July honoring the Bard. There are also very high-quality classic and contemporary plays available throughout the year, compliments of the Williamsburg Players, who perform in their playhouse on Hubbard Lane. The William and Mary Theatre also offers an excellent season of drama and comedy.

VIRGINIA SHAKESPEARE FESTIVAL
Phi Beta Kappa Memorial Hall
Jamestown Rd.
(757) 221-2659
www.vsf.wm.edu
This series has developed an enduring audience over the past 25-plus years. Sponsored each July by William and Mary's theater department, the festival season of two Shakespeare performances in repertory offers a variety of the Bard's works. The plays are performed alternately so that those in town for only a short period can attend a performance of each. The nightly curtain is at 8 p.m., and there are also 2 p.m. Sunday matinees. See our Annual Events chapter for more details about this summer tradition. Tickets range from $10 to $25.

WILLIAM AND MARY THEATRE
Phi Beta Kappa Memorial Hall
Jamestown Rd.
(757) 221-2655,
(757) 221-2674 (box office)
The college's theater, speech, and dance students stage four full-scale plays in addition to many smaller productions during the academic year. Season subscribers may see all four shows for the price of three. Matinees are at 2 p.m., and evening curtain is at 8 p.m. In addition, plays performed, written, and directed by students are presented in the Premiere Theater. The department usually stages one or two performances per semester. Past performances include *A Little Night Music* by Stephen Sondheim. Ticket prices vary and some performances are free.

THE WILLIAMSBURG PLAYERS
200 Hubbard Lane
(757) 229-1679,
(757) 229-0431 (reservations)
www.williamsburgplayers.org
From September through June the Williamsburg Players produce plays of extraordinary quality in their cozy playhouse. The season usually consists of five plays, mixing little-known and more-famous works, with emphasis on modern and contemporary authors. The casts are all volunteers, but the Players draw upon more than 30 years of experience. Their staging and performances, thanks to their willingness to risk breaking conventions to advance their art, consistently receive the highest reviews and accolades. There are only 115 seats in the theater, and tickets go fast. General admission is $17, senior citizens and students pay $15.

Dance

Whether your tastes run toward the classics or contemporary dance, ballet, or tap, you'll find fine dance performances presented in and around Williamsburg. The College of William and Mary hosts performances by national and international dance troupes throughout the academic year, and news of these performances is available through the local media. In addition, the local dance companies listed below have entertained many an enthralled audience with excellent productions, offered year-round. Venues and dates change from year to year, however, so it is best to check the *Virginia Gazette* for performance information or call the companies for updates on scheduled events.

EASTERN VIRGINIA SCHOOL FOR THE PERFORMING ARTS
1915 Pocahontas Trail
The Village Shops at Kingsmill
(757) 229-8535
www.evspa.org
This school's philosophy is to give each child correct information at age-appropriate levels about the art forms. EVSPA uses the Standards of Arts Education as its core, and offers an added bonus of providing a professional standard through the experience of the school's directors, former professional opera singer Ron Boucher and prima ballerina Sandra Balestracci, a registered dance educator. Boucher and Balestracci cofounded the school in 1996.

Under the direction of Balestracci, the Dance Division offers the highest quality of instruction and performance. The Vaganova technique is used to develop the dancer and is a full, eight-year program, beginning at age seven. The division also offers instruction in modern, jazz, tap, and lyrical dance.

Boucher heads the Theater and the Voice Division and guides students through a balanced program of strong technique and application.

The educational program is augmented by the school's outstanding productions, featuring original full-length ballets.

THE INSTITUTE FOR DANCE
3356 Ironbound Rd., Suite 201
(757) 229-1717
www.institutefordance.org
Since 1968, the institute has offered professional training for all ages. The curriculum provides expert and experienced instruction to ensure students the finest development of their skill in

ballet, offering classes in creative dance, tap, jazz, floor gymnastics, character, and ballet. Several productions are staged during the year and are very popular in the community. *The Nutcracker* at Christmastime is a long-standing local tradition. Another performance is staged during the spring.

VISUAL ARTS

Museums

DEWITT WALLACE DECORATIVE ARTS MUSEUM
Corner of Francis and South Henry Streets
(757) 220-7724
www.colonialwilliamsburg.com
It is difficult for visitors who have been in this gallery to reconcile its size and scope with the structure one sees from Francis Street in the Historic Area. Although the entrance is through the lobby of the reconstructed Public Hospital, this fascinating museum, designed by world-renowned architect I. M. Pei, is housed mostly underground. It displays prized pieces of Colonial Williamsburg's permanent collection—furniture, textiles, maps, prints, paintings, metals, and ceramics dating from the 1600s to the 1830s—in exhibits designed to instruct viewers in the aesthetics and tastes of the colonial period. Perhaps the largest collection and premier interpreter of objects from the households of early America, the gallery mounts special exhibits for several years at a time to allow large numbers of visitors to view them. Thorough research precedes each showing, and the results are presented in understandable and memorable ways. The overall effect on gallery visitors is an understanding of each object in the context of its function, design, and use.

Admission is free with any Colonial Williamsburg ticket or you can purchase single-day museums ticket ($10 for adults, $5 for children). The gallery is generally open 10 a.m. to 7 p.m. daily, but the hours vary seasonally. There is a cafe on-site, and the entire museum is wheelchair accessible. Read our chapter on Colonial Williamsburg for more information.

MUSCARELLE MUSEUM OF ART
Jamestown Road
(757) 221-2700
http://web.wm.edu/muscarelle

In the evening this museum, just west of Phi Beta Kappa Memorial Hall on the William and Mary campus, is easy to spot. Multiple columns of color are lighted along one exterior wall, and the effect is quite startling when viewed from Jamestown Road for the first time. The museum, designed by famed local architect Carlton Abbott, offers lectures, films, and tours, but the holdings are the major draw. The permanent collection includes works by European Old Masters as well as modern works, and a special holding is the collection of colonial-period portraits of Virginians. The museum also hosts several changing exhibits throughout the year. The museum is open 10 a.m. to 5 p.m. Tues through Fri, noon to 4 p.m. Sat and Sun. Docents lead tours at 1 p.m. Sat and Sun. Be sure to obtain a permit from the museum entitling you to reserved parking in the lot in front of the building. Parking spaces are at a premium on campus, and you risk having your vehicle towed otherwise. There is an admission fee that varies from a few dollars to as much as $15, depending on current exhibits.

THE WATERMEN'S MUSEUM
309 Water St., Yorktown
(757) 887-2641
www.watermens.org

Virginia's watermen, generations of them, are the focus of this small but lively museum located on Yorktown's waterfront and housed in a Colonial Revival manor house. Five galleries and a variety of outdoor exhibits chronicle the story of generations of Virginians whose livelihood stemmed from the waters of the Chesapeake Bay and its tributaries. Here visitors see ship models, paintings, photographs, nautical artifacts, and tools in permanent and rotating exhibits on this ancient trade.

The museum hopes to preserve the heritage of the watermen and to interpret their culture and their contributions to the region in an effort to provide and support educational opportunities and preserve and enhance the environment of the fragile bay. All generations are represented, from the original Native American fishermen to today's working men and women. On the grounds you can see some of the work boats and other traditional equipment once so common on our waters. The museum provides a variety of programs, seminars, activities, and special events to the public.

Admission is $5 for adults and $2 for children. Groups or individuals may make arrangements to visit anytime by calling in advance. From Apr through mid-Dec, the museum is open 10 a.m. to

---

Internationally–known artist Georgia O'Keeffe

. . . received her first honorary degree from William and Mary. Although her two brothers attended college here, women were not allowed to enroll when the family moved to Williamsburg in the early 1900s. To mark the award of her honorary degree in 1938, the college put on an exhibition of her work, including eight paintings selected by O'Keeffe's husband, Alfred Stieglitz. Another, *White Flower*, was donated to the event by Abby Rockefeller. It was O'Keeffe's first show in the South, and it remained on view for six days. In 2001 the Muscarelle Museum of Art re-created her exhibit with eight of the original nine paintings. (One was too fragile to travel.) The new O'Keeffe show was on display for five months and also included letters, documents, and a six-and-a-half-minute home movie of her visit to William and Mary to accept her honorary degree.

4 p.m. Tues through Sat and 1 to 4 p.m. Sun. The museum is closed Monday except Memorial Day and Labor Day. From Thanksgiving to Christmas the museum is open only on weekends. The Watermen's Museum Gift Shop features works by more than 40 local artists and crafters with unusual original works that will be cherished by those who appreciate folk art.

Galleries

ANDREWS GALLERY
Jamestown Road
(757) 221-1452
This exhibition gallery for the Department of Art and Art History at the College of William and Mary is behind the Phi Beta Kappa Memorial Hall. Periodic exhibits of traveling shows and of faculty and student art make the gallery an interesting window on the art scene. Hours are from 10 a.m. to 5 p.m. Mon through Fri.

NANCY THOMAS GALLERY
145 Ballard St., Yorktown
(757) 898-0738
www.nancythomas.com
A master folk artist with a national reputation and a presence in museums (and in films—her work can be seen in Jessica Lange's apartment in *Tootsie*), Nancy Thomas calls Yorktown home. This fascinating shop is where you will find her works on display: paintings and sculptures, freestanding whimsical animals, angels, trees, wreaths, Christmas decorations, and much more. You are likely also to find Thomas herself displaying a new item or ready to discuss any of the wonderful things you might find interesting. In addition, you will find antiques and other original works and prints. Hours are Mon through Sat from 10 a.m. to 5 p.m. and Sun from 1 to 5 p.m. See our Shopping entry in the Jamestown and Yorktown chapter for more information. Note,

too, that Thomas has a second gallery in Williamsburg's Merchants Square, adjacent to the city's Historic Area.

THIS CENTURY GALLERY
219 North Boundary St.
(757) 229-4949
www.thiscenturyartgallery.org
As the name indicates, the focus of this gallery, established more than 40 years ago, is work by contemporary artists, local, regional, and national. Shows featuring all media change on a regular basis, with an occasional Christmas crafts show in November/December and spring crafts exhibition. The gallery, an affiliate of the Virginia Museum of Fine Arts in Richmond, displays traveling exhibits of that museum. Hours are from 11 a.m. to 5 p.m. Tues through Sun.

A TOUCH OF EARTH
The Gallery Shops at Lightfoot
6580 Richmond Rd.
(757) 565-0425
Owned and operated by Lianne Lurie and Paul Pittman, this gallery, the oldest in the area, features fine decorative and functional crafts by more than 200 contemporary American artists and craftspeople. With a concentration on unusual works appealing to many senses, the selections include pottery, wind chimes in both clay and metal, glassworks, jewelry, lamps, musical instruments, kaleidoscopes, candle holders, and textiles—many of them signed one-of-a-kinds. The basic collection of lovely hand-built and wheel-thrown stoneware and fine porcelain includes the unique "Gloom Chasers," intricately decorated and pierced stoneware lanterns. A Touch of Earth is open from 10 a.m. to 5 p.m. Mon through Fri, 10 a.m. to 6 p.m. Sat, 11 a.m. to 5 p.m. Sun, and by appointment.

ANNUAL EVENTS

If you enjoy planning a vacation around a special event, a trip to the Historic Triangle offers plenty of options. While a summer excursion virtually guarantees a jam-packed itinerary of historic tours, sun-soaked shopping, and theme park rowdiness, the three other seasons can be just as glorious. And although the local festival season doesn't swing into high gear until April, you'll find a smattering of activities to choose from during the year's first quarter, a good time to visit if you don't like to fight crowds.

If you schedule your visit during spring break or later, your choice of fun activities pretty much runs the gamut. From the ever-popular performances of Shakespeare's plays to the rousing sounds of Scottish bagpipes to the exquisite lights of Christmas, the Williamsburg area gives you a diverse menu of events and activities from which to choose.

Below, we've listed the major—and a few more low-key but fun—celebrations that take place in and around the Williamsburg area. For those of you willing to drive a little farther for a good time, we've also included some of our favorite celebrations that take place in other pockets of Hampton Roads. Our annual events and festivals are listed month by month to make your vacation planning a little easier. The prices we provide are subject to change, but they should give you a solid ballpark figure to use when tallying up that vacation budget. We have noted where events in the Colonial Williamsburg Historic Area are included in your ticket purchase.

EVENT SCHEDULE

January

WORKING WOOD IN THE 18TH CENTURY
DeWitt Wallace Decorative Arts Museum
326 W. Francis St., Williamsburg
(800) 603-0948
The annual *Working Wood in the 18th Century* conference is cosponsored by the Colonial Williamsburg Foundation and *Fine Woodworking* magazine. Registration for the popular conference begins when the brochure is mailed in September. These programs have filled to capacity every year, so those interested are encouraged to register early. To be added to the mailing list, submit your postal address to dchapman@cwf .org or call the number listed above.

February

ANTIQUES FORUM
Williamsburg Lodge Conference Center
South England Street, Williamsburg
(800) 603-0948

In early February the Antiques Forum comes to Colonial Williamsburg, bringing collectors and experts who share their knowledge in seminars, attend lectures given by Colonial Williamsburg's curators, take special tours, and socialize. The forum brings together scholars, collectors, and antiques buffs to reexamine past judgments about American decorative arts. The five-day event cost $600 in 2009 which included all lectures, tours, special programming, opening receptions, and continental breakfasts, coffees, and afternoon teas Registration begins in October.

MID-ATLANTIC QUILT FESTIVAL WEEK
Hampton Roads Convention
Center, Hampton
(215) 862-5828
www.quiltfest.com
Explore an American art form that has developed and grown with the nation. The Mid-Atlantic Quilt Festival Week is a compilation of four exciting quilting, fiber-arts, and wearable-art shows and is the perfect place for quilters and wearable,

textile, and fiber artists of all levels and ages to explore these arts. In all, more than 500 quilts, wearables, dolls, and textiles are on exhibit; workshops, lectures, and special activities are held the last week in February.

PRESIDENTS WEEKEND
Colonial Williamsburg
(800) HISTORY
Programs throughout the weekend highlight the actions and experiences of three Virginians—George Washington, Thomas Jefferson, and James Madison—who all served as president of the United States.

March

GLOUCESTER DAFFODIL FESTIVAL
Main Street, Gloucester
(804) 693-2355
www.gloucesterva.info/pr
Considered the opening event in the busy Hampton Roads festival season, this Gloucester gala celebrates this town's long relationship with the sunny daffodil. Gloucester was once the daffodil capital of America—there are growers here who have been in the daffodil business for four generations. Held in late March or early April (depending on when Easter is) this free festival features food, arts and crafts, musical entertainment, and bus tours to Brent & Becky's Bulbs. There are children's events, games, historic displays, and the crowning of the Daffodil Festival Queen. Bring your pet along for the Magnificent Mutt Show. To get to Gloucester, follow Route 17 north from Yorktown over the Coleman Bridge. For shuttle parking, follow the signs to Gloucester High School. The shuttle ride costs $1. The money raised benefits Literacy Volunteers of Gloucester.

MILITARY THROUGH THE AGES
Jamestown Settlement
(757) 253-4838
www.historyisfun.org
Reenactment groups depicting soldiers and military encounters throughout history join forces with modern-day veterans and active units to demonstrate camp life, tactics, and weaponry. The event features a Saturday children's parade and a Sunday military pass-in-review.

ST. PATRICK'S DAY PARADE
Granby Street
Ocean View section of Norfolk
(757) 587-3548
www.norfolkparade.com
This particular wearin'-of-the-green event may not take place in Williamsburg, but if you're in the mood to celebrate your Irish heritage or simply wish to get caught up in the revelry, check out Norfolk's St. Patrick's Day Parade and Festivities. The parade, held the Saturday closest to St. Paddy's Day, is the area's oldest and largest. The route typically begins at 10 a.m. at Northside Middle School on Granby Street (about 45 minutes from Williamsburg on I-64 East on a good day) and winds up at the Knights of Columbus Hall on West Government Street for the after-party.

WILLIAMSBURG FILM FESTIVAL
Williamsburg
http://wff5.tripod.com
This might be better titled the Williamsburg Classic TV Show Festival. This three-day event in mid-March is held at the Holiday Inn on Richmond Road. In 2010, organizers were commemorating the 55th anniversary of *Gunsmoke*, "the greatest of all TV westerns." Old movies and television shows are screened, and the organizers invite actors for autograph sessions and panel discussions.

WOMEN'S HISTORY MONTH
Colonial Williamsburg
(800) HISTORY
Colonial Williamsburg celebrates the contributions of 18th-century women throughout the month. Tours, programs and special presentations explore the various roles that our foremothers filled in the creation of a new country.

April

ART ON THE LAWN
Muscarelle Museum of Art
Jamestown Road, Williamsburg
http://web.wm.edu/muscarelle
(757) 221-2700
This annual festival, typically held on a Saturday in mid-April, celebrates the arts with live music, food, and a student artwork display. Art activities, games, and museum treasures help keep the kids entertained. The event is free and open to the public.

GARDEN SYMPOSIUM
DeWitt Wallace Museum
South Henry and Francis Streets, Williamsburg
(800) 603-0948
Colonial Williamsburg's three-day crash course on cultivating a green thumb has been held for 63 consecutive years. If you want to know how to make your garden grow, join horticulturists and gardening enthusiasts for a host of lectures, tours, and master classes. Special hotel rates are available at Colonial Williamsburg hotels.

HISTORIC GARDEN WEEK
(804) 644-7776, (757) 220-2486
www.VAGardenweek.org
Sponsored by garden clubs throughout Virginia, this special week celebrating nature's beauty (and the decorating skills of a number of homeowners) is held the third week in April. On Tuesday of that week, the Williamsburg Garden Club sponsors its garden week tour of both the gardens and interiors of four or five homes in the Williamsburg area. In addition, a walking garden tour of portions of the Colonial Williamsburg gardens is offered. Since the chairperson of the local event changes annually, your best bet for more information is to contact the state Historic Garden Week headquarters at the 804 number above or the Williamsburg chairwoman of the event at the 757 number. The Web site has many details, too.

VIRGINIA ARTS FESTIVAL
200 Boush St., Norfolk
(757) 282-2800
www.virginiaartsfest.com
Introduced in 1997 as a way to provide locals and tourists with a more varied cultural menu, the festival has been deemed "an unprecedented flowering of the arts" by a writer in the *New York Times*. The festival begins in late April and runs for six weeks, staging hundreds of events in 10 Hampton Roads cities. The lineup that includes dance, theater, and all kinds of music. Performances truly are world-class—participants have included Itzhak Perlman, the National Symphony Orchestra with Leonard Slatkin, the Boys Choir of Harlem, the Stuttgart Chamber Orchestra, the Russian National Ballet, and modern dance's innovative Mark Morris Dance Group. Each of the events is separately ticketed; prices have ranged from free to a $150 orchestra seat at a world-class performance.

May

CHILDREN'S FESTIVAL OF FRIENDS
Newport News Park, Jefferson Avenue
Newport News
(757) 926-1400
A popular destination for families with young children, this one-day festival is held on a Saturday in early May. The fun includes entertainment with pint-size appeal, hands-on activities, games, and a variety of rides. Admission is free but expect to pay about a parking fee.

CONFEDERATE ATTACK ON FORT POCAHONTAS AT WILSON'S WHARF
Route 5, Charles City County
www.fortpocahontas.org
In an effort to preserve this once-forgotten fort, reenactors meet for a two-day event to restage the Civil War battle that took place here on May 24, 1864. It was the first major land-naval clash between the U.S. Colored Troops and General Robert E. Lee's Army of Northern Virginia. The weekend events include a living-history encampment, an evening lantern tour, military

demonstrations, and two battle reenactments. Sutlers—salespeople dressed in period attire—offer plenty of wares for sale. Admission is $10 for adults and $8 for students per day, or $15 for adults and $10 for students for a two-day pass. Discounts are available for groups of 10 or more.

JAMESTOWN DAY
Jamestown Settlement
Route 31, Jamestown
(757) 253-4838, (888) 593-4682
www.historyisfun.org
At Jamestown Day—an event sponsored jointly by Jamestown Settlement and Historic James-town—maritime demonstrations, military drills, and archaeology programs mark the 1607 anniversary of America's first permanent English colony. Separate admission charges apply to Jamestown Settlement and Historic Jamestown. Free parking with a shuttle is available at both sites.

MEMORIAL DAY
Colonial Williamsburg
(800) HISTORY
A modern service honors military veterans who died while serving their country. Wreaths are placed at the Governor's Palace, Bruton Parish Church, and the French gravesite to honor those interred in or near those sites who died during the American Revolution or the Civil War. A procession with Fife and Drum support begins at the palace. A brief commemorative service with musket and cannon volleys takes place at the French gravesite.

June

GREEK FESTIVAL
Saints Constantine and Helen Greek Ortho-dox Church
60 Traverse Rd., Newport News
(757) 872-8119
www.newportnewsgreekfestival.org
When more than 12,000 folks decide to have dinner at the same place, you know the food must be good. Join the crowd at this annual Hellenic festival for a few traditional favorites—moussaka, souvlaki,

pastitsio, gyros, baked chicken, and rice pilaf—and enjoy the live entertainment. Stop at the plaka, or marketplace, which sells everything from artwork and fine jewelry to Greek provisions such as filo, orzo, olives, and cheeses. Admission and parking are free. Meals typically are sold a la carte.

HAMPTON JAZZ FESTIVAL
Hampton Coliseum, exit 263B off I-64
(757) 838-4203 (Hampton Coliseum)
www.hamptonjazzfestival.com
If you like jazz and R&B, you'll love this popular Hampton festival. How much will you love it? Let us count the ways: (1) Aretha Franklin; (2) Isaac Hayes; (3) Stevie Wonder; (4) B. B. King; (5) Gladys Knight; (6) Boney James; (7) George Benson. Not all in the same weekend, of course, but there are usually a couple of major headliners performing each year. The festival typically is held in late June. Tickets can be purchased through Ticketmaster by calling (757) 671-8100. For a full lineup, see the Web site after April 1 each year.

JAMES CITY COUNTY FAIR
Chickahominy Riverfront Park
1350 John Tyler Hwy
Williamsburg, VA 23185
This free three-day fair, typically held Thursday through Saturday in late June, features rides, exhibits, crafts, music, and food. To keep the fair's local flavor firmly intact, anyone selling goods must live or work in James City County, Williamsburg, or the Bruton District of York County. Satellite parking costs $1 at Toano Middle School, with buses shuttling you to the fairgrounds.

MASONIC PROCESSION AND SERMON
Colonial Williamsburg's Historic Area
1-800-HISTORY
The Feast Day of St. John the Baptist was celebrated annually by the Masonic Lodge of 18th-century Williamsburg. Lodge members processed from the lodge to the church to hear a sermon preached for their benefit by the chaplain of the Lodge. Colonial Williamsburg's reenactment of this annual event includes costumed interpreters,

current members of Williamsburg Lodge No. 6, and masons who choose to participate.

July

INDEPENDENCE DAY CELEBRATION
Main Street, Yorktown
(757) 890-3300
Family-oriented festivities are the order of the day at the Fourth of July celebration at Yorktown. Activities include a footrace, parade, arts and crafts, musical entertainment, and, of course, a magnificent display of fireworks. Satellite parking is provided away from the waterfront, but free buses will get you to the heart of the daylong festivities. The free celebration is sponsored by the Yorktown Fourth of July Committee.

INDEPENDENCE DAY FESTIVITIES
Colonial Williamsburg
(800) HISTORY
Celebrate our nation's birthday in Williamsburg with Fifes & Drums, militia parades, and Colonial Williamsburg's famous evening program of fireworks in the Historic Area. Admission is included in your ticket to the restored area.

LIBERTY CELEBRATION
Yorktown Victory Center
(757) 253-4838
www.historyisfun.org
Tactical drills, military exercises and role-playing demonstrations salute America during the Fourth of July holiday. Visitors can see in museum galleries a rare broadside printing of America's Declaration of Independence dating to July 1776, and during a special interpretive program, learn about the sacrifices of Americans who sought to be "free and independent" from Great Britain.

August

HAMPTON CUP REGATTA
Mill Creek, Hampton
www.hamptoncupregatta.org
The oldest and largest inboard hydroplane powerboat race in the United States, the motto of these summer national championships, is "scaring fish out of their scales for 80 years." Eleven classes of boats including the Grand Prix hydroplanes, billed as the fastest piston-powered craft in the world, hit top speeds of 170 mph. There's also live entertainment and food. The races run for three days at Fort Monroe's Mill Creek. Admission is free, but get there early to grab a prime viewing spot.

September

BAY DAYS
Downtown Hampton
www.baydays.com
During the first weekend after Labor Day each September, the city of Hampton celebrates the Chesapeake Bay with its three-day Bay Days bash. Admission to Bay Days is free, but there is a fee for some special events, and parking—whether in city lots or private makeshift lots set up for the occasion—runs around $10. (Satellite parking and shuttle service are available at the Hampton Coliseum lot just off exit 263B of I-64.)

Featuring everything from hands-on Bay education activities for the kids to rides, crafts, food, and a juried art show, Bay Days has something for everyone. For those on the daring side, there's even an Extreme Arena that showcases everything from stunt bicycling, skateboarding, and in-line skating to laser tag, bungee jumping, and a rock-climbing wall. Continuous entertainment is staged at various locations throughout the celebration, which takes place along the Hampton waterfront and in the closed-off streets and parking lots of downtown. The Saturday night explosion of fireworks is a must-see. The festival concludes Sunday evening with a headline performer. Past headliners have included country star Patty Loveless and Virginia's own Bruce Hornsby.

FALL FESTIVAL AND POWWOW
Chickahominy Tribal Ground
Charles City County
(804) 829-2261, (804) 966-7043
The Chickahominy tribe hosts its annual festival at nearby Charles City County the last weekend

of September, drawing 3,000 to 5,000 visitors. Each year the powwow features Native American dancing, singing, and drumming. Not only is it an educational event for young and old alike, it's also an opportunity for shopping. There is an array of beautiful handmade Indian jewelry, pottery, and beadwork, plus books, tapes, and food. Fish sandwiches and chicken dinners are on the menu, but don't pass up a chance to try the Indian fry bread. It's a real treat. There is no admission fee, but donations are accepted. Special seating is provided for senior citizens; all others should bring their own lawn chairs or blankets. Please, leave the pets at home.

October

FALL FESTIVAL OF FOLKLIFE
Newport News Park, Jefferson Avenue
Newport News
(757) 926-1400
www.nnparks.com/fallfestival
This free event, held on the first full weekend in October, is billed as Southeast Virginia's biggest traditional craft show, featuring over 200 vendors. It's kid-friendly, too. A children's area has stage shows, hands-on crafts, and sheep-shearing, candle-making, and weaving demonstrations. There's also a folk dance stage, where spectators can see Native American, African, international, and square dancing presented in the round. The 2009 event drew 70,000, warranting two bits of advice: Arrive early because on-site parking (which costs $10) can be an extended ordeal; and eat early, as lines at the 30 food vendors tend to get really long, leaving you ravenous by the time you get a chance to dig into your pit-cooked steak sandwich and butterfly fries. Leave Fido at home. No pets are permitted.

AN OCCASION FOR THE ARTS
Duke of Gloucester St.
Merchants Square, Williamsburg
(757) 258-5587
www.anoccasionforthearts.org
Held the first Sunday in October, this annual free autumn salute to visual and performing artists boasts the oldest juried invitational art show in Virginia, limited to 150 artists and craftspeople. In addition to the art show, entertainers—magicians, musicians, dancers, mimes—are on hand, performing on a number of different stages. The festival begins at 10 a.m., with entertainment running until dark. Most performances last from 30 minutes to an hour. Food and beverages are on sale. As a finale, a professional band or musical group gives a 5:30 p.m. concert on the festival grounds. This concert, often held in the Wren Yard at the foot of Merchants Square, is dubbed "the Capper" by organizers, and typically lasts about an hour.

First held in 1969, An Occasion for the Arts now draws about 40,000 people over the course of a single day. Artists and participants may park in designated lots a few blocks away. Visitors are encouraged to park on the William and Mary campus just off South Boundary Street, although other campus parking is usually available.

POQUOSON SEAFOOD FESTIVAL
Poquoson Municipal Park
830 Poquoson Ave., Poquoson
(757) 868-3580, (757) 868-3588
www.poquosonseafoodfestival.com
The three-day Poquoson Seafood Festival is free (there's a $5 or so parking fee) and features music, fireworks, dance exhibitions, arts and crafts, children's events, and, of course, plenty of succulent seafood. Started in 1981, the event is a tribute to the working watermen of Hampton Roads and has become a tradition in the region. To get to Poquoson, which is a bit off the beaten path, take I-64 East to exit 256-B to Route 171 and follow signs for shuttle parking. Or, if you think you'll get lucky and find a parking place at the festival site, follow Route 171 for about 5 or 6 miles and follow signs to the parking area.

WILLIAMSBURG SCOTTISH FESTIVAL
Rockahock Campgrounds
Lanexa
www.wsfonline.org

This popular annual event allows festival-goers to watch or participate in Scottish games, Highland dancing, and athletic events, witness a parade of the clans and a war-cry rally, and, of course, listen to the bagpipes skirl. Individual drumming, piping, and band competitions also are held, but participants must preregister. The athletic events alone are worth the drive. When's the last time you saw athletes "toss the caber"? That's a log, a 120-pound log that measures 20 feet long. Children also get involved with their own mock athletic games, plus a few of the good old-fashioned races—a sack race and an egg-and-spoon dash. At past festivals, border collies have demonstrated their sheepherding skills, and Scottish crafts and imports—books, jewelry, weaving, woolens—have been on display. Performances by demonstration bands are among the highlights of the day's events. Visitors can sample Scottish cuisine—everything from pasties and bridies, a meat-filled popover, to shortbread and Scottish candy—or fill up on barbecue and fish and chips. Scottish soft drinks and beer are sold. Ticket prices depend on how many days you plan to attend. Saturday only is $15 for adults, $5 for children ages 6 to 11, and free for those 5 and younger. Parking at the campground is $5. A full explanation of ticket pricing and a chance to earn a discount by buying tickets in advance can be found on the festival's Web site, listed above.

YORKTOWN VICTORY CELEBRATION
Yorktown Victory Center
Route 238, Yorktown
(757) 253-4838
www.historyisfun.org
Military life and artillery demonstrations mark the anniversary of America's momentous Revolutionary War victory at Yorktown on October 19, 1781. To experience Continental Army life firsthand, visitors can enroll in "A School for the Soldier" to drill with wooden muskets and apply tactical skills in mock combat, as well as learn about soldiers' provisions and sleeping quarters. Special programs also held at Yorktown Battlefield.

Admission charges apply.

November
FOOD & FEASTS OF COLONIAL VIRGINIA
Jamestown Settlement
Route 31, Jamestown

Yorktown Victory Center
Yorktown
(757) 253-4838
www.historyisfun.org
Colonial Virginia food ways are featured during this three-day event beginning on Thanksgiving Day. At Jamestown Settlement, learn how food was gathered, preserved, and prepared on land and at sea by Virginia's English colonists and Powhatan Indians. At the Yorktown Victory Center, learn about typical soldiers' fare during the American Revolution and trace the bounty of a 1780s farm from field to kitchen. Admission charges apply.

THANKSGIVING AT BERKELEY PLANTATION
12602 Harrison Landing Rd., off Route 5
Charles City County
(804) 829-6018
www.berkeleyplantation.com
In early December 1619 a company of Englishmen arrived to settle a grant of Virginia land known as Berkeley Hundred. Their sponsor had instructed that the day of their arrival be "a day of Thanksgiving," so the settlers celebrated and gave thanks, more than a year before the pilgrims who landed at Plymouth, Massachusetts, in 1620 first did. Either a reenactment of the first Virginia Thanksgiving or a commemoration of the event has taken place the first Sunday in November since 1958 at Berkeley Plantation in Charles City County.

There is always some sort of celebration, although it varies from year to year. There is no charge to take part in the simpler commemorative ceremony. A small fee is charged during the years in which the reenactment is scheduled. Sandwiches, Brunswick stew, and other fare are available for purchase after the event in the Coach House Tavern. If the weather is temperate, the venue combined with activities makes for a poignant and lovely afternoon.

URBANNA OYSTER FESTIVAL
Urbanna
(804) 758-0368
www.urbannaoysterfestival.com
Held the first full weekend in November in scenic Middlesex County, this festival's main attraction is oysters served raw, roasted, stewed, fried, or frittered. If you tire of oysters, you can sample the clam chowder, crab cakes, or steamed crabs. While the food is the main attraction here, it isn't the only one. A variety of entertainment—including parades, visiting tall ships, fine arts, an oyster-shucking contest, live music, children's events, ship tours, pony rides, and the crowning of the festival queen—is all part of the two-day celebration. The Urbanna Oyster Festival began in 1957. To get to this somewhat out-of-the-way spot from Williamsburg, take I-64 West to Route 33 East (exit 220). Follow to US Route 17, where you will turn left and follow the signs for Urbanna. An alternate route is to take US 17 North from Yorktown across the Coleman Bridge to Gloucester then north to Urbanna and once again follow the signs.

VETERANS DAY
Colonial Williamsburg's Historic Area
(800) HISTORY
All veterans of service in America's Armed Forces are invited to participate in the parade beginning at the Capitol. After processing to the Courthouse, there will be a ceremony honoring all American veterans.

VIRGINIA LIVING MUEUM
ART SHOW AND SALE
524 J. Clyde Morris Blvd. and
Jefferson Avenue, Newport News
(757) 595-1900
www.valivingmuseum.org
The Virginia Living Museum sponsors this annual two-day tribute to our native surroundings the third weekend in November. More than 40 artists display and sell a wide range of wildlife art—from stained glass and jewelry to oils, watercolors, and one-of-a-kind photography and sculpture. Live animal shows and exhibits are part of the fun. Children 12 and younger are admitted free. Hours are 11 a.m. to 6 p.m. Sat and 11 a.m. to 5 p.m. Sun.

December

CHRISTMAS EVE TREE LIGHTING CEREMONY
Colonial Williamsburg's Market Square
(800) HISTORY
Colonial Williamsburg and the Kiwanis Club of Williamsburg cosponsor the lighting of an evergreen at 5:30 p.m. Christmas Eve on Market Square. A crowd of thousands gathers at the steps of the Courthouse on the Duke of Gloucester Street in the Historic Area. Guests will learn the story of the first Christmas tree in Williamsburg at the St. George Tucker House. The president of the Kiwanis Club of Williamsburg and the mayor of Williamsburg deliver holiday remarks.

FIRST NIGHT OF WILLIAMSBURG
Various locations
(757) 258-5153
www.firstnightwilliamsburg.org
This alcohol-free New Year's Eve celebration of the performing arts, introduced in 1993, is an event for the entire family. The First Night concept originated in Boston in 1976 and has since spread to more than 170 cities throughout the United States, Canada, and Australia. The local celebration is held from 6 p.m. to midnight in downtown Williamsburg, on the campus of the College of William and Mary, and in locations bordering the Historic Area. More than 450 artists perform, including actors, dancers, singers, musicians, jugglers, puppeteers, storytellers, and clowns. The evening's grand finale is a spectacular fireworks display. While guests can easily reach the First Night grounds on foot, complimentary buses also travel a circuit around the area and connect to ample satellite parking. The celebration typically attracts 50 acts and a crowd of about 7,000. Food and beverages are available from churches, businesses, and civic groups located along the site. The fete is open to anyone, but all except the youngest participants (age 5 and under) must wear commemorative

buttons, which cost $12 in advance and $15 on December 31.

NEWPORT NEWS CELEBRATION IN LIGHTS
Newport News Park, Jefferson Avenue
(757) 926-1400
Remember when you were little and your parents would pile you in the car and drive up and down the neighborhood streets to look at all of the splendid and not-so-splendid Christmas lights? Whether they were terrific or tacky, they all served to spark a little holiday magic. Since 1993, Newport News has re-created and magnified that magic about a million times over with its annual Festival of Lights from Thanksgiving through New Year's. Two miles of animated scenes dazzle folks driving through Newport News Park. Cost is $10 per car.

WILLIAMSBURG COMMUNITY CHRISTMAS PARADE
Richmond Road
(757) 229-6511
As the official start to the holiday season, the Williamsburg Area Chamber of Commerce sponsors its annual Christmas Parade the first Saturday in December, the day preceding Colonial Williamsburg's Grand Illumination (see next entry). The ever-popular parade, which began in 1964, typically draws 100 or more floats, marching bands, and other entrants. The parade route begins at 9 a.m. in the Historic Area and proceeds down Richmond Road to William and Mary Hall.

WILLIAMSBURG'S GRAND ILLUMINATION
Colonial Williamsburg
(800) HISTORY
On the first Sunday in December, Colonial Williamsburg kicks off the Christmas season by lighting candles in hundreds of windows in Historic Area buildings. Cressets and bonfires also illuminate the evening. Locals come in droves, usually about 30,000 people attend, and visitors love this splendid and energetic Yuletide event, which includes performances by the Junior and Senior Colonial Williamsburg Fifes & Drums; the firing of cannons on the town green; dancing, caroling, and carousing at four stages scattered throughout the restored area; and fireworks displays at three locations—the Governor's Palace, the Capitol, and the Magazine. Candlelight tours are held and 18th-century plays and concerts are performed; tickets are required for some events. Outdoor activities start at noon and are free to the public. Arrive early to avoid parking hassles and bring a flashlight. When it comes to holiday programs, the Grand Illumination is the star atop the tree, so to speak.

YORKTOWN TREE LIGHTING FESTIVITIES
Historic Main Street, Yorktown
(757) 890-3300
One evening in early December, area families are invited to hold aloft candles and walk down Main Street to participate in the annual holiday tree-lighting fun. There's caroling and background music by the Fifes and Drums of York Town. Light refreshments are served. There's even a guest appearance by jolly old Saint Nick himself.

NEWPORT NEWS AND HAMPTON

Want to take in all the rich history and diversity the Virginia Peninsula has to offer while you're in Williamsburg? Then head southeast on I-64 and check out Newport News and Hampton. If the ocean fascinates you, you can submerge yourself in the sights at the Mariners' Museum in Newport News, one of the largest and most comprehensive maritime museums in the world. If you're more given to far-flung flights of fancy, the Virginia Air and Space Center in Hampton is a must-see.

Because Hampton and Newport News are next-door neighbors—and you pretty much get to each city the same way—we've combined information about them here. For convenience and ease of planning, however, we've kept listings of the attractions, restaurants, accommodations, shopping, and recreation in each city separate.

NEWPORT NEWS

Nowhere is the old adage "geography is destiny" truer than in Newport News. The long, narrow city hugs the James River for 18 miles, but is barely a mile wide at its narrowest point. The vast stretches of waterfront made it a perfect place to build ships. Industrialist Collis P. Huntington brought the Chesapeake & Ohio railroad to a terminus at Newport News in 1882, and a few years later he established the Newport News Shipbuilding and Drydock Co. along the waterfront. The company—and the city's fortunes—took off.

Today, that firm is called Northrop Grumman Newport News, part of the huge defense conglomerate, and is the only place on earth building nuclear-powered aircraft carriers. It also builds nuclear submarines for the U.S. Navy.

The economy has diversified from its roots in shipbuilding and military, however. The Oyster Point business park in the center of the city is home to a number of manufacturers and service firms, including Canon Virginia, a branch of the Japanese copier and printer company, and Muhlbauer Inc., the American arm of a German-based company, which makes high-speed machines for producing "smart cards," such as prepaid telephone cards and credit cards that contain computer chips.

Also adjacent to Oyster Point is the Thomas Jefferson National Accelerator Facility, a cutting-edge high-energy physics research lab that has made Newport News a familiar name in scientific circles.

Progress has its price. Continued residential growth and the influx of new industry have further burdened the city's major highways, already hampered by having to serve the needs of a population spread out over this long, thin city. Rush hours can be chaotic, especially on I-64 and J. Clyde Morris Boulevard, the local name for US 17. The congestion starts earlier than most places because of the shipyard's schedule (roughly dawn until midafternoon; precise hours of the first shift vary seasonally).

HAMPTON

Neighboring Hampton prides itself on being a city of "firsts." Settled in 1610, it is the oldest continuous English-speaking settlement in America. (Jamestown moved, remember.) Our nation's first free education has its roots in the city, which was also the site of America's first Christmas. The city also was the site of the nation's first formal trading post, and the first site for the National Advisory Committee for Aeronautics, the precursor of the National Aeronautics and Space Administration. Hampton's NASA Langley Research Center actually was established in 1917 to advance the nation's airplane research. Proponents of the center say the work done there in the 1930s on the design of advanced airplane wings gave the United States and its allies the advantage that made them victorious in World War II. It wasn't until the late 1950s that NASA established the Space Task Force and located its office at Langley. Engineers and scientists in that group worked on America's original manned space program.

i Newport News's somewhat curious name has an intriguing origin. It was Captain Christopher Newport who guided the *Susan Constant* and her two sister ships *Discovery* and *Godspeed* as they carried settlers to Jamestown and the rest of the New World in 1607. After his initial voyage the good captain continued to make the trek between England and America, carting supplies, additional colonists, and word from home to the struggling Jamestown residents. To say the settlers awaited his arrival with great anticipation probably would have been the understatement of the 17th century: Because the colonists' efforts to grow food and trade with the natives were so poor, the only way they kept from starving was Newport's supplies. The sight of his boat in the lower reaches of the James was very good news to all those living in the rugged New World. So good, in fact, that Newport's name became linked with the idea of news from home, both forming the moniker for the city that eventually grew along these shores.

Hampton may have been "first to the stars," as city promoters like to say, but it also boasts a rich—and rather bloody—seafaring history. It was in Hampton in 1718 that the freshly severed head of Blackbeard the pirate was stuck on a stick and left at the harbor entrance. And during the Civil War, the ironclads *Merrimac* (*CSS Virginia*) and *Monitor* battled it out in the Hampton Roads harbor, as the Confederates tried to break the

Union's naval blockade with the hope of eventually seizing Union-held Fort Monroe.

Throughout the centuries Hampton has proved itself a city of resolute spirit, having survived shelling during the Revolutionary War and twice enduring devastating fire—first during the War of 1812, and next during the Civil War, when Hampton citizens set fire to their homes rather than see the city fall to Union forces. Today's Hampton is a vibrant and colorful city where commercial fishing, military installations, and aeronautic enterprises, along with smaller businesses and industries, sustain a population of about 145,000. The downtown has at its nucleus the captivating Virginia Air and Space Center and the restaurants and bars along narrow, cobblestoned Queen's Way.

Queen's Way is also the setting—or at least the focal point—for Hampton's major annual bash known as Bay Days. This celebration, held the second weekend of September, pays homage to the bounty of the Chesapeake Bay with marine-life displays, water conservation tips, and educational materials and activities for both the young and old.

Hampton also is home to Hampton University, the nation's largest historically black private university. Each June the college, together with the city, sponsors the renowned Hampton Jazz Festival (despite the name, it's more about rhythm and blues than traditional jazz), which brings popular entertainers such as B. B. King, Aretha Franklin, and Kenny G. and thousands of jazz fans to the city for three days of soulful sounds and rousing good times. (For more on Bay Days and the Hampton Jazz Festival, turn to our Annual Events chapter.)

The festival—and other concerts and events—are held at the Hampton Coliseum, a late '60s-era arena that bears a startling resemblance to an overstuffed flying saucer. The Coliseum Central area just northwest of the arena is the *de facto* commercial center of the city—it's home to the Hampton Roads Convention Center and the revitalized Peninsula Town Center mixed-use development, which opened in the spring of 2010 on the site of the bulldozed former Coliseum Mall.

For more on Hampton's history, geography, and demographics, visit www.hampton-development.com.

Getting Started

In planning your trip to the middle and lower peninsula, there are a few logical places to start.

NEWPORT NEWS VISITOR CENTER
13560 Jefferson Ave.
(exit 250B off I-64)
(757) 886-7777, (888) 493-7386
www.newport-news.org
As you motor down I-64 from Williamsburg, stop here for brochures, directions, and general information about any city attraction. It's open 9 a.m. to 5 p.m. daily except on Thanksgiving Day, Christmas Eve, Christmas Day, and New Year's Day.

Newport News Tourism
DEVELOPMENT OFFICE
Fountain Plaza
700 Town Center Dr., Suite 320
(757) 926-1400, (888) 493-7386
www.newport-news.org
Another place to obtain a current visitor guide or other information is this downtown office. Your best bet is to call—rather than stop—here and ask to have what you need mailed to you. Staffed 8 a.m. to 5 p.m., Mon through Fri.

Hampton Tourism
HAMPTON VISITORS CENTER
Hampton History Museum
120 Old Hampton Lane
(757) 727-1102, (800) 800-2202
www.visithampton.com
Stop here for brochures on everything from restaurants and accommodations to walking tours and citywide attractions. This also is the place to purchase tickets for a Hampton waterfront cruise, which departs from docks right at the center. Open daily 9 a.m. to 5 p.m.

Getting There

Both cities are a straight shot from Williamsburg east on I-64. The interstate runs through the northern half of Newport News before bisecting Hampton and crossing over and under the water to Norfolk via the Hampton Roads Bridge-Tunnel. While traffic congestion can be troublesome from 4 to 6 p.m. in the eastbound lanes, there's a chronic traffic problem beginning west of the Victory Boulevard exit (exit 256), where a reduction in lanes from four to two causes frequent bottlenecks. This area can cram up at any hour, but it's usually stop-and-go at rush hour, so plan your trip accordingly. If the interstate is clear, it should take you about 15 or 20 minutes to get to Newport News, 30 to 40 minutes for the trip to Hampton.

An alternate route is to take US Route 60/Warwick Boulevard from Williamsburg to the attractions located in the northern end of Newport News.

ATTRACTIONS

Newport News

ENDVIEW PLANTATION
362 Yorktown Rd. (exit 247 off I-64)
(757) 887-1862
www.endview.org
One of the few remaining colonial-era homes on the Lower Peninsula is the centerpiece of Endview Plantation.

The Endview lands belonged to the politically influential Harwood family for 350 years—originally part of the holdings of Capt. Thomas Harwood, an early émigré to the Colonies who served as speaker of the House of Burgesses (the equivalent of a parliament for the colony).

His descendant, William Harwood, built a simple white clapboard house on roughly 500 acres in 1769. The home—solid, but hardly opulent—was representative of the middle tiers of the landed gentry at the time.

Since 1995, when the Newport News purchased it, historians and curators have been at work restoring it, discovering and studying artifacts, and sorting out myth from fact. Myth: George Washington did *not* stop there en route to the siege of Yorktown (though he almost certainly passed nearby). Fact: the plantation was an important element of the Confederacy's defenses during the Peninsula campaign early in the Civil WarBy the time of the Civil War, the plantation belonged to William Harwood's great-grandson, Dr. Humphrey Harwood Curtis, who opened his medical practice at the plantation. When war broke out, Curtis organized and commanded a company of volunteers, the Warwick Beaure-gards, who took part in the Confederate defense during the Peninsula campaign.

Endview served in that campaign, too—it was a field hospital briefly, and served as head-quarters for two generals. When the Confeder-ates were forced to retreat toward Richmond, the Curtis family left too; they regained possession of the home after the war.

Today, Endview is a living-history museum with both Confederate and Union camps rep-resented. A variety of programs and events are scheduled throughout the year, including a Civil War reenactment early each spring; summer camps devoted to the study of the Civil War; and holiday-season events in December.

Admission is $6 for adults, $5 for seniors, and $4 for children ages 7 through 18. Some programs may cost extra. Endview is open 10 a.m. to 4 p.m. Mon, Wed, and Sat, and 1 to 5 p.m. Sun. It is closed on Tues year-round, and Wed Jan through Mar.

LEE HALL MANSION
163 Yorktown Rd. (exit 247 off I-64)
(757) 888-3371
www.leehall.org
If nearby Endview Plantation is a fine example of colonial-era architecture for the middle class, Lee Hall is a glimpse of the lifestyle of wealthy landowners just before the Civil War shattered the "Old South."

Restored by the city of Newport News and opened as a historic house museum in Septem-ber 1998, Lee Hall affords historical interpreta-tions of the Antebellum era and of the 1862 Peninsula Campaign.

The Italianate mansion was built in the 1850s (construction finally was done in 1859)

by wealthy planter Richard Decauter Lee. Typical of those opulent times, the home was built for entertainment: Curators have restored a ladies parlor, music room, and two of the home's bed-rooms.

But Lee didn't get to enjoy his lovely home for long. By 1862, Union troops were pushing northwest from their stronghold at Hampton's Fort Monroe. The Lees fled, and Confederate Gen. John B. Magruder used the home as his field headquarters. He built earthworks as part of a network that spanned from the James to the York, and even launched tethered hot-air bal-loons from the mansion's front yard to provide reconnaissance of the advancing Yankees.

Today, the home features artifacts and histor-ical interpretations of that campaign (which very nearly ended the war three years early). Among the artifacts are a tablecloth from the *USS Monitor* and items recovered from a nearby battle site.

Lee Hall Mansion is open Mon and Wed through Sat from 10 a.m. to 4 p.m., Sun from 1 to 5 p.m. Admission is $6 for adults, $5 for seniors 62 and older, and $4 for children 7 and older. The museum also hosts a variety of educational events throughout the year.

MARINERS' MUSEUM
100 Museum Dr. (exit 258A off I-64)
(757) 596-2222, (800) 581-SAIL
www.mariner.org
This world-renowned museum boasts the nation's most extensive international marine collection. Founded in 1930, the museum has preserved and interpreted the culture of the sea for millions of visitors over the decades. Its col-lection contains more than 35,000 maritime trea-sures including ship models, scrimshaw, maritime paintings, decorative arts, carved figureheads, navigational instruments, and working steam engines.

But the hallmarks of the museum are the arti-facts from the USS *Monitor,* the Union's first iron-clad and the key Union combatant in the Battle of Hampton Roads. Just months after that battle, the *Monitor* sank in a storm off the coast of Cape Hatteras, North Carolina. Divers finally located the wreck in the 1990s and brought up artifacts, including the ship's massive rotating gun turret. Museum curators have spent years painstakingly preserving the artifacts; they—and exhibits setting the historical context for the battle—are the centerpiece of an addition to the museum that opened in 2004.

The museum is also a key source for scholars: Its research library and archives house more maritime-related documents than any other American institution—more than 650,000 photographs and negatives, 5,000 nautical charts and maps, nearly 50,000 plans to build craft from warships to pleasure boats, more than 800 ships' logs, and thousands of other archival items, including Mark Twain's pilot license. The library is open from 9 a.m. to 5 p.m. Mon through Sat. If you plan to do extensive research, call ahead for an appointment.

The museum also has a gift gallery that offers maritime books, prints, and sea-related gifts, and a vending area where sandwiches, snacks, and soft drinks may be purchased. Throughout the year the museum stages a number of special lectures, presentations, and demonstrations. The gift gallery, (800) 259-3916, is open 10:30 a.m. to 5:30 p.m. Mon through Sat and noon to 5:30 p.m. on Sun.

After visiting the museum, explore the 550-acre Mariners' Museum Park on the Noland Trail, a 5-mile amble around Lake Maury featuring 14 pedestrian bridges, or have lunch in shady picnic areas. The park also features boat rentals for fishing.

The museum is at the end of J. Clyde Morris Boulevard and is open 10 a.m. to 5 p.m. Wed through Sat, noon to 5 p.m. Sun. Admission is $14 for visitors 13 and older, $12 for senior citizens age 65 and older, $8 for children ages 6 to 12, and free to those younger than 6. AAA and active duty military discounts are available, with ID. Closed Mon, Tues, Christmas, and Thanksgiving.

THE NEWSOME HOUSE MUSEUM AND CULTURAL CENTER
2803 Oak Ave. (exit 3 off I-664)
(757) 247-2360
www.newsomehouse.org

Built in 1899, the Newsome House is a modified Queen Anne structure that was home to Joseph Thomas Newsome, one of the first black attorneys to argue before the Virginia Supreme Court. Newsome also was the editor of a black newspaper, cofounded a Newport News church, and formed the Colored Voters League of Warwick County. His home, on Oak Avenue in the city's East End, houses an exhibit on the Newsome family and extensive archives on the African-American community in Newport News. Monthly programming on the African-American experience in Virginia is offered. Hours are from 10 a.m. to 4 p.m. Mon through Sat. Closed Sun. A $2 donation is suggested to offset operating costs.

i If kids need a break from museum-hopping, Fort Fun in Huntington Park is just the ticket. A 13,500-square-foot playground, on a bluff overlooking the James River, features a multilevel wooden structure that provides a maze, fun house, haunted castle, tightrope, bucking bronco, fire pole, sandbox, slides, swings, tunnels, balancing beams, and much more. Located in southern Newport News, off Warwick Boulevard, just north of US Route 17.

THE PENINSULA FINE ARTS CENTER
101 Museum Dr. (exit 258A off I-64)
(757) 596-8175
www.pfac-va.org
Just across from the Mariners' Museum is Newport News's fine arts center, which offers changing exhibits that showcase works by outstanding artists to help promote education and an appreciation of the visual arts. Exhibitions change every 8 to 10 weeks and feature art of regional and national interest, juried exhibitions, student shows, and touring collections of historical and contemporary works. The museum continues to enjoy growing popularity, thanks in part to the attention it is paying to budding artists. The center's Hands On for Kids Gallery lets young artists actively learn about how masterpieces are created—finger painting with sound, creating a "goof-proof" portrait, and making a flag in honor

of Flag Day. This gallery, designed for children ages 5 through 13, is open daily for self-directed arts activities. There also are weekly supervised activities that change regularly. The gallery also boasts a puppet theater and a quiet area to relax with books and puzzles.

The center's gift shop offers a selection of fine and unique decorative objects, cards, books, silk scarves, and jewelry.

Admission is good for one week beginning on the day of purchase: $7 for adults; $6 for seniors, students, and military; and $4 for children, ages six to 12. Children under six are admitted free. The museum is open Tues through Sat from 10 a.m. to 5 p.m., and on Sun from 1 to 5 p.m. On Tues and select Thurs evenings, the museum reopens for evening programming. The museum is closed on Mon, Thanksgiving, December 24–26, and New Year's Day. Free docent-led tours are available for school and community groups.

i One way to sample the exhibits at the Peninsula Fine Arts Center is to visit on the third Thursday of the month. The museum opens its doors after-hours from 5:30 to 8 p.m. for "Arts Café," with live music and tasty hors d'oeuvres from area restaurants. Admission is free to museum members, $7.50 to nonmembers.

VIRGINIA LIVING MUSEUM
524 J. Clyde Morris Blvd.
(757) 595-1900
www.valivingmuseum.org

The Living Museum is an intriguing hybrid: part zoo, part botanical gardens, part observatory and planetarium, with native bird and aquatic life exhibits thrown in for good measure. It's hard for a kid to have a bad time at the Living Museum so the place is usually crawling with that young human life, too.

Opened in May 1987, the museum underwent a $22 million expansion in 2004, which added a 62,000-square-foot exhibits building, allowing visitors to virtually walk into a Chesapeake Bay deep-water aquarium, explore a Shenandoah Valley cave, and study the environments of an Appalachian cove and cypress swamp. You'll find fossil exhibits, a touch-tank for hands-on learning about marine life, and a two-story glass aviary with native songbirds. Younger visitors get a special thrill from putting their hands in the authentic footprints of a 210-million-year-old dinosaur or from petting a docile horseshoe crab.

Outside, a half-mile boardwalk winds through a nature preserve where animals—everything from regal bald eagles to coyotes to endangered red wolves—can be viewed in their natural habitats. In the Coastal Plain Aviary, a net canopy encloses a marshy ecosystem for herons, egrets, ducks, pelicans, cormorants, and other birds, as well as turtles and a variety of plants indigenous to wetland areas.

In a separate building (part of the original facility), the planetarium is your ticket to the greater universe, featuring multi-image shows and telescope observation.

Admission is $15 for adults, $12 for children. Planetarium shows carry an additional $2 charge. Summer hours are 9 a.m. to 5 p.m. daily. In the winter, the museum opens only from noon to 5 p.m. on Sun.

VIRGINIA WAR MUSEUM
9285 Warwick Blvd.
Huntington Park
(757) 247-8523
www.warmuseum.org

This fascinating museum, administered by the Historic Services Division of the city's Department of Parks and Recreation, offers a detailed look at U.S. military history from 1775 to the present. Kids will particularly like the array of artillery on the lawn allowing for close-up looks. There are more than 60,000 artifacts on exhibit, including an 1883 brass Gatling gun, a World War I Howitzer tank, and a Civil War blockade-runner's uniform. Most aspects of America's military heritage are well represented in the museum's many galleries. The primary gallery is America and War, but several smaller galleries have interesting exhibits, including The Evolution of Weaponry, Revolution to the

Gulf War, Women at War, Hampton Roads—Port of Embarkation, and Visions of War, an exhibit featuring propaganda posters from the World Wars. The newest gallery, Marches toward Freedom, honors the contributions of African Americans to America's military history from the Revolutionary War to the Gulf War.

Admission is $6 for adults, $5 for seniors, and $4 per child ages 7 to 18. The Dufflebag Giftshop offers books, posters, and shirts. The Virginia War Museum is open 9 a.m. to 5 p.m. Mon through Sat and from 1 until 5 p.m. Sun. Closed on Thanksgiving, Christmas, and New Year's Day.

Hampton

THE AMERICAN THEATRE
125 East Mellen St., Phoebus
(757) 722-2787
www.theamericantheatre.com
Although not an attraction per se, this refurbished theater is such an important part of the peninsula's arts landscape that we decided to include it here. Built in 1908 as a vaudeville and movie house, the theater underwent several transformations before closing in the 1990s. In recent years the theater has been the recipient of a $2 million makeover and offers live theater, concerts featuring international artists, classic movies, and children's programs. The theater, which also houses the Hampton Art Commission's Great Performers Series, has hosted Sierra Maestra from Cuba, Beausoleil, Portuguese performer Mariza, and John McCutcheon.

BLUEBIRD GAP FARM
60 Pine Chapel Rd.
(757) 727-6739
Not only is the 60-acre Bluebird Gap Farm a great retreat for the younger set, it's also free. About a 10-minute drive from downtown, Bluebird Gap Farm is home to numerous animals, including pigs, deer, goats, sheep, cows, and an occasional horse. There also are a variety of chickens and ducks and some of the animals that farmers might see in the wilds around their property. A playground area is perfect for picnicking, and

public restrooms and vending machines are available. The park is open Wed through Sun from 9 a.m. to 5 p.m. Bluebird Gap Farm is closed Thanksgiving, Christmas, New Year's Day, and Wed when a major holiday falls on a Monday or Tuesday. Admission is free, but you may want to bring a couple of quarters in your pocket to plunk into food machines to feed the animals. Do not bring your own food to feed the animals; it might upset their diets.

CASEMATE MUSEUM
Grounds of Fort Monroe
(757) 788-3391
Fort Monroe, which serves as headquarters for the U.S. Army Training and Doctrine Command, holds the title of the largest stone fort ever built in America. Within its walled core you'll find the Casemate Museum, which chronicles the history of the fort and the Coast Artillery Corps. During your tour of the museum, you will see the cell in which captured Confederate President Jefferson Davis was imprisoned, as well as weapons, uniforms, Frederick Remington drawings, and other military artifacts. You also will learn how "Freedom's Fortress" helped shelter thousands of slave refugees. Other nearby points of interest include Robert E. Lee's quarters, now a private residence, seacoast batteries, and the Old Point Comfort Lighthouse. The Casemate Museum is open daily, with no admission charge, from 10:30 a.m. to 4:30 p.m.

CHARLES H. TAYLOR ARTS CENTER
4205 Victoria Blvd.
(757) 727-1490
On historic Victoria Boulevard, where grand old homes dominate the landscape, sits the Charles H. Taylor Arts Center. Housed in Hampton's 1926 library, where Victoria intersects Kecoughtan Road, the center displays the work of local artists and photographers as well as traveling exhibitions. The center also is home to the Hampton Arts Commission, which stages the highly acclaimed Great Performers Series at the American Theatre. If you stop in, pick up a copy of the organization's newsletter, Hampton Arts Calen-

dar, which gives a comprehensive rundown of arts activities on the peninsula. The center is open Tues through Fri from 10 a.m. to 6 p.m. and Sat and Sun from 1 to 5 p.m. Admission is free.

COUSTEAU SOCIETY
710 Settlers Landing Rd.
(757) 722-9300
www.cousteau.org
Known internationally for pioneering underwater exploration, photography, and conservation, the Cousteau Society opened an attraction on the downtown Hampton waterfront in 2003. The waterfront gallery showcases the undersea endeavors of Jacques-Yves Cousteau using photography, artifacts, ship models, and film footage. Visitors can see world-renowned underwater photography, models of the research vessels *Calypso* and *Alcyone*, and diving equipment from the past and present. Artifacts from Cousteau's expeditions are also on display, including a hovercraft in which guests can sit and have their pictures taken. The attraction is free and open from 10 a.m. to 4 p.m. daily, and parking is free in the nearby Radisson Hotel parking garage.

HAMPTON CAROUSEL PARK
602 Settlers Landing Rd.
(757) 727-0900
Pony up a dollar and take a ride on Hampton's beautifully restored 1920s carousel. Housed in a weather-protected pavilion along the city's downtown waterfront, it is one of only 170 antique wooden merry-go-rounds still existing in the United States. Hampton's carousel was originally built in 1920 by the Philadelphia Toboggan Company, once the premier manufacturer of both merry-go-rounds and roller coasters in the United States. Its stately chariots and prancing steeds were hand-carved and carefully painted by German, Italian, and Russian immigrants. The carousel was delivered to Buckroe Beach Amusement Park in 1921, where it delighted thousands of visitors until the park closed in the 1980s. Knowing a historic gem when it saw one, the city bought the carousel and had it painstakingly restored by R&F Designs of Bristol, Connecticut.

After two years of work, the ponies—painted in elegant shades of cream, yellow, and brown—were ready to be ridden once again. The carousel officially opened for business in 1991. You can take a spin on one of its prancing steeds from noon to 5 p.m. Mon through Wed and noon to 7 p.m. Thurs through Sun in the summer. The carousel is closed mid-Dec through Mar.

HAMPTON HISTORY MUSEUM
120 Old Hampton Lane
(757) 727-1610
The Hampton History Museum, which opened in 2003, showcases the city's heritage as the nation's oldest continuous English-speaking settlement. Nine permanent galleries are organized as follows: Native American, 17th Century, Port Hampton, 18th Century, Antebellum, Civil War, Reconstruction, Late 19th Century, and Modern Hampton. The museum is open Mon through Sat from 10 a.m. to 5 p.m. and 1 to 5 p.m. Sun. Admission is $5 for adults and $4 for active military, seniors, and children ages 4 to 12. The Hampton Visitor's Center is at the same location.

> **i** Hampton Roads is rich in African-American history, culture, and heritage. The region has served as the backdrop for a people's rise from enslavement to equality, and many sites and events bring to life that journey. Call (800) 767-8782 for an African-American Heritage brochure to guide your way.

HAMPTON UNIVERSITY MUSEUM
Huntington Building, Frissell Avenue
(757) 727-5308
www.hamptonu.edu/museum
If you're still in the mood for a little cultural grooming, stop by the Hampton University campus, where you'll find one of America's most remarkable museums. Founded in 1868, the Hampton University Museum is the second-oldest museum in the Old Dominion. It contains more than 9,000 objects and works of art from cultures and nations worldwide. Among the works housed at the museum are nine paintings

by the renowned African-American artist Henry O. Tanner.

The museum is housed in a beautiful, expanded facility—a former Beaux Art–style library, which includes a Fine Arts Gallery; the African Gallery, with objects from nearly 100 ethnic groups and cultures; the Native American Gallery, with its vast collection of American Indian artifacts including everything from basketry to beadwork; the Hampton History Gallery, which traces the university's own historical contributions; plus galleries devoted to changing exhibits by contemporary artists, the Harlem Renaissance, and a studio gallery that showcases the works of Hampton's students. The museum is open Mon through Fri from 8 a.m. to 5 p.m. and Sat from noon to 4 p.m. It is closed on major holidays and campus holidays. Admission is free, and tours can be arranged. In addition to the museum, the university also is the site of six National Historic Landmarks, including the Emancipation Oak, where President Abraham Lincoln's Emancipation Proclamation was first read to the slaves of Hampton in 1863 (see the sidebar in this chapter).

ST. JOHN'S EPISCOPAL CHURCH
100 West Queens Way
(757) 722-2567

Away from the waterfront on downtown's Queens Way sits St. John's Church, the oldest continuous English-speaking parish in the United States. The church was built in 1728, but it is the fourth site of worship of Elizabeth City Parish, which was established in 1610. The tree-lined churchyard holds graves dating from 1701, including a memorial to Virginia Laydon, one of the first persons to survive an arduous birth in the New World. Communion silver made in London in 1618 and a stained-glass window depicting the baptism of the Indian princess Pocahontas are among the church's most prized possessions. The church is open weekdays from 9 a.m. to 3:30 p.m. and on Sat from 9 a.m. to noon. There are no tours at St. John's on Sunday because of services that are held at 8 and 10 a.m. Guided tours may be arranged by calling the church office, and admission is free.

Emancipation Oak

Its low branches stretch impossibly wide, creating a cool canopy over the hot, flat landscape of Hampton, Virginia. It was here, under the sturdy limbs of what is now called the Emancipation Oak, that residents of Hampton first learned of their emancipation from slavery in 1863. This was the site of the first southern reading of President Abraham Lincoln's Emancipation Proclamation, according to historians at Hampton University.

The peaceful shade of the Emancipation Oak, located at the entrance to Hampton University, also served as the first classroom for newly freed men and women—eager for an education. It had already been a classroom for slaves: Before the Civil War, Mary Peake, a prominent educator who was the daughter of a free colored woman and a Frenchman, broke the law to teach classes to slaves and free blacks under this tree.

Ninety-eight feet in diameter, the Emancipation Oak is designated as one of the 10 Great Trees of the World by the National Geographic Society. A live oak, the tree's foliage remains green year-round.

VIRGINIA AIR AND SPACE CENTER
600 Settlers Landing Rd.
(757) 727-0900
(800) 296-0800
www.vasc.org

After working off your sea legs, why not flap your wings a little? After all, the Virginia Air and Space Center is just a short stroll along the waterfront, lending credence to the popular Hampton theme "from the sea to the stars." As you approach the glass, brick, and steel structure, you'll notice that, appropriately enough, the stunning architecture does resemble a bird in flight. This $30 million museum, which opened to sellout crowds in April 1992 and is designated the official NASA Langley Visitors Center, is considered the pièce de résistance of Hampton's revitalization.

Inside, the museum features changing exhibits relating to its "from the sea to the stars" theme. Amazing artifacts on display include the *Apollo 12* command module, an astronaut's suit, a meteor from Mars, and a three-billion-year-old moon rock. In the 300-seat giant-screen IMAX theater, visitors can watch dramatic films on a variety of topics on a 50-by-70-foot-wide screen. In 1999 the Space Center installed closed-captioning in the theater that superimposes subtitles without altering the image for other viewers. With the technology, the theater can accommodate as many as 30 hearing-impaired patrons per showing.

As you walk through the museum, note the 19 vintage U.S. aircraft that hang from the 94-foot ceiling, including a Corsair F-106B Delta Dart struck nearly 700 times by lightning while flying through storms as part of NASA lightning research. A gantry that rises three stories takes visitors up for closer inspection. Why not pause and launch a rocket to new heights as part of an interactive, hands-on exhibit that allows you to master the steps of mission control. Or perhaps you might prefer to hop on board a space shuttle, assume the controls, and attempt to land the vehicle. (We guarantee after one attempt you will understand why astronauts must train extensively to execute a perfect landing!)

A permanent exhibit called **Wild, Wild Weather,** looks at everything from hurricanes to tornadoes and how all types of weather affect our daily lives.

Space Station is an interactive exhibit that focuses on the process of design and construction required to build the first international space station. The Ham Radio exhibit takes visitors from the past into the future in a world-class, fully automated, digital amateur radio satellite station.

When you're ready for some R&R or to spend a little cash, you can stop in at the museum's cafe and first-rate gift shop. The center also offers summer camp programs for children and provides live science demonstrations.

Summer hours of operation are Mon through Wed 10 a.m. to 5 p.m., Thurs through Sat 10 a.m. to 7 p.m., and Sun from noon to 7 p.m. Winter hours are Mon through Sat 10 a.m. to 5 p.m. and Sun from noon to 5 p.m. Admission prices vary depending on whether you want to take in a film while you're at the museum. For the exhibit only, tickets are $8.75 for adults, $7.75 for seniors and military, and $6.75 for children 3 to 11. Call for combination ticket prices.

RESTAURANTS

All this sightseeing is bound to stir up a hearty appetite. Lucky for you, there's a bounty of choices in both Hampton and Newport News.

Price Guidelines

The following code indicates the average price of two entrees—without appetizer, dessert, beverages, tax, or gratuity. Rates may be higher in season (generally from mid-Mar to Nov and again during the winter holidays).

$.................	**Less than $20**
$$	**$20 to $35**
$$$	**$36 to $50**
$$$$	**More than $50**

HAMPTON

GOOD FORTUNE $
225 D-1 Fox Hill Rd.
(757) 851-6888
At Willow Oaks Shopping Center, Good Fortune has a varied menu of traditional Chinese dishes. You may think once you've tasted one wonton soup you've tasted them all, but Good Fortune's is especially delicious. A variety of steamed entrees offer a low-fat dining option. A lunch buffet is a filling midday repast. A dinner buffet is offered on Fri and Sat.

HARPOON LARRY'S OYSTER BAR $$
2000 North Armistead Ave.
(757) 827-0600

This is the kind of restaurant you'd expect to find at the beach. Its long wooden tables, massive bar, and casual atmosphere all make it a favorite after-work spot for locals. The menu includes all types of "killer" seafood prepared just about any way you can imagine. A Thursday night shrimp special—buy a half-pound and get the next half-pound for a penny—jams the place, but it's worth the wait. You might want to brave the crowds and check it out. Or, better yet, come for lunch when the lines are shorter, but the food is just as good.

MARKER 20 $$
21 East Queens Way
(757) 726-9410

Pub grub with an emphasis on things from the sea mark this downtown Hampton nightspot, also notable for its great wraps and sandwiches and the spacious outdoor patio—a perfect place from which to people watch.

SIX LITTLE BAR BISTRO $$
6 East Mellen St.
Hampton
(757) 722-1466

This funky tapas restaurant is reason enough to visit Phoebus, a once-bustling town of its own, now a neighborhood of Hampton, struggling to stay afloat. (The gorgeous American Theatre is just down the street—a Phoebus landmark with terrific programming.) Six is small, and popular, so it can be crowded on the weekends. The wide variety of small plates are worth a wait—unusual selections, delectably prepared. Order a lot of little plates for the table to share. It's not really a place for kids, but if you can time it right, a real kid-pleasing treat is the s'mores dessert, which comes with its own little can of sterno and a little grate over which to melt your chocolate.

> **i** America's first seven astronauts trained at NASA Langley Air Force Base in Hampton.

SHOPPING

Both Newport News and Hampton have overhauled their shopping districts in recent years—and in all cases they've opted for the "mixed-use" model of retail blended with apartments, condos and homes.

Two such centers in Newport News straddle either side of Jefferson Avenue in the center of the city—Port Warwick, a mixed-use development with shops and businesses arranged pleasingly around a village green, and the new City Center development, which has the same mix of homes, shops, restaurants, plus many government offices and a sparkly new Marriott hotel and conference center. Port Warwick opened first, but its no-national-chains approach may have contributed to its apparent difficulty to pull in crowds so far. City Center, by luring national brands like Talbots, Chico's, Coldwater Creek, and the Marriott, seems to have had more success.

The stores and restaurants are more unique in Port Warwick, but if you're looking for familiar favorites, City Center is a better choice.

Newport News

PORT WARWICK
On Loftus Boulevard at Jefferson Avenue
www.portwarwick.com

Located on the west side of Jefferson Avenue; turn at Port Warwick Boulevard (near the Sonic hamburger restaurant) and go straight. Parking around the square is free.

CITY CENTER
Thimble Shoals Boulevard
www.citycenteroysterpoint.com

From I-64, exit J. Clyde Morris Blvd. (258A) and turn right at Thimble Shoals Boulevard. (You can't miss the incredibly huge, neon-lighted spears above the gold-lettered sign.) Continue for one mile. The first structure you'll see is the parking garage. You might want to circle around the area once to figure out where your interest lies and park somewhere else—this is a rather sprawling complex although the most popular stores—Talbots, Coldwater Creek, and local favorites, The

Mole Hole and Sisters Unique, are on Mariner Row.

HILTON VILLAGE
From Warwick Boulevard to the James River
The big loser in the shopping shift, at least temporarily, may be Hilton Village, a humble but charming two-block shopping district on the southern end of the city. The 2008–2009 recession left many storefronts empty here, and some of the more successful businesses were lured away to the shiny, new facilities further west.

But this human-scale district—sort of the original "mixed-use" development—has been around since 1918, when the neighborhood was constructed to create a place for shipyard workers to live during the World War I shipbuilding boom. The lovely streetscape, brick-paved walkways and well-maintained landscaping make this an attractive place to stroll. A community theater stages regular productions at the Village Theater on one end of the district; a new bakery (details below) offers sumptuous treats, at the other. People who live in Hilton easily understand why the American Planning Association named it one of "America's Top 10 Neighborhoods" in 2009. It will undoubtedly revive again.

Some shops to visit:
ACT II
10253 Warwick Blvd.
(757) 595-0507
Billed as the "Peninsula's premier consignment shop," this huge store offers quality reruns at discount prices. Well-organized and clean, the atmosphere here is more like a department store than you'll find at most second–time-around places. Bargains are to be had and it's all for a good cause—profits support Women's America ORT. Open 9 a.m. to 5 p.m. Mon to Sat.

THE BEAD STORE
10375 Warwick Blvd.
(757) 591-0593
Everything you need to make your own beaded jewelry is available here. There are so many beautiful and unique beads in all shapes, sizes, and materials that even non-beaders will suddenly get inspired. Check out the ever-changing "Wall of Beads," an array of offerings in every color, shape, texture, and finish. The Bead store carries six-inch tubes of Japanese seed beads as well as Czech seed beads in hanks, and they offer free classes for novices. If you've got a tween, a make-your-own-bracelet class here with her pals makes a unique birthday party. Open 11 a.m. to 5:30 p.m. Tues through Sat.

CHELSEA'S CLOSET
10375 Warwick Blvd.
(757) 596-5369
Quality children's consignment. Owner Connie Nemec has so much stuff she could easily use a bigger store. You may have to do a little digging but there are bargains to be had. Open 10 a.m. to 4 p.m. Tues through Sat.

COUTURE CAKES
10373 Warwick Blvd.
(757) 599-6452
Master baker Nika Covington (the cake diva) opened her stand-alone bakery at a daring moment—the doldrums of the 2009 recession. What's she offering is luxurious baked goods at a price almost anybody can afford—chocolate overload cupcakes (you could easily split this, even three ways!) for $2.75, made-from-scratch cookies the size of a bread plate for $1.50. The real specialties of the house, however, are Nika's designer cakes—productions so beautifully constructed you may feel bad about eating them. A baby shower cake in the shape of a diaper bag looks like you could walk off with it slung over one arm. Open Tues through Sat 10 a.m. to 7 p.m., Sun 10 a.m. to 6 p.m.

PLANTIQUES
10377 Warwick Blvd.
(757) 595-1545
This rambling, multi-room house at the very northern end of Hilton's shopping district is like a mini antique mall under one roof. Owner Pam Phillips rents rooms out to individual purveyors, who offer jewelry, vintage clothing, home

accents, decorative items and collectibles. Pam will also whip you up a cappuccino from her coffee bar. Open 10 a.m. to 5 p.m. Mon through Sat.

PRIMROSE
10353 Warwick Blvd.
(757) 369-4697
Jennifer Gambill runs this funky gift shop while her husband, Sean, cuts hair in the back room. Sounds like an odd combination but it works. Jennifer is also the go-to gal for all things Hilton—she organizes the annual Fall Festival and other merchant events. Her shop reflects her elegant taste—unique jewelry, accessories for the home, treats for your canine friends, baby gifts, and many handpainted (some by Jennifer herself) and one of a kind items. Open Tues & Thurs 10 a.m. to 7 p.m., Wed & Sat 10 a.m. to 5 p.m., Fri 10 a.m. to 2 p.m.

Hampton

In Hampton there's Old Hampton (or downtown), and the bustling Coliseum Central corridor along Mercury Boulevard. If you're looking for ambience while you browse, stroll along the quaint brick, tree-lined streets in Old Hampton. Here you will find dozens of specialty shops selling everything from British imports to elaborate doll collections. Our favorites are listed below. For more information on downtown shopping, check out the Web site www.downtownhampton.com.

OLD HAMPTON

BLUE SKIES GALLERY
26 King St.
(757) 727-0028
This popular gallery offers 5,000 square feet of creative work by more than 100 established artisans. Its selection includes sculpture, paintings, clothing, and crafts in silver, acrylic, wood, fiber, fabric, paper, and glass. You can even browse among some selections of antiquarian books and furniture.

LA BODEGA HAMPTON
22 Wine St.
(757) 722-VINO
This delightful addition to the downtown Hampton scene sells glassware, linens, gourmet foods, gift items, a variety of freshly made sandwiches and salads, many unusual beers, and shelves and shelves of wine. The staff is knowledgeable and helpful. Grab a quick lunch and browse to your heart's content.

SHABBY CHIC
47 East Queens Way
(757) 727-0100
If it's old, you'll find it here. This fun and eclectic shop stocks everything from vintage furniture and iron fencing gates to decorative arts and dried flowers.

Coliseum Central

For all intents and purposes, this is the main business district in Hampton. Located on either side of Mercury Boulevard, the area is named after the nearby Hampton Coliseum, a circular arena and concert venue that's highly visible from I-64.

PENINSULA TOWN CENTER
1800 West Mercury Blvd.
(757) 838-1505
The new centerpiece of Coliseum Central is this mixed-use development, built on the site of a bulldozed '70s-era enclosed mall. It's anchored by Macy's, Target, JCPenney, and Barnes & Noble, with a blend of local shops, national chains and restaurants. The project was completed in early 2010, and the full array of shops is expected to open in stages throughout the year.

BEACHES

Newport News

HUNTINGTON PARK BEACH
5500 West Mercury Blvd.
(foot of James River Bridge)
(757) 886-7912
Newport News also has its own free public beach, located in the same park that is home to Fort Fun and the James River Fishing Pier (see Fishing later in this chapter). The sandy strip fronts the James

River, of course, and is open from sunrise to sunset. Lifeguards are on duty from 11 a.m. to 7 p.m. daily during the summer, but at other times you're allowed to swim at your own risk. There's a nice little snack bar with a deck and picnic tables, and restrooms are available. Two swing sets and a few volleyball nets offer a couple of other diversions.

Hampton

BUCKROE BEACH
End of Pembroke Avenue at First Street
(757) 850-5134, (757) 727-8311
If you're interested in a day at the beach, there's no reason to trek all the way to the Virginia Beach resort strip. Hampton's own Buckroe Beach is an ideal spot for a little family R&R. Bordering the Chesapeake Bay, Buckroe's gentle surf and sandy shore are perfect for family frolicking and castle building. A paved boardwalk attracts strollers and cyclists, while an outdoor pavilion is the setting for plenty of warm-weather entertainment. A bustling resort back in the 1930s, Buckroe Beach's fortunes declined when the 1957 opening of the Hampton Roads Bridge-Tunnel provided easier access to ocean attractions. In the late 1980s the city invested millions to build Buckroe Park, complete with a stage, picnic shelters, and public restrooms. During the summer the beach pavilion frequently is the scene of free concerts on Sunday, while family movies are shown on a big outdoor screen on Tuesday evenings. Films start at sundown but there is prefilm entertainment at 7 p.m. Lifeguards are on duty at the beach from 10 a.m. to 6 p.m. from Memorial Day to Labor Day.

To get to the beach, take the last Hampton exit from I-64 before the bridge-tunnel (exit 268). Turn left on Mallory Street. Follow it to its end, then turn right on Pembroke Avenue. The beach will be right in front of you. There's a small parking lot next to the beach, but on hot summer days it typically is full. Paid parking is available in makeshift lots on fields across the street.

FISHING

If you want to get an angle on some outdoor fun, toss a line off one of the peninsula's many fishing piers. Depending on the time of year, you'll probably pull out spot, croaker, flounder, bluefish, and an occasional trout. No license is needed for fishing at any of these piers (it's included in the fee), and equipment rentals are available at most of them. One of the best places for your hook, line, and sinker is listed here.

Newport News

JAMES RIVER FISHING PIER
Huntington Park
5500 West Mercury Blvd.
(757) 247-0364
This popular fishing pier is located at the foot of the James River Bridge. To fish the waters beneath will cost adults $8 and seniors and children ages 7 through 12, $6. Nearly a mile long, this is a great place to fish for croaker and spot. During the right season, you might even land striped bass, flounder, gray trout, or red drum. There also is a bait shop on hand that will provide you with the necessities: snacks, bait, and some tackle. If all that casting and reeling works up an appetite—or if the fish aren't biting and you have a hankering for some fresh seafood—**The Crab Shack** restaurant, (757) 245-2722, is located at the entrance to the pier. Here you can get everything from soft-shell crabs to shrimp at reasonable prices.

PARKS

Newport News

HUNTINGTON PARK
Off Warwick Boulevard
(757) 886-7912
In addition to the largest public tennis facility on the lower peninsula, this sprawling park has a well-maintained rose garden, baseball fields, a beach, a boat ramp for access to the James River, and Fort Fun—a 13,500-square-foot playground built on a bluff overlooking the James and featuring a multilevel wooden structure with maze, fun house, tightrope, bucking bronco, fire pole, sandbox, slides, swings, tunnels, balancing beams, and much more. Fort Fun was built in only five

days by some 1,500 community volunteers with more than $85,000 in donated materials and supplies. The playground, designed by Robert S. Leathers & Associates of Ithaca, New York, is wheelchair accessible, free, and guaranteed to keep children happy for long periods of time, though parental supervision is advised: The fort's nooks and crannies make it almost impossible to keep an eye from afar on young children—and if you chase them through the mazelike walkways, watch your head! While you're at it, take along a picnic lunch and some fishing poles and try out the children's fishing pier on nearby Lake Biggins, or visit the swimming beach that's also part of the Huntington Park complex. The park is open from sunrise to sunset.

NEWPORT NEWS PARK
13560 Jefferson Ave.
(exit 250B off I-64)
(757) 886-7912, (800) 203-8322
This beautiful oasis in the northern tier of the city—the second-largest municipal park in the United States—has more than 8,000 acres of woodlands and two freshwater lakes. While entrance to the park is free, 188 individual campsites are available for rent. A primitive area also is available for Boy Scout troops only. Each of the standard campsites includes a picnic table and charcoal grill, 24-hour registration, and security. Heated restrooms with hot showers, a laundry room, pay phones, sewage dumping station, playground equipment, ice, general store, and water and electrical hookups also are available. Campsites are open year-round. With 188 sites, there are plenty of choices. A five-star archery range located near the campsites is open to the public. To use this facility you must furnish your own bows and arrows and successfully complete a free archery safety class.

The park also offers 20 miles of hiking trails, a 5.3-mile mountain bike trail, and a variety of trails that serve as bridle paths. Bicycles and helmets may be rented on a daily basis. While exploring the park, keep a sharp eye out for the many species of birds, flowers, trees, plants, and animals that inhabit the park. You may be rewarded by the sight of a bluebird that has nested in one of the houses erected by the Hampton Roads Bird Club.

For the angler in the family, there are two reservoirs stocked with bass, pickerel, pike, bluegill, perch, and crappie. Boats are available for rent for an entire day of fishing fun (bring sunscreen). Make sure you have a valid fishing license before you cast your line for the first time.

One of the highlights in the park is the 18-hole disk golf course, one of the first of its kind in Virginia. The championship range will have you sailing your disk 5,450 yards, while the regulation, or white, course is 4,165 yards.

For you history buffs, Dam No. 1, Confederate gun positions, and remaining Union trenches are evidence of the area's involvement in the 1862 Peninsula campaign. The park's visitor center interprets the action that took place there and offers a free park map and literature on other pertinent sites nearby. Across from the Dam No. 1 Bridge is the park Discovery Center, which displays flora and fauna exhibits as well as Civil War artifacts.

The park also hosts the annual Fall Festival in October and is the site of Celebration in Lights during the holiday season. For more information on these and other nearby festivals, turn to our Annual Events chapter.

Hampton

GRANDVIEW NATURE PRESERVE
Intersection of Beach Road and
State Park Drive
(757) 727-6347
Another place sure to please the outdoor enthusiast is the Grandview Nature Preserve in northeast Hampton, with its 578 acres of marshland and beach area. Grandview is home to endangered species of birds and wildlife. It's the perfect place to stroll a 2-mile stretch of bayfront beach to observe all of nature's glory. Off the beaten path a bit, you get to Grandview by taking Mercury to Fox Hill. Travel Fox Hill for a few miles— past the Willow Oaks development—and turn left onto Beach Road. You'll find Grandview just

where you would expect—at the end of Beach. No admission fee is charged.

SANDY BOTTOM NATURE PARK
1255 Big Bethel Rd.
(757) 825-4657
Hampton's public park, Sandy Bottom Nature Park, on Big Bethel Road, has 456 acres of woodland, two lakes, play and picnic areas, walking and interpretive trails, a wildlife area, nature center, paddleboats, and concessions. Built almost entirely by volunteers, this park has room for overnight guests, too. There also are two primitive group sites (popular with Boy Scout troops) and four tent cabins. The park also offers environmental education programs and special programming in astronomy, wildlife observation, and environmental field-testing. To get to the park, take exit 261A off I-64 and follow Hampton Roads Center Parkway to Big Bethel Road. The park entrance will be on your left. Admission to the park is free.

PARKS AND RECREATION

Williamsburg area localities take recreation seriously and offer residents myriad options. Anyone interested in sports and recreation information should consult the *Virginia Gazette*'s sports section, which gives extensive coverage to local sports. Another good source of information is the James City County Parks and Recreation's comprehensive seasonal publication, which is available at the JCC-Williamsburg Community Center, listed later in this chapter, and at other sites. Both the Williamsburg and York parks and recreation departments also publish lists that will let you know about recreational opportunities.

For those of you hoping to hit the links during your stay, please turn to our Golf chapter for information on area courses.

PARKS DEPARTMENTS

JAMES CITY COUNTY PARKS AND RECREATION
5249-C Olde Towne Rd., Williamsburg
(757) 259-4200
www.james-city.va.us/recreation
This department oversees a wide range of recreation programs throughout the county including those at the James City County–Williamsburg Community Center, the James River Community Center, Little Creek Reservoir, Mid County Park, and Upper County Park. Office hours are 8 a.m. to 5 p.m. Mon through Fri.

WILLIAMSBURG PARKS AND RECREATION DEPARTMENT
202 Quarterpath Rd., Williamsburg
(757) 259-3760
www.ci.williamsburg.va.us
Numerous recreation programs are available through this department, which also oversees Quarterpath Park, Waller Mill Park, and Kiwanis Park. The department's regular office hours are 8 a.m. to 5:30 p.m. Mon through Fri, although someone is on duty whenever the recreation center is open.

YORK PARKS & RECREATION
100 County Dr., Grafton
(757) 890-3500

Located at the York County operations center off Goodwin Neck Road, the office of York Parks & Recreation oversees the operation of six parks, the Yorktown Beach waterfront, and county public boat landings at various sites. The offices are open 8:15 a.m. to 5 p.m. Mon through Fri, except on holidays.

Park Locations and Activities

BACK CREEK PARK
Goodwin Neck Road, Seaford
(757) 890-3850
A free boat-launching facility keeps this 27-acre York County park hopping year-round. It is a U.S. Tennis Association award-winning park that also features a picnic area, restrooms, and six, well-maintained, lighted tennis courts.

CHARLES BROWN PARK
Route 238, Lackey
(757) 890-3500
Named in memory of a Lackey resident and York County educator who demonstrated a keen interest in youth, this 10-acre park includes a baseball field, two basketball courts, two tennis courts, picnic shelter, playground area, and restrooms. A 3,000-square-foot community center on-site

includes two small meeting rooms, one large meeting room, restrooms, and a small kitchen.

CHISMAN CREEK PARK
Wolf Trap Road, Grafton
(757) 890-3852

This 13-acre park was reclaimed from a fly ash site in 1991. It has two lighted softball fields, restrooms, and a parking lot. It includes skinned infields and irrigated outfields. It is used primarily for York County's adult softball program in the spring and summer, and is used in the fall for youth soccer.

COLLEGE LANDING PARK
South Henry Street, Williamsburg
(757) 220-6170

This small park on the southern edge of town off South Henry Street is always open. It is built alongside a marsh and has picnic areas, a boat ramp, and a quiet boardwalk. It is wheelchair accessible.

DIASCUND RESERVOIR
US Route 60 West, Toano
(757) 259-4200

This James City County reservoir, operated jointly with Newport News and the Division of Game and Inland Fisheries, is open to the public for boating and fishing. Public boat-landing hours are one hour before dawn to one hour after sunset. Electric trolling motors are the only ones allowed on the reservoir.

THE GREENSPRINGS TRAIL
Route 5, behind Jamestown High School, Williamsburg
(757) 259-4200

The 4.7-mile Greensprings Trail is a soft-surface hiking trail that consists of three interconnecting loops through rural landscapes. It includes a boardwalk over a beaver pond. It can be reached by parking at the tennis courts at Jamestown High School and following the dirt road to the left of the courts.

JAMES CITY COUNTY DISTRICT PARK SPORTS COMPLEX
Off Centerville Road, Williamsburg
(757) 259-4200

This new 675-acre park being built by James City County is under development; plans call for numerous trails for hiking, biking, and horseback riding. It will also have picnicking facilities as well as tennis, basketball, and volleyball courts. Long-range plans include an outdoor education center and an indoor/outdoor pool. The project is ongoing.

KILN CREEK PARK
Kiln Creek Subdivision, Yorktown
(757) 890-3500

Located in the Kiln Creek community, this 21-acre York County park opened in 1999. The park features a lighted soccer field, lighted baseball field, youth softball/baseball field, two outdoor basketball courts, a playground, a picnic shelter, parking, and restrooms. The park is used primarily for the Little League baseball program and the youth soccer program.

KIWANIS MUNICIPAL PARK
123 Longhill Rd., Williamsburg
(757) 259-3760

Little League baseball fields, basketball courts, lighted tennis courts, a picnic shelter, and a playground and playground equipment make this Longhill Road park a local favorite. Besides a convenient location and many leisure activities, the park offers tennis classes (see the entry under Tennis for further information on this park).

LITTLE CREEK RESERVOIR PARK
180 Lakeview Dr., Toano
(757) 566-1702

Located off Forge Road, this park is a fisherman's paradise featuring year-round fishing and boating on the 996-acre reservoir, which is stocked with largemouth bass, bluegill, crappie, stripers, walleye, perch, pickerel, and a variety of sunfish and catfish. If you don't have a boat, you can rent one here, by the hour, and choose among jon boats with or without motors, kayaks, canoes, and paddleboats, or you can use the fishing pier, for which there's no charge. Use of the boat ramps costs a nominal amount. All fishermen must have a Virginia fishing license. The park is a nice place for a picnic, too, and offers a concession facility and shelter with grills. It's open daily 7 a.m. until sunset (6 a.m. until sunset on weekends) Mar through Nov and 7 a.m. to 5 p.m. weekends only from Dec through Feb. (See also the entry for Little Creek Reservoir in this chapter's Fishing and Hunting section.)

MID COUNTY PARK
3793 Ironbound Rd., Williamsburg
(757) 229-1232
Fitness trails, soccer, baseball, basketball, softball, tennis, and volleyball are a few of the recreational activities available at this James City County park, which is open daily from sunrise to dusk. Located off Route 199, Mid County also offers picnic shelters and Kidsburg, an all-volunteer, community-built children's play area, parts of which are modeled on area attractions. For more on Kidsburg, see our Kidstuff chapter.

NEW QUARTER PARK
Lakeshead Drive, York
(757) 890-3500
Near the Queens Lake area of Williamsburg, this 545-acre York County park is especially good for group activities. Family reunions, company picnics, business meetings, and the like often take place here, where people can enjoy boating, hiking, fishing from the piers, playing horseshoes, and picnicking in the pavilions. The park is open from Memorial Day to Labor Day, 7:30 a.m. to 7 p.m.

POWHATAN CREEK ACCESS
Jamestown Road at Powhatan Creek, Williamsburg
(757) 259-4200
Listed on the Natural Resources Inventory, this facility provides access to Jamestown Island and the James River. It consists of a small-boat and canoe launch with parking for 20 vehicles.

QUARTERPATH PARK AND RECREATION CENTER
202 Quarterpath Rd., Williamsburg
(757) 259-3760
This park is home to some huge area sports leagues, and for good reason. Its facilities include free tennis and basketball courts (which are being renovated), an outdoor pool that's open through Labor Day, three softball fields, a playground, and indoor courts for basketball or volleyball. For open-play volleyball, stop by between 6 to 9 p.m. on Thurs in the summer and 6 to 8 p.m. Sun the rest of the year. Or, if you prefer basketball, come by for open play daily from 1 to 5 p.m. Cost for either is $2. Morning aerobics classes are offered for a fee.

UPPER COUNTY PARK
180 Leisure Rd., Toano
(757) 566-1451
This James City County facility is open from Memorial Day to Labor Day and boasts an outdoor pool, bathhouse, community room, picnic shelters, and playground. Entrance to the park is free, although use of the pool costs $2.50 per day for resident adults, $3.50 for nonresidents, $2 for resident children, and $3 for nonresidents. Children five and younger are admitted free. Families can purchase season pool passes for $70. The park is open from 11 a.m. to 7:45 p.m. daily.

WALLER MILL PARK
Airport Road (Route 645)
Williamsburg
(757) 259-3778
On Route 645 west of Williamsburg, Waller Mill is the place to go for a picnic or a lazy paddle around the lake. Open from sunrise to sunset year-round, Waller Mill offers shelters, tables, nature trails, jogging and fitness trails, a 5.5-mile mountain bike trail, and fishing, plus canoe, rowboat, and pedal-boat rental (boat rates range from $4 to $8 per hour). Boats for fishing rent for $5 per licensed angler per day. For a nominal fee you can launch your own fishing boat at the boat ramp. There's also a walking course for senior citizens. (See also our entry under the Fishing and Hunting section.)

WILLIAMSBURG INDOOR SPORTS COMPLEX
5700 Warhill Trail, Williamsburg
(757) 253-1947
www.thewisc.com
This 50,000-square-foot indoor sports facility is owned by the Williamsburg Indoor Sports Complex, a private organization that went into partnership with James City County. The complex sits on county park property. The Williamsburg Indoor Sports Complex, or WISC as it is known, offers summer camps for soccer (see more about soccer a little later in this chapter), in-line hockey (youths—various age groups, 10 weeks for $90), and field hockey (Saturday mornings for high school students and adults for $40). It offers flag football and karate, and plans are in the works for volleyball and lacrosse. The organization also hosts a variety of activities including parties, dances, and open skate times. There are sports activities throughout the year and no residence restrictions. In order to participate in WISC programs, individuals must purchase an annual membership for $15, plus $5 for additional family members. WISC is run by Chris Haywood, a former collegiate All-American and professional soccer player as well as a high school soccer coach.

WOLF TRAP PARK
Wolftrap Road, Grafton
(757) 890-3500
This 28-acre park hosts the Yorktown United Soccer Club's matches. It features four soccer fields, restrooms, and a parking lot. Two ponds also are located here. It is home, too, to the York County Memorial Tree Grove, which provides an opportunity for friends, relatives, and organizations to commemorate deceased local citizens.

YORK RIVER STATE PARK
5526 Riverview Rd., Williamsburg
(757) 566-3036
The Virginia Department of Conservation and Recreation operates this 2,505-acre tract of land year-round. The park lies alongside the York River, which is formed by the joining of the Pamunkey and Mattaponi Rivers at West Point. On the park property is Croaker Landing, an archaeological site listed on the National Register of Historic Places. The park is on what was once Taskinas Plantation. In the 17th and 18th centuries, it was the site of a public tobacco warehouse, where local planters stored their crops to be shipped. Remnants of wooden "corduroy" roads dating from the period can still be seen at low tide.

York River State Park opened in 1980 and is a great place to see firsthand the rare and delicate coastal estuarine environment, where freshwater and salt water merge to create a habitat rich in marine and plant life. You'll find excellent outdoor opportunities here, including 25 miles of hiking, biking, and horseback-riding trails through the park's diverse natural areas. The 1.75-mile Taskinas Creek Trail gives hikers a fascinating look at the Chesapeake Bay estuary. The Taskinas Creek area is one of four sites along the York River designated as a Chesapeake Bay Estuarine Research Reserve site. The park also has excellent picnicking facilities, with three shelters that overlook the scenic marsh or York River. The shelters, which have grills, picnic tables, and access to restrooms and the playground, may be reserved by calling the state park reservation office at (800) 933-PARK. In addition to the shelters, the park has 40 picnic tables that are available first-come, first-served.

York River State Park offers many interpretive programs, including pontoon boat tours, guided canoe trips on the Taskinas Creek, night canoe trips, ranger-guided programs, ghost night hikes, Junior Rangers, fossil hikes, wildlife observations, nature hikes, and campfire programs in the fall, as well as environmental education programs for groups of 10 or more. The guided canoe trips are provided May to October. Some programs do involve extra fees and require reservations.

The park has an interesting equipment rental policy: Once you pay the rental fee, you can swap equipment, which includes bikes, canoes, paddleboats, jon boats, and kayaks, as well as horseshoes, volleyballs, Frisbees, and badminton equipment. Rental equipment is available May through October.

While the park hours are 8 a.m. to dusk, the visitor center, park office, and gift shop are open from 8 a.m. to 6 p.m. during the week and 10 a.m. to 6 p.m. on Sat and Sun. The gift shop sells snacks, drinks, and ice cream. There are also primitive group tent camping sites available for up to 48 people. At York River there are three areas to fish, take your pick: freshwater, salt water, or brackish water. A valid fishing license is required (see our entry in this chapter under Fishing and Hunting).

York River State Park hosts several events through the year, including Harvest Day at the end of October. Admission is regular price, though some events may cost extra. During this festivity the park offers colonial and American Indian games, arts and crafts, old-fashioned games, such as the potato sack race and three-legged race, hayrides, and a maze for the children to wander through.

Located about 10 miles west of Williamsburg on Riverview Road (also known as Route 606), York River State Park can be reached by taking the Croaker exit 231B off of I-64.

i   A favorite biking trip is the 23-mile Colonial Parkway, which passes through various landscapes and provides wonderful views without the heavy traffic of local streets and highways. Observe Virginia biking laws, which require bikers to ride in the same direction as the flow of traffic at all times.

YORKTOWN WATERFRONT
Water Street
Yorktown
(757) 898-3500

This two-acre beachfront is open to the public year-round free of charge. However, there are no lifeguards on duty. Water lovers can swim, fish, and boat here and even take a shower afterward. Restrooms are located on-site. Showers and restrooms are open Apr 1 to mid-Oct.

RECREATION

GREATER WILLIAMSBURG YMCA
630 South Henry St., Williamsburg
(757) 258-3830

This small but active center is the first foray of the YMCA into Greater Williamsburg. Before- and after-school programs and a summer camp program are held in this building, located across from the Marshall Wythe School of Law of the College of William and Mary on South Henry Street.

The state-licensed before- and after-school program is held Mon through Fri from 6 a.m. until school opens, and then again from 2:30 until 6 p.m. It is open to all students ages 6 to 12. Students participate in various activities, including fitness, homework time, free play, multicultural projects, character-building programs, and nature studies. Children can also try out the computer room.

The YMCA also offers a 10-week summer camp for children ages 5 to 12. The camp, which runs from the end of June until mid-August, offers a variety of age-related activities.

In addition, from March to June the YMCA sponsors Neighborhood Basketball League (NBL), a youth basketball program for students ages 6 to 12.

The YMCA also operates the accredited Preschool Childcare Program at Colonial Williamsburg for kids ages six weeks to five years. The program operates 6:30 a.m. to 6 p.m. Mon through Fri. Placement is on a space available basis. For more information call (757) 220-7045.

JAMES CITY COUNTY–
WILLIAMSBURG COMMUNITY CENTER
5301 Longhill Rd., Williamsburg
(757) 259-4200

This large facility has just about anything a person could want in recreation: a gymnasium with two basketball courts, four volleyball courts, a two-lane indoor suspended track, a 25-meter-by-25-yard swimming pool with three lap-lanes, locker rooms with showers and saunas, racquetball courts, a whirlpool for 16 people, and a fitness room with free weights, two circuits of Cybex, and 23 pieces of cardiovascular equipment. There's also a teen area equipped with TV and games, and a senior area with pool table and game table. The center also has a craft room, a kiln and pottery wheels, and a dance and aerobics room. Hours of operation are Mon through Fri 6 a.m. to 9 p.m., Sat 9 a.m. to 6 p.m., and Sun 1 to 6 p.m.

The center offers senior activities provided in conjunction with the Historic Triangle Senior Center, and rehabilitation and health education programs in conjunction with Williamsburg Community Hospital. Also, trainers are on-site to offer fitness assessments and personal fitness training.

A notary public is on site 8 a.m. until 5 p.m. Mon through Fri.

The Greater Williamsburg Branch YMCA provides child care for children ages 6 months through 10 years in the Community Center while their parents are using the facility. Reservations may be made by phone or in person up to one week in advance and must be made at least 24 hours in advance.

Patron services include orientation on weight equipment, on-site registration for division-wide programs and services, rentals for picnic shelters, soccer and softball field rentals, and corporate passes for local businesses.

Annual access passes for residents are as follows: family, $360; adult, $180; youth (ages five and older), $55; senior citizens, $145. The daily admission fee is $10 for adults and $4 for youth ages 17 and younger. Semiannual and quarterly access fees for residents are also available. The center closes for Labor Day, Thanksgiving, Christmas, New Year's Day, Easter, and the Fourth of July.

JAMES RIVER COMMUNITY CENTER
8901 Pocahontas Trail, Williamsburg
(757) 887-5810

The center includes a gymnasium, a multipurpose room with game tables and large-screen TV, a glass-backed racquetball court, fitness room, table tennis and pool table, three tennis courts, basketball courts, a sand volleyball court, soccer field, softball field, and a nature trail. The fitness room is equipped with a circuit of Cybex equipment, dumbbells, a weight bench, and a pull-up dip station. Patrons have access to a cafeteria and kitchen area.

The multipurpose rooms, cafeteria, and gym are available for rent for small parties or large gatherings. Patron services include orientation on weight equipment, on-site registration for division-wide programs and services, rentals for picnic shelters, soccer and softball field rentals, and corporate passes for local businesses. A notary public is on-site noon until 8 p.m. Mon through Fri. The center also offers a wide variety of classes, such as karate, CPR, tennis, and oil painting.

The center is open Mon through Thurs from noon to 9 p.m., Fri noon to 8 p.m., Sat 9 a.m. to 6 p.m., and Sun 1 to 6 p.m. One-year resident access passes cost $30 for adults, $45 for families, $20 for seniors, and $15 for youth. An annual resident combination pass to James River Community Center and the James City County–Williamsburg Community Center is $385 for families, $210 for adults, $155 for seniors, and $60 for youth. All resident patrons without a monthly access pass must purchase a $5 access pass to use the center. This pass must be shown each time the patron visits the center and pays the daily admission fee. The daily admission fee is $3 for adults and free for youth. Semiannual access passes are also available. The charge for nonresidents to use the facility for the day is $5 for adults and $2 for children, or they can buy an annual or semiannual pass. The center is closed Labor Day, Thanksgiving, Christmas Eve and Christmas Day, New Year's Day, Memorial Day, and the Fourth of July.

Activities
Biking

Many visitors enjoy biking through the Historic Area, especially on quiet and picturesque back streets where the illusion of a return to the past is most complete. Bikes are available from the following private businesses:

BIKES UNLIMITED
759 Scotland St., Williamsburg
(757) 229-4620

Near both the college and the west end of the Historic Area, this company offers complete biking services, including rentals for $15 a day. Hours are 9:30 a.m. to 6:30 p.m. Tues through Fri, 10 a.m. to 5 p.m. Sat, and noon to 4 p.m. Sun (summers only). The store is closed Mon.

WILLIAMSBURG AREA BICYCLISTS
Williamsburg
www.wabonline.org
If you bring your bike to town and are looking for companions to ride with, check out this club, which encourages the use of the bicycle for recreation, fitness, and transportation, while also encouraging the development of facilities for bicycling on public lands. A calendar of rides is kept up to date on its Web site and provides phone numbers for ride leaders. Scheduled rides vary from the casual ride that is good for beginners and families (up to 11 mph, level terrain, and a distance of 10 to 25 miles) to an A grade, in which cyclists ride steadily at 18 to 22 mph. Rides take place at York River State Park, the Colonial Parkway, Jamestown, and around Williamsburg. Annual membership is $15; $20 for families. Riders are required to wear helmets for all rides.

Bowling
AMF WILLIAMSBURG LANES
5544 Olde Towne Rd., Williamsburg
(757) 565-3311
Regular hours here are 9 a.m. to midnight Sun through Thurs, 9 a.m. to 2 a.m. Fri and Sat. Colorful excitement is offered in the form of the Extreme Bowl Package. The fun begins at 10 p.m. Fri and continues until 2 a.m. Sat and again 10 p.m. Sat until 2 a.m. Sun. During these events regular lighting is turned off, the music is turned up, and black lights provide special effect lighting on the pins, which glow in the dark. Three times a year Williamsburg Lanes hosts tournaments, which may make getting a lane difficult. The Virginia Women's Tournament takes place over several weeks in October and November. Colonial Virginia's Men's Tournament comes along during March and April. During the Colonial Virginia's Mixed Tournament in June, July, and August, they really mix it up. Special rates are offered to children, senior citizens, and groups. This is an excellent spot for a child's birthday party since they offer special packages.

i Fishing is a year-round pursuit in the greater Williamsburg area. Even when popular fishing holes at area parks are closed, the bountiful James and York Rivers are always open for business. Of course, it's potluck what you catch, depending on the time of year.

Fishing and Hunting
Water surrounds the Historic Triangle—rivers, tributaries, lakes, ponds, wetlands, estuaries, and the bay. A complete guide to area fishing would require a hefty volume. Here we offer merely some local fishin' holes and information about licenses. If you're a die-hard angler, check with the **Department of Game and Inland Fisheries** in Richmond, (804) 367-1000, for a copy of its annual state fishing guide and the facts on seasons and creel limits, etc. Or call (800) 986-2628 to purchase Virginia licenses by phone.

Used to be you could toss your line in the ocean or Chesapeake Bay for free, but since 1992 a license for fishing in salt water is required for all those between the ages of 16 and 65. The cost is $19 for residents, $37 for nonresidents. A freshwater license is required for those 16 and older all over the state of Virginia, and the Tidewater area is no exception. A five-day, nonresident freshwater license is $10. Licenses are valid for the calendar year during which they are bought and are available at local bait and tackle shops, marinas, sporting goods counters of larger stores, and county circuit court clerks. For more information on fishing licenses or for boat licenses, contact the Department of Game and Inland Fisheries.

If hunting is your sport, you'll need a license, too. Hunters 16 and older who have previously had a license can purchase one valid in Virginia by phone through **Bass Pro Shops** at (800) 986-2628 for $12.50. If you've never had a hunting license before or are between the ages of 12 and 15, you must first take a hunter safety course to obtain a Virginia hunting license. These courses are given by the state for free. Again, contact the Department of Game and Inland Fisheries.

LITTLE CREEK RESERVOIR
180 Lakeview Dr., Toano
(757) 566-1702

Little Creek Reservoir in Toano, covering 996 acres, has a boat ramp, a dock, and a fishing pier. You can also fish from the shore. Crappie, largemouth bass, pickerel, bluegills, stripers, and walleye can be hooked here. Little Creek is open daily Mar through Nov; Dec through Feb it opens weekends only, weather permitting. Season passes are available for $60 a year. Boats can be rented for $8 per boat per day, and that includes fishing privileges. Children younger than 16 fish for free. Boat rentals for pleasure riding range from $3 to $8 per hour or $20 per hour with motor and battery. This wonderful, practically secret lake is a bit hard to find for the new resident: From US Route 60 in Toano, take Route 610 (Forge Road) 2 miles to the first left, which is Lakeview Drive. (See also the Little Creek Reservoir Park entry in this chapter under Park Locations and Activities.)

i The temperate climate that makes outdoor life so enjoyable for humans also spawns a variety of tiny wildlife that can get you itching and scratching. This includes mosquitoes, ticks, and spiders, among others. Insiders will strongly urge you to use a bug repellent for comfort and safety when spending time outdoors.

POWHATAN CREEK ACCESS
Jamestown Road at Powhatan Creek, Williamsburg
(757) 259-4200

Listed on the Natural Resources Inventory, this simple facility provides access to Jamestown Island and the James River. It consists of a small-boat and canoe launch with parking for 20 vehicles. It is located along Jamestown Road across from Cooke's Greenhouse.

WALLER MILL PARK
Airport Road (Route 645)
Williamsburg
(757) 259-3778

For freshwater fishing, try Waller Mill Park, which has one of the area's deepest lakes, known for large striped bass, crappie, largemouth bass, perch, pickerel, and channel catfish. There is no charge to fish from the pier. The fee to rent a boat is $5 per day per person. That charge includes fishing privileges. For more information on Waller Mill, see our earlier entry under Park Locations and Activities.

YORK RIVER STATE PARK
5526 Riverview Rd., Williamsburg
(757) 566-3036
www.dcr.state.va.us/parks/yorkrive.htm

The Virginia Department of Conservation and Recreation operates this large tract 10 miles west of Williamsburg off I-64 and adjacent to the York River. Here you'll find excellent fishing and boat ramps. A broad spectrum of fish are here for the catch, including saltwater fish (croaker, spot), brackish-water fish (largemouth bass, sunfish, spot, croaker), and freshwater fish (primarily bluegill, largemouth bass, and catfish). The park is open from 8 a.m. to dusk. During the week visitors enter the park for a $2 parking fee per car. They then pay to rent boats. On weekends visitors pay $2 per adult and $1 for kids with a limit of $3 per car. The cost of renting any sports equipment, including boats, is $5 for adults for the whole day. This includes jon boats, canoes, kayaks, and paddleboats. An appropriate fishing license is required for both saltwater and freshwater fishing.

Health and Fitness Clubs
IRON-BOUND GYM
4325 New Town Ave.
New Town
(757) 229-5874
www.ironboundgym.com

This coed fitness center, located in New Town, features indoor cycling and fitness classes, free weights, circuit training, cardio equipment, a smoothie bar, and more. Daily and weekly rates are available. Open from 5:30 a.m. to 10:00 p.m. Mon through Fri, 8 a.m. to 7 p.m. Sat, and 9 a.m. to 5 p.m. Sun.

Horseback Riding

CARLTON FARMS
3516 Mott Lane, Williamsburg
(757) 220-3553
Carlton Farms offers lessons, boarding, summer camp, and sales, and has an indoor, lighted arena. It specializes in hunter horses and has a special package for beginning riders. Instructors at the farm suggest that beginning riders have at least three private lessons to get used to being on a horse. Those lessons are $35 an hour. From there, the rider would be given group lessons at $25 an hour.

CEDAR VALLEY FARM
2016 Forge Rd., Toano
(757) 566-2621
Off Lightfoot Road, Cedar Valley Farm gives private lessons to groups or individuals in English riding. Summer camps are offered sometimes, and horse owners can obtain permission to ride at the farm. Cedar Valley Farm also runs the College of William and Mary riding program and equestrian show team.

Jogging and Running

Joggers will find that many area parks offer some kind of fitness path. Waller Mill Park offers four trails—its mile-long trail is one of the best—and the trail at the James City County–Williamsburg Community Center is also very popular. But Insiders love running along the Colonial Parkway best of all.

JAMES CITY COUNTY–WILLIAMSBURG COMMUNITY CENTER
5301 Longhill Rd., Williamsburg
(757) 259-4200
The center includes a two-lane indoor suspended track. The inside lane is reserved for walking and is also accessible to wheelchairs and canes. The

outside lane is reserved for joggers and speed walking. The facility also has 2 miles of walking and bicycling paths on the grounds.

WALLER MILL PARK
Airport Road (Route 645)
Williamsburg
(757) 259-3778
This park offers a wide range of trails for the jogger, walker, and bicyclist. All of them wind through a wooded setting. The mile-long Fitness Trail is especially popular because it features fitness stops along the way for different exercises. The other trails include the 1.5-mile Bayberry Nature Trail; the 3-mile Lookout Tower Trail; the 5.5-mile Dogwood Trail, which is used by joggers and bicyclists; and the 1-mile senior walking course.

Soccer

The sport of soccer is thriving here, with the number of youth soccer clubs on the increase.

JAMES CITY COUNTY DIVISION OF PARKS AND RECREATION YOUTH SOCCER LEAGUE
5249 Olde Towne Rd., Williamsburg
(757) 259-4200
James City County offers a youth soccer league in the spring and fall for boys and girls in grades one through nine. This program is for fun and educational purposes and is noncompetitive. Registration takes place in September. The Half-Pint soccer classes are offered for children ages 3 to 5.

WILLIAMSBURG INDOOR SPORTS COMPLEX
5700 Warhill Trail, Williamsburg
(757) 253-1947
www.thewisc.com
This private facility on county land is operated by Chris Haywood, a former collegiate All-American and professional soccer player and a Lafayette High School boys soccer coach. He started the Colonial Football Club, which operates out of the Williamsburg Indoor Sports Complex (WISC). The sports complex offers numerous sports activities, including soccer. In the summer, there is a 10-week adult soccer league, a men's division,

and a coed division ($65). There's also an eight-week Indoor/Outdoor developmental league for boys and girls ages 6 to 12 ($55). Then there is the Little Rascals soccer program, a six-week class designed to introduce children ages 2 to 5 to the joy of soccer and help them develop fundamental motor skills. This class is $40 per session. There are also various soccer programs throughout the rest of the year.

WILLIAMSBURG SOCCER CLUB
(757) 220-3794
www.williamsburgsoccer.com
The Williamsburg Soccer Club has been around for years and promotes the development of girls and boys as individual soccer players within a team environment. It sponsors travel teams for kids ages 5 to 17. It also offers a girls' independent league, a beginner clinic for 4-year-olds, and boys' classic teams. There are also the boys' premier teams and the girls' premier teams, which play league games in the Virginia Club Champions League. The club offers summer training camps, a half-day session for ages 4 to 12. The club's Annual Williamsburg Cup, a premier tournament in the mid-Atlantic area, draws more than 200 youth teams each year, with games played at the recreation center, area parks, schools, Fort Eustis, and Anheuser-Busch. Richard Butler, the primary coach, formed the club. He was an assistant coach to the Blazers and played professional soccer after being a starter at the University of Alabama at Birmingham.

YOK COUNTY DIVISION OF PARKS AND RECREATION
100 County Dr., Grafton
(757) 890-3500
Boys and girls in kindergarten through 12th grade from York County can participate in the Youth Soccer Program sponsored by York County Division of Parks and Recreation. There are spring and fall programs. Practices take place at area elementary and middle schools and county parks. Registration begins at the end of August and February. Fees are $30 for the first child, $25 for each additional child. Coach certification pro-

grams are also offered. A weather hotline at (757) 890-3501 keeps participants informed of weather cancellations.

Tennis
PUBLIC COURTS
BACK CREEK PARK
3000 Goodwin Neck Rd., Seaford
(757) 890-3850
This beautiful 27-acre USTA award-winning tennis facility, accessible year-round, features six lighted tennis courts. Fees are charged when the park is staffed—on weekends in the spring through late November. The fee is $2 per couple to play before 5 p.m. and $4 to play after 5 p.m. Players can use the courts for free from the end of November through late March. Courts can be reserved up to a week in advance by calling the park. Lessons are available in the spring, summer, and fall.

CHARLES BROWN PARK
Route 238, Lackey
(757) 890-3500
This 10-acre park has two tennis courts, open year-round. There is no fee for using these courts.

KIWANIS MUNICIPAL PARK
123 Longhill Rd., Williamsburg
(757) 220-6170
Kiwanis Municipal Park has seven hard-surface courts that are free. Call (757) 220-6176 about availability. Tennis lessons are offered in the spring, summer, and fall. The USA Tennis class is extremely popular. This six-week course, which costs $50 per player, includes three weeks of instruction and three weeks of supervised play.

MCCORMACK-NAGELSEN TENNIS CENTER
College of William and Mary
705 South Henry St.
(757) 221-7378
www.wm.edu/mntc
This gorgeous facility is home to the nationally ranked William and Mary Men's and Women's Tennis teams, and the only place to play when the weather's bad. The complex offers six air-

conditioned indoor hard-Tru courts, locker rooms with changing facilities and showers.

Adult programs offered year-round include Friday night mixers and holiday socials. Instructional clinics, from beginners to advanced, are offered each week, as are match arranging and ball machine practice time. The desk keeps a sub list for players available to fill in when needed for league play.

On the second floor is spectator seating for nearly 400 and the Intercollegiate Tennis Association's Women's Tennis Hall of Fame, a collection of artifacts and records pertaining to collegiate women's tennis, and shrines to the players, coaches and contributors that have impacted the sport. The Hall of Fame also functions as a library, archive and research center for intercollegiate women's tennis.

MID COUNTY PARK
3793 Ironbound Rd., Williamsburg
(757) 229-1232
Three asphalt surface courts, available at no charge on a first-come, first-play basis.

QUARTERPATH PARK
202 Quarterpath Rd., Williamsburg
(757) 259-3200
There are three asphalt surface courts available at no charge on a first-come, first-play basis.

KINGSMILL TENNIS CENTER
931 Kingsmill Rd.
Williamsburg
(757) 253-3945
The Kingsmill Tennis Center offers 15 courts, including six Hydro Courts™ and two lighted for evening play. A player's lounge and locker facilities are located in the pro shop, which has a nice assortment of the latest tennis wear and equipment. Court fees are $16 a person per day for adults and $8 a person per day for teens ages 13 to 19. For persons wanting a court in the morning, the club suggests making reservations a day or two in advance. Regular tennis shoes, not running shoes, must be worn.

THE WILLIAMSBURG INN
136 East Francis St., Williamsburg
(757) 220-7794
Colonial Williamsburg provides Colonial Williamsburg hotel guests with access to tennis courts on the property of the Williamsburg Inn near Providence Hall. Memberships for area residents are available. Two hard and six clay courts can be rented at $24 per hour. Call ahead for reservations, especially in the morning. Lessons are available for $45 an hour or $25 a half-hour from the resident pro. Rackets can be rented, $5 for adults, free for youths.

GOLF

The temperate weather allows golf courses in southern Virginia to stay open nearly year-round—a natural advantage that has helped Williamsburg become one of the premier golf destinations on the Eastern Seaboard. Another factor has been the annual splash of glamour provided by hosting PGA and LPGA tournaments at Kingsmill for nearly three decades. Here we have a hit a small divot, however. In 2010, Kingsmill lost its marquee event when InBev, the new owners of Anheuser-Busch, withdrew its sponsorship of the LPGA Michelob Ultra Open.

Life goes on, and so do the duffers. The recent purchase of the Brickshire course in Providence Forge, west of Williamsburg, brings the number of courses owned and operated by Traditional Golf Clubs to four. Packages which offer golfers to sample all four courses, dubbed "The Traditional Golf Trail," are available with one-stop-shopping at www.traditionalgolftrail.com or by calling (888) 825-3436, ext. 4. Details about each course are listed below.

Naturally, the courses in the area also cater heavily to the communities with which they are associated, which includes a growing local retired population. Though greens fees can be steep, there are bargains to be had, especially in the nonpeak months. It's even worth checking the sports pages of the *Virginia Gazette* for discount coupons.

In this chapter we give you an overview of the courses, including yardages (from the men's tees), special features, and driving directions for courses that are not in town. Reduced rates, based on time of year, time of day, and so on, are available at most of the courses so greens fees can vary quite a bit. Carts are required at most courses, but the price is included in the greens fee. As elsewhere, soft spikes have become the rule here.

THE COURSES

THE COLONIAL GOLF CLUB
8281 Diascund Rd., Lanexa
(757) 566-1600, (800) 566-6660
www.golfcolonial.com
Designed by Lester George (with the help of PGA pro Robert Wrenn) and opened in 1995, this course is situated in Lanexa, on Diascund Road (which is off US Route 60, 7 miles west of the Williamsburg Pottery). It is a daily-fee course, carved out of dense woods and wetlands, with several holes overlooking the Chickahominy River. The daunting par 3 sixth hole is all carry over marshland to an elevated green. This championship course plays to a par 72 and is 6,886 yards long. Unique features include a three-hole practice course ($18, with cart and practice balls) and the Teaching Center and Golf Academy. Different rates apply for the various teaching and clinic packages, and reservations are appropriate. A round with cart (a must) ranges from $35 (weekday afternoons) to $70 (weekend mornings). Call for details.

FORD'S COLONY COUNTRY CLUB
240 Ford's Colony Dr., Williamsburg
(757) 258-4130, (800) 334-6033
www.fordscolony.com/golf
Fifty-four holes of world-class golf, designed by Dan Maples, are set on verdant hills with water, water everywhere. Choose from three 18-hole layouts—the Blackheath course plays 6,621 yards, and with rolling hills and water on seven holes, it is a real challenge. The Marsh Hawk course is 18 holes over 6,650 yards; the Blue Heron course offers 18-holes over 6,266 yards.

Greens fees at Ford's Colony vary seasonally, so inquire about fees when calling for a tee time. Lessons are available, and guests of the Marriott Manor Club, a resort within the Ford's Colony development, can purchase golf packages at a discounted rate. The clubhouse facilities are first-rate, and after your round, world-class dining awaits.

THE GOLDEN HORSESHOE GOLF COURSE
South England Street, Williamsburg
(757) 220-7696
www.goldenhorseshoegolf.com

Choose from three challenging courses here, including the Gold Course, first opened in 1963 and designed by Robert Trent Jones. In 1998, the course underwent a multimillion-dollar redesign by Jones's son, Rees, aimed at expanding the appeal for higher-handicap players and lengthening the course from the back tees. Nationally renowned, the course features numerous elevation changes, tight fairways, and plenty of water. Its signature hole, the par 3 16th, boasts the first island green ever built in America. Playing to a par of 71, the 6,817-yard layout's five closing holes are a test for any golfer. (Jack Nicklaus holds the course record of 67.)

The Golden Horseshoe—known locally as "the Shoe"—offers full clubhouse amenities, including a pro shop, locker rooms, and a lounge.

The Green course opened in 1991. Designed by Rees Jones, this is a 7,120-yard, par 72 course where mounds abound and the par 5 18th hole requires a 200-yard carry off the tee. More wide open than its sister course, this design still offers a stiff test for hackers of all levels. Like the Gold Course, the Green features a first-class clubhouse, pro shop, and restaurant.

The third course, also designed by Jones Sr., is named for **Colonial Governor Alexander Spotswood.** Its executive-length design allows golfers to get around its nine holes in quick order, perfect for a late afternoon of fun.

Greens fees vary seasonally, ranging from $79 to $165.

KINGSMILL GOLF CLUB
1010 Kingsmill Rd., Williamsburg
(757) 253-1703
www.kingsmill.com

The three courses at this golf club have something to satisfy every golfer. The neighborhoods of Kingsmill on the James and resort property surround the courses, but the wide, exceptionally well-landscaped vistas and breathtaking views of the river remove you from any sense of encroachment—one reason why PGA and LPGA tournaments have been held here for three decades.

The River Course is the crown jewel. Designed by the legendary Pete Dye, the par 72, 5,001-yard course is both challenging and scenic. The design requires accuracy off the tee and precise shots into greens which are well-protected by strategically placed bunkers. Holes 16, 17, and 18 are not only challenging—they have river views.

The Plantation Course, par 72, is a 6,432-yard Arnold Palmer design. Undulating greens make for a putting challenge, and a couple of the par 4s will test you off the tee. In 1993, the 18th hole was redesigned to feature a new fairway and green. Considered a challenging but fair layout, the Plantation Course has been ranked by *Golf Digest* as one of the "Top 50 Courses for Women."

Lastly there is the **Woods Course,** designed by Tom Clark and two-time U.S. Open Champion Curtis Strange. East of the other courses, this 6,659-yard achievement looked like a course that had cured for 20 years on the day it opened. It features its own clubhouse with all the amenities you would expect at a world-class resort such as Kingsmill.

The courses are open to the public. Greens fees range from $85 to $160, depending on which course you play. A nine-hole par 3 is $12 for adults and $6 for children 17 and under. All fees include the mandatory golf cart. Golf clinics are available to resort guests for $20 per person. One-, two-, and three-day Golf Academy programs are also available. Visitors can reserve a tee time 24 hours in advance.

NEWPORT NEWS GOLF CLUB AT DEER RUN
Newport News Park
901 Clubhouse Way, Newport News
(757) 886-7925
www.nngolfclub.com
Golfers looking for a budget day on the links often take advantage of Deer Run, a challenging 18-hole course located in an 8,000-acre park. (The city's Department of Parks and Recreation manages the course.) Whether you tackle Ed Ault's 7,206-yard wooded course or opt for the middle-length 6,645-yard links (this one is really suited to all levels of play), the greens fees are the same: $31. The clubhouse has a snack bar and restaurant, driving range, putting greens, and pro shop. The course is an easy 15-minute drive east on I-64. Take exit 250B, go straight through the light, and turn left at the golf club entrance.

THE TRADITION CLUB AT BRICKSHIRE
5520 Virginia Park Dr.
Providence Forge
(804) 966-7023, (888) 825-3436, ext. 4
www.traditionalclubs.com
The popularity of this course, the most recent addition to the Traditional Club fold in the Williamsburg area, can be explained in two words: "player friendly." Wide inviting fairways, artfully sculpted, true-rolling greens, and dramatic elevation changes mark the layout, designed by U.S. Open Champion Curtis Strange who has replicated some of his favorite holes from around the world at this course, located between Richmond and Williamsburg. The 15th hole is a wickedly picturesque par 3; the 18th, a par 5 with panoramic views that has been called one of the best finishing holes in the mid-Atlantic. *Golf Digest* readers rate Brickshire four and a half stars; *Golf Styles* named it one of the mid-Atlantic's "Must Play" courses.

Carts are not required but strongly suggested—the course is 7,291 yards. Greens fees vary seasonally and discounts are offered to military, VSGA card holders, and senior citizens, but expect to pay $99 on a summer weekend. A clubhouse, pro shop, and restaurant round out the amenities.

The course is about 30 minutes west of Williamsburg; follow I-64 to exit 214 (Providence Forge). Take Route 155 south one-half mile to the course entrance.

TRADITION GOLF CLUB AT KISKIACK
8104 Club Dr.
(757) 566-2200, (888) 825-3436, ext. 4
www.traditionalclubs.com
This John LaFoy–designed course opened in the fall of 1997. Created from woodlands and rolling terrain, Kiskiack has quickly become a favorite among local golfers. Ten minutes west of Williamsburg, at the Croaker Road exit (exit 231B) on I-64, this 6,405-yard, par 72 layout is a treat. The par 3 11th hole, requiring a hefty carry over water, is the signature hole. Greens fees, including cart, range from $29 to $75, and getting a tee time in advance is a must.

THE TRADITION GOLF CLUB AT ROYAL NEW KENT
Route 155
Providence Forge
(804) 966-7023, (888) 825-3436, ext. 4
www.traditionalclubs.com
This par 72 course, two miles south of Brickshire, has been compared to Ballybunion and Royal County Down in Scotland, two of the world's greatest links courses. Among other things, it features stone walls, hidden greens, and blind fairways, giving this course a particularly natural setting. Greens fees with a cart, which we recommend, range from $83 to $100. The course is about 30 minutes west of Williamsburg; follow I-64 to exit 214 (Providence Forge). Take Route 155 south 2.5 miles to the course entrance.

TRADITION GOLF CLUB AT STONEHOUSE
9700 Mill Pond Run
Toano
(757) 566-1138, (888) 825-3436, ext. 4
www.traditionalclubs.com
This course, located 15 miles west of Williamsburg, is one of the most beautiful courses in the Mid-Atlantic region. It features deep bunkering; awesome vistas; and undulating, fast greens

comparable to Cypress Point in Pebble Beach, California. Some greens sit atop cliffs, while others meander along spring-fed creeks. The par 71 design measures 6,111 yards. Greens fees range from $30 in the winter to $99 on weekends in high season. Lesson costs vary. Carts are required. The quickest route to the course is via I-64 West to exit 227. The entrance is a half-mile north on the right.

WILLIAMSBURG NATIONAL GOLF CLUB
3700 Centerville Rd., Williamsburg
(757) 258-9642, (800) 859-9182
www.wngc.com

Located within the Greensprings neighborhood, this semiprivate golf club offers two 18-hole courses—the Jamestown, which opened in 1995 with a design by Jack Nicklaus's Golden Bear Associates, and the Yorktown, designed by Tom Clark, which opened in 2007. *Golf Digest* gave the courses here a four-star rating, and the Yorktown course has been named a "Top 50 Fifty Courses for Women in America."

DAY TRIPS

While Williamsburg is one of a kind, other pockets of Hampton Roads have plenty to offer the would-be wanderer. The Old Dominion, after all, is a land of vast diversity.

What we've outlined below are some of our favorite adventures, places you can go by simply hopping behind the wheel and heeding our directions. Whether you ferry across the James River, grab some R&R on Tangier or Smith Island, or stroll along the historic streets of downtown Smithfield, all of these favorites are worth a good 8 to 12 hours of your time and most (with the exception of the islands) take well under two hours of driving time. (Although we can't promise you won't run into traffic. Sorry.)

JAMESTOWN-SCOTLAND FERRY
End of Jamestown Road
(800) 823-3779

This free, state-run service, the last of a once-thriving ferry commerce in Hampton Roads, crosses the James River from Jamestown to Scotland Wharf in Surry County in Southside (many contend that the South doesn't really begin until one is securely below the James). For a large number of residents, this scenic ride is a twice-daily commute, either to the Surry nuclear power plant across the river or to jobs on the peninsula. For many others, especially on weekends in good weather, it's a favorite day trip.

You can reach the ferry by traveling either Jamestown Road or the Colonial Parkway to its southernmost end, near Jamestown Settlement. The schedule varies with the season and the time of day. Typically, in the summer you can hop aboard every 25 minutes to half an hour from 1 a.m. to midnight. The ferry gets under way every 20 minutes to half an hour from 1 a.m. to midnight Fri, Sat, and Sun.

While on the concrete dock waiting to board, you'll notice the three restored ships of Jamestown Settlement to your left: the *Susan Constant*, the *Godspeed*, and the *Discovery*. You don't get a better waterside view of all three ships than this, and your wait might be a prime opportunity to pull out the camera.

The trip takes a little less than 20 minutes from castoff to docking and offers beautiful views, especially on clear autumn days or during late-summer sunsets.

Once you have boarded one of the ferries of the fleet, you may leave your vehicle (being careful, of course, not to ding your neighbors' car doors) and enjoy the view from the railing or from bow or stern. There is a small cabin upstairs with water fountains and restrooms as well as good views, but there is no seating on most of the ferries.

The unique experience of riding a ferry is periodically threatened with extinction by studies that call for a replacement bridge spanning the river, either here or upstream. Each year approximately 936,000 vehicles use the ferry service.

SURRY COUNTY

After you're across the James and docked at Scotland Wharf, you'll drive off into Surry County. Many people choose to go directly down Route 31 to the Surrey House (yes, that's the spelling) or Edwards' Ham for delicious southern cooking. Others prefer exploring Smith's Fort Plantation, traveling to Bacon's Castle, or going to Chippokes Plantation State Park and Chippokes Farm and Forestry Museum. Whatever your choice, you'll find that a voyage across the James is a trip into the quiet, rural southern landscape of Surry County that offers a last picture of what the peninsula used to be. Miles of farmland and two-lane highways separate small, historic communities. Weathered tobacco barns, more tall than wide, occasionally are visible in fields where prized Virginia peanuts are now the major crop. It's a world away from generic fast-food restaurants, hotel chains, and the sometimes frantic pace of an established tourism industry.

Attractions

BACON'S CASTLE
465 Bacon Castle Rd. (Route 617), Surry
(757) 357-5976
www.apva.org/baconscastle
Williamsburg may have a palace, but Surry has its own castle—Bacon's Castle on Route 10. You might think you heard all about the Virginia colonists' rebellion as you toured Williamsburg, but did you know that, 100 years before the Revolution, another rebellion occurred? In 1676 Nathaniel Bacon began the colony's first act of insurrection against Governor William Berkeley's harsh rule. The struggle spread to Surry County, and, on September 18, Bacon's commander, William Rookings, captured this building, home to Major Arthur Allen, in a siege.

Major Allen built the house in 1665, and now, more than 340 years later, it is the oldest documented brick house in English North America. Architecturally, it is of extreme interest. Unlike its surviving, typically Georgian, contemporaries, the building has curving Flemish gables and triple chimneystacks. Its front and rear facades also are unusual in that they are broken midpoint by an entrance-and-porch tower in front and a corresponding stair tower in back. This gives the building a cruciform shape, the first house in the colony so designed. A formal garden has been excavated and restored, giving the whole estate a sense of antiquity and a peace that contrasts with its most famous historical event.

The house is closed Mon, and open noon to 5 p.m. Wed through Sun, Apr through October 31. It is open weekends only in Nov and Mar,

and closed in Jan and Feb. Admission is $8 for adults, $6 for senior citizens, and $5 for students ages 6 to 18. Tickets for both Bacon's Castle and Smith's Fort can be purchased for $12 (adults), $10 (seniors). Group tours can be arranged by appointment. Closed July 4.

CHIPPOKES PLANTATION STATE PARK
695 Chippokes Park Rd.
Secondary Route 634 off Route 10 East, Surry
(757) 294-3439, (757) 294-3625
The 1854 manor house at Chippokes Plantation State Park might be a welcome change from the Georgian architecture on which this part of Virginia prides itself. Formal gardens surround the house and contain one of the largest collections of crape myrtles on the East Coast. This plantation, named after a Native American chief friendly to the settlers, has been continuously farmed for more than 370 years, which makes the model farm and the adjacent Farm and Forestry Museum a fitting part of the state park. There are biking and hiking trails, picnic shelters, a swimming pool, and fishing. Some folks on the peninsula are unaware of the fine public swimming pool, but a day trip to swim here is well worth the effort. Swimming fees run about $2 to $4.

If you would like to lengthen your outdoor stay, the park also has 32 campsites with water and electrical hookups, plus additional primitive campsites. Camping is open from Mar through Oct and costs $25 a night for sites with water and electricity; $18 for the others. If you prefer a less rugged stay, Chippokes also has three air-conditioned cabins. It's a good idea to make plans well in advance if you want to camp. To reserve a spot, call (800) 933-PARK.

The park is the site of the Steam and Gas Engine Show in June; the Pork, Peanut, and Pine Festival in July; and Halloween at Haunted Chippokes and the Plantation Christmas in late fall, all of which draw huge crowds from around the region for a variety of activities that primarily focus on food and fun. (For more on the Plantation Christmas celebration, please turn to our Close-up in this chapter.)

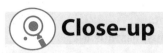 **Close-up**

Party at the Plantation

You're going to have to work a little to get there, but if you like a festival that has something of an Old World feel to it, don't pass up Plantation Christmas at Chippokes in Surry County. This three-day event, which typically takes place the last weekend in October, offers a unique array of crafts, a diverse assortment of food, and some truly unusual entertainment.

A relatively new celebration (it was started in 1997), Plantation Christmas is a juried invitational crafts festival that delights visitors with original offerings. Exhibitors show handcrafted wares that range from 18th-century furniture reproductions, exquisite wooden vases, and hand-braided rugs to marionettes, wooden toys, and children's clothing.

To create an inviting atmosphere, vendors' booths are set up along curving paths that either front the James River or encircle the Chippokes Plantation mansion (which also is open to festival visitors for tours).

Many craftspeople work their trades while selling their wares, and most are pleased to have visitors come up and ask questions.

Also contributing to its "place-out-of-time" feel, the festival hosts strolling musicians. The Stowehaven Strings, for instance, is a trio that walks the grounds throughout the event, pausing to play holiday and traditional entertainment on violins and viola, while the Colonial Christmas quartet wear traditional colonial garb and raise pints of "ale" as they serenade festivalgoers with 18th-century holiday music.

The food, too, is a bit unusual. While you still can purchase typical festival fare like Italian sausage and foot-long hot dogs, those with more adventuresome palates can sample vegetarian crepes, smoked turkey legs, sweet-potato fries, and peanut raisin pie. Our favorite taste treat: a buckwheat crepe brimming with spinach, mushrooms, and tomatoes, then slathered with a light basil-garlic sauce. (We recommend washing it down with the homemade mint iced tea sold at the same food booth.)

General admission to the festival is $5 for adults and children older than 12. Parking is free. To get to the festival, board the ferry at Jamestown and take it to Scotland Wharf in Surry County. Upon debarking follow Route 31 to Route 10. Head east on Route 10, then follow Secondary Highway 634 (and the signs) to Chippokes Plantation State Park. For more information call (757) 294-3728.

Since seasonal hours for both the manor and farm vary, call ahead for an exact schedule and admission fees.

SMITH'S FORT PLANTATION
Route 31, Thomas Rolfe Lane, Surry
(757) 294-3872
www.apva.org/smithsfort

You may be surprised to note that the Smith in the name of this historic plantation is none other than Captain John Smith, who built a fort on high land at nearby Gray's Creek in 1609 as protection for Jamestown, directly across the river.

The land has other famous connections as well, having been part of Chief Powhatan's wedding gifts to Pocahontas and John Rolfe. The building currently on the site was built in 1765 and is considered a fine example of a Georgian brick manor house with its typical one and a half stories and central entrance.

The plantation is closed Mon, and open noon to 5 p.m. Wed through Sun, Apr through Oct 31. It is open weekends only in Nov and Mar, and closed in Jan and Feb. Admission is $8 for adults, $6 for senior citizens, and $5 for students ages 6 to 18. Tickets for both Bacon's Castle and

Smith's Fort can be purchased for $12 (adults), $10 (seniors). Group tours can be arranged by appointment. Closed July 4.

S. WALLACE EDWARDS & SONS
11381 Rolfe Hwy. (Route 31), Surry
(757) 294-3121, (800) 222-4267 (for mail order)
www.vatraditions.com
If you like ham, plan to stop in at S. Wallace Edwards & Sons, just down the street from the well-known Surrey House and the source of the ham served at the restaurant. For three generations the Edwards family has been creating some of the finest hams you can find anywhere in Virginia. Their smokehouse offers a fascinating glimpse into how the curing process, taught to settlers by Native Americans, has become a modern art. Each ham, selected for its high quality, is hand rubbed with a special dry cure, then aged perfectly. A notable mahogany color is achieved with days of exposure to hickory smoke and supervised aging. While some long-cut hams are aged for a year, the company's most popular hams are ones that have aged between four and six months.

Edwards' hams have a wide following. The company has its own mail-order catalog and also receives orders from mail-order merchandisers like Williams-Sonoma, Harry & David, Winterthur, and Neiman-Marcus—especially during the busy holiday months. They won a top honor from *Gourmet* magazine in 2005, and every September those same hams capture blue ribbons at the state fair in Richmond. Surry's most famous pork products have even earned a stamp of approval from none other than celebrated chef and cookbook author Julia Child.

We recommend that you spend some time in the retail shop: Your taste buds will demand it. If you can't make it to Surry, check out **Edwards' Virginia Ham Shoppe of Williamsburg** (757) 220-6618. Located at 1814 Richmond Rd., it's open 9 a.m. to 9 p.m. seven days a week.

Restaurants
SURREY HOUSE RESTAURANT
11865 Rolfe Hwy., Surry
(757) 294-3389, (800) 200-4977
www.surreyhouserestaurant.com
Somehow it wouldn't seem right if you left Surry County without stopping in at the Surrey House Restaurant, a favorite destination for Williamsburg residents, especially on a sunny Sunday after church. Established in 1954, the Surrey House specializes in ham, seafood, pork, and poultry dishes as well as other regional fare. We recommend that you begin your meal with peanut soup, a creamy delicacy full of chunky bits of world-famous Virginia peanuts. As a main dish, the Surrey House Surf and Turf is typically Virginian, featuring a combination of ham and crab cakes. Other regional dishes include apple fritters, delicious ham hocks, great southern fried chicken, and homemade desserts. For the latter, we prefer the peanut raisin pie, a proudly served local variation on the South's ubiquitous pecan pie. It's delicious. Entrees range from $3.99 to $18. This restaurant has a waiting list on weekends and holidays, so we recommend reservations. Just tell them what ferry you'll arrive on, and they'll tailor your reservation to meet your arrival. The restaurant is open daily from Easter through Nov 1, 7:30 a.m. to 9 p.m. During the winter, closing time is one hour earlier.

SMITHFIELD

While you're over in Southside, you might want to head to Smithfield in Isle of Wight County, the true home of the world-famous Smithfield ham. While ham has placed Smithfield on the map in recent years, the town actually grew up around the trade and commerce that flourished on the Pagan River. Its rich past provides Smithfield with much to tempt the day-tripper. The city's charming downtown is a National Historic District, and the restored pre–Revolutionary War homes that line Main Street are a delight to behold. In recent years a downtown improvement project has added new brick sidewalks, old-fashioned street lamps, and attractive landscaping.

While Smithfield isn't exactly next door to Williamsburg, it's just down Route 10 from Bacon's Castle and Chippokes Plantation. Take the ferry to Scotland Wharf, then follow Route 31 to Route 10 in Surry County, where you'll turn left. Drive down this road for another 18 miles or so until you come to a stoplight. Turn left, and you'll be on Smithfield's Main Street. If you hit the ferry at the right time, the whole trip should take about 50 minutes. (One word of advice: As you approach Smithfield on Route 10, disregard the signs that direct you to the Smithfield business district. This is a roundabout route that takes you past the area's meatpacking plants. Following our directions, you'll reach downtown much more quickly.)

SMITHFIELD AND ISLE OF WIGHT CONVENTION AND VISITORS BUREAU
335 Main St.
(757) 357-5182, (800) 365-9339
www.smithfield-virginia.com
To start your visit, stop by the old Isle of Wight Courthouse and pick up brochures and a walking map from the county tourism bureau. The courthouse was built in 1750 and is owned by the Association for the Preservation of Virginia Antiquities. If you follow the walking tour guide, you'll stroll past dozens of gorgeous old houses, actually a blend of 18th-century colonial, Federal, Georgian, and Victorian period houses sitting side by side. There are more than 65 structures on the tour—and they really are within comfortable walking distance of one another—including the Oak Grove Academy at 204 Grace St., which was built in 1836 as Oak Grove Academy for Young Ladies. You'll also see the Keitz-Mannion House at 344 South Church St., which was erected in 1876 as the Methodist parsonage and was originally located across the street from where it now stands. Other points of interest are Smithfield Academy, 205 South Mason St., once a private school for young men; and Christ Episcopal Church, 111 South Church St., which was built in 1830. Its bell was said to have been tendered to the Confederate Ordnance Department in 1862 during the Civil War.

ISLE OF WIGHT COUNTY MUSEUM
103 Main St.
(757) 356-1223, (757) 356-1014
This museum, housed in a former bank built in 1913, offers archaeological displays that highlight county history. It features imported marble and tile and an impressive Tiffany-style dome skylight. Exhibits include Civil War displays, a video presentation on Isle of Wight County's past and present, and a country store, complete with old post office boxes, a potbellied stove, a checkerboard, and old pharmacy and hardware supplies. The newest addition to the museum is a fully furnished miniature colonial plantation house patterned after an existing plantation in Surry County. Other exhibits focus on Smithfield's famous meatpacking industry and archaeological digs that have been conducted throughout the county. The museum is open Tues through Sat from 10 a.m. to 4 p.m. and Sun from 1 to 5 p.m. Admission is free.

FORT BOYKIN HISTORIC PARK
7410 Fort Boykin Trail
(Secondary Hwy. 673)
(757) 357-5182, (800) 365-9339
Out in the country along the banks of the James River sits Fort Boykin Historic Park, which was created in 1623 to protect the settlers from Indians and raiding Spaniards. The fort, shaped in a seven-point star, has been involved in every major military campaign fought on American soil and still retains earthworks dating from the Civil War. According to legend, the guns of Fort Boykin sunk two British men-of-war in 1813. A gazebo overlooks the river, and a picnic area is available. The fort is a tad off the beaten path, so your best bet is to pick up a brochure and map at the Smithfield Convention and Visitors Bureau. Its regular hours are 8 a.m. to dusk seven days a week. Admission is free.

SAINT LUKE'S SHRINE
14477 Benns Church Blvd.
(Route 10)
(757) 357-3367
www.historicstlukes.org
As you leave town and head about 2 miles east on Route 10, you'll come to Saint Luke's Shrine.

Built in 1632 and nicknamed "Old Brick," this Episcopal church is the country's only original Gothic church and the oldest church of English foundation in America. The church features its original traceried windows, stepped gables, and a rare mid-17th-century communion table. Since 1957 Saint Luke's has been home to the oldest intact English organ in America. Constructed ca. 1630, the organ recently had its beautifully painted doors restored. This National Shrine is open Tues through Sat from 10 a.m. to 4 p.m. and Sun from 1 to 4 p.m. The shrine is closed during Jan; admission is free.

Restaurants

C. W. COWLING'S
1278 Smithfield Plaza
(757) 357-0044

Located in a shopping center just east of downtown, Cowling's has everything for lunch and dinner, from Cajun specialties and seafood pasta dishes to fajitas, steaks, chicken, and ribs. A variety of burgers and sandwiches—from catfish to chili cheese dogs—round out the menu. Dinners range from $7 to $16. A kids' menu has a number of options—all for less than $5—and desserts include such temptations as fried apple pie and a chocolate peanut butter pie topped with whipped butter frosting. Cowling's is open seven days a week.

KEN'S BAR-B-Q
Route 258
(757) 357-5601

Ken's is a popular and friendly roadside restaurant that serves up great barbecue and ribs. If you love beef, the pit-cooked steaks are a good choice and come in regular and large sizes (for the heartier appetite). But even if you order the regular size, portions are huge and prices reasonable (an average entree is less than $10). Ken's is open 11 a.m. to 9 p.m. Tues through Fri, 8 a.m. to 9 p.m. Sat, and 8 a.m. to 8 p.m. Sun.

SMITHFIELD CONFECTIONERY & ICE CREAM PARLOR
208 Main St.
(757) 357-6166

A family-run business since 1982, this old-fashioned ice-cream shop sells subs, deli sandwiches, salads, and, of course, ice-cream dishes. Belly up to the traditional soda fountain counter and please your palate with a banana split or triple scoop of chocolate chip mint. If you'd like to chow down on a sandwich or salad instead, you can expect prices to run from $3 to $7. The shop is open 9 a.m. to 7 p.m. Mon through Sat and 11:30 a.m. to 5 p.m. Sun.

SMITHFIELD GOURMET BAKERY AND CAFE
218 Main St.
(757) 357-0045

Since the spring of 1993, this delightful little eatery has served up tasty and unusual sandwiches to an adoring public. All breads are Smithfield Gourmet recipes, baked fresh daily. Cold pasta dishes and salads also are served, and specials start at $6.49. A variety of fresh-baked items—cookies, pies, cinnamon rolls, muffins, and a cake of the day—are available. Cheesecakes, in just about any flavor imaginable, are a house specialty. The cafe is open from 9 a.m. to 6 p.m. Mon through Sat and 11 a.m. to 5 p.m. Sun. It is also open for dinner Thurs through Sat from 6 to 9 p.m.

THE SMITHFIELD INN & TAVERN
112 Main St.
(757) 357-1752
www.smithfieldinn.com

This elegant dining spot in the heart of downtown Smithfield was built in 1752. Fine food—seafood, pork, lamb, beef, and chicken—is served in an atmosphere of candlelight, flocked wallpaper, and crisp linens. While your average entree runs more than $15, there's a less expensive tavern menu available. Lunch is served Tues through Sun, dinner Wed through Sat. The restaurant is closed Mon. Reservations are advised.

SMITHFIELD STATION
415 South Church St.
(757) 357-7700
www.smithfieldstation.com

A popular destination for boaters, Smithfield Station is one of our favorite haunts. It sits at the foot of a small bridge overlooking the Pagan River. The restaurant serves seafood, pork, pasta, and daily specials for lunch and dinner (the average price of an entree is $18). We especially like the house salad, which is prepared with a slightly sweet Italian-style dressing and baby shrimp. The stuffed flounder also comes highly recommended. After dining, stroll out on the deck that surrounds the restaurant and connects it to the marina or mosey along the boardwalk. Hours are 11 a.m. to 9 p.m. Mon through Thurs, 11 a.m. to 9:30 p.m. Fri, and 8 a.m. to 4 p.m. Sat and Sun.

TANGIER ISLAND

An excursion to fancifully named Tangier Island makes for an enjoyable day trip from Williamsburg. It was Captain John Smith who chartered this remote island in 1607, naming it for the Moroccan region he thought it resembled. Twenty miles from the mainland and only 1 mile wide by 3.5 miles long, Tangier Island actually is part of Accomack County on the Eastern Shore.

During the Revolutionary War the British used Tangier as a base for raiding American ships. Pirates also frequented the island, finding it a great hideaway from enemies. After the war the island's population began to swell as more and more people settled down for the long haul and began working the bay. Today, Tangier Island is home to some 700 inhabitants, most of whom rely on the Chesapeake Bay for a living. You'll hear the accents of 17th-century Elizabethan English here, as isolated residents have retained some of their ancestors' ways of speaking.

A variety of boats will get you to Tangier Island. The Tangier Ferry leaves Onancock, Virginia, at 10 a.m. daily from Memorial Day to Oct 15. Tickets are $24 for adults and $12 for children ages 6 through 12. Call (804) 453-4434 for information and tickets. If by chance you want to take this trip from Maryland's eastern shore, the *Steven Thomas*, a 300-passenger ship with an air-conditioned cabin and snack bar, leaves from Crisfield, Maryland, at 12:30 p.m. daily from May 15 through Oct. Tickets are $24 for adults and $12 for children ages 6 to 12. Call (800) 863-2338 for information.

As you approach the dock via the water, take the time to look around you. You will see dozens of crab farms, neat little sheds rising above the water on stilts. In small wooden pens inside these farms, crabbers hoard their catch until the crustaceans have molted and can be sold as soft-shell crabs. The work is tedious, as the pens must be checked every three hours around the clock throughout the entire season. A missed "peeler," as the soft-shells are called, turns into a quick meal for fellow captives.

Once on the island, you will have several hours to sightsee, take a golf cart or bike tour (there are only a handful of cars on the island), and grab lunch before it's time for departure. The island's pathways lead past charming white frame houses, and you'll probably notice only one school, which serves about 170 youngsters from kindergarten through high school.

Restaurants

HILDA CROCKETT'S CHESAPEAKE HOUSE
P.O. Box 232, Tangier Island 23410
(757) 891-2331

When you start hunting down a place for lunch, you'll find your choices are limited. But as long as you like seafood, you can't go wrong trying out Hilda's, which serves breakfast and lunch family-style with crab cakes, clam fritters, Virginia ham, vegetables, potato salad, coleslaw, applesauce, homemade rolls, pound cake, and endless refills of iced tea. The cost of your meal—served from 7 a.m. to 5 p.m.—is $19 per person for lunch, $7 for breakfast. The restaurant is closed Nov through Apr 15.

SMITH ISLAND

Smith Island in the Chesapeake Bay is actually a chain of marshy islands with a fascinating history. Pirates once hid their boats in the tricky waters surrounding this archipelago, waiting to raid passing ships. Dissenters from the Jamestown colony settled here, eventually forming the three villages of Ewell, Rhodes Point, and Tylerton. Today, Ewell, the island's largest town, is sometimes referred to as its capital. Here, commercial fishermen catch hard- and soft-shell crabs and send them to the mainland to serve markets throughout the world. Life for these islanders is often harsh but is guided by a strong religious faith. Joshua Thomas established the Methodist church here and on several other Chesapeake Bay islands during the late 1800s; it continues to be the only organized religion on the island today.

Once you get to the island, go to the **Smith Island Center** (410) 425-3351, and ask for a copy of the brochure describing the island. The pamphlet includes a detailed self-guided walking tour of Ewell, along with maps, historical information, and important tips on island etiquette (for example, the island is dry, meaning islanders don't appreciate public consumption of alcohol). At the center you can watch a 20-minute film featuring the people of Smith Island and view a number of exhibits on the history, environment, watermen, women, and church. Admission to the center, which is open from noon to 4 p.m. daily Apr through Oct, is $2.50 for those 13 and older; younger children enter free. For more information about the island before embarking, visit www.smithisland.org.

Cruises to Smith Island leave from the Chesapeake Bay/Smith Island KOA Campground in the Smith's Point area of Reedsville. To reach the KOA from Williamsburg, take the Colonial Parkway east to Yorktown. Follow US Route 17 North to Saluda, then Route 33 to Route 3 and Kilmarnock. From here follow Route 200 North to US Route 360, which leads to Route 652. Go east on Route 652 until it becomes Route 644, then turn northeast on Route 650. It sounds complicated, but signs for the Smith Island cruise provide adequate directions. The drive takes about an hour and 45 minutes.

The cruise, aboard the *Captain Evans*, leaves the dock at 10 a.m. and pulls in at Ewell around 11:30 a.m., allowing visitors several hours to roam at will and grab lunch before departing around 2 p.m. or so. Current round-trip rates for the Smith Island cruise are $24.50 for adults and $13 for children 3 to 12. Children younger than 3 ride free. Reservations are required; for more information call (804) 453-3430.

If you decide to spend the night in one of the campground's 11 rustic, air-conditioned cabins, you'll have access to a swimming pool and pavilion, a bathhouse with private showers, canoe and bike rentals, and a number of planned weekend activities, including hayrides, lollipop hunts, pet shows, and crab races for the kids. Cabin rental rates start at $40 for a cabin for two. KOA discounts apply. For more information about the campground, call (804) 453-3430.

Once you arrive, the main attraction, of course, is the island itself. The leisurely pace of life here is a welcome change from the hustle and bustle of mainland existence. This is a place where you can put your feet up on a back porch railing and enjoy the soft breezes off the Chesapeake Bay. If it's spring, you might catch the fragrance of blossoming fig, pear, mimosa, and pomegranate trees, which grow in all of the island's towns.

Once you're rested, there is plenty to do and see. A walking tour of Ewell will take you past Cape Cod–style homes, rustic country stores, and the sunken remains of the Island Belle I, one of the earliest island ferries. Goat Island, across Levering Creek, is home to a herd of about 20 formerly domestic goats. Natives rely on the goats' migration to the water's edge to obtain salt from the marsh grasses as a sign that rain or snow is imminent. Other attractions include Pitchcroft, the island's first settlement, and the wooden keel remains of the 60-foot bugeye sailboat C. S. *Tyler*, built for islander Willie A. Evans.

You can also tour, by foot or bicycle, Rhodes Point, the island's center for boat repair. This small town originally was called Rogue's Point because of the pirates who frequented the area. Here you'll see boats being made and repaired and see the ruins of some of the earlier vessels that plied their trade on the bay.

During your visit you also may notice how friendly everyone seems. Islanders in cars and trucks honk their horns and wave to greet every vehicle and pedestrian they meet. This hospitality also is extended to a hefty population of stray cats, which seem to be everywhere, but look especially well fed and comfortable despite their rather nomadic existence.

Restaurants

BAYSIDE INN
4065 Smith Island Rd.
(410) 425-2771
Located on Ewell's Harbor, this charming restaurant serves up a bountiful buffet from 11 a.m. to 4 p.m. daily. A typical menu includes a vegetable crab soup, crab cakes, baked ham, clam fritters, baked corn pudding, stewed tomatoes, macaroni salad, coleslaw, homemade rolls, iced tea, and homemade pie.

NORFOLK

On the eastern edge of Hampton Roads in the world's largest natural harbor, Norfolk has been a sailors' city for more than 200 years. Norfolk Naval Base is the world's largest navy base, and the numerous posts and bases that support it have been temporary home to thousands of men and women from around the nation over the years, particularly during World War II. While Uncle Sam has always played a key role in the city's economy and demographics, Norfolk also serves as the region's financial hub: Within a 2-block radius of downtown Norfolk are the Hampton Roads headquarters for all of the state's major banks. But business often takes a backseat to culture, as Norfolk also is home to the area's four dominant arts organizations: the Virginia Stage Company, the Virginia Symphony, the Virginia Opera, and Chrysler Hall. (See our Nightlife chapter for more information.)

During the past 15 years or so, the city has undergone a renaissance of sorts, transforming a decaying waterfront into an attractive gathering spot with the addition of the Waterside Festival Marketplace and new hotels, parks, and office buildings.

Although Williamsburg residents tend to turn toward Richmond for employment and for large-city conveniences, many residents commute to Norfolk for jobs, and still others make the trip for an evening out.

The approach to Norfolk from the Historic Triangle is stunning by any criteria: I-64 moves out over the mouth of Hampton Roads on a bridge-tunnel that affords a breathtaking view of the harbor and the navy base on the far shore. To get downtown once you've crossed the water, follow I-64 to I-264 West, then take I-264 until it becomes Waterside Drive. The Waterside Festival Marketplace will be on your left, and parking will be to your right. If you're feeling adventuresome or just want to see a little more of Norfolk, an alternate—and more direct—route is to take the Granby Street exit from I-64, then follow Granby Street (a six-lane highway for much of the drive) through the neighborhoods of Norfolk until Monticello Avenue splits off to the right. Follow Monticello downtown. Several downtown garages offer public parking.

The drive takes about an hour from Williamsburg, longer if traffic is backed up at the tunnel—and it frequently is during rush hour, on summer weekends, and on holidays. Signs along the interstate refer travelers to a radio band for traffic advisories well before the tunnel, and an alternate route to Southside via the James River Bridge is marked with checkered attachments to highway signs. I-664, which also spans the James River via a tunnel and a bridge, is a scenic—though somewhat roundabout—route into Norfolk.

There are special times of year when a trip to Norfolk has added interest. In late April through early May, the Virginia Arts Festival brings world-class music, dance, theater, and visual arts to the Norfolk waterfront; the late-April International Azalea Festival is staged amid the blossoms at Norfolk Botanical Garden; and, during the first weekend in June, you can join a crowd of thousands for Norfolk's annual Harborfest celebration, which brings music, food, and entertainment to the downtown waterfront for three days of fun in the sun. For more on the Virginia Arts Festival, turn to our Annual Events chapter.

Before venturing south to Norfolk, you may want to pick up a copy of the *Insiders' Guide to Virginia's Chesapeake Bay* for more detailed listings of restaurants, accommodations, and attractions. (Or you may want to purchase the *Insiders' Guide to Virginia Beach*, which will have the same information.)

NORFOLK CONVENTION & VISITORS BUREAU
232 East Main St.
(757) 664-6620, (800) 368-3097
www.visitnorfolktoday.com
This is the best place to stop in during weekday business hours for brochures and pamphlets. Or call the number above and ask to have a visitor's guide sent to you. The bureau also operates a Visitor Information Center just off I-64. Take exit 273, the second exit after you come east through the Hampton Roads Bridge-Tunnel. The center offers brochures and a hotel reservation service; staff members there can answer all your questions. The center is open 8:30 a.m. to 5 p.m. Mon through Fri.

Attractions

Once you drop anchor in Norfolk, you will wish you'd reserved an entire day to take in all this seafaring city has to offer. Many of the city's attractions are in the heart of downtown, but along its western fringe is an area known as Ghent, the place where the downtown crowd likes to hang out. It's no wonder. Colley Avenue, the main corridor in Ghent, is home to many small specialty shops, some very good restaurants, and a bona fide old-fashioned movie house. Another Norfolk neighborhood is Ocean View, with 7.5 miles of public beaches bordering the Chesapeake Bay. Especially popular from the turn of the 20th century to the 1950s, Ocean View's three city beaches offer a place to swim, sun, and picnic. Ocean View is one of the first areas of Norfolk you'll come to after crossing the Hampton Roads Bridge-Tunnel; an exit is marked for it on the interstate.

THE CHRYSLER MUSEUM
245 West Olney Rd.
(757) 664-6200
www.chrysler.org
If you appreciate visual arts, this is the cream of the crop in Hampton Roads. The Chrysler is considered one of the top 20 art museums in the country. Its collection contains more than 30,000 pieces from all time periods. Holdings include works by Renoir, Matisse, and Gauguin, and its art library is the largest in the southeastern United States. The Chrysler also is known for its 8,000-piece glass collection, which includes the works of Tiffany, Lalique, and other masters; its superb collection of 19th-century sculpture; and its well-recognized collection of photographs. Changing exhibits are excellent: In the past few years, the museum has hosted a gorgeous display of original illustrations from children's literature; Rembrandt and the Golden Age, on loan from the National Gallery of Art; and the widely acclaimed Hot Glass and Neon, which helped redefine the limits of sculptural glass.

On average, The Chrysler brings 15 special exhibitions to Norfolk each year. The outstanding collections have ranged from *Rodin: Sculpture from the Iris and B. Gerald Cantor Collection* to *The Art of Andy Warhol*.

All told, the award-winning museum houses 60 galleries, the library, auditorium, gift shop, and a restaurant. The Chrysler hours are 10 a.m. to 5 p.m. Thurs through Sat, 10 a.m. to 9 p.m. Wed, and 12 to 5 p.m. Sun. The museum is closed Mon, Tues, and major holidays. Admission is free for the permanent exhibitions, although donations are appreciated. Special visiting exhibitions may charge an entry fee; call for details or visit the Web site for more information.

D'ART CENTER
208 East Main St.
(757) 625-4211
www.d-artcenter.org
Wander through this cooperative center and enjoy the creations of the 36 or so artists who sometimes will work their magic before your very eyes. You'll see painters, sculptors, and jewelry

makers in their studios and can negotiate with most of the artists to purchase what catches your fancy. The center has been open since the late 1980s. Summer art classes are offered for adults and children.

Hours are 10 a.m. to 5 p.m. Tues through Sat and from 1 to 5 p.m. on Sun. Admission is free.

DOUGLAS MACARTHUR MEMORIAL
198 Bank St.
(757) 441-2965
www.macarthurmemorial.org
For those intrigued by our nation's military history, the Douglas MacArthur Memorial honors the life and times of General MacArthur. The controversial general is entombed here, and his signature corncob pipe and the documents that ended the war with Japan are on display in the galleries. A 25-minute film featuring newsreel footage of MacArthur is shown in the memorial's theater, and the gift shop even displays the general's shiny 1950 Chrysler Crown Imperial limousine. Other exhibits include one on segregated military forces and another on female prisoners of war during World War II. No admission is charged for any of the exhibits, but donations are requested. The museum is open from 10 a.m. to 5 p.m. Mon through Sat and 11 a.m. to 5 p.m. Sun.

HARBOR PARK
150 Park Ave.
(757) 622-2222
http://norfolktides.com
Just a baseball throw from Waterside is Harbor Park, home base for the Norfolk Tides, a Triple A farm team of the Baltimore Orioles. Designed by the same firm that built the Baltimore Orioles park at Camden Yards, Harbor Park was selected as the minor leagues' best stadium in 1995 by the publication *Baseball America*. Catch the boys of summer in action from early April through Labor Day. Tickets cost $11 for box seats, $9.50 for an adult reserved seat, and $8 for a child's reserved seat. Tickets can be purchased at the park, or you can order them through www.ticketmaster.com.

HISTORIC GHENT
Colley Avenue and 21st Street
www.destinationghent.com
About a mile from downtown, this intriguing neighborhood is a mix of cafes, boutiques, and a bona fide old-fashioned movie house called the **Naro,** (757) 625-6295. This is where the folks who work downtown like to mix and mingle on any given evening. Join the crowds and enjoy a little people-watching while you sip espresso in an outdoor cafe!

MACARTHUR CENTER
300 Monticello Ave.
(757) 627-6000
www.shopmacarthur.com
We have to admit—we don't usually think of a mall as an attraction. But in the case of Norfolk's MacArthur Center, we just have to make an exception. For one thing, the center, which opened in March 1999, is a destination in its own right. You can spend hours and hours browsing through this three-level land of wonder and still not see everything. The 70-foot atrium is a good place to start and maybe meet if you get separated from your traveling companions. All told, MacArthur houses more than 150 stores, 21 eateries and coffee shops, and a movie theater with 18 screens. In fact, once you get here, you don't even have to shop. Instead you can chat with a friend at a quiet corner cappuccino bar, unleash energy with the kids at a picnic-themed play area with giant foam hot dogs and cupcakes, or collapse into one of the overstuffed chairs in the lobby lounge and read a book. Other center amenities include valet parking, package carryout, complimentary strollers and wheelchairs, and three ATMs. As for the stores? The list includes Nordstrom, Dillard's, Abercrombie & Fitch Co., Pottery Barn, Restoration Hardware, and Williams-Sonoma, to name a few. Mall hours are 10 a.m. to 9 p.m. Mon through Sat and noon to 6 p.m. on Sun. Parking is available in the attached garage.

NAUTICUS
1 Waterside Dr,
Downtown Waterfront
(757) 664-1000, (800) 664-1080
www.nauticus.org

Norfolk's newest museum is the National Maritime Center, more commonly called Nauticus. This $52 million attraction opened in the spring of 1994 on the western edge of the downtown waterfront, adjacent to Town Point Park. And with the arrival of the battleship *Wisconsin*, one of the last and largest battleships of the U.S. Navy, things have only gotten bigger.

The 120,000-square-foot science center showcases more than 150 exhibits, including everything from the latest interactive computer technology to a touch-tank with sharks! The center was designed to have an equal appeal for both adults and children with displays focusing on maritime commerce, the navy, exotic sea creatures, and the weather. The Changing Gallery even houses the bridge from the USS *Preble*, while three theaters show films that help explain the maritime experience.

If you just want to drop in for a bite to eat at the Galley Restaurant or for a peek into the Banana Pier Gift Shop, you can enter the museum's ground floor for free. Access to the Hampton Roads Naval Museum, which moved from the Norfolk Naval Base to Nauticus and is operated by the U.S. Navy, is also free. The city of Norfolk took over operation of the facility in January 1997 and has been rethinking its approach to exhibits. The USS *Wisconsin*—an 887-foot battleship that earned five combat stars during World War II—set down anchor in its permanent berth right beside Nauticus. Now visitors go on board and can stand beside the massive 16-inch guns and take self-guided or audio tours of the historic ship's main deck.

In conjunction with the free ship's tour, Nauticus has created three exhibits of its own to honor one of the last battleships built by the U.S. Navy. "Design Chamber: Battleship X" lets you race against top designers to create a battleship. "City at Sea" shows what life was like on board the *Wisconsin*, while "BattleScopes" takes you on a virtual tour of the impressive vessel that survived kamikaze attacks and went on to assist in Desert Storm.

Nauticus and the *Wisconsin* are open from 10 a.m. to 5 p.m. Tues to Sat, Sun noon to 4:45 p.m., closed mon. The ship will not have tours on Thanksgiving, Christmas Eve, or Christmas Day. You can tour the ship's deck for free, but admission to Nauticus is $10.95 for adults, $8.50 for children between the ages of 4 and 12. Children under 4 are free. Special discounts are offered to senior citizens, AAA members, and military personnel.

NORFOLK BOTANICAL GARDEN
6700 Azalea Garden Rd.
(757) 441-5830
www.norfolkbotanicalgarden.org

The great outdoors in all its splendor beckons at the Norfolk Botanical Garden near the Norfolk International Airport. This 155-acre garden began in 1938 as a Works Progress Administration grant. Today it boasts more than 12 miles of pathways and thousands of trees, shrubs, and flowering plants arranged in both formal and natural gardens. There are more than 20 themed gardens, including the 3.5-acre bicentennial rose garden, healing and herb gardens, and the fragrance garden for the visually impaired. We think the best time to go is in spring when the more than 250,000 azaleas are so spectacular they take your breath away, but there's something blooming just about any time of year. (Even during the winter months you can enjoy camellias, witch hazel, wintersweet, and colorful berries.) Newer gardens include the Bristow Butterfly Garden, a perennial garden, a wildflower meadow, and a renovated Japanese garden. There's even a "surprise" garden with changing blooms that always offer a hint of color and something new for visitors. One of the best ways to view the gardens during the warm-weather months is by a 30-minute boat or tram ride. The gardens are open from 9 a.m. to 7 p.m. mid-Apr through mid-Oct and until 5 p.m. the rest of the year. The cafe is open for a light lunch and snacks. Admission to the gardens is $9 for adults, $8 for seniors, $7 for youth ages

3 to 18, and free for children 2 and younger if accompanied by a paying adult. Tickets to the boat rides are sold separately. The boat tour costs $5 per adult, $3 per child ages 3 to 12. The tram ride is free with your paid admission to the garden. The Botanical Garden offers family programs throughout the year.

i The tiger swallowtail is Old Dominion's state insect. This beautiful yellow and black butterfly, which feeds on buddleia, honeysuckle, bee balm, and sunflowers, is one of many that can be found in plentiful supply at the Bristow Butterfly Garden, which opened in 1998 at Norfolk Botanical Garden, 6700 Azalea Garden Rd., Norfolk. For more information call (757) 441-5830.

VIRGINIA ZOO
3500 Granby St.
(757) 624-9937
www.virginiazoo.org
If you like to take a walk on the wild side—and if you have small children along—a stop at the Virginia Zoo is a must. Situated on 55 acres along the Lafayette River, the zoo is small but certainly charming. It is home to some 340 animals, including reptiles, nocturnal animals, rare Siberian tigers, primates, llamas, rhinos, and a pair of elephants who like to toss around tires and douse each other with water. The zoo was singled out for praise by former Attorney General Janet Reno for making its facility more accessible to persons with disabilities. A 10-year, $15 million improvement plan resulted in a new entry and educational complex and the African Okavango River Delta exhibit. In the summer of 1999, the zoo opened its doors for a pair of gelada baboons—Joe-Joe and Tommy—as the first residents of the African exhibit. Joe-Joe and Tommy have since welcomed a third baboon to the zoo, Hoss. Also opened with the baboon habitat was the Xaxaba village, which featured structures similar to those found in the Okavango Delta in Botswana. The focal point of the African village

is the Xaxaba Restaurant, which offers traditional fast food and specialty items such as catfish and chicken-fried steak.

Special children's programs are offered year-round. Zoo hours are 10 a.m. to 5 p.m. daily. Admission (cash only) is $8 for anyone older than 11, $6 for children ages 2 to 11, and $7 for seniors 62 and older.

WATERSIDE FESTIVAL MARKETPLACE
333 Waterside Dr. on the Elizabeth River
(757) 627-3300
www.watersidemarketplace.com
No trip to Norfolk is complete without a visit to Waterside, the city's festival marketplace overlooking the Elizabeth River. In fact, sometimes this is the only destination visitors have in mind when they come to Norfolk. Since opening in June 1983, the marketplace has provided the downtown waterfront with a colorful mix of retail shops and restaurants. The marketplace is constructed of steel and glass on two levels and is connected to a parking garage across the street by a second-level walkway.

A few years ago Waterside shifted its focus from a tourist attraction to an entertainment destination, welcoming a number of new tenants, including Jillian's, a vast entertainment complex that includes a hibachi grill restaurant, a sports video cafe, a blues and jazz club, a dance club, a sit-down restaurant, and an area where adults can play virtual-reality games. Other restaurants include Outback Steakhouse, Dixie's Tavern, Bar Norfolk, Have a Nice Day Cafe, and Crocodile Rocks, a South Carolina–based operation that features a dual piano bar.

Retailers include gift shops and boutiques, including Hat Rack, Christmas Attic, Dollar Tree, and Lillian Vernon. In season, boat tours leave daily from the premises, and an attached marina makes the place convenient for pleasure sailors. From Waterside it's an easy stroll to Nauticus, Harbor Park, and other downtown attractions. The marketplace is open from 10 a.m. to 9 p.m. Mon through Sat and noon to 6 p.m. Sun, with extended hours during the summer and for special events. Restaurants and nightclubs maintain their own individual hours. Admission to the marketplace itself is free.

Restaurants

While Norfolk has pretty much anything your heart—and palate—desires, we have a few favorite haunts we want to mention. If you're looking for a satisfying meal in appealing environs, you can't go wrong with any of the eateries listed here.

DOUMAR'S CONES & BARBECUE
19th to 20th Streets and
1919 Monticello Ave.
(757) 627-4163
www.doumars.com
We couldn't decide if this was an attraction or a restaurant, but since you'd be hard-pressed to drop in and leave without eating, we've listed it here. What makes Doumar's so special? For one thing, it is one of the only remaining Hampton Roads eateries that still has carhops. For another, it has been at the same location since 1934. It has been visited *twice* by Food Network's Guy Fieri on "Diners, Drive-Ins & Dives." But, perhaps most interestingly, restaurant founder Abe Doumar invented the ice-cream cone back in 1904 during the St. Louis Exposition.

Doumar's serves up outstanding, inexpensive pork barbecue, burgers, fries, and milk shakes in old-fashioned soda fountain glasses. And the limeade is superb. In 1999 Doumar's was a James Beard Award winner, recognized as one of America's eight regional classics that are "timeless, grass-roots restaurants that serve memorable food and are strongly embedded in the fabric of their communities." The restaurant is closed on Sun but is open 8 a.m. to 11 p.m. Mon through Thurs and 8 a.m. until after midnight Fri and Sat. Doumar's does not accept credit cards.

RAJPUT INDIAN CUISINE
742 West 21st St.
(757) 625-4634
www.rajputonline.com

The name of this eatery refers both to royalty and to a region in western India. But the food here is surprisingly diverse, including seafood and vegetarian dishes, a tandoori mixed grill with chicken, lamb, fish, and shrimp, and a smattering of curry offerings.

TODD JURICH'S BISTRO
(inside the SunTrust Building)
150 West Main St., Suite 100
(757) 622-3210
www.toddjurichsbistro.com
This award-winning restaurant serves some of the most creative fare in town. Innovative creations by chef/owner Todd Jurich include free-range Piedmont boneless sirloin with crispy buttermilk onion rings. Much of the menu, however, will vary with the season. A dinner for two—entrees only—will set you back about $50. Bistro serves lunch Mon through Fri 11:30 a.m. until 2 p.m., and dinner Sat and Sun from 5:30 p.m. to 10 p.m.

VIRGINIA BEACH

You say you're from western Ohio, central Pennsylvania, or some other landlocked region and the last time you saw the Atlantic Ocean was on a postcard sent to you by a vacationing friend? Well, then by all means schedule a day trip to Virginia Beach. After all, it isn't every day you get to dip your toes in the ocean, bury your spouse in the sand, or sip a piña colada while watching the waves break on shore.

A day at the beach also is the perfect addition to your itinerary if you have small children. In fact, it may be the only opportunity you have to stretch out in the sunshine as the kids frolic in the surf and sand. (Although we advise you to keep a very close eye on the little ones. The surf may, on occasion, appear gentle, but the ocean's undertow is unpredictable.)

The route to the beach is pretty direct. Hop on I-64 and head east through the Hampton Roads Bridge-Tunnel until you hook up with I-264, which heads either to Norfolk or Virginia Beach. Follow I-264 toward Virginia Beach, staying on the highway until it ends. Continue to head straight until you intersect with Atlantic Avenue. Turn right and you're cruising the beachfront. (The entire trip should take you about 90 minutes.) You'll find there's plenty of parking space—both free and metered, depending on how close you are to the water—on side streets all up and down the beach, but they fill up fast. There's also paid parking in a number of municipal lots. Your best bet is to get to the beach early on a weekday so you can grab a prime spot for parking—and sunning.

Virginia Beach prides itself on being a family destination, and over the last several years has backed up its claims with a $94 million modernization of both the boardwalk and Atlantic Avenue that includes new landscaping, whimsical sculptures, attractive signs, streetlights, and a special bike-riding lane along the boardwalk. City officials also are putting the finishing touches on an extensive beach erosion and hurricane protection project that has widened and reinforced the shoreline to withstand storms like 1999's Dennis and Floyd, which brought high winds and devastating rainfall to the region.

As part of the $117 million five-year plan, the city began pumping in more sand in June 2001—an extra 3.2 million cubic yards—to turn Virginia Beach into one of its widest, sandiest beaches in recent memory. The last time the city's beach measured 300 feet wide was in 1700. To get an idea of how much sand Virginia Beach is bringing in, imagine a football field stacked 1,920 feet high with sand. That's one and a third times as tall as the Empire State Building.

If you prefer to plan your visit around a special event, you're in luck. In mid-June the city hosts its annual Boardwalk Art Show and Festival, which brings close to 400 artists to the oceanfront to display and sell the fruits of their creative endeavors. In mid- to late September, the Neptune Festival salutes summer's end with free musical entertainment, a world-famous sandcastle contest, and a military air show; and around Christmastime the boardwalk is ablaze with more than 200 displays of 450,000 lights as part of Holi-

day Lights at the Beach. Or, you can always take in a concert at the VerizonWireless Virginia Beach Amphitheater. The outdoor complex brings big-name entertainment to the "Beach" throughout the warmer-weather months. Of course, there's always the possibility that you may not want to do much more than turn over while you're at the beach. But, if you have a hankering to take in some of the sights, there are a number of places to visit along the waterfront and its side streets.

VIRGINIA BEACH CONVENTION & VISITORS BUREAU
2100 Parks Ave.
(800) VA-BEACH
www.vbfun.com
If you'd like to find out exactly what this city on the ocean has to offer, call the toll-free number above or visit Virginia Beach on the Internet. The Web site is particularly helpful as it offers a convenient "trip planner," a feature that helps would-be vacationers customize their itinerary.

i If you're a lover of the great outdoors, why not try one of these Virginia Beach back-to-nature excursions: dolphin-watching boat trips sponsored by the Virginia Marine Science Museum, (757) 425-FISH or www.vmsm.com; nature tours aboard the 50-passenger Coastal Explorer, a pontoon boat that travels Owls Creek Salt Marsh near the marine science museum, (757) 437-BOAT; or a guided kayak tour in some of the scenic waterways, (757) 480-1999.

Attractions
ATLANTIC WATERFOWLHERITAGE MUSEUM AND DEWITT COTTAGE
1113 Atlantic Ave.
(757) 437-8432
www.awhm.org
This museum looks at wildfowl—everything from ducks and geese to songbirds—through art exhibits, interactive displays, and special demonstrations. The museum's five galleries feature

artwork and decoy carvings, including some that date from the turn of the 19th century. Overlooking the ocean, the museum is located in the 1895 deWitt Cottage, the last remaining oceanfront cottage from the late 19th century. The museum is open Tues through Sat from 10 a.m. to 5 p.m. and Sun noon to 5 p.m. From Oct through Feb the museum is closed on Mon. Admission is free, although donations are accepted.

EDGAR CAYCE'S ASSOCIATION FOR RESEARCH AND ENLIGHTENMENT (A.R.E.)
215 67th St. and Atlantic Ave.
(800) 333-4499
www.edgarcayce.org
This intriguing attraction is the headquarters for the work of the late psychic Edgar Cayce, who resided in Virginia Beach and was best known for falling into a trance and diagnosing and prescribing cures for medical ailments. Each year A.R.E. hosts thousands of international visitors and researchers who have an interest in Cayce's remarkable talents. There are free lectures, video and film presentations, ESP demonstrations, and daily tours. There's even a meditation room overlooking the ocean and a bookstore with overflowing shelves. A.R.E. is open 8 a.m. to 7 p.m. Mon through Fri, 10 a.m. to 7 p.m. Sat, and 12 a.m. to 7 p.m. on Sun. Admission is free. Take care to park in the lot and not on the road as the local police are quick to ticket, especially in summer.

FIRST LANDING STATE PARK
2500 Shore Dr.
(757) 412-2300, (800) 933-PARK
www.dcr.virginia.gov
This 2,888-acre campground and sanctuary has more than 336 species of trees and plants, a self-guided nature trail, and a visitor center with books for sale and exhibits. Nine trails, including one that is wheelchair accessible, cover 19 miles and are part of the National Scenic Trails System. Located in the park is the Chesapeake Bay Center, an environmentally focused, inter-

active visitor information center that also offers aquariums, environmental exhibits, and a touch-tank developed by the Virginia Marine Science Museum. A 5-mile bike trail connects to the city's bike trails.

If you didn't bring a bike, don't worry, the park's camp store will rent you one by the hour or for the day. The camp store has all types of rental items, including fishing poles, umbrellas, chairs, four-wheelers, and two-person tents.

If you would like to extend your stay, First Landing has ample camping facilities with 213 sites along the Chesapeake Bay to pitch your tent—an inexpensive alternative to the cost of a hotel. You can even rent a cabin, if you prefer not to deal with tent stakes, but don't delay, the cabins are hot commodities. If you are interested in cabin rentals, call the Reservation Center at (800) 933-PARK. There also are places here to picnic, so if you're planning a visit, you might want to pack a lunch.

FRANCIS LAND HISTORICAL HOUSE AND HISTORY PARK AND NATURE TRAIL
3131 Virginia Beach Blvd.
(757) 431-4000
http://virginiabeachhistory.org/land.html
This 18th-century plantation home was designed by Francis Land, a wealthy landowner and political activist, and retains some of the original architecture and family heirlooms. Costumed tour guides help transport visitors to a time when the plantation was bustling with family members and the servants that helped keep the farm running.

As an extension of the plantation, visitors trek along a scenic trail that offers glimpses of the city's once vast wilderness. Interpretive signs help make the journey an educational experience, while native plants and the wildlife of the woodland provide opportunity for year-round discovery. Admission to the Francis Land House is $4 for adults, $3 for seniors, and $2 for children ages 6 through 12. Park admission is free. Hours are 9 a.m. to 5 p.m. Tues through Sat and 11 a.m. to 5 p.m. on Sun. Closed Mon.

OLD CAPE HENRY LIGHTHOUSE
583 Atlantic Ave.
(Fort Story, extreme north end of
Atlantic Avenue)
(757) 422-9421
www.apva.org/capehenry
Construction of this lighthouse was authorized by George Washington and was completed in 1791 at a cost of $17,500. The edifice continued to guide mariners until it was replaced in 1881. The stone used in the structure came from the same Virginia quarry that supplied the White House, the Capitol, and Mount Vernon. Over the years the edifice has become the official symbol of Virginia Beach. The lighthouse is open from 10 a.m. to 5 p.m. beginning in mid-Mar and continuing through Oct. From Nov 1 to Mar 15 the hours are 10 a.m. to 4 p.m. Closed Thanksgiving, Dec 24, 25, 31, and Jan 1.

OLD COAST GUARD STATION
24th St. and Boardwalk
(757) 422-1587
www.oldcoastguardstation.com
A former U.S. Life-Saving/Coast Guard Station built in 1903, this simple wooden structure is reminiscent of an earlier, simpler oceanfront era. Inside, two galleries give glimpses into the history of the people who risked their lives to save strangers during shipwrecks. A permanent display focuses on the impact of World Wars I and II on Virginia Beach. A TowerCam, a roof-mounted video camera, can zoom in on passing ships spied on the Virginia Beach horizon. The camera transmits its pictures to a 27-inch television monitor, providing visitors with the same view crewmen had from the station tower almost a century ago. The museum is open Mon through Sat from 10 a.m. to 5 p.m. and Sun from noon to 5 p.m. From Memorial Day to Oct 1 the museum is closed Mon. The station is also closed for Thanksgiving, Christmas, New Year's Eve and New Year's Day. Admission is $4 for adults, $3 for seniors and military personnel, and $2 for children 6 through 18. Members and children under 6 visit for free.

Group tours and rates are available with advance notice.

VIRGINIA AQUARIUM & MARINE SCIENCE CENTER
717 General Booth Blvd.
(757) 385-FISH
www.vmsm.com
An extremely popular destination for the entire family, the marine science museum completed a $35 million expansion in 1996. This fine facility—which continues to draw huge crowds throughout the year—features three buildings and dozens of exciting exhibits, from the Atlantic Ocean Pavilion, which showcases schooling fishes, sharks, and other deep-sea creatures in a 300,000-gallon aquarium, to the Family Channel IMAX 3-D Theater. Visit the Owls Creek Marsh Pavilion, where you can view a live river habitat and outdoor marsh bird aviary. Dozens of hands-on exhibits give children the opportunity to tong for oysters or make a few waves. And, by all means, stop and pet the rays, which may look a tad odd but are as friendly as any well-loved puppy. Plans are in the works for an additional facility that will highlight animals and plants from both the ocean and coastal regions. This facility also will house the museum's stranding program, which rescues endangered dolphins, seals, fish, and coastal birds. The museum is open 9 a.m. to 6 p.m. daily during the summer. The Osprey Cafe, which serves a variety of sandwiches and hot foods, is open from 10 a.m. to 5 p.m. daily and from 10 a.m. to 6 p.m. during the summer. Admission for the museum only is $17 for adults, $16 for seniors, and $12 for children ages 3 to 11. Admission to the IMAX theater is $8.50 for adults, $7.50 for children, and $8 for seniors. Combination tickets are $23 for adults, $18 for children ages 3 to 11, and $22 for senior citizens.

VIRGINIA BEACH SPORTSPLEX
2181 Landstown Rd.
(757) 427-2990
www.vbgov.com
The Sportsplex is America's first stadium built specifically for soccer, but it is also used for football, rugby, and lacrosse. Home to the Piranhas, a women's professional soccer team, the $10.5 million facility seats 6,000 spectators, but can

be expanded to hold 30,000. Features include an 18-by-20-foot instant replay screen behind one goal and a high-tech sound system that can monitor the noise level of the stadium crowd and adjust the volume level accordingly. Ticket prices for soccer games range from $7 to $15. Rugby tournaments are held here also, and those tickets are $10 and up.

ℹ️ Horse-racing fans can trot up I-64 to Colonial Downs, a racetrack in New Kent County, about 25 miles west of Williamsburg. The track offers two seasons of equestrian racing. Harness season typically starts in late spring and ends in midsummer. Thoroughbred racing starts on Labor Day and continues through the first week or so of October. General admission is usually $2, $5 for a box seat. To reach Colonial Downs take I-64 West to exit 214. Turn left and the racetrack will be on your left. For more information call (804) 966-7223 or (888) 482-8722.

VIRGINIA LEGENDS WALK
13th Street, between Atlantic and Pacific Avenues
www.va-legends.com
This outdoor monument between Atlantic and Pacific Avenues pays tribute to famous Virginians who have made significant contributions to the country and the world. When the walk was dedicated on July 19, 1999, 13 of the original 24 inductees were represented at the ceremony, including representatives for Arthur Ashe, Pearl Bailey, Patsy Cline, Ella Fitzgerald, Patrick Henry, Robert E. Lee, Douglas MacArthur, James Madison, George C. Marshall, Edgar Allan Poe, Bill "Bojangles" Robinson, Captain John Smith, and Woodrow Wilson. Each year nominations are accepted for future honorees. The plaques on the walk are lit from above so that it can be viewed at night. Future plans call to expand the walk across Atlantic Avenue to the oceanfront boardwalk.

Restaurants

All that splashing around in the ocean is sure to work up an appetite. While "the Beach," as locals call it, has a well-rounded selection of restaurants for your dining pleasure, we've singled out a handful sure to please.

BEACH BULLY BAR-B-QUE
601 19th St.
(757) 422-4222
www.beachbully.com
For some of the best open-pit barbecue in town—for lunch or dinner—stop in at Beach Bully. Grab a beef platter for $7.99, or dig into a half a chicken with two sides for $6.99. The restaurant is open seven days a week, and the dress code is casual, so just come as you are after a day in the sun and the surf. It's open from 10 a.m. to 9 p.m. Sun through Thurs, an hour later on Fri and Sat.

PASTA E PANI
1805 Laskin Rd.
(757) 428-2299
www.pastaepanionline.com
If you like Italian, you'll thoroughly enjoy this restaurant, whose name translates to pasta and bread. Both are homemade and delicious, making this restaurant a perennial favorite of Insiders who come here for lunch or dinner. A dinner for two should run about $30 to $40. Lunch is served weekdays from 11 a.m. to 2 p.m. Dinner is served from 5 to 9 p.m. Mon and 5 to 10 p.m. Tues through Sun. The on-site Deli-Shoppe is open 11 a.m. to 6:30 p.m. daily.

ℹ️ If you decide you just can't "do" Virginia Beach in one day, you have plenty of sleepover options. The city has more than 11,000 hotel and motel rooms—5,000 of them on the oceanfront. A central reservation service is available at (800) ROOMS VB.

LIVING HERE

In this section we feature specific information for residents or those planning to relocate here. Topics include real estate, education, health care, and much more.

RELOCATION

The 2000s saw what can only be described as explosive growth in the Williamsburg area. Population nearly doubled; so did the median price of home sales.

Several factors contributed—suburban development in the Lower Peninsula started sprawling north as available land ran out. But the major factor was a boom in relocations from the northeast—retirees and second-home/early-retiree buyers who cashed out of expensive homes there. They were lured by more-affordable prices and planned communities featuring resort-like amenities (and weather that allows golf 10 or 11 months a year).

The result wasn't quite a bubble—but it was close. In 1999, the median price of a home in the Williamsburg area was a mere $156,000; by the peak of the market in 2005, it was $321,500. Like elsewhere, the market plateaued, then dropped, though not as severely as other places. Home sales dropped from a high of more than 2,000 a year in the middle years of the decade to just 1,400 in 2009, but prices modulated only slightly. By 2009, the median was still at nearly $300,000.

A side note: Any discussion of growth in the area will use "Williamsburg" as shorthand—but very little of the growth actually has occurred in the city itself. Williamsburg is small, landlocked and largely developed. So its population growth has been limited, from 11,600 in 1990 to an estimated 12,500 in 2008. The real growth as occurred in the two suburban counties that ring the city, especially James City County, which arcs around Williamsburg from the south to the northeast. James City County's population has essentially tripled from 1980 to today, from 22,000 to 62,400 today.

To the east, growth is somewhat constrained by the large government land holdings—the Naval Weapons Station, and the CIA (oops! Sorry! The Defense Department—really!) base at Camp Peary. Still, significant growth also occurred on the available land near those installations. That area is colloquially known as upper York County to differentiate it from the rest of York on the other side of the government installations.

While the recession slowed the pace of growth, it hasn't stopped. The building of the 1990s and early 2000s filled most of the available land immediately west of Williamsburg, along the Route 199 beltway. Now the growth is spreading northwest, toward Lightfoot and Toano. (The luxury Stonehouse community, near Croaker, is actually closer to downtown Richmond than it is to Hampton.)

The new building in those suburban areas has been dominated by single-family subdivisions. They cover the range of the market— starter homes jammed together, middle-market family communities on quarter-acre lots, and estate homes in master-planned country club communities like Kingsmill, Governor's Land at Two Rivers, and Ford's Colony.

If you're thinking of relocating to the area, there are plenty of resources to consult. The real-estate ads in the Saturday edition of the *Virginia Gazette* were long considered the best way to keep track of new listings—but nowadays, nearly all the brokerages have excellent Internet databases that contain all the homes in the local multiple listings service. The **Williamsburg Area Association of Realtors** is a good place to start, at www.waarealtor.com.

Don't want a detached single-family home? Plenty of other options are available. Most of the new mixed-used developments (like New Town, or the High Street project off Richmond Road near downtown) have rental apartments, condominiums, or both. Condo listings are available from Realtors. Apartment listings can be a bit tougher—there's no single great resource for them. A variety of free-distribution magazines contain listings, as do the *Gazette* and the *Daily Press*. Internet services like Apartments.com and Craigslist are useful, too.

Looking to come to Williamsburg frequently—but . . .

. . . you don't want the expense and hassle of a second home? Ten timeshare resorts have popped up in the area over the past 20 years. Think about your decision carefully—plenty of consumer resources caution against buying timeshares because of lack of flexibility, a thin resale market, and sales tactics that can cross the line to high pressure.

That said, for people who like visiting the same place at roughly the same time each year, timeshares can be more home-like than hotels. Among the local timeshares: Colonial Crossing; Diamond Resorts Greensprings Plantation; King's Creek; Marriott Manor Club at Ford's Colony; Powhatan Plantation; Westgate Historic Williamsburg; Williamsburg Plantation; Wyndham Williamsburg at Governor's Green; Wyndham Williamsburg at Kingsgate; and Wyndham Williamsburg at Patriots Place.

NEIGHBORHOODS

Adam's Hunt

This subdivision off Centerville Road, about midway between US Route 60 and Longhill Road, fea-

tures modest homes on good-size lots in heavily wooded, rolling terrain. The one- and two-story houses are in a mixture of styles. It is a good beginner neighborhood for people interested in getting into the single-family housing market.

Banbury Cross

About 5 miles west of Williamsburg, this lovely, sprawling neighborhood is accessible by I-64, exiting at Route 646 North. Large lots, mostly an acre or more, are the rule here. An abundance of natural woods with tall pines, oaks, and mountain laurel make this an ideal setting for those interested in living near town but beyond the suburbs of Williamsburg. Homes are large and colonial or transitional in style.

Baron Woods

Offered by Sash Digges, a prominent local builder, this property proved so popular that lots sold about as fast as they could be subdivided. The charming neighborhood features modest homes on small lots with many tall trees. It's on Ironbound Road, just north of Route 5 at Five Forks.

Berkeley's Green

Proving to be one of the area's most popular subdivisions, Berkeley's Green is off Route 5 and Greensprings Road. Tucked discreetly behind a facade of tall oaks and pines, this neighborhood features several carefully executed home designs, colonial as well as transitional.

Birchwood Park

Birchwood is one of Williamsburg's established neighborhoods, located off Route 199. Its modest homes, many of them ranch-style, have landscaped yards and established gardens. It is especially accessible to shopping and schools, as well as I-64.

Brandon Woods

Located on John Tyler Highway (Route 5) in Five Forks, this subdivision is characterized by rolling, wooded homesites on tree-lined streets and easy, quick access to shopping and services. Home styles are transitional, and have either brick or "hardy plank" low-maintenance exteriors. These single-family detached homes are condominium ownership, which means the homeowner's association is responsible for all exterior maintenance, including roofs, and the upkeep of all common areas.

Canterbury Hills

Also an established, small neighborhood, this charming area boasts winding roads shaded by large, old trees, neatly tended yards, and larger, well-maintained homes. Off Route 5 and very accessible to the Williamsburg Crossing Shopping Center, it is bounded by Indigo Park and Mill Creek Landing.

Chanco's Grant

A few years ago this neighborhood began as a two-street, starter-home subdivision with low-priced homes on small lots. It proved so vastly popular that it has developed by leaps and bounds to include an abundance of attractive colonial-style homes on several well-tended streets. It is on Ironbound Road, midway between Route 5 and Jamestown Road, close to Clara Byrd Baker Elementary and convenient to shopping.

Chickahominy Haven

Chickahominy Haven started out as a recreational community with small summer homes tucked away on the river from which it gets its name. Now it boasts numerous year-round residents who have built a mix of large and small transitional or contemporary homes interspersed among the summer cottages. It's a drive back through the James City County woods to get there, but take Forge Road off US 60 West, keep bearing right, and wind your way to the river.

Cobble Creek

Located in York County, immediately off the Colonial Parkway and near Queens Lake, is this relatively new community close to shopping and convenient to I-64. Single-family homes are transitional in style, though some offer traditional colonial floor plans and exteriors. Some homes feature vaulted ceilings, kitchen islands, Jacuzzis, and other amenities. All have fireplaces. This community offers a choice of floor plans in new construction, and here you'll find an updated version of the traditional split-level concept. A choice of ravine lots or level tracts give this wooded community visual appeal.

The Coves

Off South Henry Street, after it winds its way past the College of William and Mary's Marshall-Wythe School of Law, is this pristine little subdivision along two short lanes. Most homes here are masterpieces, custom-designed and meticulously maintained by their owners. Every once in a while, someone will put a lot up for sale in this extremely desirable area, but not very often—and they are pricey when they do become available. But its location—within walking distance of Colonial Williamsburg, Merchants Square, the college, and more—is ideal. It also offers easy access via Route 199 to I-64.

Cromwell Ridge

One of several new condominium communities that have emerged in the greater Williamsburg area, Cromwell Ridge is part of the Powhatan Secondary complex, situated just a short walk from the Monticello Marketplace. The three-bedroom condos here feature private garages, first-floor master suites, 9-foot ceilings on the first floor, and fireplaces.

Druid Hills

An established neighborhood off Jamestown Road, Druid Hills features a mix of large and small homes—two-story Colonials as well as contemporary ranches—on winding lanes shaded by old trees. Because of its proximity to the campus of the College of William and Mary, many professors, students, and their families live here.

Fernbrook

Large, heavily wooded lots in James City County's Fernbrook development off Greensprings Road will appeal to families seeking to be within 10 minutes of the heart of Williamsburg. Colonial and transitional homes populate the area.

Fieldcrest

This upscale neighborhood offers luxurious living in a country setting. Large, new homes line its wide streets. Old, stately trees shade Greensprings Road as it leaves Route 5 and leads to the entrance of this lovely subdivision. Homes are primarily transitional in style and usually brick.

Ford's Colony

If you're looking for an elegant home in a gated community replete with golf, lighted tennis courts, fine dining, and one of the state's most extensive wine lists (turn to our Restaurants chapter for details about The Dining Room and The Grille), this expansive planned community is for you. The homes are large and luxurious; the condominiums, townhomes, and cluster homes are equally elegant. The two golf courses here are outstanding and will provide continual challenges (see our Golf chapter for more information). Ford's Colony is a gated community of 2,500 acres on Longhill Road, a couple of miles west of the Historic Area. Lots run in size from a third-acre to a half-acre.

Fox Ridge

Still one of the most affordable subdivisions in the greater Williamsburg area, Fox Ridge is off Centerville Road between Longhill Road and US 60. Charming, smaller homes are interspersed among tall trees, dogwoods, and mountain laurel on rolling hills.

The Governor's Land at Two Rivers

This is, without reservation, the most elegant subdivision in western James City County. Smaller than Kingsmill but no less impressive in its ameni-

ties and terrain, this developing subdivision offers large homesites, many along the river's edge. Off Route 5 at the confluence of the James and Chickahominy Rivers, it offers the last riverfront acreage in the county. A professional golf course, beach facilities, nature trails, a swimming pool, and tennis courts are in place, and the clubhouse offers all one could wish to complete the high quality of the neighborhood.

Graylin Woods

Understated is the best description of this charming, elegant, albeit small subdivision off Route 5 between Route 199 and Five Forks. Large, stately homes on modest, lovely wooded lots and rolling hills give this neighborhood charm and character.

Greensprings Plantation

Williamsburg's newest golfing community is an excellent option for anyone, but especially the golf enthusiast looking for a home-based golfing community. Lots range in size from a third-acre to a half-acre, sometimes a bit larger. Homes in the wooded hills are adjacent to the Williamsburg National Golf Club, an 18-hole championship golf masterpiece designed by Jack Nicklaus's Golden Bear Associates. In addition to the wonderful golfing, amenities include a full-size pool, tennis courts, a recreational center, and two children's play areas.

Heritage Landing

This elegant subdivision off Route 5 west of Five Forks features large brick and wood custom homes on spacious lots. Rolling hills, winding lanes, and flowering trees and shrubs make this an exquisite venue just far enough out of town to make you feel like you're on vacation.

Holly Hills of Williamsburg

Upper-end new property within the city limits is at a premium. Holly Hills on Jamestown Road is the last development to serve the city market. It is located on nearly 300 acres of heavily wooded property just a mile from the Historic Area and the College of William and Mary. Homesites range in size from 0.4 to 2 acres. Strict architectural guidelines ensure that the appearance and value of properties will remain high.

Hunter's Creek

This family-oriented subdivision is small but attractive with its modest colonial homes and well-tended gardens. Off US 60 west of Williamsburg on the edge of Toano, it offers easy access to I-64.

Indigo Park

One of the Route 5 area's earlier developments, Indigo Park has endured as a charming neighborhood of well-maintained homes along rolling, winding lanes shaded by large, old trees. A family-oriented neighborhood with a private pool for residents, Indigo Park is within a five-minute drive of Williamsburg Crossing Shopping Center and schools, as well as Williamsburg's Historic Area and other shopping areas. Two-story ranch homes in brick or wood are a good buy.

Kingsmill on the James

One of Williamsburg's most prestigious neighborhoods, this multifaceted development of 2,900 acres includes everything from riverfront estates to tidy condos overlooking lush fairways on one of three world-class golf courses. Kingsmill residents enjoy on-site tennis, a spa, several superb restaurants, an outstanding recreation and conference center, a private marina, dry-dock facilities, and a riverside beach. Developed by the Anheuser-Busch Corporation, security is provided by the Kingsmill Police Department and limited-access entrances. Prices vary widely.

Kingspoint

This quiet, established neighborhood is tucked away at the foot of South Henry Street just across Route 199. Bounded by the Colonial Parkway on one side and College Creek on the other, it is a wide, tree-covered peninsula. Kingspoint is noted for its friendliness as well as its convenience to the heart of town via Henry Street. It also offers quick access via Route 199 to other parts of

James City County and the interstate. You'll find an eclectic mix of sizes, styles, and ages from '60s to new construction.

Kingswood

Conveniently located off Jamestown Road, about halfway between Merchants Square and the Jamestown Ferry, this idyllic, quiet neighborhood is the choice for those seeking convenience and solitude. Well-tended yards and an assortment of older contemporary and traditional homes line the area's streets and lanes. The neighborhood has a private pool that is open for a fee each summer to guests from nearby developments as well.

Kristiansand

The Norwegian name pays tribute to the town of Norge, which is adjacent to this small subdivision. Off US 60 West, it is just down the road from the Williamsburg Pottery Factory. It offers quick and easy access to Ewell Station Shopping Center and I-64 as well as local schools.

Lake Toano

If you don't mind driving about 15 minutes west of Williamsburg along US 60 West, you can find this subdivision situated in a heavily wooded area surrounding a quiet reservoir in the Toano area. Large and small homes, both contemporary and traditional, line the streets and cul-de-sacs that make up this country neighborhood. It is just minutes from the I-64 exit for Toano.

Landfall at Jamestown

Talk about a lush setting! This upscale subdivision is located on prime real estate, off Jamestown Road, about half a mile from the James River. Some lots sit amid meandering streams and creeks; others front the James River. New construction includes transitional and contemporary as well as traditional colonial design, most with brick exterior.

Longhill Gate

Located on Longhill Road just before the entrance to Ford's Colony, these attached homes range in size from moderate to fairly large. Sidewalks, manicured landscapes, and winding streets are indicative of the low-key family ambience that sets the tone of this charming neighborhood.

The Meadows

Looks are deceiving as you approach this small community of small- to moderate-size homes, between Strawberry Plains and Ironbound Roads. At the back edge of a wide-open field, the streets of this neighborhood dip and wind, curve and wander. Neatly kept yards and pristine houses characterize this subdivision, halfway between downtown Williamsburg and Jamestown via Sandy Point Road.

Mill Creek Landing

Without a doubt, this elegant subdivision of custom-built homes (nearly all of them brick) situated around a 7-acre fish-stocked pond is one of the area's best-kept secrets. Limited in size, it is off Route 5 and Stanley Drive. It offers a country setting less than 2 miles from Williamsburg's Historic Area, with easy access to schools, Williamsburg Crossing Shopping Center (which is within walking distance), and I-64.

Mirror Lake Estates

About 15 minutes west of the Historic Area, this inviting neighborhood features small, moderate, and larger starter homes, all built fairly recently. It can be reached via Richmond Road or from I-64, which is less than a mile from the entrance of the subdivision.

North Cove

Off Route 646 in York County, this large-lot subdivision features rolling hills, large homes, lots of trees, and quick access to I-64. About 10 minutes west of Williamsburg, it is a charming setting that seems far removed from the bustle of downtown. It is also near York River State Park and a public boat ramp on the York River. You'll find homes in brick, cedar, and stucco.

Peleg's Point

Conveniently located off Neck-O-Land Road in James City County, this relatively new neighborhood features larger homes, many brick, in colonial, transitional, and contemporary styles. It is only a few miles from downtown Williamsburg, but also offers proximity to the James River and Colonial Parkway.

Piney Creek Estates

Two of the area's most renowned builders, Ronald T. Curtis and Joel S. Sheppard, offer owners a prime city address—and low taxes. This new development is within a mile of the James City County–Williamsburg Community Center and Kiwanis Park, and it's a short drive from all area attractions and shopping.

Poplar Hall

About 8 miles east of downtown Williamsburg, this meandering neighborhood is tucked discreetly away from the traffic of US 60 East, off of which it is located. This subdivision offers a variety of sizes and styles and boasts both older and new homes. It is midway between two I-64 interchanges and is just minutes from Busch Gardens and the Anheuser-Busch brewery.

Port Anne

One of the last subdivisions in the city where you can still purchase land and build a custom house, this neighborhood is for the discerning homeowner in search of an idyllic setting above College Creek. Large, custom-designed homes on smaller lots provide the perfect place to settle down in style. A clubhouse, tennis courts, and pool are among other amenities. It offers quick access to I-64 and is within biking and walking distance of the city's Historic Area.

Powhatan Crossing

One of the developing moderate-income neighborhoods in James City County, this small but charming subdivision is just east of Route 5 at Five Forks. It features affordable, small to moderately sized homes along a cozy lane that stretches into the woodlands. Residents enjoy easy access to downtown Williamsburg or I-64 via Route 5.

Powhatan Place

Located near Monticello Marketplace off News Road, this three-bedroom luxury townhome community offers excellent location and all amenities. Two floor plans are offered. The 2,700-square-foot end units feature first-floor master suites. The 2,500-square-foot interior units feature master bedrooms with spacious his/her master baths. All units feature gas heat and hot water, as well as gas-log fireplaces, single-car garages, and laundry rooms. All units are prewired for security systems.

Powhatan Secondary of Williamsburg

On the site of the early-17th-century Powhatan Plantation off Ironbound Road at Mid County Park, this popular and growing subdivision offers choice wooded homesites at reasonable prices. The attractive, custom-built homes are a mix of contemporary and traditional styles, all meticulously maintained and landscaped. The community includes 45 acres of recreational land and lakes for homeowners to enjoy. Buyers can choose from a variety of floor plans from nine quality builders.

i Over the years some land in James City County has tested positive for hydric soil (water-soaked soil with a tendency to shift). This is no big deal provided your builder knows about it and takes precautions when doing the foundation of a new home. If you're buying an existing home, you'll want to have a "shrink-swell" test to find out if the land is hydric. If it tests positive, have a home inspector make sure this was taken into account when the home was built.

Powhatan Shores

While most neighborhoods offer some attractive amenities to their homeowners, this charming

family neighborhood has them all, especially for the boating enthusiast. Most lots have private access via a creek to the James River. It is just a few minutes from the city's Historic Area and is close to Route 199 and I-64.

Queens Lake

This stately, established neighborhood, bounded by Queens Creek and the Colonial Parkway, is one of the most prestigious neighborhoods in the greater Williamsburg area. Tennis courts, a pool, a recreation center, and a marina are among the amenities. Some of the area's loveliest homes are situated on the rolling, wooded lanes of this charming subdivision. It offers country living just minutes from I-64, Colonial Williamsburg, and area schools.

Queenswood

Off Hubbard Lane, this family-oriented neighborhood features newer homes on moderate-size lots away from the activity of downtown Williamsburg and major roads. Ranches and two-story Colonials are the norm here, and meticulously landscaped and maintained homesites are typical. It is within minutes of Colonial Parkway, James York Plaza Shopping Center, and Route 143, which leads to I-64.

Richmond Hill

This is a small, high-end neighborhood in the city limits very close to the Historic Area. All brick homes are Federal architectural designs similar to those on Richmond's Monument Avenue. Three golf courses, indoor tennis, and the shopping and dining of Colonial Williamsburg are all within walking distance.

Rolling Woods

Lovely midrange homes with brick, vinyl, and cedar exteriors tucked away under stately oaks and pines make this hilly subdivision much sought after. Off Lake Powell Road in James City County, it offers seclusion just minutes from the congestion of downtown Williamsburg. It is near Route 199 and I-64.

Seasons Trace

One of the most popular planned communities in the area is this neighborhood with its neatly maintained townhomes, condos, cluster homes, and small private homes. Off Longhill Road, adjacent to Lafayette High School and across the road from the Windsor Forest subdivision, Seasons Trace features winding lanes and a pond stocked with fish and populated with ducks. Also offered are such amenities as a pool, tennis courts, a basketball court, and dry-dock storage for boats and RVs.

Settler's Mill

Off Jamestown Road approximately halfway between Route 199 and Jamestown, Settler's Mill has emerged as a very popular development. Located in a heavily wooded community, it features a lake, ponds, and rolling hills. It is a joint venture of four of the most prestigious names in residential building and development in the area: Larry McCardle, Sterling Nichols, Joel Sheppard, and Ron Curtis. Homes feature a variety of traditional and transitional styles.

Skimino Hills

Developed in the late 1970s and early 1980s, this large subdivision is situated on gently rolling hills in western York County. Off I-64 at Route 646, it offers large lots with trees and lush growths of mountain laurel and dogwood. A mix of large and small contemporary and traditional homes lines its narrow streets.

Skimino Landing Estates

Large lots—from an acre up—and lots of trees, including hardwoods, characterize this subdivision in upper York County. The neighborhood features a boat ramp with access to the York River. Construction reflects a mix of styles, many transitional, most with brick facades.

Skipwith Farms

This was the City of Williamsburg's first real subdivision, built in the 1950s and '60s, and it features modest single- and two-story homes. Few areas are more centrally located or offer easier access to shopping, recreation, and area schools. It is off Richmond Road, less than 3 miles from the heart of the city's Historic Area.

St. George's Hundred

One of the area's most popular, family-oriented neighborhoods, St. George's is off Route 5 about 5 miles west of Williamsburg. Charming homes, mostly colonial style, line the streets. Established more than two decades ago, this neighborhood continues to grow. In addition to its easy access to area shopping and schools, it features a recreation area with picnic tables, basketball courts, and a softball field.

Stonehouse

Located along the I-64 corridor in both James City and New Kent Counties is Stonehouse, a 5,700-acre development that offers homeowners an all-digital residential community in a beautiful natural setting. A joint venture of the real estate divisions of Dominion Resources Inc. and Chesapeake Corp., Stonehouse is offering large single-family homes, golf villas on the Legends of Stonehouse Golf Course, patio homes, and town houses. The project includes lots ranging in size from a third of an acre to more than an acre. Stonehouse homeowners have access to a variety of technological services, from digital TV with more than 200 audio and video channels to state-of-the-art security systems and high-speed Internet service. The community is being developed on a 25-year plan and eventually will offer an aquatic and sports center, retail shops, churches, offices, grocery stores, movie theaters, and more. More than 50 percent of the property will remain in its natural state. For more information visit the Web site at www.stonehouseva.com.

The Vineyards of Williamsburg

Off Neck-o-Land Road, this subdivision of large, stately homes is quickly becoming one of Williamsburg's most prestigious addresses. Larger houses are the rule, but there are a few areas offering smaller, exquisitely constructed dwellings. Most are tucked away discreetly among old shade trees. Breezes from the nearby James River and proximity to both Jamestown Road and the Colonial Parkway make this a much-sought-after location.

Westgate at Williamsburg

In a community where condominiums are quickly catching a foothold, this complex is one of the most reasonably priced options. Located off US 60 just west of the Prime Outlets, it's convenient to Williamsburg and I-64. Placed along quiet streets, the charming two- and three-bedroom condos here are large, measuring about 1,600 square feet. They feature natural gas heat and water, vaulted ceilings, walk-in closets, and lofts. Some have gas fireplaces and sunrooms. The community also offers owners use of a pool and cabana.

Westmoreland

Off Olde Towne Road near its intersection with Long Hill Road, this small development currently has 15 single-family lots on richly wooded property developed by the Hornsby family (relations of Bruce Hornsby). Convenient access to shopping and amenities on the Richmond Road side of town, proximity to the Historic Area (a 10-minute drive), and convenient access to I-64 are strong advantages to this neighborhood.

Westray Downs

Rolling hills, winding lanes, and charming homes characterize this relatively new neighborhood off Route 5 in James City County. Ranch-style homes, traditional two-story homes, and some charming colonial-style homes add interest to the landscape. It is minutes from the county's Law Enforcement Center and Fire Station on Route 5 and offers quick, easy access to Williamsburg Crossing Shopping Center, Five Forks, the Jamestown Ferry, and I-64 via Route 199.

Windsor Forest

Before Ford's Colony joined the ranks, this was the most upscale subdivision on the northeast side of James City County. It is off Longhill Road, and large homes—some contemporary, most traditional colonial-style—are the norm here. Amenities include a community pool. Nearby are the county recreation center and lots of shopping. There is easy access to I-64 via Airport Road, and the city's Historic Area is just a few miles away.

> **i** Thinking about building in greater Williamsburg? Think you've narrowed your list of potential builders? Before selecting, make a call to the Peninsula Housing & Builders Association, (757) 595-1600. They can discuss each builder's track record—and perhaps save you some money in the long run.

The Woods

This handsome, upscale subdivision is quickly establishing itself as one of distinction. Large, stately homes are situated on rolling hills amid lush woods and tall, old oaks and pines. Off Jamestown Road and within a brisk walking distance of the city's Historic Area, this fine subdivision offers easy access to just about everything, including I-64 via Route 199.

Yorkshire

Nothing short of elegant is this small albeit stately subdivision, located conveniently off Jamestown Road near the Route 199 intersection. Large custom homes are located on quiet meandering streets and cul-de-sacs set inside rolling hills and woodlands. The neighborhood is less than a mile from the city's Historic Area and is located within the city limits.

REAL ESTATE COMPANIES

It stands to reason that there are plenty of Realtors to bring housing seekers and sellers together, and there are. We have listed below a sample of some of the area Realtors. (All Realtors are located in Williamsburg unless otherwise noted.)

ABBITT REALTY COMPANY INC.
104 Bypass Rd.
(757) 253-7600, (757) 827-1144
Established in 1946, Abbitt Realty is a recognized leader in the peninsula real estate market, with five offices, one in the Williamsburg area. A member of RELO, the nation's largest and oldest effective relocation network, Abbitt has reinforced its leadership with a full complement of associated divisions, enabling the company to offer buyers an integrated array of real estate ervices.

> **i** Looking for a reputable real estate company and agent? Call the Williamsburg Area Association of Realtors at (757) 253-0028 or visit www.waarealtor .com.

BERKELEY WILLIAM E. WOOD
& ASSOCIATES REALTORS
1326 Jamestown Rd.
(757) 229-0550

926-A J. Clyde Morris Blvd.
Newport News
(757) 599-8449, (800) 866-3201

907 Richmond Rd.
(757) 253-8150
Berkeley is one of the community's largest and longest-established companies, handling commercial, residential, and land sales, and has a reputation for client satisfaction.

COLDWELL BANKER
PROFESSIONAL REALTORS
312-A Lightfoot Rd.
(757) 564-9595
www.coldwellbanker.com
This firm, one of the area's largest with 25 Realtors, represents buyers and sellers throughout the greater Williamsburg market.

EXECUTIVE HOMES REALTY
124 Quaker Meeting House Rd.
(757) 565-1963
Executive Homes Realty handles properties in prestigious golf, waterfront, and gated commu-nities surrounding historic Williamsburg. Their specialty is buyer representation while purchasing a homesite or an existing home as well as buyer representation during the construction of a new home.

GSH REAL ESTATE, WILLIAMSBURG OFFICE
264 McLaws Circle, Suite H
(757) 253-2442
GSH has a major presence in the Tidewater area and is heavily involved in commercial real estate and property management. The local office provides full and expert representation in commercial, residential, and land transactions. They've been in business for more than 50 years.

HORNSBY REAL ESTATE CO.
4732 Longhill Rd., Suite 1101
(757) 565-1234
This is a long-established (more than 50 years) and highly respected company handling commercial, residential, and land transactions throughout the greater Williamsburg area. Currently, the firm is developing the upscale Westmoreland subdivision off Olde Towne Road. (See the Westmoreland listing under Neighborhoods in this chapter.)

KINGSMILL REALTY INC.
100 Kingsmill Rd.
(757) 253-3933, (800) 392-0026
While other companies represent properties in Kingsmill, Kingsmill Realty is an obvious option for those seeking to own in the Kingsmill on the James planned community. On top of what's available as well as what's coming onto the market in all of Kingsmill's neighborhoods, the company's agents can help clients find the ideal location.

> **i** While homes in the city of Williamsburg aren't as plentiful as in James City or upper York Counties, they are available. In addition to closer proximity to downtown, homes in the city are taxed at a much lower rate than those in the counties. This will directly impact your monthly house payment.

LONG & FOSTER REALTORS
4655-101 Monticello Ave.
(757) 229-4400

Associated with the company that's been selling real estate since 1968, this office has had a presence in the Williamsburg area for about a decade. The staff of about 30 agents can help you find the home or condominium you're looking for anywhere in the greater Williamsburg area.

PRUDENTIAL MCCARDLE REALTY
1201 Jamestown Rd.
(757) 253-5686

811 Richmond Rd.
(757) 229-6151

3449 John Tyler Hwy
(757) 220-9500
www.mccardlerealty.com

This independent, locally owned company with more than 25 years of experience associated with Prudential in early 1999. Three convenient offices have approximately 60 full-time Realtors to ensure customer service and satisfaction.

McCardle belongs to RELO, a national and international network of independent companies that can assist those leaving for or moving from other parts of the country. McCardle handles commercial, residential (new and resale), and land transactions.

WILLIAMSBURG REALTY INC.
4519 John Tyler Hwy
(757) 564-0988

Jerry and Pam McCardle, the owners of Williamsburg Realty in the Five Forks Shopping Center, have more than 25 years of local real estate experience. He knows his territory well. Before selling homes, Jerry McCardle helped build 300 of them in the Williamsburg area. The helpful and friendly staff at Williamsburg Realty specializes in both residential and commercial properties. Pam McCardle also serves as a broker.

RETIREMENT

The Historic Triangle continues to grow in popularity as a retirement destination, drawing older Americans from across the nation. Why? you may wonder. Well, for starters, our temperate climate is a significant draw. We enjoy four distinct seasons, yet winters here generally are mild and short. The brunt of wintry weather doesn't begin until mid-December and is over by late February or early March. Snow may fall, but it rarely lingers. Ice may form, but it quickly melts. Colorful redbud and dogwood are harbingers of spring, which often arrives early. Summers can be sultry, but elongated falls, replete with nearly summerlike weather well into October, make the impending winter easier to swallow.

People retiring from military service in the Hampton Roads area are familiar with the amenities to be had, and many are quick to settle here. The cost of living is relatively low when compared to many other parts of the country, particularly the northeast urban centers. Recreational opportunities are numerous. Local health-care options are many and good. And, as a college town, Williamsburg offers a broad spectrum of generally inexpensive cultural activities senior citizens are invited to enjoy.

Perhaps the most important contact point for seniors here is the **Historic Triangle Senior Center,** located in the James City County–Williamsburg Community Center. The center, open to persons age 50 and older, is a meeting and greeting place, the site of special events and many regularly scheduled monthly events, and the starting point for varied daytrips and longer excussions for seniors. Additionally, the center offers tai chi, sewing circles, fitness classes, Scrabble, chess, movies, mah-jong, card games, readers' theater, book club, spanish language instruction, and other activities for interested seniors. Particularly Popular are the four annual themed socials. Call (757) 259-4187 for more information or visit the website at www.theseniorcenter.com

The center also is particularly concerned with health issues related to aging. It offers special workshops on such topics as growing younger, and Wellness Days programs, which focus on such themes as maintaining good health through smart physical activity, risk factors for coronary artery disease, and what to expect when you undergo joint replacement surgery. Many of these programs are offered in conjunction with Williamsburg Community Hospital's home health-care program. And an added bonus: The center offers free blood pressure and glucose screenings. Call (757) 259-4187 for scheduled dates and times.

A good place to look for more information on programming (and discounts) is the *Senior Times*, published quarterly by the senior center.

All senior residents are eligible for **Good Neighbor passes** from Colonial Williamsburg. These $10 tickets entitle them to admissions, bus service, and shopping discounts in Colonial Williamsburg's properties. They can purchase admission tickets for up to 20 guests each year at a 25 percent discount, and holders receive a helpful newsletter published seasonally by Colonial Williamsburg. Senior residents of York County, James City County, and Williamsburg are also entitled to free admission to Jamestown Settlement and Yorktown Victory Center. Proof of address is required.

SERVICES

COMPUTER LITERACY TRAINING
Historic Triangle Senior Center
5301 Longhill Rd.
(757) 259-4187
Volunteer instructors will assist seniors, provide access to computers for practice, or arrange a self-paced course between the instructor and the pupil.

MEALS ON WHEELS
Williamsburg Baptist Church
227 Richmond Rd.
(757) 229-9250
Operated out of an office in the Williamsburg Baptist Church, this volunteer group serves more than 100 local senior citizens a nutritionally balanced, hot meal prepared by Williamsburg Community Hospital from Mon through Fri. Recipients are charged on a sliding-scale, ability-to-pay basis. Anyone wishing to call should use the number listed above. Those who prefer to write for more information can send their inquiry to Meals on Wheels, P.O. Box 709, Williamsburg, VA 23187. This service is not only for the elderly. The program serves all who meet its criteria.

RIDES (MEDICAL ESCORT SERVICE)
312 Waller Mill
(757) 259-4182
This organization provides non-emergency transportation to doctors' offices, medical clinics, and the hospital for seniors. Transportation must be arranged 48 hours in advance. There is no fee but a $2 donation is appreciated.

PENINSULA AGENCY ON AGING (PAA)
739 Thimble Shoals Blvd.
Suite 1006, Newport News
(757) 873-0541
www.paainc.org
The central source of information on services for senior citizens throughout the entire area, this office provides services and programs covering needs such as housing, health, income or financial aid, community services, adult day care, legal services, nutrition and meal programs, transportation, recreation, in-home support, and social services. The staff will make an appropriate referral for the closest service that meets your needs.

RIVERSIDE ADULT SERVICES
1010 Old Denbigh Blvd.
Newport News
(757) 875-2033
This organization provides a structured environment for seniors Mon to Fri from 7:30 a.m. to 5:30 p.m. While this group caters to seniors with physical limitations and mental disorders such as Alzheimer's disease, the center is open to all interested seniors, including those in good health. Although there is no transportation provided to the center located in upper Newport News, Medicaid patients can make use of the Medicaid Cab.

i The Williamsburg Area Chamber of Commerce has embraced its local retirees, who participate in SCORE (Senior Corps of Retired Executives), a group that helps small local businesses get established. SCORE resources are offered free of charge to qualifying businesses, but the knowledge members impart is invaluable. For more information on how to get involved, call the chamber at (757) 229-6511 or go to www.williamsburgcc.com.

PUBLICATIONS

WILLIAMSBURG REGIONAL LIBRARY
515 Scotland St.
(757) 259-4070
7770 Croaker Rd.
(757) 259-4040
Williamsburg Regional Library and the satellite library in upper James City County keep on file a variety of published resources of interest to senior citizens. These resources include publications especially for older Americans, such as *Modern Maturity*, which is the magazine published monthly by AARP.

SENIOR TIMES
Historic Triangle Senior Center
5301 Longhill Rd.
(757) 259-4187
This newsletter, published quarterly by the Historic Triangle Senior Center, lists all activities and programs for senior citizens, at the center and beyond. Nearly 1,000 copies are mailed each issue, and others are distributed at the center.

Activities

Active seniors interested in participating in social, civic, and special-interest activities don't have to look very far. The College of William and Mary sponsors concert series, theater productions, exhibits, and gallery talks, usually for a small admission fee or no charge at all. We describe some of these in The Arts chapter. Call (757) 221-4000 for details. What follows is a list of some of the more active clubs and programs in this area.

THE CHRISTOPHER WREN ASSOCIATION
FOR LIFELONG LEARNING
College of William and Mary
(757) 221-1506
www.wm.edu/cwa
No report on retired living in the Historic Triangle would be complete without mention of the Christopher Wren Association for Lifelong Learning, an innovative educational program begun at the College of William and Mary in 1991. Any Williamsburg area resident of retirement age who loves learning is welcome to take part in this course of study. Don't worry, there are no grades or tests here, though intellectual challenge is amply present.

The association, founded by retired college professors Ruth and Wayne Kernodle, is peer-run and peer-taught. By tapping the area's reservoir of retired persons with expertise in art, literature, history, social sciences and other fields, the program is able to offer courses on government, comparative religions, photography, music, and many other subjects. The enrollment fee is $85 per semester.

In addition, the association sponsors the Town and Gown Brown Bag luncheon-and-lecture series, held weekly at William and Mary's Campus Center. This program attracts many area retirees, who gather to hear speakers from near and far give informal talks after a catered luncheon on topics of sometimes general, sometimes specialized, interest. The series is open only to regular and associate members of the Christopher Wren Association. (Associate members pay a $25 fee and may attend the luncheons, social events, and day trips, which carry an additional fee. Associate members are not eligible to enroll in classes.)

A full schedule of course offerings and additional information is available by visiting the Web site, listed above.

THE 50 PLUS GROUP
P.O. Box BB, Williamsburg, VA 23187
(757) 229-1771
This ecumenical program, sponsored by Williamsburg United Methodist Church, is open to all interested persons ages 50 and older. The group meets on the second Wednesday of each month, September through May, for lunch and a program. The group is open to any one over 50. Bring a small donation to offset the cast of lunch. Call for more information.

RETIRED SENIOR VOLUNTEER
PROGRAM (RSVP)
12388 Warwick Blvd., Suite 201
Newport News
(757) 595-9037
RSVP responds to community needs through a network of senior citizen volunteers. Although local work had been coordinated out of Newport News, it has a branch in Williamsburg as well. This office recruits and places people ages 55 and older who are interested in providing community service. The office usually is open 8 a.m. to 5 p.m. Mon through Fri, and seniors who want to check out their options are welcome to drop by. Volunteers give their time to more than 250 places such as Meals on Wheels, nonprofit agencies, convalescent centers, and hospitals in the area.

> **i** Retired military officers and their families can keep abreast of what's happening through the Virginia Peninsula Chapter, Retired Officers Association. This organization puts out a monthly newsletter, holds local chapter meetings, and enjoys social events. To learn more about this special group, call (800) 234-6622.

SENIOR CENTER OF YORK
5314 George Washington Hwy
Yorktown
(757) 898-3807

This center offers myriad activities for citizens ages 55 and up. Seniors can participate in such activities as quilting, dominoes, bridge, line dancing, and computer classes. A free monthly calendar, available at the center, lists scheduled activities and events, including special senior citizen trips.

RESIDENTIAL LIVING

While many seniors choose to live in conventional, mixed-age neighborhoods, others prefer the more exclusive, secure, or convenient atmosphere of the retirement community. Currently, Williamsburg can provide several such options for retirees in search of a community lifestyle.

CHAMBREL AT WILLIAMSBURG
3800 Treyburn Dr.
(757) 220-1839
www.brookdaleliving.com

Located across the street from Williamsburg Community Hospital is this attractive, well-maintained senior community (formerly known as Brookdale), built on 56 acres in James City County. Active seniors can choose from a number of lifestyle options, including apartments or cottage homes. All units feature washers and dryers, and many have screened porches.

In addition, Chambrel offers assisted living in both efficiencies and full-size garden apartment arrangements. Brandon House and York Manor are the special-care needs section offering assisted-living services tailored to the specific needs of each resident.

Amenities at Chambrel include biweekly housekeeping and weekly linen service. The elegant Village Center includes a dining room, library, swimming pool, and wellness center. Chambrel residents can take advantage of scheduled transportation, maid service, travel opportunities, social and cultural events, walking trails in natural woodlands. Several shopping areas, Colonial Williamsburg, the College of William and Mary, and many golf courses are nearby. Chambrel charges residents a monthly fee determined by the category of their living arrangement, with no admission charge or endowment required.

> **i** Fore! If you're a golfer, you're really in luck. With more than 15 golf courses in the Historic Triangle, golfers have a grand selection of links from which to choose. Better yet: Most offer senior citizen discounts. Call ahead and inquire about discounts and reservations at the same time.

DOMINION VILLAGE
4132 Longhill Rd.
(757) 258-3444
www.firestarcommunitycare.com

Many seniors in need of long-term, assisted-living care opt for this fine facility, conveniently located about 5 miles from the city's Historic Area across Longhill Road from the entrance to Ford's Colony. It provides permanent and short-term residence options in private and semiprivate rooms. The center is conveniently near shopping, bus lines, and several area churches, making it extremely convenient to visiting family members and friends.

Dominion Village offers three levels of care, ranging from minimal to more extensive assistance with activities of daily living. It also offers a secure, positive atmosphere for residents with Alzheimer's disease or dementia. The monthly rental fee covers nearly everything: three meals; afternoon and evening snacks; around-the-clock nursing care; assistance with bathing, dressing, and personal care as needed; medications monitored by the nursing staff; daily activities, programs, and monthly outings; church services;

housekeeping and linen services; cable TV; and all utilities except telephone. Amenities include a dining room; living room; cozy sitting areas; an activity room for crafts, art, reading, and conversation; an outdoor garden patio for cookouts; and an emergency call system in each room.

The Bridge to Discovery is a special-care unit designed for those with Alzheimer's, dementia, or related disorders.

ENVOY OF WILLIAMSBURG
1235 Mount Vernon Ave.
(757) 229-4121

Owned by Consulate Healthcare, Envoy offers long-term and skilled nursing and respite care, varied activities, and physical, occupational, respiratory, and speech therapies. Services and amenities include a dining program tailored to each resident's dietary needs, a dessert cart that circulates throughout the living area, and an extensive volunteer program that brings in church groups, civic groups, students, and local musical entertainment on a regular basis. This center offers an enclosed courtyard for those residents who wish to spend time out-of-doors in nice weather.

PATRIOTS COLONY
6000 Patriots Colony Dr.
(757) 220-9000, (800) 716-9000
www.patriotscolony.com

Retired military officers and their spouses can investigate this gated, continuing-care retirement community with 158 private villas and apartments and 24 freestanding homes. Located adjacent to the Greensprings Plantation National Historic Site on historic Route 5 west of Williamsburg, Patriots Colony offers residences and a community center featuring fine dining, a fitness and wellness center, and recreational areas. Other amenities include all utilities, weekly maid service, one meal per person per day, total interior and exterior building maintenance, and a community greenhouse, pool, and tennis courts. In addition to independent-living facilities, the community offers long-term care on-site. Long-term health care includes assisted living, assisted living for residents with Alzheimer's disease and other dementia, and a convalescent care

center. While the independent-living community is open to retired officers of the seven uniformed services and retired federal civil service employees only, the assisted-living and convalescent care centers are open to everyone.

TANDEM HEALTH CARE AT WILLIAMSBURG
1811 Jamestown Rd.
(757) 229-9991
www.tandemhealthcare.com

This senior nursing-care facility is staffed by a team of health professionals providing care for physical and mental well-being in a supportive, homelike setting. The center's design features a number of living areas and courtyards, as well as spacious dining and activity rooms. The center offers three levels of care: intermediate, skilled, and Alzheimer's. Residents are accepted for both short- and long-term stays. On-site services include comprehensive rehabilitative services as well as physical therapy, occupational therapy, and speech-language pathology. It also offers optometrist and podiatry services, daily recreational therapy, beauty/barber services, cable TV, and a code alert security system.

WILLIAMSBURG LANDING
5700 Williamsburg Landing Dr.
(757) 565-6505, (800) 554-5517
www.williamsburglanding.com

At this lovely, upscale community that must be seen to be believed, seniors can choose home or apartment independent living and take advantage of health services that range from a minimal wellness program to licensed nursing-home care. The gated community offers around-the-clock security, housekeeping, all interior and exterior building maintenance, all appliances in each unit, all utilities except cable TV and phone, trash removal, one meal per day, shuttle bus service to doctors' offices, and access to local shopping and special events in town. The Landing also offers on-site banking, shopping, library, computer room, woodworking shop, billiards, health spa, outdoor pool, tennis court, and more.

Situated on 135 woodland acres next to College Creek, this long-term care facility offers social, recreational, and cultural activities such as concerts, tours, physical fitness classes, and events presented in conjunction with the College of William and Mary. Outpatient clinic services of outpatient services and a medical director, include care by physicians and registered nurses. Many locals, upon retirement, sell their homes and move to the Landing to live out their senior years in style, comfort, and convenience. There are 310 independent-living units, a mixture of cluster homes and apartments. A monthly service fee covers meals, utilities, and other items. Those who need to move temporarily or permanently into the Woodhaven Hall health-care complex can choose private or semiprivate care. The Landing is a pet-friendly community, but there are some restrictions—call for detailed information.

EDUCATION

One of the finest universities in America is located in the heart of Williamsburg, the **College of William and Mary,** the second oldest institution of higher learning in the United States (Harvard is the oldest.) King William III and Queen Mary II granted the charter in 1693. Although many out-of-state visitors assume William and Mary is a private school, it is actually a state-supported, four-year university with a prestigious reputation. Often referred to as a "public ivy," William and Mary offers its students the diverse resources of a large institution with the community atmosphere of a smaller town.

The campus is at the western end of Duke of Gloucester Street between Jamestown and Richmond Roads, a landmark known locally as College Corner. Near this intersection you'll find the Sir Christopher Wren Building, which typically has served as the starting point for any self-guided walking tour. It is well worth spending a few hours of your stay in Williamsburg to survey the gracious campus of this school, whose earliest alumni, Thomas Jefferson among them, were the first leaders of our nation.

As you approach the Wren Building, you'll notice the brick wall surrounding the triangular College Yard, which also holds two other pre–Revolutionary War structures: the President's House and Brafferton, formerly an Indian school. While the college was chartered by the Crown in 1693 in response to a 1691 petition from Virginia's General Assembly, bricks weren't laid for the Wren Building (originally known as "The College") until two years later, making it the oldest academic building in continuous use in the United States.

For several years the building served as temporary headquarters to Virginia's colonial government. Then, in 1705 and again in 1859, fires destroyed portions of the building, which was twice rebuilt by using the remaining foundation and walls. Alas, in 1862, Federal soldiers set the building afire again. Despite such damage, the original exterior walls survived to be restored during the 1920s and '30s, and the Wren Building visitors see today has the appearance of the pre–1859 fire structure. Today the Wren houses William and Mary's religion department. Visitors also will see early classrooms, the 1732 chapel—under which noted Virginians such as Sir John Randolph and Lord Botetourt are buried—and Great Hall, where the Burgesses assembled.

North of the Wren Building in the College Yard is the President's House, built in the early 1730s. Besides serving as a home to such famous college presidents as James Madison and James Blair, it also housed British General Cornwallis before his Yorktown surrender to Revolutionary forces led by Washington. The building is still in use as a residence for College of William and Mary presidents.

The third and smallest structure facing the College Yard is The Brafferton, now used for offices, but originally an Indian school. The Brafferton was built in 1723 with funds provided by an English scientist determined to bring Christianity to area Indian youths, who already were forced to attend a training school in Williamsburg. Apparently, the young boys were not at all happy about living in town, learning English, or wearing uniforms, and they longed for their villages and tribes. A William and Mary myth holds that one of these Indian students can sometimes be seen running quick as the wind across campus at night, as if trying to regain his freedom.

You can stroll in the Sunken Garden west of the Wren Building or through shady Crim Dell with its footpaths and small pond. Other buildings worth noting on campus include Phi Beta Kappa Memorial Hall, Earl Gregg Swem Library, and the Muscarelle Museum of Art.

Its long history, appealing campus, and strong national reputation for top-notch academics have made admission to William and Mary, a state university, highly competitive. A record number of applicants—12,500—sought admission in 2009, up 3 percent from the previous year. (The Tribe football had one of its best seasons in recent memory in 2009. That helps, too!) They're hoping to join the 7,650 students already enrolled here in the schools of Arts and Sciences, Business Administration, Education, Law, and Marine Sciences.

Student-led tours of the college campus for prospective students are available throughout the year. For information on tours call (757) 221-4223.

ℹ️ One of the best-kept secrets in Williamsburg is the Earl Gregg Swem Library at the College of William and Mary. The public is welcome to use the materials found here, including copies of most major American newspapers. In addition, you'll find more than one million books, even more microforms, and a half million items in the government publications collection. For more information call (757) 221-4636 or look up www.swem.wm.edu.

CHRISTOPHER NEWPORT UNIVERSITY
1 University Place, Newport News
(757) 594-7000
www.cnu.edu
Once part of the College of William and Mary, CNU split from the larger college in the 1980s and since has developed an identity of its own. Located on a verdant, 125-acre campus about 25 miles southeast of Williamsburg in Newport News, this four-year institution offers a wide variety of undergraduate and graduate courses and degrees.

"We are a young university on the move that enjoys a growing reputation for really caring about students, great teaching, small classes, and having Virginia's safest campus," said CNU President Paul S. Trible, a former U.S. senator.

In short, CNU is a young college offering 80 undergraduate and graduate programs to 4,800 students in business, science, technology, education, government, and the performing arts. Once known primarily as a commuter school, the campus has undergone a massive transformation in the past 10 years, adding a state-of-the-art sports and convocation facility, a new library, additional campus housing, and the the Ferguson Center for the Arts, designed by the architectural firm founded by I. M. Pei. Local wags have suggested the school mascot been changed from the Captains (for Christopher Newport) to the Bulldozers, since construction of all these new facilities has made the Warwick Boulevard corridor (US Route 60) along which the university is situated a demolition zone for most of that decade.

CNU's intercollegiate sports program includes NCAA Division III contests in 18 sports including a 12-time national championship women's track and perennial nationally ranked men's basketball team.

HAMPTON UNIVERSITY
East Hampton off Settlers Landing Road
Hampton, VA 23668
(757) 727-5000
www.hamptonu.edu
Privately supported Hampton University opened its doors on April 1, 1868, known as the Hampton Normal and Agricultural Institute. It had a few buildings on 120 acres of land, little equipment, two teachers (who earned $15 a month), 15 students, and a dormitory retrofitted from a converted hospital barracks. In 2010, the man who agreed to give the commencement address accepted only two such invitations: President Barack Obama. You've come a long way, Hampton U.

General Samuel Chapman founded the school with a plan to educate the newly emancipated African Americans. Today Hampton University is one of the most popular black colleges in America, boasting a student population of more than 5,000.

Hampton has a $180 million endowment, the highest SAT scores of entering freshmen for any historically black college, state-of-the-art facilities, a distinguished faculty, and an innovative curriculum. It offers a variety of programs including especially strong ones in science, engineering, pharmacy, business (including an MBA degree), architecture, and nursing.

Hampton offers a strong athletic program as well with 14 sports, including a men's and women's sailing team.

The university, which stresses the importance of leadership through its Leadership Institute, also reaches out to the community with its A Plus (A+) Summer Program for Pre-College Students. The monthlong program for 13- to 15-year-olds offers everything from mentoring and mathematics to art and scuba diving.

Listed among famous graduates is Booker T. Washington, class of 1875, who took what he learned here south, where he founded Tuskegee Institute. Other grads include Spencer Christian (class of '70 and former weatherman on ABC's *Good Morning America*), Ms. Frankie Freeman (class of '37 and former U.S. Civil Rights Commissioner), and Vanessa D. Gilmore (class of '77 and a federal judge in Texas).

The Hampton University Museum (detailed in the attractions section of our Newport News and Hampton chapter) is worth seeing. And no visit to Hampton University would be complete without a stop at the Emancipation Oak—a massive shade tree on the northeast side of the campus. It was under this tree in 1863 that Hampton's black community—people who the law then prohibited from attending school—gathered to hear the first southern reading of President Abraham Lincoln's Emancipation Proclamation.

THOMAS NELSON COMMUNITY COLLEGE
99 Thomas Nelson Dr., Hampton and
Historic Triangle Center
161-C John Jefferson Square
Williamsburg
(757) 825-2700
www.tncc.cc.va.us

Thomas Nelson was a signer of the Declaration of Independence. The community college in Hampton that bears his name was established in 1967, granting associate degrees in 36 fields and more than 38 certificates in career-related areas, including administrative support technology, automotive career studies, and information systems technology. Six of the associate degree programs are transferable to a four-year college. (*NOTE*: If you are looking for a place to stay while you are in Hampton Roads, try the Marl Inn in Yorktown. Owner Tom Nelson is a direct descendant of this college's namesake.)

A satellite campus opened in Williamsburg in 1999 to provide service to residents in the Williamsburg–James City County–York County area after having offered a limited schedule of evening classes at various locations in the area for 30 years.

Located in the Busch Corporate Center off US Route 60 near Busch Gardens, the office provides one-stop admissions, registration, academic assessment, counseling, and book ordering so students do not have to go to the Hampton campus, about 30 miles away, for any services. The new location allows TNCC to offer classes at the Historic Triangle location on both day and evening schedules. Additional evening courses are offered at Lafayette High School and Jamestown High School and on the campus of the College of William and Mary. Students also are able to enroll in a growing number of distance learning courses the college now offers via television and the Internet.

Like the campus in Hampton, the Historic Triangle operation provides a full range of workforce training, economic development, and employment skills to its community. It also offers courses that transfer to other colleges and universities and count toward degrees past the associate degree. In fact, it's possible for students to complete three transfer degrees—in liberal arts, science, and business administration—at the Historic Triangle Center and to take many other courses, ranging from computing and small-business development to childhood development, without leaving Williamsburg.

Another benefit of Historic Triangle campus is dual enrollment arranged through the high schools, allowing students in certified high school courses to take those courses for college credit. Senior citizens may take courses at TNCC on a space-available basis without paying tuition under a program the college offers.

ELEMENTARY AND SECONDARY EDUCATION

Anyone who's visited the Williamsburg area within the last couple of years can confirm that the area is experiencing a growth phenomenon unlike anything since the founding of the colonial capital city in 1699. With the influx of new homes and businesses come children—in all developmental stages and grade levels. Area school systems have had to grapple with the dilemma of where and when to build new schools and, of course, how to pay for them. As the public schools get more crowded, the private schools have had more applications than ever, and all have waiting lists. To accommodate a growing population, even the private schools have expansion projects in the works.

Two public school systems serve the Williamsburg area's kids: The **Williamsburg–James City County Public Schools** division is a unified system that serves the majority of students in the area from kindergarten through high school. The York County school system serves the balance of students from families living in the northern and eastern portions of the Historic Triangle.

Williamsburg–James City County operates 14 schools: 3 high schools, 3 middle schools, and 8 elementary schools. Students are assigned to schools through a districting formula that is revisited regularly to ensure enrollment balance for each school.

A seven-member school board governs the system, which is run by a superintendent and staff. The five representatives of James City County are elected, while the two city representatives are appointed to the school board. All public meetings of the school board are televised on the W-JCC Schools cable channel.

The system is fully networked and computerized, with each school sporting a Web site of its own. More important, interested individuals can access information on anything from curriculum, the school calendar, block scheduling, sporting events, and programming by surfing the Internet. The Web address is www.wjcc.k12 .va.us/. Here you can learn about everything from the teacher evaluation process to the division's Strategic Plan. There are links to each school Web site, all administrators, and allied organizations such as parent organizations, scholarship groups, and more. Information is available on programs such as Bright Beginnings, a W-JCC preschool program based at Rawls Byrd Elementary School that helps promote the achievement of at-risk children, and programs designed for gifted and talented children as well as preschoolers with a wide range of disabilities.

One of the most important online features of W-JCC Schools is its 24-hour Information Hotline, which also can be accessed by calling (757) 259-4154. Here parents and students can get up-to-the-minute information on school closings and delayed openings in case of inclement weather. They can offer suggestions and pick up school-related announcements and, of special interest to students, birthday listings. Student birthdays also are televised on the W-JCC Schools cable channel.

Options for high school students include advanced-placement courses, vocational education, technology education, business, practical nursing, and fine arts sequences. The school district's graduation rate is about 97 percent. Approximately 90 percent of its graduates go on to some form of higher education.

Student services are multitudinous and include special education, psychological services, the Pre/GED Program, substance abuse prevention, health services, school social work services, adult education, and dropout prevention.

For information on specific schools, you can call the school directly or visit each school's Web site, which is accessed through the Web address listed earlier.

An important component of local public education is the Williamsburg–James City County Education Association, an active advocate for high-quality public education locally. It supports rigorous standards and seeks to develop, maintain, and strengthen meaningful partnerships between parents, the community, and educators. It is a local affiliate of the Virginia Education Association and the National Education Association. WJCEA is governed by an executive board, which is elected each year by the membership.

York County Public Schools

The York County school system is a large division that covers a vast area. It includes the territory bounded by Hampton on the south and east and Newport News and James City on the western and northern perimeters, and encompasses several military installations such as Langley Air Force Base, Cheatham Annex, the Yorktown Coast Guard Station, and Yorktown Weapons Station.

The system operates 21 schools, including 6 high schools, 4 middle schools, and 11 elementary schools. It is a large system, governed by a five-member school board and run by a superintendent and staff. One member represents each of the county's five election districts. The board meets monthly, usually on the fourth Monday of each month, for its regular meeting. The public is welcome to attend; the meetings are also televised on local cable television.

Known for academic excellence, the York schools division was listed by *Money* magazine as one of the "Top 100" school divisions nationwide in towns you can afford. It has achieved 100 percent accreditation by the Southern Association of Colleges and Schools and is a seven-time winner of the What Parents Want award given by *SchoolMatch* magazine to less than 15 percent of all school divisions nationwide.

While there are more than 12,000 students who attend York public schools, the vast majority of them live outside of the greater Williamsburg area. Residents of upper York County near Williamsburg enjoy a zoning plan designed to let children attend the schools that are closest to their homes. This plan routes students of Waller Mill and Magruder Elementary Schools to Queens Lake Middle School and Bruton High School.

The system is computer networked and the division has a large, easily accessible Web site at http://yorkcountyschools.org. On the site, you can access administrators and learn about each school and the vast array of special programs the division offers. This includes such special programs as adult education, gifted education, the Governor's School, the honors program, New Horizons, NJROTC, the York County School of the Arts, the TV Broadcast Center, the Lifelong Learning Center, special education, and vocational education programs.

For information on registration call the school board office, located at 302 Dare Rd., at (757) 898-0300. For information on specific schools, log onto the Web site.

Private Schools

Approximately 1,300 children in the Williamsburg area attend private schools. These include the oldest private school—Walsingham Academy—and two other private institutions, one local, the other on the lower peninsula.

Neither Williamsburg Christian Academy nor Walsingham Academy provide transportation for students. Hampton Roads Academy, about 25 miles east, does have bus service available for students in the Williamsburg area.

Christ Church School, which is a coeducational, private boarding school on the Northern Neck in King and Queen County, recently has enrolled a couple of Williamsburg area students as well.

HAMPTON ROADS ACADEMY
739 Academy Lane, Newport News
(757) 884-9100
www.HRA.org

Founded in 1959, Hampton Roads Academy, or HRA as it's referred to locally, celebrated its 50th anniversary in 2009. It has an enrollment of more than 475 students, many of whom commute 30 miles from the Greater Williamsburg area to attend school. The academy offers a curriculum for students in grades 6 through 12. From its inception HRA has stood for excellence in college preparatory education and has earned the designation as a "Blue Ribbon School" from the U.S. Department of Education. Hampton Roads Academy is fully accredited by the Virginia Association of Independent Schools. HRA appeals to a wide cross section of students because of its broad-based athletics, arts, and music programs; commitment to community service; small class size; active Honor Council and honor code; and reputation for sending 100 percent of its graduates to four-year colleges and universities. It offers bus service from Williamsburg. HRA completed a $2 million wing that houses a new library, computer center, and classrooms.

i The College of William and Mary offers a youth enrichment program each summer. The Center for Gifted Education at the School of Education runs the activity in July. Gifted and talented students in pre-K through 10th grade are eligible for the course, which offers 20 hours of content instruction. Call (757) 221-2362 for more details.

WALSINGHAM ACADEMY
1100 Jamestown Rd.
(757) 229-6026, (757) 229-2642
www.walsingham.org
Established in 1948 and directed by the Sisters of Mercy in partnership with a lay faculty, Walsingham is committed to the education and development of the whole person through a caring, value-centered, high-standard curriculum, emphasizing responsible leadership in an increasingly complex world. This independent, coeducational institution offers an elementary as well as a college preparatory high school, and while it is a Catholic academy, it is open to students of various faiths. Its spirit of ecumenism and a strong sense of community, which provides an environment of friendship, care, and concern, characterize the quality of life at Walsingham. The academy stresses academic distinction and self-discipline, encouraging all to rise to their fullest potential. The Mercy heritage of compassion and service is reflected in the school's outreach programs, which extend to the larger community of town, nation, and world. The student/teacher ratio is 20 to 1. This fully accredited school completed a multimillion-dollar sports facility and indoor gym complex for the Upper School and a $1 million renovation of the Lower School. Nearly all of Walsingham's graduates move on to excellent colleges and universities. Enrollment is limited. We recommend application at the earliest possible time: for the Lower School, when students are a year or two out; for the Upper School, at the end of the year prior to the fall in which they wish to attend.

WILLIAMSBURG CHRISTIAN ACADEMY
309 Waltz Farm Dr.
(757) 220-1978
Another private school option is Williamsburg Christian. Opened in 1978, this school focuses on Christian values and Biblical viewpoints. The academy, which in 1992 became an independent, interdenominational Christian school with no church affiliation, is located in the former Jamestown Academy adjacent to Skipwith Farms. New additions to the school have enabled it to increase enrollment and expand on the variety and scope of programs offered students. The school accepts students from four-year-old preschoolers through 12th graders. Williamsburg Christian Academy boasts a 13 to 1 student/teacher ratio.

HEALTH CARE

The Williamsburg area has become known for things other than tourism in the past 20 years—as a bedroom community for both Richmond and Hampton Roads, and as a mecca for second-home owners and early retirees (must be that "play golf 11 months a year" thing).

Those two factors have combined to nearly double the region's population, and to skew its age higher than the median for Virginia. In turn, that has led to an explosion in health-care facilities in the area. Two competing groups—Norfolk-based Sentara Healthcare, and Newport News–based Riverside Health Systems—have fought to years to become the dominant system in the area, building or planning a range of new facilities—specialty physician offices, outpatient surgery and treatment centers, and not one but two full-service hospitals.

As a result, the Williamsburg area offers virtually every medical service available in major metro areas.

The centerpiece of medical services, at the moment, is the new Sentara Williamsburg Regional Medical Center. It opened in 2006 as part of a 120-acre medical campus off Mooretown Road in York County.

The $96.4 million facility has 145 acute-care beds, and is surrounded by an outpatient care center, physician offices, and other ancillary services. It replaced the Williamsburg Community Hospital, originally built in 1961, near the William and Mary campus.

Riverside is building, too, convincing state officials in 2009 of the need for a second hospital in Williamsburg. Doctors Hospital—a $72 million, 40-bed facility near the junction of US Route 60 and Virginia Route 199, not far from Kingsmill and Busch Gardens, is expected to open in early 2012.

HOSPITALS

SENTARA WILLIAMSBURG REGIONAL MEDICAL CENTER
100 Sentara Circle
(757) 984-6000
www.sentara.com/williamsburg
Needs that can't be met in Williamsburg are provided at other regional hospitals, including the Medical College of Virginia in Richmond; the Children's Hospital of the King's Daughters in Norfolk; Mary Immaculate and Riverside hospitals in Newport News; and Riverside Walter Reed Hospital in Gloucester.

Emergency transport services include state-of-the-art ambulances and Nightingale helicopters, depending upon the urgency of care.

URGENT HEALTH CARE

The best location for a true medical emergency is the emergency room of Sentara Williamsburg Regional Medical Center, but minor and immediate-attention medical issues—minor cuts, injuries, or illnesses can be handled at these "urgent care" centers. All offer a variety of diagnostic tools, including X-rays, and can see patients without appointments.

FIRST MED OF WILLIAMSBURG
312 Second St.
(757) 229-4141
On the side of the city closest to Busch Gardens and Water Country USA, this clinic is open 9 a.m. to 6 p.m. Mon through Fri and 9 a.m. to 1 p.m. Sat. Closed Sun.

MEDEXPRESS WILLIAMSBURG
120 Monticello Ave.
(757) 564-3627
This facility is just northwest of downtown, not far from the intersection of the US 60 bypass and Richmond Road. Open daily 9 a.m. to 9 p.m., except Thanksgiving and Christmas.

RIVERSIDE URGENT CARE CENTER
Williamsburg Crossing Shopping Center
5231 John Tyler Hwy
(757) 220-8300
Riverside is particularly convenient to the James-town Road side of town and the Route 5 corridor. The hours are 8 a.m. to 6 p.m. Mon through Fri, 10 a.m. to 4 p.m. Sat, and noon to 4 p.m. Sun.

SENTARA NEW TOWN URGENT CARE
4374 New Town Ave., Suite 100
(757) 259-1900
This facility, affiliated with the hospital, opened in 2008 in the New Town mixed-use development, just west of downtown off Ironbound Road. It's part of a 50,000 square-foot complex of doctors' offices and medical facilities. Hours are 8 a.m. to 8 p.m. Mon through Fri; and 10 a.m. to 4 p.m. weekends.

CHILD CARE

While word of mouth remains one of the best ways to find good child care, newcomers may not be sure whose recommendations to trust. The majority of child care centers are licensed by the state, and there are two ways to get current information about providers in whom you have an interest. Several options for finding local care providers are available as parents begin their search. In the Williamsburg area, **Child and Family Connection** is your best bet for accurate, up-to-date information on daily child care or babysitting services. A locally based research and referral agency, it maintains a list of commercial and private day-care providers. Of course, you can also contact the **National Association for the Education of Young Children**, which also can provide information on child care options.

i Need assistance with an issue that doesn't necessarily involve a doctor—a support group, for example, or a referral to an agency that can help you deal with a loved one's issue? Any number of support groups and service agencies are available in and around Williamsburg. A good starting point to find one is the United Way of Greater Williamsburg and its Information and Referral Center. It's available 9 a.m. to 3:30 p.m. weekdays, at (757) 229-2222; more information, including a downloadable directory of organizations, is available at www.uwgw.org.

MEDIA

Williamsburg's location smack between two metro areas leaves it in an odd position: It can get radio and TV from both—but has relatively few sources of truly local information. Here's a quick review of the media sources available to visitors and newcomers.

NEWSPAPERS

DAILY PRESS
7505 Warwick Blvd.,
Newport News
(757) 247-4800, (757) 247-4600
www.dailypress.com

The *Daily Press* is the daily newspaper serving the Virginia Peninsula, including Williamsburg, and Gloucester and Isle of Wight Counties. It's owned by Tribune Company, a multimedia company that owns newspapers and television stations throughout the United States. The newspaper has a small team of reporters assigned to cover Williamsburg and York County and is widely circulated through the Historic Triangle.

FLAT HAT
College of William and Mary
P.O. Box 8795, Williamsburg, VA 23187
(757) 221-3281
http://flathat.wm.edu

The *Flat Hat,* the college's student paper, is published each Friday during the regular academic year. It's a quintessential student newspaper, expounding on events useful and controversial from the student perspective. It also lists upcoming performances, lectures, and programs presented by faculty, students, national performing troupes, and artists, as well as by myriad local organizations.

RICHMOND TIMES-DISPATCH
401 Duke of Gloucester St.
Williamsburg
(757) 229-1512
www.timesdispatch.com

The Richmond paper, owned by Media General, is the daily newspaper in the state capitol of Richmond. It's widely available at news boxes and stores in the Williamsburg area, but has a limited amount of local news. Home delivery is available.

VIRGINIA GAZETTE
216 Ironbound Rd., Williamsburg
(757) 220-1736, (800) 944-6908
www.vagazette.com

Virginia Gazette, is a twice-weekly newspaper that covers only local news. Like many small-town weeklies, it has its quirks—but for decades no one has covered Williamsburg as well. The paper, like the town, also takes its history very seriously: The *Gazette* was first published in 1736, and likes to style itself as America's oldest non-daily newspaper. It hits the streets each Wed and Sat.

The paper is regarded as a public forum where readers comment freely and regularly on everything from local politics to their experiences as visitors. (The anonymous comments in the Last Word section, typically published on the back page, can range from amusing to downright scurrilous.) While it is owned by Tribune Company, the same owner as the nearly *Daily Press* in the Lower Peninsula, the papers have separate newsrooms and content.

The *Gazette* it is also a gold mine for information on attractions, local restaurants, places to stay, what special events are on tap during your stay in the area and the real-estate market.

VIRGINIAN-PILOT
150 West Brambleton Ave., Norfolk
(757) 446-2000, (800) 446-2004
www.pilotonline.com

Owned by Norfolk-based Landmark Communications, the *Pilot* (as it's known) is the largest daily newspaper in Virginia. It covers all of Hampton Roads and the northeastern portion of North Carolina, but no local coverage of Williamsburg. It's available at newsstands and stores only.

WILLIAMSBURG-YORKTOWN DAILY.COM
5000 New Point Rd., Suite 2201
Williamsburg, VA 23188
(757) 565-1079

We could get all philosophical with questions about whether a newspaper is a newspaper if it's not published on paper. Instead, we'll simply highlight this terrific Web site, which publishes a flow of continuously updated, professionally produced news. Unlike the *Gazette*, whose Web site is rarely updated between print editions, WYDaily.com publishes several stories a day as they become available.

The site was launched in 2008 by Tom Davis, owner of two local radio stations, to provide another source of local news. It also features a variety of special offers from advertisers, including 30 percent off gift certificates at many area merchants.

MAGAZINES

HAMPTON ROADS MAGAZINE
1264 Perimeter Parkway
Virginia Beach, VA 23454
(757) 422-8979, (800) 422-0742
www.hrmag.com

This glossy regional magazine covers features, dining, arts, and entertainment throughout Hampton Roads, with a particular focus on Norfolk and Virginia Beach. Because of the upscale nature of Williamsburg, however, Williamsburg restaurants and entertainment are frequently featured. It's available on newsstands throughout the region, and is published eight times a year by the same company that now produces *The Official Williamsburg/Jamestown/Yorktown Visitors Guide*.

THE OFFICIAL WILLIAMSBURG/JAMESTOWN/ YORKTOWN VISITORS GUIDE
1915 Pocahontas Trail, Suite E-3
Williamsburg
(757) 229-8508

Helpful and readily available, especially in area hotels and motels, is this free, glossy magazine for visitors. It's produced by the publishers of *Hampton Roads Magazine* in cooperation with the Williamsburg Area Hotel & Motel Association. It comes out three times a year with updates on what's new at local attractions, and the advertising is especially helpful when you're looking for something specific.

WILLIAMSBURG MAGAZINE
216 Ironbound Rd., Williamsburg
(757) 220-1736
www.williamsburgmag.com

The monthly *Williamsburg Magazine*, published by the *Virginia Gazette*, is designed for tourists and those relocating to the area. It includes a variety of feature stories about the region and its attractions, lists of upcoming events—and is a great source of coupons and special offers from regional merchants. It's free, and is widely distributed at news racks, stores, hotels, and tourist attractions.

RADIO STATIONS

Three radio stations are based in Williamsburg, but because of its proximity to both the Hampton Roads and Richmond media markets, more than two dozen are available. We'll touch on the local stations in depth, and list the others by their program format.

WCWM, 90.1 FM
www.wcwm.org

College radio in all its glory: An eclectic mix running from indie rock to techno and hip-hop. The station also programs a variety of locally produced news and public affairs shows.

WTYD, 92.3 FM, THE TIDE
www.tideradio.com

"The Tide" is the primary locally programmed FM serving Williamsburg. It plays what it likes to call "hand-picked music"—a blend of contemporary and older rock, blues and folk, reminiscent of free-form FM stations from the early 1970s. It wears its localness on its sleeve—primary owner Tom Davis moved to the region when he bought the station, and lined up a group of local investors (including musician Bruce Hornsby). The station also covers local news in a way most radio groups don't any more, and uses its news updates to power a news website, WYDaily.com.

WXGM, 99.1 FM, XTRA 99.1, GLOUCESTER
While not technically a Williamsburg station (it's actually headquartered in Gloucester, across the York River), this station includes the Historic Triangle in its target audience. It plays a mix of light pop and rock, known in the trade as "adult contemporary."

WBQK, 107.9 FM, "BACH-FM"
As the name implies, "Bach-FM" plays classical music. It's owned by the same group as The Tide, and also broadcasts local news updates mornings and afternoons.

WMBG, 740 AM
This locally owned AM plays "golden oldies"—nostalgic music from the 1930s through 1950s. It has relatively low power, especially at night, making reception tricky.

Elsewhere on the dial, you can find these types of music and programming (this isn't a complete list; it attempts to cover the stations with the best signal into Williamsburg and the most-popular programming styles).

NOTE: Most stations carry the same traffic reports from an outside provider; but the State Department of Transportation offers updated traffic alerts at 610 AM in Hampton Roads and at 1620 AM in Richmond.

Adult contemporary/R&B
WKJM, 99.3/105.7 FM, Kiss-FM, Richmond
WKUS, 105.3 FM, 105.3 Kiss-FM, Norfolk

Adult contemporary/soft rock
WTVR, 98.1 FM, Lite 98, Richmond
WVBW, 92.9 FM, The Wave, Norfolk
WWDE, 101.3 FM, 2WD, Norfolk

Christian
WAUQ, 89.7 FM, Richmond
WRJR, 1010 AM, Norfolk

Classical
WHRO, 90.3 FM, Norfolk

Classic rock/classic hits
WAFX, 106.9 FM, The Fox, Norfolk
WKLR, 96.5 FM, 96-5 KLR, Richmond
WNOB, 93.7 FM, Bob FM, Norfolk
WWLB, 98.9 FM, 98-9 Liberty, Richmond

Contemporary Christian/inspirational
WGH-AM, 1310 AM, Star 1310

Contemporary hits/Top 40
WBTJ, 106.5 FM, The Beat, Richmond
WCDX, 92.1 FM, iPower 92-1, Richmond
WMXB, 103.7 FM, Mix 103-7, Richmond
WNVZ, 104.5 FM, Z104, Norfolk
WOWI, 102.9 FM, 103 Jamz, Norfolk
WPTE, 94.9 FM, The Point, Norfolk
WRVQ, 94.5 FM, Q94, Richmond
WVHT, 100.5 FM, Hot 100.5, Norfolk
WVKL, 95.7 FM, 95-7 R&B, Norfolk

Country
WGH, 97.3 FM, 97-3 The Eagle, Norfolk
WKHK, 95.3 FM, K-95, Richmond
WUSH, 106.1 FM, US106, Norfolk

Modern Rock
WDYL, 100.9 FM, Y-101, Richmond
WNOR, 98.7 FM, FM99, Norfolk
WROX, 96.1 FM, 96X, Norfolk
WRXL, 102.1 FM, The X, Richmond

National Public Radio/public affairs
WCVE, 88.9 FM, Richmond
WHRV, 89.5 FM, Norfolk

News/talk
WLEE, 990 AM, Richmond
WNIS, 790 AM, Norfolk
WRVA, 1140 AM, Richmond
WTAR, 850 AM, Norfolk
WTPS, 1240 AM, Richmond

Smooth Jazz
WJCD, 107.7 GM, Smooth Jazz 107.7, Norfolk

Spanish Language
WTOX, 1480 AM, La Equis
WVNZ, 1320 AM, Selecta 1320
WVXX, 1050 AM, Selecta 1050

Sports/Talk
WRNL, 910 AM, Richmond's Fox Sports, Richmond
WVSP, 94.1 FM, 94.1 ESPN, Norfolk
WXGI, 950 AM, ESPN 950, Richmond
WXTG, 102.1 FM and 1490 AM, The Game, Norfolk/Hampton

TELEVISION STATIONS

As with radio, residents of Williamsburg and the surrounding area can pick up television stations from both Norfolk and Richmond. (The dominant local cable-TV provider, Cox Cable, only carries the Norfolk stations, however.)

WTKR Channel 3 (CBS), Norfolk
WSKY Channel 4 (Independent), Norfolk
WTVR Channel 6 (CBS), Richmond
WRIC Channel 8 (ABC), Richmond
WAVY Channel 10 (NBC), Norfolk
WWBT Channel 12 (NBC), Richmond
WVEC Channel 13 (ABC), Norfolk
WHRO Channel 15 (PBS), Norfolk
WCVE Channel 23 (PBS), Richmond
WGNT Channel 27 (UPN), Norfolk
WTVZ Channel 33 (MyNetwork), Norfolk
WRLH Channel 35 (FOX), Richmond
WVBT Channel 43 (FOX), Norfolk
WZTD Channel 45 (Telemundo), Richmond
WUPV Channel 47 (CW), Richmond
WPXV Channel 49 (Ion), Virginia Beach

INDEX

A

Abbitt Realty Company Inc., 217

Abby Aldrich Rockefeller Folk Art Museum, 94

Aberdeen Barn, 45

accommodations, 15. See bed-and-breakfasts and guest homes

Act II, 169

Adam's Hunt, 209

African American Experience, The, 95

African-American Music, 96

AirCanada, 12

Airport Express, 10

AirTran, 8

air transportation, 8

Alamo car rentals, 9, 12

Alice Person House, 30

American Airlines, 9, 12

American Indian museums, 135

American Indian tribes, 134

American Theatre, The, 164

AMF Williamsburg Lanes, 132, 180

Amtrak, 12

amusement parks, 103

Andrews Gallery, 148

annual events, 149

Antiques Forum, 149

antiques stores, 75

Applewood Colonial Bed and Breakfast, 30

Archer Cottage, 120

Aroma's Coffeehouse, Café and Bake Shop, 45

Artcafé26, 46

art galleries, 76, 148

art museums, 146

Art on the Lawn, 151

arts, the, 143

arts venues, 143

Astronomical Pancake House, The, 65

Atlantic Waterfowl Heritage Museum, 203

Attic Collections, 75

attractions, 84

attractions for kids, 130

Augustine Moore House, The, 120

Avis car rentals, 9, 12

B

babysitting services, 21

Back Creek Park, 174, 183

Backfin Seafood Restaurant, The, 47

Bacon's Castle, 190

Baker's Crust, 47

Banbury Cross, 209

bar-b-que, 42

Barnes and Noble, 77

Barnes & Noble, 77

Baron Woods, 209

Bassett Hall, 94

Bassett Motel, 16

Bassett's Christmas Shop, 78

Battle of Yorktown, 122

Bay Days, 153

Bayside Inn, 197

Beach Bully Bar-B-Que, 206

Bead Store, The, 169

bed-and-breakfasts, 30. See accommodations

Belle Aire Plantation, 99

Bently Manor Inn, 31

Berkeley Plantation, 99

Berkeley's Green, 209

Berkeley William E. Wood & Associates Realtors, 217

Berret's Seafood Restaurant and Taphouse Grill, 47

Bertram & Williams Books and Fine Art, 76, 77

Best Western Historic Area Inn, 16

Bikes Unlimited, 179

biking, 179

Binn's, 73

Birchwood Park, 209

Black Angus Grille, 48

Bluebird Gap Farm, 164

Blue Skies Gallery, 170

Blue Talon Bistro, 48

Book Exchange, 77

Bookpress Ltd., The, 77

Books-A-Million, 78

bookstores, 76

bowling, 180

Boxwood Inn of Williamsburg, A, 31

Brandon Woods, 209

Bray Bistro, The, 59

breweries, 109

Brunswick stew, 41

Bruton Parish Church, 88, 98

Buckroe Beach, 171

Budget car rentals, 9, 12

Budget Inn, 16

Busch Gardens, 103

bus transportation, 12

C

Camp Peary, 140

Campus Shop, The, 73

Candy Store, The, 79

Canterbury Hills, 210

Capitol, 89

Captain George's Seafood Restaurant, 49

Carlton Farms, 131, 182

Carousel Children's Clothier, 73

car rentals, 9, 12

Carrot Tree Kitchens, 49, 118, 125

Casemate Museum, 141, 164

Cedars of Williamsburg, The, 32

Cedar Valley Farm, 131, 182

Center Street Grill, 49

Chambrel at Williamsburg, 222

Chanco's Grant, 210

Charles Brown Park, 174, 183

Charles City Tavern, 44, 50
Charles H. Taylor Arts Center, 164
Charlie's Antiques and Amazing Stones, 75, 80
Charly's, 50
Cheese Shop, The, 50
Chef's Kitchen, A, 51
Chelsea's Closet, 169
Chez Trinh, 52
Chickahominy Haven, 210
Chickahominy tribe, 134
Child and Family Connection, 21, 232
child care, 232
children's activities. See kidstuff
Children's Festival of Friends, 151
Chippokes Plantation Christmas, 191
Chippokes Plantation State Park, 190
Chisman Creek Park, 175
Chowning's Tavern, 54
Christiana Campbell's Tavern, 54
Christmas all year stores, 78
Christmas Eve Tree Lighting Ceremony, 156
Christmas in Colonial Williamsburg, 93
Christmas Mouse, 78
Christmas Shop, The, 76, 78
Christopher Newport University, 226
Christopher Wren Association for Lifelong Learning, The, 221
Chrysler Museum, The, 198
churches, 98
Cities Grille and Wine Shop, 52
City Center, 168
Civil War and Native American Store and Gallery, 83
Clarion Hotel—Historic District, 16
Classic Cravats, 73
clothing stores, 73
Cobble Creek, 210

Coffeehouse, The, 52
Coldwell Banker Professional Realtors, 217
Coliseum Central, 170
College Delly, 53
College Landing Park, 175
College of William and Mary, 225
Colonel Waller Motel, 16
Colonial Capital Bed and Breakfast, 32
Colonial Gardens Bed & Breakfast, 33
Colonial Golf Club, The, 185
Colonial Houses, 18
Colonial Nursery, 72
Colonial Pancake House, The, 65
Colonial Parkway, 10
Colonial Post Office, 72
Colonial Williamsburg, 84
Colonial Williamsburg annual events, 97
Colonial Williamsburg Brickyard, 96
Colonial Williamsburg buildings, 88, 92
Colonial Williamsburg churches, 98
Colonial Williamsburg evening events, 96
Colonial Williamsburg exhibits, 92
Colonial Williamsburg family programs, 95
Colonial Williamsburg Fifes & Drums, The, 97
Colonial Williamsburg gardens, 91
Colonial Williamsburg lodgings, 18
Colonial Williamsburg mercantile shops, 92
Colonial Williamsburg taverns, 54
Colonial Williamsburg trade shops and demonstrations, 92
Colonial Williamsburg Visitor Center, 87
Comfort Inn—Central, 17

Comfort Inn—Historic Area, 17
Comfort Suites, 17
Comic Cubicle, 78
Computer Literacy Training, 220
Confederate Attack on Fort Pocahontas at Wilson's Wharf, 151
Continental Airlines, 9, 12
Cooke's Christmas, 78, 118
Corner Pocket, The, 53, 67
Country Hearth Inn & Suites, 17
Country Inn & Suites by Carlson Williamsburg East, 20
Country Inn & Suites by Carlson Williamsburg Historic Area, 20
County Grill & Smokehouse, 42
Courthouse, 92
Cousteau Society, 165
Couture Cakes, 169
Coves, The, 210
Crab Shack on the James, 45
craft stores, 76
Cromwell Ridge, 210
Crowne Plaza Williamsburg Hotel and Conference Center, 20
Cry Witch, 96
cuisine, regional. See regional cuisine
C. W. Cowling's, 194

D
Daily Press, 233
dance, 145
Dance, Our Dearest Diversion, 97
d'Art Center, 198
Days Inn—Central, 20
Days Inn—Colonial Downtown, 20
Days Inn—Colonial Resort, 21
Days Inn—Historic Area, 21
day trips, 189
Delta Airlines, 8, 9, 12
DeWitt Cottage, 203

DeWitt Wallace Decorative Arts Museum, 95, 146
Diascund Reservoir, 175
Dining Room at Ford's Colony, 45, 53
dinner theater, 69
Discovery, 116
Dollar car rentals, 10, 12
Dominion Village, 222
Doraldo's, 53
Douglas MacArthur Memorial, 199
Doumar's Cones & Barbecue, 202
driving directions to Williamsburg area, 7
Druid Hills, 210
Duke of York Motor Hotel, 126

E
Eagles, 59
Eastern Chickahominy tribe, 134
Eastern Virginia School for the Performing Arts, 146
Econo Lodge Parkway/ Historic Area, 22
Edgar Cayce's Association for Research and Enlightenment (A.R.E.), 204
Edgewood Plantation, 33, 100
education, 225
Edwards' Virginia Ham Shoppe of Williamsburg, 79
18th-Century Play Series: Polly Honeycombe, 97
elementary and secondary education, 228
Emancipation Oak, 166
Embassy Suites— Williamsburg, 22
Emerald Thai, 54
Endview Plantation, 160
Enterprise car rentals, 9, 10, 12
Everything Williamsburg, 74
Envoy of Williamsburg, 223
Executive Homes Realty, 217

F
Fairfield Inn and Suites, 22
Fall Festival and Powwow, 153

Fall Festival of Folklife, 154
Family Life at the Benjamin Powell Site, 96
Family Life at the Geddy Site, 96
Farmhouse, The, 80
Fat Canary, 55
Fernbrook, 211
Fieldcrest, 211
Fife and Drum Inn, 34
50 Plus Group, The, 221
First Baptist Church, The, 98
First Landing State Park, 204
First Med of Williamsburg, 231
First Night of Williamsburg, 156
fishing and hunting, 180
Flat Hat, 233
Food & Feasts of Colonial Virginia, 155
Food for Thought, 56
food stores, 73
Ford's Colony, 211
Ford's Colony Country Club, 185
Fort Boykin Historic Park, 193
Fort Eustis, 140
Fort Fun, 162, 171
Fort Monroe, 141
Founding Fathers, 127
Fox & Grape Bed & Breakfast, 34
Fox Ridge, 211
Francis Land Historical House and History Park and Nature Trail, 204
Fresh Market, 79
Frontier Airlines, 8

G
Gabriel Archer Tavern at the Williamsburg Winery, 56
Garden Symposium, 151
Gazebo House of Pancakes and Waffles, The, 65
G. Bates Studio Workshop, 74
George Wythe House, 89
gifts and accessories stores, 73
Gin Tail Antiques, 127

Giuseppe's Italian Cafe, 56
Gloucester Daffodil Festival, 150
Godspeed, 116
Go-Karts Plus, 130
Golden Ball Shop, 72
Golden Horseshoe Clubhouse Grille, 57
Golden Horseshoe Golf Course, The, 186
golf, 185
golf courses, 185
Good Fortune, 167
Governor's Land at Two Rivers, The, 211
Governor's Palace, 89
Governor's Trace, 34
Grace Episcopal Church, 120
Grand Medley of Entertainments, A, 97
Grandview Nature Preserve, 172
Graylin Woods, 211
Greater Williamsburg YMCA, 178
Great Hopes Plantation, 93
Great Wolf Lodge, 22
Greek Festival, 152
Greenhow Store, 72
Green Leafe Cafe, 57, 68
Greensprings Plantation, 211
Greensprings Trail, The, 175
Greyhound Bus System, 12
groceries and specialty food stores, 79
Groome Transportation, 12
GSH Real Estate, Williamsburg Office, 217
Guardhouse, 90
guest homes. See private guest homes

H
ham, 42
Hampton, 70, 158, 164, 167, 170, 171, 172
Hampton attractions, 164
Hampton beaches, 171
Hampton Carousel Park, 165
Hampton Coliseum, 70
Hampton Cup Regatta, 153

Hampton History Museum, 165

Hampton Inn & Suites—Central, 23

Hampton Inn & Suites—Historic District, 23

Hampton Inn & Suites—Williamsburg, 23

Hampton Jazz Festival, 152

Hampton National Cemetery, 141

Hampton parks, 172

Hampton restaurants, 167

Hampton Roads Academy, 229

Hampton Roads Magazine, 234

Hampton shopping, 170

Hampton Tourism, 160

Hampton University, 226

Hampton University Museum, 135, 165

Hampton Visitors Center, 160

Harbor Park, 199

Harbour Coffee, 57

Harpoon Larry's Oyster Bar, 168

Harrison Opera House, 70

Haunted Dinner Theater, 69

Hayashi Japanese Restaurant & Sushi Bar, 57

health and fitness clubs, 181

health care, 231

Heritage Landing, 211

Hertz car rentals, 9, 10, 12

Hickory Neck Episcopal Church, 98

Hilda Crockett's Chesapeake House, 195

Hilton Garden Inn, 23

Hilton Village, 169

Historic Area attractions, 88

Historic Area shopping, 72

Historic Garden Week, 151

Historic Ghent, 199

history, 2

Holiday Inn—Gateway, 24

Holiday Inn—Patriot, 24

Holly Hills of Williamsburg, 211

home furnishings stores, 79

Homewood Suites by Hilton, 24

Hornsby Real Estate Co., 217

horseback riding, 182

horseback riding for kids, 130

hospitals, 231

hotels and motels. *See* accommodations

Howard Johnson, 24

Hughes Guest Home, 39

Hunter's Creek, 212

Huntington Park, 171

Huntington Park Beach, 170

I

I Must Say, 74

Independence Day Celebration, 153

Independence Day Festivities, 153

Indigo Park, 212

Inn at 802, The, 35

Institute for Dance, The, 146

Iron-Bound Gym, 181

Isle of Wight County Museum, 193

J

James City County District Park Sports Complex, 175

James City County Division of Parks and Recreation Youth Soccer League, 182

James City County Fair, 152

James City County Parks and Recreation, 174

James City County—Williamsburg Community Center, 131, 178, 182

James Fort, 117

James Geddy House and Foundry, 94

James River Community Center, 179

James River Fishing Pier, 171

James River plantations, 99

Jamestown, 112

Jamestown attractions, 114

Jamestown Day, 152

Jamestown driving directions, 113

Jamestown history, 112

Jamestown interpretive programs, 115

Jamestown National Historic Site, 114

Jamestown Pie Company, 58, 118

Jamestown restaurants, 117

Jamestown-Scotland Ferry, 189

Jamestown Settlement, 116, 135

Jamestown Settlement cafe and gift shop, 117

Jamestown ships, 116

Jamestown shopping, 117

Jefferson Restaurant, The, 58

JetBlue, 12

jewelry stores, 75, 80

J. Fenton Gallery, 74

Jimmy's Oven and Grill, 58

J. M. Randalls Classic American Grill & Tavern, 58

J. M. Randalls Restaurant & Tavern, 68

jogging and running, 182

Johnson's Guest Home, 40

K

Ken's Bar-B-Q, 194

Kidsburg, 131

kidstuff, 130

Kiln Creek Park, 175

Kimball Theatre, 69, 143

King's Arms Tavern, 55

Kingsmill Golf Club, 186

Kingsmill on the James, 212

Kingsmill Realty Inc., 217

Kingsmill Resort, 24

Kingsmill Restaurants, 58

Kingsmill Tennis Center, 184

Kingspoint, 212

Kingswood, 212

Kinks, Quirks and Caffeine, 76

Kinks & Quirks Contemporary Handcrafts, 127

Kitchen at Powhatan Plantation, The, 59

Kiwanis Municipal Park, 175, 183

Kristiansand, 212

Kyoto Japanese Steak & Seafood House & Sushi Bar, 59

L

La Bodega Hampton, 170
Lake Toano, 212
Lakewood Trails, 131
Landfall at Jamestown, 212
Langley Air Force Base, 141
La Tolteca, 59
Lee Hall Mansion, 161
Legacy of Williamsburg Bed and Breakfast, The, 35
Le Yaca, 60
Liberty Celebration, 153
Liberty Rose Bed and Breakfast, 36
Lightfoot Antiques Mall & Country General Store, 75
Listen My Children: Legends, Myths, and Fables for Families, 97
Little Creek Reservoir, 181
Little Creek Reservoir Park, 175
Long & Foster Realtors, 218
Longhill Gate, 212

M

MacArthur Center, 199
Magazine, 90
magazines, 234
Mama Steve's House of Pancakes, 65
Manhattan Bagel, 60
Marina Bar & Grille, 59
Mariners' Museum, 136, 161
Marker 20, 168
Marl Inn, 126
Marriott's Manor Club at Ford's Colony, 25
Masonic Procession and Sermon, 152
Master Craftsmen, 80
Mattaponi Indian Museum and Minnie Ha Ha Educational Trading Post, 136
Mattaponi Reservation, 134
Matthew Jones House, 140

Maurizio's, 60
McCormack-Nagelsen Tennis Center, 183
M. Dubois Grocer's Shop, 72
Meadows, The, 213
Meals on Wheels, 220
MedExpress Williamsburg, 232
media, 233
Memorial Day, 152
Merchants Square, 72
Mermaid Books, 78
Mid-Atlantic Quilt Festival Week, 149
Mid County Park, 176, 184
military heritage, 137
Military Life at the Magazine, 96
Military Through the Ages, 150
Mill Creek Landing, 213
Mill, The, 59
Mirror Lake Estates, 213
Miyako Japanese Restaurant, 61
modern attractions, 103
Monacan Indian Nation Headquarters, 135
Moody's Tavern, 59
Moss Cottage, 127
movies, 69
Movie Tavern, 69
Mr. Liu's Chinese Restaurant & Lounge, 61
Muscarelle Museum of Art, 132, 147
music, 144
Mystery Dinner Playhouse, 69

N

Nancy Thomas Gallery, 74, 128, 148
Nansemond tribe, 135
National Association for the Education of Young Children, 232
National car rentals, 9, 10, 12
National Pancake House, 65
National Park Service Yorktown Battlefield Visitor Center, 121

Native Americans. *See* Virginia's Indian Culture or American Indian
Nauticus, 200
Naval Station Norfolk, 141
Naval Weapons Station Yorktown, 142
Navy Weapons Station, Cheatham Annex, 142
Nawab Indian Cuisine, 61
neighborhoods, 209
Nelson House, The, 120
Newport House, 36
Newport News, 158, 160, 168, 170, 171
Newport News attractions, 160
Newport News beaches, 170
Newport News Celebration in Lights, 157
Newport News fishing, 171
Newport News Golf Club at Deer Run, 187
Newport News Park, 172
Newport News parks, 171
Newport News shopping, 168
Newport News Tourism, 160
Newport News Visitor Center, 160
Newport News/Williamsburg International Airport, 8
New Quarter Park, 176
Newsome House Museum and Cultural Center, The, 162
newspapers, 233
New Town, 81
New Town Cinemas 12, 70
New York Deli, 61
Nick's Riverwalk Restaurant and Rivah Café, 125
nightlife, 67
Norfolk, 70, 197
Norfolk attractions, 198
Norfolk Botanical Garden, 200
Norfolk Convention & Visitors Bureau, 198
Norfolk International Airport, 9
Norfolk restaurants, 202
Norfolk Scope and Chrysler Hall, 70

Norge shopping, 80
North Bend Plantation, 37, 100
North Cove, 213
Northwest, 12
Northwest Airlines, 9
Norva, The, 70

O

Occasion for the Arts, An, 154
Official Williamsburg/ Jamestown/Yorktown Vistors Guide, The, 233
O'Keeffe, Georgia, 147
Old Cape Henry Lighthouse, 205
Old Chickahominy House Restaurant & Antiques, 62, 83
Old Coast Guard Station, 205
Old Custom House, 120
Old Hampton, 170
Old Mill House of Pancakes & Waffles, 65
Opus 9, 62
Order in the Court, 96
Original Ghosts of Williamsburg Candlelight Tours, The, 69
outlet shopping, 81

P

Pamunkey Indian Museum, 136
Pamunkey Reservation, 134
pancake tour, 65
Papa Said, Mama Said, 97
Papillon A Bistro, 62
parks and recreation, 174
parks and recreation for kids, 131
parks departments, 174
Pasta E Pani, 206
Patriot Inn & Suites, 25
Patriots Colony, 223
Paul's Deli Restaurant & Pizza, 62, 68
peanuts, 45
Peanut Shop, The, 45
Peking and Mongolian Grill, 62

Peleg's Point, 213
Peninsula Agency on Aging (PAA), 220
Peninsula Fine Arts Center, The, 162
Peninsula Town Center, 170
People of the Past, 96
performing arts, 144
Period Designs, 128
Peyton Randolph House, 90
Phi Beta Kappa Memorial Hall, 143
Piano–Organ Outlet, 81
Pierce's Pitt Bar-B-Que, 43, 63
Piney Creek Estates, 213
Piney Grove at Southall's Plantation, 37, 101
Pirate's Cove Adventure Golf, 130
Plantation Christmas. *See* Chippokes Plantation Christmas
plantations, 99
Plantiques, 169
Poor Potter Site, 120
Poplar Hall, 213
Poquoson Seafood Festival, 154
Port Anne, 213
Port Warwick, 168
Powhatan Creek Access, 176, 181
Powhatan Crossing, 213
Powhatan Place, 214
Powhatan Secondary of Williamsburg, 214
Powhatan Shores, 214
Precious Gem, The, 75
Prentis Store, 72
Presidents Park, 101
Presidents Weekend, 150
Prime Outlets at Williamsburg, 81
Primrose, 170
Prince George Art and Frame, 76
private guest homes, 39
private schools, 229
pronunciation guide, 13
Providence Hall Guesthouses, 18

Prudential McCardle Realty, 218
Public Gaol, 91
Public Hospital of 1773, 95
public schools, 228
public tennis courts, 183

Q

Quality Inn—Colony, 25
Quality Inn—Historic Area, 26
Quality Inn—Kingsmill, 26
Quarterpath Inn, 26
Quarterpath Park, 184
Quarterpath Park and Recreation Center, 176
Queen Anne Dairy Snack, 43
Queens Lake, 214
Queenswood, 214
Quilts Unlimited, 74

R

radio stations, 234
rainy day activities for kids, 132
Rajput Indian Cuisine, 202
Raleigh Tavern, 91
Raleigh Tavern Bakery, 72
Ranger Rick's, 130
Rappahannock Tribal Office, 135
Rare Breeds of Livestock, 96
R. Bryant Ltd., 73
real estate companies, 216
recreation, 179
recreation centers, 178
Regatta's Café, 59
regional cuisine, 41
relocation, 208
Residence Inn by Marriott, 26
restaurants, 45
Retired & Senior Volunteer Program (RSVP), 221
retirement, 219
Retro's, 63
Richmond Hill, 214
Richmond International Airport, 11
Richmond Times-Dispatch, 233
RIDES (Medical Escort Service), 220
River Room, 126

Riverside Adult Services, 220
Riverside Urgent Care Center, 232
Riverwalk Landing, 128
Rocky Mount Bar B-Q House, 43
Rodeway Inn & Suites, 27
Rolling Woods, 214

S

St. George's Hundred, 215
St. John's Episcopal Church, 166
Saint Luke's Shrine, 193
St. Patrick's Day Parade, 150
Sal's by Victor, 63
Sal's Ristorante Italiano, 63
Sandy Bottom Nature Park, 173
Scotland House Ltd., 74
Seafare of Williamsburg, The, 64
seafood, 43
Seasons Cafe Restaurant, 64
Seasons Trace, 215
semiprivate tennis courts, 184
senior activities, 221
Senior Center of York, 222
senior publications, 220
senior services, 220
seniors residential living, 222
Senior Times, 221
Sentara New Town Urgent Care, 232
Sentara Williamsburg Regional Medical Center, 231
Settler's Mill, 215
Shabby Chic, 170
Sherwood Forest Plantation, 102
Shields Tavern, 55
Shirley Metalcraft, 83
Shirley Pewter Shop, 74
Shirley Plantation, 102
shopping, 72
Shops at Carolina Furniture of Williamsburg, The, 79
Silver Vault Ltd., 75
Six Little Bar Bistro, 168
Skate Park, 131
Skimino Hills, 215

Skimino Landing Estates, 215
Skipwith Farms, 215
Sleep Inn Historic, 27
Smithfield, 192
Smithfield and Isle of Wight Convention and Visitors Bureau, 193
Smithfield Confectionery & Ice Cream Parlor, 194
Smithfield Gourmet Bakery and Cafe, 194
Smithfield Ham Shoppe, 73
Smithfield Inn & Tavern, The, 194
Smithfield restaurants, 194
Smithfield Station, 195
Smith Island, 195
Smith Island Center, 196
Smith Island restaurants, 197
Smith's Fort Plantation, 191
soccer, 182
Southwest Airlines, 9
Spring Hill Suites by Marriott, 27
Stars and Stripes Forever, 129
Stonehouse, 215
Stonehouse Stables, 131
Summer Breeze Concert Series, 144
Super 8 Motel—Williamsburg/ Historic Area, 27
Surrey House Restaurant, 192
Surry County, 189
Surry County attractions, 190
Surry County restaurants, 192
Susan Constant, 116
Suter's Handcrafted Furniture, 80
S. Wallace Edwards & Sons, 192
Swan Tavern Antiques, 129

T

Tandem Health Care at Williamsburg, 223
Tangier Island, 195
Tangier Island restaurants, 195
Tarpley's Store, 72
television stations, 236
tennis, 183

Thanksgiving at Berkeley Plantation, 155
theater, 145
Theater for the Young, 96
This Century Gallery, 76, 148
Thomas Everard House, 94
Thomas Nelson Community College, 227
Thompson Guest Home, 40
Thrifty car rentals, 10, 12
timeshares, 209
TK Asian Antiques, 80
Toano shopping, 80
Todd Jurich's Bistro, 202
Touch of Earth, A, 76, 148
Toymaker of Williamsburg, The, 74
Tradition Club at Brickshire, The, 187
Tradition Golf Club at Kiskiack, 187
Tradition Golf Club at Royal New Kent, The, 187
Tradition Golf Club at Stonehouse, 187
train transportation, 12
transportation, 7
Travelodge—Historic Area, 27
Trellis, The, 64
Trevillian Furniture and Interiors, 80

U

United Airlines, 9
United Way of Greater Williamsburg, 232
universities and colleges, 225
Upper County Park, 176
Upper Mattaponi tribe, 135
Urbanna Oyster Festival, 156
urgent health care, 231
U.S. Airways, 8, 9, 12
U.S. Army Transportation Museum, 140

V

Vernon Wooten Studio & Gallery, 76
Veterans Day, 156
Victoria's, 66
Victory Monument, 123

Vineyards of Williamsburg, The, 215

Virginia Air and Space Center, 166

Virginia Aquarium & Marine Science Center, 205

Virginia Arts Festival, 151

Virginia Beach, 70, 202

Virginia Beach Amphitheater, 70

Virginia Beach attractions, 203

Virginia Beach Convention & Visitors Bureau, 203

Virginia Beach restaurants, 206

Virginia Beach Sportsplex, 205

Virginia Gazette, 233

Virginia Legends Walk, 206

Virginia Living Museum, 163

Virginia Living Museum Art Show and Sale, 156

Virginiana stores, 83

Virginian-Pilot, 233

Virginia Shakespeare Festival, 145

Virginia's Indian cultures, 133

Virginia War Museum, 163

Virginia Zoo, 201

visual arts, 146

W

Waller Mill Park, 176, 181, 182

Walsingham Academy, 230

War Hill Inn, 38

Water Country USA, 106

Water Country USA entertainment and dining, 109

Water Country USA featured attractions, 107

Water Country USA safety features, 109

Watermen's Museum Gift Shop, The, 129

Watermen's Museum, The, 124, 147

water parks, 106

Waterside Festival Marketplace, 201

Wedmore Place, 38

weekend getaways. See also day trips

Westgate at Williamsburg, 216

Westmoreland, 216

Westover Plantation, 102

Westray Downs, 216

Wetherburn's Tavern, 94

Whitley's Virginia Peanuts and Peanut Factory, 45

William and Mary Theatre, 145

Williamsburg Alewerks, 109

Williamsburg Antique Mall, 76

Williamsburg Area Bicyclists, 180

Williamsburg area transport, 14

Williamsburg at Home, 74

Williamsburg Choral Guild, 144

Williamsburg Christian Academy, 230

Williamsburg Community Christmas Parade, 157

Williamsburg Courtyard by Marriott, 28

Williamsburg Craft House, 74

Williamsburg Doll Factory, 82

Williamsburg Film Festival, 150

Williamsburg Hospitality House, 28

Williamsburg Indoor Sports Complex, 177, 182

Williamsburg Inn Regency Room, The, 66

Williamsburg Inn, The, 18, 184

Williamsburg–James City County public schools, 228

Williamsburg Landing, 223

Williamsburg Lodge Bay Room and Cafe, The, 66

Williamsburg Lodge, The, 19

Williamsburg Magazine, 234

Williamsburg Manor Bed and Breakfast, 38

Williamsburg Marriott, 28

Williamsburg National Golf Club, 188

Williamsburg Outlet Mall, 82

Williamsburg Parks and Recreation Department, 174

Williamsburg Players, The, 145

Williamsburg Pottery Factory and Outlets, 82

Williamsburg Realty Inc., 218

Williamsburg Regional Library, 68, 132, 220

Williamsburg Regional Library Art Center, 144

Williamsburg Sampler Bed and Breakfast, 39

Williamsburg Scottish Festival, 154

Williamsburg's Grand Illumination, 93, 98, 157

Williamsburg Soccer Club, 183

Williamsburg Symphonia, 144

Williamsburg Trolley, 9

Williamsburg White House, A, 39

Williamsburg Wicker and Rattan, 80

Williamsburg Winery, The, 110

Williamsburg Women's Chorus, 144

Williamsburg-Yorktown Daily .com, 234

Windsor Forest, 216

wine and wineries, 109

Wolf Trap Park, 177

Women's History Month, 150

Woodlands Hotel and Suites, 19

Woods, The, 216

Working Wood in the 18th Century, 149

Wythe Candy and Gourmet Shop, 73

Y

York County Division of Parks and Recreation, 183

York County public schools, 229

York Parks & Recreation, 174

York River Inn Bed & Breakfast, 127

York River State Park, 177, 181

Yorkshire, 216

Yorktown, 112, 118

Yorktown accommodations, 126

Yorktown attractions, 121

Yorktown celebrations, 121
Yorktown driving directions, 118
Yorktown historic buildings, 119
Yorktown history, 119
Yorktown National Cemetery, 139
Yorktown Pub, 126
Yorktown restaurants, 125
Yorktown Shoppe, The, 129
Yorktown shopping, 127
Yorktown today, 121
Yorktown Tree Lighting Festivities, 157
Yorktown trolley, 125, 128
Yorktown Victory Celebration, 155
Yorktown Victory Center, 124
Yorktown Waterfront, 132, 178